The Context of Self

*A Phenomenological Inquiry
Using Medicine as a Clue*

Richard M. Zaner

Easterwood Professor, Southern Methodist University

Ohio University Press
ATHENS, OHIO

Library of Congress Cataloging in Publication Data

Zaner, Richard M.
  The context of self.
(Series in Continental Thought; v.1)
  Bibliography: p.
  Includes index.
  1. Man. 2. Body, Human. 3. Self
(Philosophy) 4. Medical literature. I. Title.
[DNLM: 1. Body image. 2. Self concept.
3. Ego. 4. Philosophy. BF697 Z28c]
BD450.Z36   128   80-18500
ISBN 0-8214-0443-1
ISBN 0-8214-0600-0 pbk.

For Alfred Schutz
and Aron Gurwitsch
In memoriam

Contents

Preface

PHILOSOPHICAL discourse, Ortega y Gasset once pointed out, is essentially "hermetic." Elaborating on this, and contrasting philosophical with literary expression, he continued:

> Even in the most favorable case of the most lucid thinker the little doors of the sentences are firmly shut, their meaning does not step out on its own feet. To comprehend them, there is no means but to enter. Yet once inside, we understand the reason for this strange condition of philosophical sentences which, being expression—and that means a saying—are also, and more, silence and secrecy. Philosophical thought is systematic, and in a system each concept carries all the others within it. But language can at one moment say only a few things; it cannot say them all at once. It is discourse, a going on saying and never having finished saying. Philosophical sentences cannot be expansive, for they are essentially inclusive. In this they are like love and great grief which, when striving to become manifest in words, seems to choke the throat with the avalanche of all that should be said. *

For better or worse, this study is philosophical in that complex way: it is systematic. But the "systematic" here is not without its history and even idiosyncrasies. I had set out to develop some few thoughts that had slowly grown out of my modest and all too episodic encounters with the world of medicine. I had hoped especially to be able to say something clear on the reasons within medicine itself which would make our prominent concern for "ethics" and "values" in it more understandable. But as I began, there appeared a veritable avalanche of themes which, it seemed, were quite necessary to address before I could properly even pose the initial question. What was to have been a rather more perfunctory than extensive discussion of the person as embodied, turned out to be in serious need of a much more detailed discussion of its own.

With that, still other issues immediately appeared as quite decisive. Of key importance for making fuller sense of the phenomenon of embodiment, to say

---

* José Ortega y Gasset, "A Chapter From the History of Ideas," in José Ortega y Gasset, *Concord and Liberty*, tr. Helene Weyl (New York: W. W. Norton and Company, 1946), p. 136.

nothing of a good deal of medicine, is the idea of "wholeness" or "integrity"—talk of which abounds in so many discussions within (and outside) medicine. The challenge of such talk could best be met, it seemed to me, through a critical understanding of Aron Gurwitsch's seminal theory of the "field of consciousness," the core part of which concerns the nature of "contextures." At the same time, the systematic analysis of this—to the extent I could undertake it—made it evident that two other foundational ideas, within (and outside) medicine, could then be taken up in a fresh way: "self" and the "relationship" of self to the "other self." Properly to consider these incredibly complex themes, however, required a far more extensive study than anything I had initially envisaged.

What thus began with modesty, wound up, perchance immodestly, as an effort to set down a full theory of the embodied self. Still, however "full" this study seeks to be, I can hardly claim to have had the last word on these important and complex themes. As with all philosophical discourse, this too is a "saying and never having finished saying." Much, of course, is not said here, and it may be that much is improperly, or even wrongly, said. Judging these matters is an essential part of philosophical discourse as well. Nevertheless, it is also true of such discourse that it is "systematic"—not everything can be said on the first page, in the first chapter. Each section builds on the preceding and is integral to it; each lays the basis for subsequent ones, and is similarly integral; and only, I dare say, after the final word of the study has been said can the sense of it all be grasped and judgments rendered. There is no surprise in saying that, for in light of the more extensive analysis of context and contexture included herein, it is perfectly obvious that this study is itself an instance—however imperfect—of a contexture within its own context.

An important "part" of the "background" (field or context) of this "whole" (contexture) is the ambience of medicine as I came some time ago to know it. That context was first made available to me by the kindness, foresight, and continuously critical presence of Dr. Edmund D. Pellegrino, who is now President of Catholic University. Through his own writings, our lively conversations, and our joint efforts to develop a curricular model for making "the humanities" a strong presence in the health sciences, I came to see and appreciate as never before just how crucial is a rigorous and sensitive phenomenological study of such issues as this study is concerned with—not only for medicine and medical theory, but for other eminently "practical" spheres of life as well. I am deeply appreciative of his responsive and generously encouraging support over the years. And there is another philosopher-physician whom I must acknowledge, and thank for all he did to help make medicine more accessible to me than it otherwise was or could have been: H. Tristram Engelhardt, Jr., whom I am delighted to count as among the finest of the students with whom I have worked, and now count as well among my teachers and respected colleagues.

The dedication of this work to Aron Gurwitsch and Alfred Schutz, themselves close friends and great thinkers, and whom I am fortunate to have had as my teachers, speaks for itself. Their work, and that of Edmund Husserl, is the ground upon which I try to build, and with which I am in continual critical dialogue. Others of those philosophers who have been important for this work are evident, for it is their work with which I am continually in critical engagement herein. I want especially to mention, however, one who was also one of my teachers, and who directed my Master's Thesis, the work which in many ways initiated this set of themes: Hans Jonas, whose work in philosophical biology is continually encountered here.

Two of my close friends and colleagues at Southern Methodist University deserve special mention—at once for their great encouragement in the writing of this study, and for their immense patience in providing a needed hearing and reading from time to time of portions of the book: Osborne Wiggins and Lonnie D. Kliever. And for providing me with the needed time to pursue these issues, I wish to thank Southern Methodist University, especially the Deans of the Schools of Humanities and Sciences, A. Lee McAlester and James Early; their understanding of the need for such time, in approving a research leave for me, is gratefully acknowledged.

I must say a word of thanks, too, to the Secretary of the Department of Philosophy, Mrs. Cecilia B. King, whose patience with my quirks and the flurry that too commonly follows me has been profoundly appreciated, although too infrequently spoken. Finally, for the skill and expertise in typing this manuscript, a well-earned note of thanks goes to Rebecca K. Gracy and Kathleen Triplett.

My hope is the hope of anyone who engages in tasks such as this: that while no one else is to be held responsible for it—such responsibility being mine to assume—this study fulfills the confidence and trust of all those who have encouraged me through the years.

RMZ
Dallas, Texas
November 10, 1978

Part I

THE EMBODYING ORGANISM

Introduction

I AM fully cognizant of how many works, great and small, have been devoted to the questions pursued in this study. It has also been much on my mind whether yet another bundle of words should be committed to print. In the end, I suppose, some sort of confession is in order—and the beginning of the study seems as good a place as any.

The confession is a simple one and has two parts. One: the persons in philosophy and medicine whose ideas are mainly considered here are, in my judgment, among the most seminal of our times—hence amply deserving of serious critical engagement. For me, as for them, that is the highest respect which can be paid to them. Two: these issues, these ideas, are among the most significant for our times—hence they require as much serious philosophical reflection and discussion as we are capable of giving them.

The central problematic which engaged Wilhelm Dilthey throughout his career is one which, though perchance going under different names, is still with us: an axial antithesis that

> . . . arises when historical consciousness is followed to its last consequences. The finitude of every historical phenomenon . . . the relativity of every kind of human apprehension of the totality of things is the last word of the historical *Weltanschauung* . . . . And over against this both the demand of thought and the striving of philosophy for universal knowledge assert themselves. The historical *Weltanschauung* liberates the human spirit from the last chains that natural science and philosophy have not yet broken. But where are the means to overcome the anarchy of opinions which threatens to befall us? To the solution of the long series of problems which are connected with this, I have devoted my whole life. (*16*, V, p. 9)

Dilthey had early recognized that whatever else must be done to solve this antithesis, it required a careful probing of mental or psychical life. To secure the very possibility of historical knowledge, one must be able to understand why and how mental life manifests itself outwardly in objective expressions: ideas, values, works, laws, institutions, documents, culture. Hence he unequivocally called for, and even set out the program for, a "descriptive" psychology—a

1

disciplined study of the textured complexus (*Zusammenhang*) of instinctual, emotive, volitional, and ideational processes (*Erlebnisse*) thanks to which subjectivity lodges itself in an equally rich and complex set of objective manifestations. To *understand* historical traces and expressions of particular past figures and peoples, one must take these as the outward revelations of the subjective life or lives that produced them. They stand as interpretative clues and tokens. But that psychology proved to be a formidable undertaking.

For one thing, the psychology for the most part extant in his times was hardly concerned with the problematic Dilthey saw as basic. Concerned instead with becoming a natural, explanatory science, its energies were taken up mostly with piecemeal quantitative analyses of visual and auditory perception. Little of the richness of creative and artistic life, axiological experience, much less historical awareness, was studied. Clearly it was necessary not merely to point up the merely hypothetical character of that psychology, but much more to set out exactly what *had* to be focally studied if historical knowledge—and with it, the whole spectrum of *Geisteswissenschaften*—was to be firmly grounded, and the antithesis resolved. Knowledge must be rescued from the increasing frustrations of utter relativism. This Dilthey attempted in many of his works, but especially in his signal essay of 1894, "*Ideen über eine beschreibende und zergliedernde Psychologie.*"[1]

It is not within my present purposes to give any critical exposition of Dilthey's splendid work; Rudolph Makkreel's thorough study (*72*) has in any case done this. My concern is rather with the issues which Dilthey so clearly framed, and the directions in which he pointed.

Husserl, too, grappled with these problems throughout his career, striving on the one hand to reconcile his definitive critiques of "psychologism" (*49*, I, pp. 90–222; *45*, pp. 149–75) and of "logicism" (*45*, pp. 156–61, 259–61, 282–89, etc.), and on the other hand to establish an authentic *logos* of *psyche*. To confront the "crisis of European science," as he attempted in every phase of his philosophical life, meant to confront the question of "the demand of thought," or of reason, and "the striving of philosophy" to secure universal, rigorously self-responsible knowledge: the norms of rationality. But this could not be accomplished without a radical understanding of the flaws not only of psychologism, but equally of logicism: the force of Husserl's searching phenomenological explications of the depths of consciousness is, in one respect, to bring into question the sense and range of "a priori" and "a posteriori" cognition. To bring them under scrutiny and fundamentally alter them: the antithesis Dilthey set out is squarely at the heart of the Husserlian project, and its resolution hangs on two critical points, both presupposing (as does everything in his work) the core phenomenon of *Intentionalität*. On the one hand, the problematic of *Evidenz*, in its fullest reach, must be mastered; on the other, the key motion of "free-phantasy variation." Without these, there simply is no way of articulating, much less of resolving, the antithesis, the enigmatic impasse of finitude and universality. I do not, however, propose to develop these themes in any direct, expository way; there are efforts such as these aplenty, including some of my own. I rather want to enter the arena by way of what has become so problematic during the course of the past five centuries.

As Ortega y Gasset has shown, the key to Dilthey, and the issue on which subsequent thinking must be tested, is *life* (*85*, pp. 129–82). Hence we have here an unprobed enclave inherited from modern thought; we find ourselves in a quandary when we try to comprehend the sense of life itself—in our own case most of all, but life in the wider sphere of things as well. *This* theme is the core concern of Hans Jonas' work, to which I shall have to devote serious study at the outset. Expressing the antithesis as being between freedom and necessity— echoing Spinoza—Jonas' way of confronting this manifests the same concern for the tension between finitude and infinitude that may be discerned in Dilthey or Husserl. For freedom is locused in the bodily empowered individual (especially, but not only, in human embodied persons); and necessity's root is found there as well. Hence the issue for Jonas is the same: how is it possible for an essentially temporal, biologically enrooted and finite creature (man) to know the lay of what-is, to achieve a viable view of being as such? As will have to be seen, Jonas insightfully shows at once why and how "life" has emerged as the central theme of our times.

The issues which have largely occupied psychology, though, have not generally been any of these—as Dilthey had already seen. Man, after all, is a creature who is not only "alive" but *complexly alive:* bodily life and psychical life at the very least. And whatever may have been said, or will be said, in the service of no matter which version of materialistic monism, that complex aliveness is noticeably and urgently in need of understanding. For even if all things are "matter," there are at least two sorts of "matter" which stubbornly resist being taken as *merely* material. It "matters," if you will, that their radically different statuses be recognized. The first, as will be seen, is the living body embodying; the second, the subject (self, mind). Even if all things are postulated as material, two things cannot be material in the very terms of that monism: the "that which utters the claim," which "knows" and "judges" about matter; and the "that by virtue of which" there is at all any encounter or experience with matter.

Hence if these are termed "matter," it is perforce still necessary to notice that they are curious bits of matter indeed: not mere occupants of space, not mere impenetrables, but experientially grounded knowing and saying, giving even such terms as "matter" their sense. The critical distancing requisite to know, to name, to experience the material world fundamentally betrays the flaw, and sets up the issues: what is "self"? What is that by virtue of which this creature is "here," "now," enrooted irrevocably—i.e., embodied? And how shall we understand these, how shall we gain access to them so as to ground whatever claims will then be made? If self is not only historical, not only finite, but—as a

condition for both—is embodied, how is any knowledge, value, or hope beyond
the mere passing moment at all possible? Or, in slightly different terms, it being
the clear case that we all without exception and without hesitation in our usual
careers *believe* that we somehow get beyond the ephemeral here and now—to
the past, the future; to things around us; even to affairs purely imaginary—what
is it about this magical, forceful "custom and habit" which so natively tugs us
dimensionally out of the passing moment and manipulatory range? We think
we experience and know far more than this or that; indeed, we stake enormous
odds on it; battle and slay for it; plan and contrive on its behalf, devote our lives
to it; and strive to get rid of ourselves when it seems a mere mirage.

Jonas focuses his regard on these, therefore. But as soon becomes plain, there
are serious problems. Not only is it puzzling what a *living body* is; far more is it
enigmatic that *this one* living body is *experienced* (felt, perceived, treasured,
distrusted, cared for, etc.) *by me as "mine."* How shall we account for this? And
who or what is this "me" who says "mine"? How is it possible that "I" "have"
this "body"? That "I" am aware of "myself" as such, or to whatever extent?
While focusing on some of these issues, Jonas' work leaves us more deeply
puzzled. Thus to maintain a disciplined focus on the issues, and not be diverted,
it is unavoidable to turn again to the self and to its embodying organism.

The understanding of these phenomena, it is soon obvious, is not possible
without a crucial pause, an interlude: this body is in some way a *whole*
comprised of *parts* of very different and subtle sorts; "I," too, seem at once
dispersed among a vast number of activities and awarenesses, a "manyness,"
and yet am somehow "the same" throughout. It seems that we here confront
two deeply puzzling whole/part complexes. Aron Gurwitsch, criticizing and
building on the work of Husserl, has produced a seminal analysis of just this
issue—finding its roots in the psychology of the late 19th century and early 20th
century. But he did not elaborate his theory of *contexture* beyond the theme of
perception. I have felt it completely natural and necessary to try just that: body
and consciousness (mind, mental life), like the perceptually experienced object,
are also contextures. But they differ in crucial ways; hence the "interlude" in the
study is necessary to get the bearings needed for carrying out the remainder of
the study.

I used the phrases "body and self" and "body and mind." That was too
casual; however closely intertwined, body is not self, nor mind nor world; self is
not body nor mind nor world; world is not self nor body nor mind. Thus the
critical pause in the study is extended, while I try to get straighter on these
issues, their interlacings and differences. Paul Ricoeur has devoted considerable penetrating effort to them—and, believing it essential to "self" that it
can only manifest itself in indirect ways, calls for a conception of philosophy as
rigorous hermeneutics. This call returns us to the antithesis Dilthey worried
about: subjectivity expresses itself objectively in words, actions, institutions,
and the like, hence the understanding of self must apparently be an
interpretative one: hermeneutics.

It would seem that full circle is reached. I think not: hermeneutics, it will appear, or at least Ricoeur's version of hermeneutics, is found wanting in crucial ways—ways which fundamentally affect the understanding of self, reflection, embodiment, and other self. The concluding sections of this study attempt to set out the outlines at least of a phenomenological theory of concrete embodied life vividly presenced along with the other concrete embodied life: the other self. For this task, there are some central notions employed: context, contexture, reflexivity, presence, awakening, and still others. These, it is to be hoped, will attain their sense in their particular contexts.

1

The Body and Embodiment: Hans Jonas

I INITIATE this study with a consideration of one of Hans Jonas' most fascinating and important discussions: his project to establish a philosophical biology. Jonas' work provides an unusually skillful delineation of a central issue in contemporary science and philosophy, and a discerning analysis of the historical setting out of which that issue emerges. The problem of our times is *life*, and it is problematic because of fundamental shifts in what Susanne Langer once appropriately termed "generative ideas" in modern times. The careful study of this shift, and the preceeding shifts from classical thought, has occupied Jonas throughout his career.

But I am not concerned to give an exposition of the whole of Jonas' thought, even if this were possible. His thought is very much in the making with the theme of the foundation of ethics, based in responsibility, at the forefront of his current concerns.[1] Hence such a comprehensive exposition is just not possible. In any case it is only one facet of his work that my study directly benefits from: his discussions of those issues which may properly be regarded as the core moments of his philosophical biology. I propose to give his ideas the respect and merit they are manifestly due—indeed, overdue—by confronting them philosophically: that is, critically. This will require both careful exposition and subsequent criticism in order to make the relevant issues clear.

THE HISTORICAL MATRIX

Dualism, in whatever form—Gnostic (*56*, pp. 263–348; *53*), Cartesian (*55*, pp. 9–19, 54–63), or even that cognitive frustration, epiphenomenalism (*54*, pp. 146–54)—is not merely one of the passing points of view which pop in and out of the historical panorama of metaphysics, like some wacky Punch and Judy show. Nor is it simply an intractably persistent *bête noir*, forever dogging the tracks of monism's thrust to more pristine regions, where one might hope to be ethereally innocent of the vexing questions of otherness. Dualism, Jonas has brilliantly shown, is "so far the most momentous phase in the history of thought" (*55*, p. 16), "the vehicle of the movement which carried the mind of man from the vitalistic monism of early times to the materialistic monism of our own. . . . " (*55*, p. 12). Historically bound, both idealism and materialism (in all their variations) are inherently "postdualistic"—partial products, merely, of the dualism which by essence inhabits, shapes, and determines them by leaving behind itself a "nature" (*res extensa*) bereft of life and quality, and a "mind" (*res cogitans*) incorporeally stripped of concrete locus in the world (*55*, pp. 17–18, 54).[2] It is thus no accident that, with dualism's positing that just as matter can be without mind, so mind can be without matter, idealism and materialism became the two subsequent, historically possible forms of monism. Both emerge from and presuppose dualism's ontological polarization, a bifurcation which cannot on principle be ignored, and which necessitates a highly specific epistemological problematic—that of *necessary illusion*. We do not experience what we would experience, were we to experience what nature "really" is. Accordingly, what must be accounted for, as Husserl showed, is why our sense experiences do not deliver that "true" nature (*42*, pp. 21–100). Here the notorious *Vorstellungstheorie* comes into play, the roots for which are, first, the potent assumption that Nature is as it is posited by physical science (extension and motion, both mathematizable quantities), and second, that sense perception is in its essence incapable of "truth," of delivering what truly exists. As Brentano remarked, *Wahrnehmung* (perception; but literally, "truth-taking") is in truth *Falschnehmung* (literally, "false-taking") (*9*, I, pp. 28, 110, 129). Perception consists of the passive reception of "impressions" or "data" and these are denizens of subjective life ("in" the mind). To become perception in the proper sense, they require *non*-sensory processes (memory, judgment, association, etc.) before they can be "taken" as actually corresponding to material things. The developments of modern thought are in part built on the twin assumptions of an implicit *trust* of (mathematical) cognition, and a fateful *mistrust*, a suspicion, of sensory life *tout court*.

Nor is it accidental that both idealism and materialism, each in its own way, leave something central out of joint, something incomprehensible which mutely but insistently bespeaks its unaccountable presence: *the living body*. If taken as pure, extended matter, then its being alive is not understood; if taken as the sensible field of feeling of which it is one of a number of the ideas of consciousness, then its "being *my* body, my extended I and my share in the world of extension, is not understood" (*55*, p. 18).

It is thus, Jonas writes, that

the organic body signifies the latent crisis of every known ontology and the criterion of "any future one which will be able to come forward as a science." As it was first the body on which, in the fact of *death*, that antithesis of life and nonlife became manifest whose relentless pressure on thought destroyed primitive panvitalism and caused the image of being to split, so it is conversely the concrete unity manifest in its *life* on which in turn the dualism of the two substances founders, and again this bi-unity which also brings to grief both alternatives branching off from dualism, whenever they—as they cannot help doing—enlarge themselves into total ontologies. . . . The living body that can die, that has world and itself belongs to the world, whose outward form is organism and causality, and whose inward form is selfhood and finality: this body is the memento of the still unsolved question of ontology, "What is being?" and must be the canon of coming attempts to solve it. (*55*, p. 19)

An exact declaration-of-intent, and a telling formulation of the problematic which was[3] to occupy Jonas throughout his distinguished career: a philosophical biology whose major theme is "life" centered in the problematic of the living body. No mere partial monism, and certainly no dualism, can hope to solve it, much less even clearly articulate it. The surmounting of both can be accomplished only by a new, integral monism, which must seek to "absorb" the radical polarity "into a higher unity of existence from which the opposites issue as faces of its being or phases of its becoming" (*55*, p. 17). The "problem" at the root of dualism must be taken up, freed from the partiality and distortions of monism, as also from the intrinsic riddles of dualism: "the existence of feeling life in an unfeeling world of matter which in death triumphs over it" (*55*, p. 17).

By no means an arbitrary invention, Cartesian dualism emerged in part as a response to difficulties encountered with early modern efforts to mathematize Nature. To understand the "Book of Nature" as written by a hand mathematical, it was necessary to exclude, in principle, all elements or features which did not seem to be amenable to this expression. It also required that mathematics itself be conceived in a certain way, and of course that its applicability be secured (that things to be mathematized be susceptible of this understanding, indeed were thus truly understood).

Without going into the difficult historical interpretations called for here (*42; 65; 102*), it seems clear enough that one key move (whatever its historical motives and expressions) involved conceiving matter as equivalent to *extension* (*65*, pp. 111–12, 114, 121–22), and making this the sole category of Nature. Coupled with this, as Husserl has shown (*42*, pp. 21–67, 353–78), mathematics (especially geometry) was taken to be the science of *measurement* (indeed, a "science" whose own origins were not questioned, but which was taken over as full-bodied and already-delivered as Athena from Zeus). Nature as extended, or as a system of measurable particles in motion and defined by mathematical means, found its perfect match in mathematics. The difficulty (which Galileo had already seen) was that not everything was definable in such terms: the perceptual contact with Nature yielded "appearances," "secondary qualities," which, although merely apparent, resided in a subject whose "inside" consisted of these "ideas" (and the mental activities working on and with them)—and these nonextended affairs could only be extrusions of nonmathematizable things into the world of mathematizable extension.

Just here, Jonas points out, Descartes' dualism had its place: there are *two* substances, each of them self-existent, self-subsistent, and *sui generis. Matter*, defined as extension (*cum* motion), depends neither for its *being* nor its *being known* on *mind*, defined as thinking, and vice versa. What mattered here, of course, was the mutual *isolation* of the two: "the isolation of the *res cogitans* was the most effective way of securing the complete ontological detachment of external reality from what was not extended and measurable" (*55*, p. 54).

And yet, the stroke of genius (or ingenuity) became the mortal weakness. The theory "self-confidently *clashes* with experience" (*55*, p. 62, n. 5). As already indicated, it generates the experiential and epistemological oddity of shunting into the dungeon of subjectivity, into the sphere of mere appearances of material things, everything save extension and motion. What in concrete experience we believe and inveterately act upon turns out to be the least reliable index to what is real. And with this is generated the postulation of "ideas" as epistemic entrepreneurs whose guarantee of efficacy can only be an indirection: approximations merely to mathematical ideals, while only the latter can be certain, and this thanks strictly to the benevolent underwriter, God. As regards the living body, there is correspondingly created the enigma of how a person could possibly move even his own arm, or how an arm, struck by a physical thing, not only could be in its turn moved but be *felt* as moving and hurt. The living body of the thinker is the obdurate unaccountable: the mechanics of the body cannot comprehend its life, and the ideational theory of mind leaves its plain physical placement in the world the faintest shadow, an "idea" merely. Of course, with Descartes this crops up only in the case of man, for the rest of the "organic" world is pieced in with *extensa*. This, though, is fully enough to undo, rudely but definitively, the whole cloth. For even if "the exemption of man was," as Jonas believes, "a mere inconsistency" (*55*, p. 74), it is nonetheless decisive, as he also emphasizes.

And yet again: there are haunting vascillations in Descartes' words, curious clues which trickle through the otherwise sealed door between these substances. The reach of matter includes organisms, the human body, too; hence the human body as an organism within the material milieu is *essentially* extension—and thereby is it barred from direct commerce with the human person, so far as this signifies the *res cogitans*. Yet—and this reservation ("mere inconsistency" though it may be) is immense, as I see it—the soul is *not* in the body in a way a boatman is in his boat: i.e., removably, accidentally, revocably. Indeed, so much to the contrary is it that it seems a matter of *essence*, too: throughout, Descartes insists that the body is "intimately unioned" with the mind. Here the stress is not at all on the *isolation* of extension from mind (whatever the benefits science, and later monisms, tried to glean from that), but rather on the "*intimacy*" which was not grasped again until the late 19th and early 20th centuries (*120* ; *127*). But what are we, Descartes' explicitly invited readers, to make of this, if not that the "union" is essential?

"Body" seems a wonderful enigma indeed (as Pascal acidly noted), within the very system of the dualism: shifting, equivocal, at once *both* "mental" *and* "material," yet *neither* the one *nor* the other simpliciter. After all has been said, there remains the *factum brutum*: the human body is the only affair within the entire *res extensa* which reveals this "intimacy," and thereby the only affair in the whole of reality which is "both . . . and . . . " and yet "neither . . . nor . . . "!

This, surely, must make the reader pause. What is impossible here—an impasse of the first order—is that such "intimacy" can hardly be more than merely announced. In a universe where everything is *either* matter *or* mind, nothing can be *both* mind *and* matter: the logic undergirding and giving life to the Cartesian metaphysics permits no devolving of the principle of non-contradiction into one of conjunction or disjunction. For that matter, even if it could, such a logic would not enable us to grasp the sense of "union," much less "intimacy." Thus there emerges the central problematic (Jonas is clearly correct) of subsequent philosophy: what is it we are called upon to think, when we meet—in Descartes' works or in our own experiences—this "intimate union"? What is it, to think "union"? And to think of it as "intimate"? Descartes' ontology collapses under the weight of its own insight.

THE LIVING BODY: METABOLISM

Just this issue seems crucial for Jonas' quest, too; all I have suggested thus far is that it is vitally within Descartes' as well. Clearly, too, it will not do merely to repeat metaphysical dualism, nor to smuggle in covertly any brand of monism. Whether Jonas is correct in calling for a "new" and "mediated" monism or not, I shall have to assess later. The more immediate concern is to pose the problem clearly, and to see Jonas' proposed solution. There are, as I see it, several significant moments to this, and I want first to lay them out carefully, in order then to give them critical attention.

Unmistakably, there is a profound problem of "union." Still, as I read Jonas, that notion harbors serious difficulties unless it is purged of its dualistic overtones. The "two-ness" Descartes found is, for Jonas, "grounded in reality itself" (*55*, pp. 16–17), but even if my suggestion is right that Descartes seemed to be onto the main problem (the "living organism"), it is clear enough that he could do nothing about it. "Union," to put it bluntly, is literally unthinkable in his final system. Descartes' generative idea, his "great discovery, that of the essential opposition between mind and extension" (*65*, p. 121) generates as well the fateful subversion of that discovery. That essential scission has cut out its own ground: the "intimate union" of mind and body gainsays the dualism. How, then, are we to conceive that "two-ness"?

In the first place, Jonas rightly stresses that it is only thanks to our being "living material things ourselves" (*55*, p. 91), or on "the strength of the immediate testimony of our bodies" (*55*, p. 79), that we can say anything at all about the body (I shall return to this point later). Without that source, "life itself would not even become visible, nor yet a blank in its place" (*55*, p. 87). What we face with the genuine "intimate union" is "the fact that the living body is the archetype of the concrete, and being *my* body it is, in its immediacy of inwardness and outwardness in one, the *only* fully given concrete of experience in general" (*55*, p. 24).[4]

Secondly, this extensive outwardness and intensive inwardness "in one" are not only "genuine aspects of myself" (*55*, p. 23), and thus give *concrete* significance to one side of the "two-ness," but also give the same significance to the other side. For it is not at all possible, in any traditional dualist or monist position, to find any legitimate ground for the causal interpretation of natural regularities. Hume was perfectly correct in his own way, for there *is* no perception or impression of causality; nor is the nexus between data a perceptual content: neither "force" nor "cause," hence neither "regularity" nor "connection," and hence *no idea of Nature at all* (*55*, pp. 26–33). But upon carefully consulting our own actual bodily life as embodied persons, we find that *only this actual bodily life* could possibly yield the very ideas which play such central roles in the scientific account of nature. Force, cause, connection, and regularity are in no way a priori *bases of* experience, but are *themselves basic experiences.* Their root is the experience of "*effort,*" resistance of things to my bodily acting on them, and undergoing the impact of things on myself as embodied (*55*, pp. 22–23, 99–107). Thus just as "causality" is a "finding of the practical, not of the theoretical, self, of its activity, not of its perception" (*55*, p. 23), so force "is not a datum, but an 'actum' humanly present in effort" (*55*, p. 25).[5]

Hence if one renders life, especially bodily life, unintelligible, one renders both the world of Nature and the world of "mind" or "soul" unintelligible. "In the body, the knot of being is tied which dualism does not unravel but cut. Materialism and idealism, each from its end, try to smooth it out but get caught in it" (*55*, p. 25). From this, as I see it, the conclusion seems evident: the "union" is ultimately an abortive notion, for its very sense effectively buys into a dualism, if only incipiently. Or, differently expressed, what in Descartes is a sort of desperation (the intimate union, which was grasped then allowed to slip through) turns out to be, for Jonas, the insight that there truly *is* no "union" but rather the "one"living body whose "extensiveness" locates it within the actual world (and grounds subsequent knowledge of that world), and whose "intensiveness" is the "efforting" estate of subjectivity. The dual*ism* is wrong for it renders the dual aspects of reality, grounded in the dual*ity* of the organism, into ontological substances. *Both the aspects are myself* in the core sense of what alone "my life" can mean. There are not two *things*, then, to be by some legerdemain welded together; there is rather the one and only embodied person, whose being is, however, *intrinsically complex, dual.*

But in this complexus, what is it which answers to "life"? By virtue of what is it an "organism"? We have to do here with a "whole," but it is a "living" whole. This "selfhood with which 'organism' originally dared indifferent nature" (55, p. 107), this "ontological surprise" nature springs with living things (55, p. 79): what is it? The fundamental key, for Jonas, to unlock what must otherwise remain utterly closed, is *metabolism.*

> In this remarkable mode of being, the material parts of which the organism consists at a given instant are . . . only temporary, passing contents whose joint material identity does not coincide with the identity of the whole which they enter and leave, and which sustains its own identity by the very act of foreign matter passing through its spatial system, the living *form.* It is never the same materially and yet persists as its same self, *by* not remaining the same matter. Once it really becomes the same with the sameness of its material contents . . . it ceases to live; it dies. . . . (55, pp. 75–76)

Anything else which occurs in and for the living organism—for instance, with human life: the emergence of the full person through motility, emotion, perception, image-making, etc.—could not occur without the functioning of metabolism. At the same time, the peculiar kinds of transcendence which appear at higher levels are already conditioned by and prefigured within, metabolic activity. Thus after recognizing and showing the differences between plant and animal life, Jonas insists that the dynamics of animal metabolism itself make possible the distinctive sort of mediate actions in animal life (55, pp. 100, 102, 103),[6] and on this ground the still richer levels of human life and freedom become possible. The understanding of the complexus (extensive outwardness / intensive inwardness) will find its most *general* but also its most *fundamental* principles in the activity of metabolism, since this is all-pervasive in life as such.

Jonas contends, in effect, that this root of life answers the double question of life and living organism qua "system." Metabolic activity is not merely peripheral, but "is the total mode of continuity (self-continuation) of the subject of life itself" (55, p. 76, n. 13). As against the machine, no matter how sophisticated cybernetically (55, pp. 108–34), the organism is a system whose very character is at once the result and the agency of its metabolism, wholly and continuously. Hence the organism is the peculiar self-referential center it is, solely by means and on the basis of its continuous interchanges with its material environs. The "unity" here is totally innocent of "synthesizing activities" of thought and/or perception, as also of the concurrence of forces binding parts into a manifold: it is strictly "self-unifying, by means of changing multiplicity. Sameness, while it lasts . . . is perpetual self-renewal through process, borne on the shift of otherness" (55, p. 79). This conception alone, for Jonas, can give significance to the ontological notion of "individual," a conception beyond the reach of phenomenology (55, p. 79). As will be seen in detail later, however, while Jonas' notion of "self-unifying" holds a crucial insight (which will only come out fully in the development of the notion of contexture), the idea that phenomenology is somehow "by nature" restricted from understanding the notion of "individual" can only be a judgment from plain bias, not evidence.

Here, in any case, we find a striking reversal in the ontological relationship of "matter" and "form:" where inert, purely physical "wholes" are "identities" thanks to their *matter*, for organisms, *form* is the essence and matter the accident. Thus "the organic form stands in a dialectical relation of *needful freedom* to matter" (55, p. 80). Form in living things is efficacious (i.e., "real"), and even though enjoying a certain independence from its material—precisely by preserving self-identity through continuous metabolic change of matter—it is thereby ineluctably *bound* to its matter. The "reality" of the organism's form is an "ontological revolution" in respect to matter: while the latter's "identity" is fixed, the organism's is mediate and functional, revealing always changing and shifting substrata: an *act* incessantly accomplished, a genuine "self"-continuation.

This complexus, then, is the ontologically basic sense of "self": emergent self-identity of form which thereby is singled out as distinct from the environs, from all the rest of reality. "Profound singleness and heterogeneousness within a universe of homogeneously interrelated existence mark the selfhood of organisms" (55, p. 83). An identity whose being is to continue, maintain, and assert *itself* is always within a milieu set off against it, polarized by otherness: and "self," too, is a polarized identity within the context of otherness (an insight which will have to be taken up again later).

Ceasing to *be thus* is tantamount to ceasing to *be at all*. The very freedom of the living form *from* matter is also the (dialectical) necessity of being *bound to* matter. To be self-continuing, the living form *stands in need of* the material world, and thus assumes the richer forms of "outwardness," being-at-world, while yet that very being-turned-outward is an "inwardness," a "for-itself" whose form is thus complexly inner/outer.[7] The *turning-outward*, however, is of necessity (for the form *to be* what it is) a *taking-into-inwardness* of its other: foreign matter. That rudimentary activity is what ultimately gives sense to higher-level modes of interaction (pursuing food, fleeing danger, etc.). The "primary antinomy of freedom and necessity," at all levels of life as such, is "inherent in organism as such" (55, p. 84).

For this self-continuation of efficacious form to be, some modality of sensitivity, awareness, or interest is requisite. Self-continuation of the metabolic process signifies the presence, however minimal, of a *needful self-concern*, active by way of *selective* modes of relation to the world. Affection by foreign matter brings about the sense of being-affected, impinged upon, hence of *self-feeling*, and thereby of sensitivity to what affects this "self"—viz., the other. Thereby emerge the germinal senses of "within-ness" and "without-ness" (the self of organism), in space (without) and time (within, as stretched to what "will" be brought into the metabolic process). The incorporating of what is other is already an encountering of a "there" (meshing it with the "here"), but it is a "there" which also signifies a *time* necessary to bring it to the "here." Self-transcendence and purposiveness thus express the fact that "life is facing forward as well as outward and extends 'beyond' its own immediacy in both directions at once" (55, p. 85). In different terms, the very fact of metabolism signifies that *purposiveness* is essential to the being of this form. Jonas goes on "to add the implications: there is no organism without teleology; there is no teleology without inwardness; and: life can be known only by life" (55, p. 91). All higher modes of life, which open up peculiarly animal forms of "distance" and thus ground specifically human forms of relatedness to the world, even theory itself, are constitutively grounded in this elemental activity of metabolism. With their emergence in motility and emotion (55, pp. 99–107), perception (55, pp. 135–56), and image making (55, pp. 157–82),[8] there emerge as well the richer modes of the dialectic of freedom and necessity, risk and dependency, which single out the human world itself.

There is thus a far richer world beyond what has been indicated up to now. Enough is at hand, though, to give pause for reflection—indeed precisely *before* one could go any farther with Jonas. It is imperative here to take seriously his claim that what he has maintained stems from "the evidence of each one's own organic awareness"; this "evidence we find in ourselves is an integral part of the evidence concerning life which experience puts at our disposal" (55, p. 91). It is *this evidence* which is continually, albeit most often silently, operative in every biologist's and behaviorist's *actual* work and study—without it, they would, like Sir James Jeans' "mathematical God," utterly miss the very "life" and "behavior" they seek and claim to know.

CRITIQUE: ONTOLOGY AND THE BODY

A brief rehearsal of the issue is needed to secure the terrain of our reflection. As Jonas shows, the panvitalism of classical times saw life everywhere and thus rendered death enigmatic; to acknowledge death was effectively to negate it by making it a transformation, a stage along life's way. In modern materialism precisely the reverse holds: not death—a merely "natural" event among others—but life becomes the riddle. But materialism and its necessary counterpart, idealism, are creatures born of the Cartesian sectioning, carrying always within themselves, each in its own way, the crippling marks of their parentage. What stands as the stubborn impasse of dualism, becomes in its post-dualistic offspring an egregious misfit, a cunning disguise to be unmasked: *the living body*.

Accepting the imperative to think from within one's own historical context, it is inevitable that one situate oneself with respect to that history—to the origins of Cartesian dualism. The major theme of contemporary thinking is perforce the theme of life, for that dualism, stripping the material world of human presence, forcefully deprived the realm of life of any *effective* status (hence, reality) in the scheme of things. As Koyré shows, the only exception to the sweeping conception of material extension as the substance of Nature, hence to the absence of analogy between God and world (indeed, God's absence from the world even of his own making), is the pure soul—the *res cogitans*, wherein alone is there a presence, albeit only as a tenuous "idea," of God. There are otherwise "no *imagines* and *vestigia Dei in mundo*." Accordingly,

> teleological conceptions and explanations have no place and no value in physical science, just as they have no place and no meaning in mathematics, all the more so as the world created by the Cartesian God, that is, the world of Descartes, is by no means the colorful, multiform and qualitatively determined world of the Aristotelian, the world of our daily life and experience—that world is only a subjective world of unstable and inconsistent opinion based on the untruthful testimony of confused and erroneous sense-perception—but a strictly uniform mathematical world, a world of geometry made real about which our clear and distinct ideas give us a certain and evident knowledge. There is nothing else in this world . . . but extension and motion. (*65*, pp. 100–01)

Identifying "matter" with "extension" also foreclosed the issue of *space*: for Descartes, there simply *is* no "space," no "void" somehow "filled" with material objects. Space is strictly an abstraction: as Descartes put it, body and space "are not different otherwise than in the mode in which they are conceived of by us" (*15*, I, p. 259). Hence, too, all sensible qualities are divested from extended matter; all that remains is extension in length, breadth, and depth (*15*, I, p. 260). Indeed, beyond moving to the then obvious conclusion that matter is infinite, Descartes holds to the companion implication that, as Koyré puts it, matter in no way depends on human perception or cognition, for matter "would be the same if there were no men in the world" (*65*, p. 115). The *res extensa* is thereby radically leveled, denuded of everything which in our usual experiences we believe it to be, and the way is cleared for subsequent rationalism, even Kant's version of the forms of sensibility. Since it is necessary to find a "place" for these usual experiences nonetheless, there is no choice but to locate them one and all *in the mind*: space, quality, value, goal, life, and the rest are relegated to subjectivity. The question then arises: why do we not experience what we would experience if we did experience what Nature "really" is? Modern epistemology—"the problem of the external world"—is thus a *phenomenon consequent* upon the acceptance of the Nature posited by the newly emerging sciences and their philosophical apologists.

By cluttering up "subjectivity" with all the leavings of that leveling-out of nature *à la bas* (to extension and motion), in short, by directly clashing with the evidence of concrete experience, dualism necessarily created a demanding impasse. In the terms of that theoretical posture, man becomes a puppety caricature; but so, too, does the wealth of animate life, its marvel of complex organization, observable opulence, and plain display of difference. Theory, Jonas reminds us, became as it hitherto had never been: an ingenious, inventive, even sportive effort to solve "a difficulty never faced before and itself an invention of theory" (55, p. 63). However much one must admire its inventors, one must nevertheless be thoroughly suspicious of their problem.

"The problem": what is it, for Jonas? What is the "evidence" I am supposed to have, and what does it disclose? On the one hand, I am asked to focus my unprejudiced attention on *my own experience as embodied*. Only life can understand life; but more than that: for this "evidence" I have in my own case is "an integral part of the evidence concerning life which experience puts at our disposal." Thus, on the other hand, I am asked to take this evidence I obtain in my own case and presumably make use of it "critically": i.e., to avoid the pitfalls of possible anthropomorphism (55, p. 91), but also to enable me to know what *life itself*, beyond *my own* and other *human* life, truly is. Here several puzzles make themselves felt.

First, as for possible anthropomorphism: why not? Or, rather: within Jonas' own "new monism," what else could there be? While anthropomorphism is not exactly ruled *out* in the passage cited, in his "Note on Anthropomorphism,"[9] on the other hand, it seems clear that it is most definitely ruled *in*. The history of anthropomorphism, Jonas argues, is the same as the history of dualism/ post-dualistic monism, a history of struggle against teleology (final causes). In modern materialism, as we know now, we are left in the same dilemmas and with the same caricatures: alienation of man and obfuscation of the reality of life. The other alternative mentioned in this "Note" (presumably the alternative Jonas is disposed toward, and in any case, the one implied in his emphasis on "evidence") is "to take the presence of purposive inwardness in one part of the physical order, viz., in man, as a valid testimony to the nature of that wider reality that lets it emerge, and to accept what it reveals in itself as part of the general evidence . . . " (55, p. 37). In fact, in the immediately preceding Appendix concerning the source of causality in the bodily experience of force and effort, he clearly embraces this alternative: " . . . the right of extrapolation from this source beyond its immediate range of deliverance is a question to be studied, without fear of the blame of anthropomorphism" (55, p. 33).[10]

I gather that it is with an aim to clarifying this and related issues that Jonas points out the two major tasks of his study: a philosophical biology and a philosophy of Nature. It is, he states here, *solely on the basis of* the philosophical biology that the philosophy of man is at all possible. Thus the "charge" of anthropomorphism is turned into a positive acceptance by Jonas, but solely in the context of philosophically grounding it in philosophical biology (55, p. 92).

But here things quickly become more obscure. On the one hand, Jonas appeals to the evidence we find "in ourselves," the evidence which gives us (presumably) "purposive inwardness" in the most direct and incontrovertible way, on the basis of which we shall then move to "life itself": it is taken as valid testimony to the wider reality, and is the sole basis and condition for biology and behavioristics being able to do what they do (55, p. 91).

On the other hand, however, the philosophy of man is said to be strictly dependent on philosophical biology. Anthropomorphism is effectively embraced; but then it is submerged with what may as well be called biologism. In the first case, the "evidence" can only come from within *reflection*,[11] for in no other way could one possibly become cognizant of "my own organism" as mine, "my own self," and the like. In the second, it is at least uncertain what role reflection might play, if any, and thus uncertain, too, precisely which "evidence" comes into play. If we wonder about this latter issue, so far as I can tell Jonas merely refers us back to the evidence mentioned: I am able to know "life" because, in the strongest sense, I myself am "alive," an organism. But *this* evidence seems clearly to imply precisely the reverse relation between the anthropology and the biology!

This seems not only full circle; it seems on the face of it vicious. For if philosophical anthropology is itself not possible except on the basis of philosophical biology, then neither can the evidence for the first figure in the securing of the latter; it must rather presuppose the latter. Thus only the reverse relation could possibly hold: the biology is what can alone inform and ground the anthropology, *and therefore the evidence in question*. It cannot be had both ways, and this is nonetheless the proposal.

This is no small quibble, neither irrelevant nor irreverent. It concerns not only the possibility of Jonas' ontology; it concerns more immediately the status and nature of that "evidence" and the "method" for grounding judgments made on behalf of the philosophical biology and the anthropology. All that I have suggested thus far is that, given the difficulty mentioned, the problem of method must loom large in his project, precisely to the extent that the sense of the evidence appealed to here remains uncertain, at the least, with respect to what it is supposed to establish, or give access to. (I return to this in a moment.)

The point has another relevance. Might it not be that the very history Jonas unravels so well has a quite different significance? For him, it signifies the necessity of a "new, integral monism" whose mission is to "absorb" the conflicts of dualism, idealism, and materialism "into a higher unity of existence." Thus do equally integral and purportedly comprehensive visions of the real become "stages," chapters merely, in the future history of metaphysics. But is that step really necessary? Might it not be, rather, that the history has the significance, negatively, of precisely *not* repeating the urge to comprehensiveness? That "a new monism"—whatever it may purport to do—is yet but *another* monism, and thus suspect from the very beginning? It may be that the very yearning for totality is what is so awry in the issue Jonas critiques, and that the "partiality" of every monism is not merely an historical mark of particular parentage but also of the very effort itself! Partiality may be the inevitable result of totalism; perhaps, too, *any* subsequent effort to conceive and write the "oneness" within "twoness" bears the inevitable mark of that very same parentage. I only note that at the most rudimentary levels of life, for Jonas, there is yet *the radically alien*: ephemeral or not, "matter" stands not just as "other" but as a radical stranger to "form"; and "form," however efficacious, however needful of "matter," is yet its radical opposite. What is different here—that "form" rides the crest of "matter," and that "nature" springs forth with "form"—may not make all that much difference for resolving the dilemmas of dualism. In the effort to construct the new monism, the duality of matter and form seems but to return, assuming only a new kind of tension and opposition. Jonas' dialectical move may thus not at all escape the dilemmas of dualism or monism, wherein "having it both ways" seems but native air.

But the doing of that skillful feat may well be the very thing our recent history, from Descartes on, has made impossible: the urge to comprehensiveness surely requires far stronger curbs than even Kant envisioned. I thus rephrase what Jonas calls the "crisis of every human ontology" in, not dialectical, but *reflexive* terms: every future ontology which will be able to come forth as a science must be capable of *accounting for and justifying itself* first and foremost.[12] This reflexive inquiry, however, may only show the impossibility of making good on the wager of comprehensiveness. However that may turn out, the main thing is that there cannot on principle be such efforts in the absence of *continuous and radical, i.e., transcendental, self-criticism*. Taking Jonas' appeal to "evidence" with philosophical seriousness thus leads directly to the transcendental grounds for "one's own awareness of organism," and in this specific sense to the *transcendental-phenomenological problematic*.

This returns me to my initial concern about evidence, and to the shifting character of Jonas' study. To what am I directed in the case of "evidence" of living organism in my own case? One would think that front and center would be precisely this *body which is mine*. And here it would seem that this is the issue: by virtue of what is this one organism uniquely singled out, from the universe of objects and organisms, *as mine*?

I "want" to eat, and *I* "move" *my* arm. . . . While Jonas insists that this daily action is bequeathed to us as a profound riddle by Descartes (e.g., 55, pp. 60–62), his analysis in the meantime leaves us wondering. That central question is quickly submerged, for what he presents is not at all a study meeting and redressing the Cartesian legacy, uncovering critically why it is that *this* body is so "intimately unioned" to me, but rather an exercise in philosophical biology: *metabolism* and its implications for understanding "life" and "organism."

Fascinating, profound, and subtle, his analysis, however, can hardly be warranted on the grounds of the very evidence he appeals to. For it is in this study that he appeals to "my own living organism" and, so it seems to me, the evidence here can in no way penetrate to the *metabolic* activities *of my own* organism, nor does this instruct us on the grounds for my experiencing *this* one body as uniquely *mine*. Our attention is deflected from the latter to the former, and we no more follow up that move than we find the sense of "self" and of "my body" understood, not on the basis of the evidence in one's own case, but on the scientific-biological model of metabolism—at best a highly indirect, intellectually sophisticated and abstract procedure, presumably introduced to reach the most concrete of all, the living organism! Indeed, either that is the case, or Jonas has all along presupposed that we *already know* the answer to the question, that we have, to express it better, *already done* the philosophic work necessary to understand the very categories of his analysis of metabolism: "self," "other," "foreign," "freedom," "necessity," and the like.

To be clear about this, we need to ask: what is the status of the inquiry into metabolism and its results? It may be that its significance lies in its *illustrative* character—viz., that, already having some knowledge ("evidence") about the sense of "body" and "self" (for instance), one can better understand the kind of activity metabolism is or reveals. It may be, on the other hand, that the inquiry's status is in effect a *regression* from the "evidence" in my own case to its roots in metabolic activity (in which case, as far as I can see, there is a crucial departure *from* the "evidence" of one's own embodiment, *to* what can be garnered from the highly abstract and sophisticated sciences of biology, bio-medicine, and the like).

But Jonas would endorse neither of these, I think. It seems rather that he is maintaining that the inquiry into metabolism is *foundational* for an understanding of "*life*," and therefore for understanding *one's own "life"*: the disclosure of the fundamental sense of self and body is to be found first at this level, he maintains, and helped by that one can then move to the specifically human life (philosophical anthropology). In this case, however, it must needs be emphasized that the appeal to evidence has no formal status in the way claimed; at best, it can enter only subsequent to the philosophical biology.

Either, then, the latter inquiry grounds that which would be indicated by the "evidence of each one's own organic awareness"; *or* this evidence (the anthropology) grounds and guides the biology, in which case the status of the claims made about metabolism must be radically altered.

In fact, however, it seems to me that Jonas' arguments, while expressly departing from "mere" phenomenology (55, p. 79), *trade* on it—or, if not on it, then on our common understanding of the central terms. As it were, I "know" what he means when he writes about the subtle workings and weavings of metabolism, *just because I "know" ahead of time about "self," "continuation," "transcendence," and the like, from my own experience.* Or, perhaps more accurately, thanks to the "evidence of my own organic awareness," the inquiry into metabolism makes sense, can be checked out, confirmed, or disconfirmed, and the like. But Jonas just does not give what is promised in his appeal to the "evidence." The evidence, taken seriously, concerns phenomena which the inquiry takes for granted have *already* been delivered to us.

If we step back a bit to assess what has transpired, it might be suggested, without appearing in the least bizarre, that the logic which had trapped Descartes, despite his insight, may well be at work in Jonas' effort to set up a "new monism." I mean: Jonas' strenuous and frequently brilliant double-edged effort to refute any materialist interpretation of "life," and to secure the "different nature altogether" (55, p. 82) of "organic identity," can succeed only at the substantial cost of reintroducing a kind of dualism. Now dubbed "form/matter," there seems little doubt that Jonas' analysis reinstates a gap between the two, hardly less formidable than the one Descartes had made. Not only is the sense of the "identity" of each radically different, not only is the source of that identity radically different, but so too is the principle or essence: for the physical world, matter is the principle; for life, it is form. And throughout the analysis of life, matter is taken as the "alien," the "foreign," the "accidental." Indeed, so profound is the chasm that Jonas is led to argue that no mere analysis of the physical record could possibly yield "life"; and, on the other hand, only a being itself alive could possibly know life, even in the indirect ways of inference (55, p. 82).

Of course, what Jonas calls "form" in organic life *does* take "matter" (of *some* sort, but *not all* sorts) into itself; it literally "incorporates" its other, it bodily transforms matter. But I fail to see how *in principle*, granting this description of the emergence of self and world from the rudimentary reaches of metabolic activity, there could be the *initial*, much less the *continuous contact* between two such radically opposed "things." Within Jonas' study, at its initiating point, there seems clearly the very "dualism" he has in other contexts rigorously refuted. And, as Descartes had indeed had a glimmering of the significant issue—"intimate union"—so Jonas has, with much greater force and clarity, seen the issue—the "living body" which is *mine*. The turn to metabolism, with the ontological categories of "form" and "matter" in hand, however, seems to generate or to include an equally enrooted dualism.

In a telling footnote to the analysis, however, he writes:

> . . . when we call a living body a "metabolizing system," we must include in the term that the system itself is wholly and continuously a result of its metabolizing activity, and further that none of the "result" ceases to be an object of metabolism while it is also an agent of it. For this reason alone, it is inappropriate to liken the organism to a machine. . . . But metabolism is more than a method of power generation, or, food is more than fuel: in addition to, and more basic than, providing kinetic energy for the running of the machine (a case anyway not applying to plants), its role is to build up originally and replace continually the very parts of the machine. Metabolism thus is the constant becoming of the machine itself—and this becoming itself is a performance of the machine: but for such performance there is no analogue in the world of machines (55, p. 76, n. 13).

Here, independently of the problems raised earlier about the formal status of "evidence," Jonas seems to me perfectly correct. But just as it is inappropriate to liken the organism to a machine, so also does it seem inappropriate to take this systemic activity as a dialectical relation between form and matter. No matter how, if at all, dialectically conceived, a form of dualism seems inevitable with that move. *The above passage, however, does not use that distinction*; instead, the living body is a "metabolizing system" whose "parts," continually changing and being replaced, are integral to the body itself as a consequence, and as the agency, of metabolism. *It is thus not a relation of form to matter which is revealed here, but of "part" to integral "whole"*; or rather, one can speak of a relation of "form" and "matter" only insofar as they are both understood as constituents of the integral, living system (the "whole"). So understood, however, this represents a major overhaul of these traditional categories, so major as to warrant their exclusion from the analysis of the body as a "living whole." The "life" of this integral whole is thus expressed by the specific and distinctive "activity" which continuously exhibits that complex and reflexive self-maintaining and self-enhancement. In these terms, it is not so much that the "form" rides on the "crest of a wave" composed of changing "matter"; nor that the latter comprises merely a "passing collection" whose individual "unity" (unity of matter) is of no particular consequence as regards the sustaining (self-sustaining) unity of the organism (unity of form). So understood, as I will later show, the very idea of "organization" collapses precisely to the extent that one argues that "matter" is in itself devoid of "organization" (i.e. form), or that "form" *somehow* comes to impose organization on otherwise formless matter. What we will find, rather, is that the "whole" itself is precisely nothing other than the system of mutually self-referencing constituents, which are themselves nothing outside their functional role (place, or significance) within that whole.[13] To take the "parts" of the organism, or of the metabolizing activity, as somehow "different altogether," as forming a "collection" all their own, and the like, is to vitiate the very "system" itself, to fragment it into a dualism easily as profound and consequential as any Descartes constructed.

* * * * * * * *

It is thus not so much that "the" organic body signals the "latent crisis of every known ontology." It is rather that *"my"* organic body does. The ease with which Jonas glides from the one to the other is striking, and suggestive, I think, of the temptations of ontological thinking itself: the urge to comprehensiveness, so deeply rooted and so apparently endemic, may nevertheless be profoundly inimical to what we (with Jonas) so mightly seek to know and be. The breakdown of traditional ontologies—dualistic and monistic alike—is signaled preeminently by "the *only* fully given concrete of experience" (*55*, p.

24), *my* own living body, which forms an integral, living, and incredibly complex whole—a veritable *contexture* achieved and sustained continuously by its own unique activity. And *this* "concrete" can by no epistemic stretch be reached by appeal to the *abstract* sciences of *bios*.

But having once posed the issue, one cannot let it slip away in the embrace of whatever totalism it may be—surely not, at the least, until its concreteness and fully presented contexture have been explicated. Only that evidentially guided and grounded task can possibly be what is "used" in the understanding of life more generally and thence be "testimony" for the wider reality beyond it. And, it seems to me, that critical, phenomenological explication of the "evidence of each one's own organic awareness" is exactly what lies beneath Jonas' otherwise penetrating analysis of metabolism—what stands under and makes it possible to understand it. Philosophical biology is thus based in philosophical anthropology, and that, in turn, finds its ground and continual critical accompaniment in the phenomenological explication of the "evidence" at hand.

Embodiment and Integrity

2

THE "knot of being," Jonas has shown, is bound in the living body, and dualism's trial at ontological dissection results in a radical disruption of the integral whole itself. The schism, calculated to heal the disorders of the newly emerging sciences, ends by producing a caricature of human life and begets a profound forgetfulness. Dualism is left with the hollow sound of "intimate union," subsequent idealism with a mere specter for a body, and materialism a mere ghost in a machine.

But that "knot," as was seen, is not so much directly grasped by Jonas as it is shunted aside on behalf of the admittedly important issue, "life as such." Hence another forgetfulness sets in, in the service of another "monism." This monism is not without its irony. While admonishing us to attend to evidence each of us garners from his or her own embodied life, our attention is immediately deflected to "life" itself, to metabolism. Necessarily incorporating a claim to ultimacy and comprehensivness, this is as well a claim to exclusivity, hence (perchance with vengeful dialectics) it sets the stage for a struggle among other, equally integral totalisms (*38*, pp. 8–9, 160, 237–39). And with this we are squarely back to the antinomy Dilthey anguished over for so long: how shall we, in the midst of a pluralistic bedlam, be able to stay the anarchy of opinions that then befalls us? Are we to pit "life" against "being"? "Being" against "mind"? "Mind" against"matter"? For when we read the richly hued texts of life, of Nature, of spirit, of history, of matter, of mind, every interpretation we might give seems intractably to give rise to still another, quite opposed interpretation. As Ricoeur has indicated, intrinsic to the very nature of interpretation is a conflict, a veritable war of opposites.[1] Yet the direction of such thought seems just as intractably to demand not simply *an* interpretation, but *the* comprehensive and exclusive one. How, indeed, shall we find the means to overcome what seems inherent in the very effort to overcome?

On the other hand, it was suggested already that there is an even more cutting irony here. In the urge to seek wholeness (the "all" of "what-is"), there is a moment of "double-think," a kind of knifing seduction which one thereby yields to: believing that one has found the "source" of all things (whatever name it be given), one finds oneself a mere pawn in some grand scheme, responding and responsible *to* its requirements, and seeing (or trying to see) oneself in its embracing mirror. And one forgets, fatally, that it is oneself who made the model, who thought the source. All such dreams and schemes wear a uniquely human face, even when defaced by double-think.[2] The echo of Dilthey's quandary is never absent: the "finitude of every historical phenomenon . . . the relativity of every kind of human apprehension of the totality of things. . . ."

Two things, then. First, the core sense of an authentic *problēma*, an impasse, is its *demand for discipline*; it invokes the necessity to stay with it rigorously and responsibly, wherever it may lead, not allowing other issues to come into view unless and until the problem itself demands that. Second, whatever may be the truth of whichever comprehensive view, the inevitable question such views generate must be squarely faced: how are we to decide, in principle, the question of truth and falsity, and thus decide between conflicting views? The question, therefore, is the question of *evidence*. For every such view is in a sense a *wager* (98, pp. 355–56): the bet is that one "view" will yield a better understanding of things than any other. But, and here the issue is a strict and hard one, how are we to judge the sense of "better"? Ricoeur is at least explicit on this usually concealed issue: we shall have that better understanding if the things in question are "better illumined" and "ordered" than otherwise. Here, however, is the rub, indeed the Achilles' heel: what are we to understand by "illumined" and "ordered"? and how are we to know whether the things really are thus better illumined and ordered? The wager is thus a hedged bet: it supposes all along that these things have already been delivered in their fullness to us, for only that deliverance could serve as the test for "better illumined and ordered."

In different terms, the wager inherent to such totalisms depends for its payoff on the phenomenological explication of the "things themselves" at issue. Whether, after having done the "dirty work" of detailed explication, one or another comprehensive view is possible, is a question to be left open. For, as Dilthey soon discovered in his own attempt descriptively to disentangle the complex nexus of mental life, that task is a formidable one indeed, requiring a major effort. The task here, however, is both clear and demanding: not "life," not the "living body," but that by virtue of which this one animate organism is uniquely singled out as "mine"—that is the issue which, from Jonas' own brilliant analysis of the past few centuries, is unequivocally delivered to us for our thinking. It is to this, then, that we must turn.

* * * * * * * *

As with most issues, there are several points of entrance to this one. I have shown elsewhere (*127*) that the question is by no means a new one; it has, in fact, been explored in considerable depth by numerous thinkers during the past few decades. But already at the end of the 19th century, Henri Bergson had stressed that this body, my own, even regarded as a physiological entity, is not simply an object like other objects. It is peculiarly *"mine"* (*4*, pp. 11, 14–16). This *one* organism, as no other, is a *center*: that by reference to which other worldly things are arranged, organized, displayed and placed. Moreover, inasmuch as these worldly things are never simply, passively "given" but *essentially* appear only within specific kinds of activities in which I am bodily engaged, my body is an "actional center" (*centre d'action*). Perception is not a preliminary gathering of information, then, not a prelude to action, but already arises within and through action. Things are not first of all conglomerations of "qualities" and only later taken up into contexts of bodily action; perception is not a matter of "data-reception" (or "input") followed by "internal neural translation" and then by "externalization" ("output"). These notions, to the contrary, are *abstractions away* from concrete bodily life, for which things are "menacing," "useful," "handy," "dangerous," and the like. In short, things are, as Jean Piaget stressed, "poles of action," appearing as what they are only in and through specifically organized schemes of activity (*89*, Ch. I).

Although Bergson had more to say, it remained for later thinkers to probe the phenomenon in greater depth.[3] Yet there is a significant area of contemporary discussion where the contributions of these authors have yet to be explicitly applied. It is important to do so, for this approach is not only relevant to a host of pressing problems, but will also, I believe, help to show that embodiment is in no sense a contrived, or merely intellectual, issue. The area I have in mind is what has come to be called "medical humanities," and the specific discussion is "medical ethics." I should make it clear, however, that while I cannot, within the limits of the present study, directly engage the crucial issues of medical ethics, the study should help to provide the philosophical framework, the proper context, for those problems—a context they presently lack in large measure.

BIOLOGY AND ETHICS

The thesis has been advanced by H. T. Engelhardt that "moral claims emerge and withdraw in step with the process of embodiment," a process involving "the genesis of personal being and worth" (*20*, pp. 486–87). Engelhardt's case is well made and cogent. Despite this, indeed despite the fact that the phenomenon of embodiment has been shown to be of decisive significance for human reality, and despite the obviously focal place of the human body in medicine and biomedical science, one rarely finds close scrutiny given to it in discussions of the ethical and value dimensions of medical practice and biomedical research. Why is this so?

Some part of the reason may well have to do with a prevailing tendency engendered by what Paul Ramsey calls our "resolutely biologizing age" (*93*, p.

59). Considering almost any bioethical issue—abortion, euthanasia, fetal research, selective treatment of deformed neonates, etc.—the discussions invariably come to the point where, it seems, biological and medical evidence becomes crucial to have on hand, and doctors are often called on for answers. For instance, in cases of abortion, the question concerning "the beginnings of life" seems unavoidable, and biological evidence is thought to be important. As André Hellegers puts it, however,

> the assumption is that the medical information is pertinent, or even important. Doctors are supposed to pronounce "death," and conversely may be expected to pronounce "life," or at least to be capable of doing so. Diagnosing life and death may factually be expected from physicians, but . . . this may not be the crux of the abortion debate. Terms like "personhood" . . . have no meaning in biology.
>
> What evidence science can bring to the debate must be restricted to that in which it has competence. This competence is restricted to describing biological facts. (35, p. 11)[4]

Thus, for Hellegers, while it may well be that such problems as abortion at some point *concern* the medical diagnosis of life and death, it must be clearly understood that such problems are simply not medical problems:

> . . . many have thought that the ethics of abortion may in some way depend on medical facts. I think this is an error. The fetus is an undoubted biological human being in the medical sense. It is human because it falls in the category of the human rather than in that of cats, rats, or elephants. It is a being because it is there. If it were not, no abortion would be necessary. The biological term human should not be confused with such unscientific terms as personhood, soul, value, dignity, or those words denoting societal attitudes toward biological life. (35, p. 14)

Whether one is "for" or "against" abortion, fetal research, etc., both stances "involve," in the words of Roger Shinn, "a metaphysical judgment about what it means to be a person" (113, p. 61). Such judgments, so far as many physicians and researchers are concerned, are related to non-medical issues. Even though it is true that the view of a physician such as Hellegers manifestly involves serious philosophical assumptions precisely about "person," "value," and the like, these are, as often as not, left simply unstated—and I shall have to come to grips with at least some of these unstated problems.

For the moment, however, it is necessary to press further into this discussion. The view commonly espoused is that even though it is true that the kinds of medical and biological facts which are presented by physicians in response to requests "can, of course, affect what is perceived by others" (35, p. 11), still, bio*ethical* debates are not *medical* or bio*medical* debates at all. Physicians and scientists, therefore,

> . . . are just the scientific diagnosticians and prognosticators and the deputative technicians for carrying out society's values. In the abortion debate the physician can

only state his own perceptions on value judgments about undoubted biological human life. . . . [O]ne does well to realize that those physicians who decide to perform the abortion do so as a reflection of their personal value perception of unborn human life, rather than on biological fact or medical fact. (*35*, pp. 14–15)

In the face of such strongly advanced views, it seems quite reasonable for those concerned with ethical problems to practice a rigorous "hands-off" policy when it comes to the human body. If the abortion, or any other "bioethical" issue, is a matter of "personhood," "value," or even "meaning,"[5] this takes it out of the sphere proper to science. Thus, presumably, despite the fact that the human body is so manifestly and intimately "involved" in most bioethical discussions, it forms *no* proper part of their ethical dimension:

I believe the abortion debate is not, and never has been, about when human life starts. I think it is a debate about the degree of which one accepts a utilitarian v. some other view of life. (*35*, p. 15)

If such a view is correct, what is peculiar is not at all that one finds so little scrutiny of the human body in ethical discussions, but rather Engelhardt's thesis concerning the essential tie between the body and the moral claims. The body would then be a biological affair and, as such, properly the concern of the biological and medical sciences and practices. Ethics and values, like "persons" and "souls," are "unscientific" and properly *meta*-physical (Shinn), not *physical*, and the metaphysical cannot be considered as dependent upon the physical. Scientists, of course, surely can and do speak about ethics. Yet this is just as surely *not as scientists* that they do this, but merely because they are human like the rest of us. Even if an ethicist is also a scientist or physician, however, there is simply no way for him properly to drag the body into the context of strictly ethical matters.

THE CADAVER AND THE SOMA

It may well be asked, however, whether one can so neatly divide matters. Even if one agreed that the abortion issue is not about "when life begins," though this is surely not immune to question,[6] this and other bioethical issues do profoundly concern "human life" itself, and not simply its (possible) "meaning" or "quality." After all, it is clearly at least one dimension of the ethical problem whether "life" ought to be continued *at all* (whether specifically as regards abortion, euthanasia, or psychosurgery). Beyond this, however, it is necessary to point out that even if the abortion debate were solely about whether one accepts a utilitarian, a deontological or some other view, these are all, as Hellegers himself says, views of "life"—presumably not "life" in the abstract, but *the very same "life"* with which medical praxis is concerned.

It will not do, furthermore, to argue that what is meant here is not so much "life" as the "significance" (value, dignity, quality) of life. That is surely a prominent ethical concern, but one suppresses or rules out what is qualified thereby ("life") at the risk of cutting the qualifier from any reference: to float freely in what sort of airy limbo one knows not, nor how. In different terms, I am concerned to mark out a perilous equivocation concerning "the human body": on the one hand, it is the strictly biological organism; on the other, it is the focus of clinical diagnosis and intervention, and as such is not *somehow* merely biological *but also* experienced by the person whose body it just happens to be.[7]

I want to pursue this problem by way of an indirection, through a fascinating passage from Paul Ramsey's reflections on the indignity of death.

> In the second year anatomy course, medical students clothe with "gallows humor" their encounter with the cadaver which once was a human being alive. That defense is not to be despised; nor does it necessarily indicate socialization in shallowness. . . . Even when dealing with the remains of the long since dead, there is special tension involved . . . when performing investigatory medical actions involving the face, the hands, and the genitalia. This thing-in-the-world that was once a man alive we still encounter as once a communicating being, not quite as an object of research or instruction. Face and hands, yes; but why the genitalia? Those reactions must seem incongruous to a resolutely biologizing age. For a beginning of an explanation, one might take up the expression "carnal knowledge" . . . and behind that go to the expression "*carnal conversation*," an old, legal term for adultery, and back of both to the Biblical word "know." . . . Here we have an entire anthropology impacted in a word, not a squeamish euphemism. In short, in those reactions of medical students can be discerned a sensed relic of the human being bodily experiencing and communicating, and the body itself uniquely speaking. (*93*, p. 59)

Concerned here to evoke the "felt difference between life and death," Ramsey emphasizes that this difference makes itself felt even in the case of the cadaver: thing-in-the-world though it may be, it is not merely that, for it is still encountered as "once a man alive" and not simply as an object of instruction. To be sure, the incommensurable contrast between life and death is met most dramatically with the "newly dead": if the cadaver evokes gallows humor, the mangled body lying on the emergency room stretcher awakens dread and awe. Both, however, suggest an almost haunting presence of once enlivened flesh—bodily gestures, attitudes, movements, stances—which a "resolutely biologizing age" too easily seems to ignore or suppress.

Such encounters with corpses (newly or long dead) suggest, indeed, that there are no clean divisions possible—neither empirically in medicine, nor substantially in metaphysics—between "biological" and "personal" life. Which is not to say that there are no differences in significance or logical status. It is to say, on the other hand, that what Ramsey has pointed to is a positive phenomenon in need of an accounting, and that this remains deeply enigmatic from the perspective presented by much contemporary biomedicine. Labeling terms such as "self," "person," or "dignity" as "unscientific" does nothing to elucidate their sense. Neither does it formally recognize that the animate organism treated or investigated by a physician or researcher is in no way *simply* "there"[8] on the table, but is a far more complex affair: in some determinable sense, varying with age, biological wherewithal, and circumstance, it is the body belonging to and experienced by a "someone," a "person." The cases of the fetus, the severely handicapped neonate, as well as those of the comatose patient or one under relatively complete anaesthesia, are, doubtless, problematic ones. Perhaps they must be conceived as limiting cases, those where the processes of embodiment are either not yet able to be more than minimally or only globally (undifferentiatedly) articulated, or have been too severely curtailed to permit the embodying functions. Perhaps, even, some organisms will never be able to be fully experienced by the one whose organism it is (or was). (Certain similar cases will be discussed later on.) Nevertheless, however one eventually comes to understand them, much less to treat them, it needs to be pointed out that they are as much "sensed embodiments" as the cadavers Ramsey talks about are "sensed relics" of the human being bodily experiencing and the body itself "uniquely speaking."

Pointing to this phenomenon, Ramsey is clearly at odds with any "mind/body" dualism—either philosophical or medical—which certainly seems implicit to a "biologizing age." In an ultimately less than successful effort to surmount the dualism, Ramsey refers to St. Augustine's claim that "the body is not an extraneous ornament or aid, but a part of man's very nature" (*93*, p. 60). In the case of the alive human being, body and soul are "conjoined and closely intertwined," they "interpenetrate" each other. Thus, Ramsey insists, "for Biblical or later Christian anthropology, the only possible form which human life in any true and proper sense can take here or hereafter is 'somatic' " (*93*, p. 60).

These suggestions raise profound issues. In the first place, as already mentioned, views like that of Hellegers become very problematic. The effort to divide out human biological from human personal life may well, paradoxically and ironically, signify that such a biomedical theory has in effect taken the *dead body*—the cadaver—as the model for the human body. As Jonas masterfully demonstrates, in classical panvitalism,

> it was the corpse, this primal exhibition of "dead" matter, which was the limit of all understanding and therefore the first thing not to be accepted at its face-value. Today the living, feeling, striving organism has taken over this role and is being unmasked as a *ludibrium materiae*, a subtle hoax of matter. Only when a corpse is the body plainly intelligible: then it returns from its puzzling and unorthodox behavior of aliveness to the unambiguous, "familiar" state of a body within the world of bodies, whose general laws provide the canon of all comprehensibility. To approximate the laws of the organic body to this canon, i.e., to efface in *this* sense the boundaries between life and death, is the direction of modern thought on life as a physical fact. Our thinking today

is under the ontological dominance of death. . . . All modern theories of life are to be understood against this backdrop of an ontology of death, from which each single life must coax or bully its lease, only to be swallowed up by it in the end. (*55*, pp. 12, 15)

Not a "live" body, indeed, one animated and experienced by a person, but only a dead one seems even remotely capable of being spliced off from the "person." Yet even though death is no longer the profound shock it had to be within panvitalism, but is now a constitutive principle—the accepted norm for bodies "in a universe formed after the image of the corpse" (*55*, p. 15)—Ramsey's quick reminder is perceptive. Even with the corpse we face a "sensed relic" of the once-embodied and communicating person—whence, of course, the otherwise quite unaccountable gallows humor, that "special tension" and the felt reluctance or hesitancy on encountering corpses in coffins or cadavers on carts. We will later come across quite similar "shocks" when we consider the implications of cases of brain-injured patients or autistic children.

It seems unavoidable, as Jonas suggests, that such a biology can only be a science (*logos*) without life (*bios*).[9] The point is that no science of life or of animate being generally, much less one focusing on the human body, can be considered well-grounded or epistemically complete unless it can *systematically* take into account that the human body is most fundamentally a live organism *embodying* a human person. Or, at the very least, such a science *must not in principle exclude* this. The materialism, mechanism, and accompanying positivism which subtly infuses much of modern biomedicine, in short, renders not only its own most fundamental *issue*—"life"—highly problematic; it also, and more significantly, leaves the living human body deeply enigmatic. It will thus be necessary, in the next chapter especially, to give some consideration to biologists of a very different persuasion.

In the second place, however, Ramsey's discussion is seriously deficient itself. What, after all, is "the body itself uniquely speaking"? It may well be that the body is not an "ornament," that one cannot without decisive loss reduce bodily life to "an acceptable level of indifference to the person long before his dying" (*93*, p. 60), that in short *no* version of mind/body dualism is acceptable. As Ramsey no doubt realizes, these claims are, however, hardly sufficient. But, as will be clear soon, neither are such notions as "conjoin," "closely intertwined," or "interpenetration"—as anyone familiar with Descartes' work quickly recognizes—at all adequate for the problem of understanding the living body as "mine."

In the third place, without a theory of "wholes and parts," the claim that the body is "a part of man's very nature" must remain, if not unintelligible, then certainly most obscure. Intentions to the contrary notwithstanding, the absence of a theory capable of articulating and accounting for the sense of both "whole" and of "part" (which are even more complex, as I hope to show, when it is a question of the embodying organism) can only give the views of modern theories of "life" (based in "death") far more credence than they in fact merit. Ramsey's sensitive noticing of our encounters with corpses and cadavers—by implication, with living embodied persons as diseased, maimed, impaired, or healthy—is not, unfortunately, matched by an equally sensitive *accounting* for these encounters.

HEALTH AND WHOLENESS

One physician-scientist has made some of these issues more salient. In the course of arguing for *health* as the proper aim of medicine (quite in keeping with the logic of any "art"—that is, following Aristotle, it inherently promotes some goal, some "good" of human life), Leon Kass rightly poses the question concerning the meaning of health itself. This, he contends, has to do fundamentally with "bodily integrity" or "wholeness":

> The wholeness of man is not the wholeness of a statue of a man,[10] but a wholeness-in-action, a working-well of the work done by the body of a man. . . . Health is a natural standard or norm—not a moral norm, not a "value" as opposed to a "fact," not an obligation, but a state of being that reveals itself in activity as a standard of bodily excellence or fitness, relative to each species and to some extent to individuals, recognizable if not definable, and to some extent attainable. If you prefer a more simple formulation, I would say that health is "the well-working of the organism as a whole," or again, "an activity of the living body in accordance with its specific excellences." (*60*, pp. 27, 28–29)

It is evident—although not as carefully pursued as seems necessary—that in this fine essay Kass' concern to reconceive the "end of medicine" as health *takes him to a reconception of the body as well.* Just as he is notably reticent even to use the language of "disease" (insisting instead that with health as the norm one must speak of various stages of "unhealth"),[11] so, we can say, his understanding of the bodily organism, being built on the notion of "wholeness-in-action,"[12] has little if anything in common with prevailing biological notions of the body-as-mechanism or as-cadaver, as something radically unakin and alien to personal life. For Kass, the human body (presumably the organism of any species, such as the squirrel he uses as an instance of what he means by a recognizably live body-in-action), is a living, integral unity. The sense of body indicates a unity or wholeness *achieved solely in action,* i.e., in realizing its own specific "excellences," and is a healthy body to the extent that this activity is "in accordance with" these "excellences." Difficult as it certainly is to define this "natural norm" (supposing this is correct) of bodily conduct, it is not only attainable, but patently recognizable by each of us all the time within the context of our daily living (as are the various stages of "unhealth," as any caring mother knows well of her own child, or most physicians clearly recognize when "something is not right" about a patient's look). Ramsey draws attention to the very same point, in the extreme cases of encountering cadavers: that "sensed relic" of the human being bodily experiencing and communicating is very much like the phenomenon to which Kass points in the case of the live body.

But as with Ramsey, so with Kass: serious problems remain in spite of the sense of rightness one has in reading his discussion of bodily integrity. On the one hand, like Ramsey but more explicitly, Kass relies heavily on the concept of "wholeness," but does not indicate what one is supposed to understand by this decisive notion. What is missing is a theory of "whole/part" relations, specifically as found with the human body—and without this, the very terms of Kass' study must remain obscure, even question-begging. On the other hand, several points do advance somewhat our understanding of the human body— one explicit and one only implicit.

First, the *reference to activity* clearly differentiates the "wholeness" of the living body from that exhibited by the statue of the body (as it does from that of the cadaver, although this presentiates the human being once-embodied quite differently from the way a statue makes the viewer think of the person portrayed—the latter being depictively embodied, as opposed to being a "sensed relic"). It is "wholeness-in-action" we need to understand, then, *not* a static wholeness.[13]

Second, however, precisely because of Kass' reference to bodily action, we are obliged to shift our attention as well to the one-who-is-active by means of his body. Thus if we are to understand the meaning of bodily wholeness, it is necessary to take "wholeness" itself as something effectively realized in bodily activity, and consequently as a phenomenon concretely experienced as such by the person whose body it is. This implies that *a theory of actively constituted and experienced bodily integrity or wholeness is necessary to medicine and biomedical science*—just the result I came to before.

In somewhat different terms, it is the phenomenon of *embodiment* which is the prominent issue raised by biomedicine itself and by many of the ethical deliberations pertaining to medical practice and biomedical research. Much of what has been said about human reality by both, however, is strongly reminiscent of reflections by Descartes and later philosophers on the body and the mind.

THE "INTIMATE UNION"

As already suggested briefly in the last chapter, there is a striking peculiarity in Descartes' treatment of the body. On the one hand, as is well known, he argued that mind and matter are "substances": mutually exclusive, self-subsistent and ontologically distinct entities, neither of which requires the other either to be or to be known. Since he took the human "body" to be a part of "matter," he was led to the view that, somehow, mind and body "interact," although specifying that "somehow" proved to be inordinately difficult, if not impossible—the infamous "pineal gland" argument seems more desperation than cogent argumentation.

Admitting, but for present purposes ignoring, these difficulties, it is also clear that his reflections show him, as he says, that though mind and body (as material) are separable, the mind is not "in" the body in the way a boatman is "in" the boat—i.e., not contingently or accidentally. Thus although "body" is part of the *res extensa*, it must nevertheless be conceived as also *something else*: the mind and the body, he frequently emphasizes (*15*, I, Med. V), are "intimately united." To say this, however, forces one to say that the body is *not* of a piece with the material world: it is not matter simpliciter. Nothing else in the material world can be designated as "intimate," much less "unioned," with mind. But neither can one say that the body per se is "mental" (part of the *res cogitans*): nothing of the latter can be designated as forming an "intimate union" with the material world.

Thus the human body stands out even in the Cartesian system as unique: though everything must be *either* mind *or* matter, and nothing can be both, the human body is *neither* mind *nor* matter (simpliciter, anyway). Just this peculiarity, however, is what his ontological dualism cannot account for. Hence the central question he faced: how is it at all possible for mind and body to influence, act upon, or act in concert with each other? The focal and apparently insurmountable difficulty is accounting for, correctly understanding, that very "intimacy" and "union" which are *essential* attributes of the body—and just for that reason, we have seen, does the human body, in the end, vitiate Descartes' ontology, and (as Jonas states) every post-dualistic ontology.

It has been argued by Gilbert Ryle that the difficulty is that Descartes' theory incorporates a basic "category mistake." Indeed, both "interactionists" and "reductivists" are for him guilty of the "dogma of the ghost in the machine": since "the phrase 'there occur mental processes' does not mean the same sort of thing as 'there occur physical processes,' . . . it makes no sense to conjoin or disjoin the two" (*101*, p. 22). These statements are of different logical orders, and thus the disjunctive "either/or," the conjunctive "both/and," and the identity (reductivist) thesis all fail to account for what Ryle takes to be the basic point. Namely, a person engaged in some action

> is bodily active and he is materially active, but he is not being synchronously active in two different "places," or with two different "engines." There is the one activity, but it is one susceptible of and requiring more than one kind of explanatory description. (*101*, pp. 50–51)

Ryle's point has obvious merit, especially in its negative thrust. Still, what he goes on to argue may well involve a *petitio principii*: to say that "there is one activity," which is describable in two different ways,[14] is on the one hand simply to *presume* (not to demonstrate) that such statements, though logically *different* (they "do not mean the same thing," he contends), yet can pertain somehow to the *same* thing. And, on the other hand, his argument fails to show what *legitimates* (if anything does) the presumption that there is indeed an activity which is "one and the same."

If one responds that the action is "one and the same" because, after all, one and the same person does it, this merely pushes the question back a stage: what, after all, constitutes the "person" as "one and the same" yet as *both* "mentally" *and* "physically" active? Just as importantly, since the activity is presumably experienced and believed by the person to be *his* (ultimately, *his* body), what are the grounds for, and thus what legitimates the conceiving of, the action itself (and, of course, the body) as "mine"?

Reconsidering Descartes' reflections on the peculiarity of the body, it seems reasonable to say that despite the inconsistencies and even absurdities of his ontology, he had precisely this phenomenon of "mineness" in view when he insisted on the "intimate union" of mind and body. Just this, however, is *presupposed* and not in the least dispelled by Ryle's arguments. The supposed "ghost," in other words, merely returns to haunt the would-be exorcist. Ryle wants to deny that it makes sense to disjoin, conjoin, or reductively identify mind and body, to be sure. However, he succeeds in this only by covertly readmitting the shadowy culprit of dualism through the back door, as is clear when he asserts *both* "there is mental activity" *and* "there is physical activity."

In short, Descartes' insight into the fundamental issue—the peculiarity of the body itself (the human body)—stands, and remains to be accounted for, as a positive phenomenon in its own right. I have already indicated how Jonas' analysis is deflected from the critical issue. It must be noted here that for the same reasons that Descartes fails to get a clear hold (*con-cept*) on the issue, so, too, does Ramsey, as his references to Augustine's terms make obvious: terms such as "conjoining," "intertwining," and "interpenetrating" take us no further than does the Cartesian "intimacy" of "union." What is at issue, to repeat, is the *sense* of "intimacy" and the *sense* of "union": what is it about the human body that in principle enables it and the mind (whose body it is) to be so "unioned"?

In the same way, Hellegers' and others' attempts to carve out the biological organism as the exclusive domain of the biological and medical sciences, leaving that of "personal life" and "values" to ethical and social concerns, fares no better than Descartes' earlier bifurcation of reality into physical and mental substances. Finally, although Kass' concept of the integrity of the body as a "wholeness-in-action" is surely a sound notion, not only must "wholeness" be theoretically grounded, but, it seems clear, his study does not take us very far in understanding the specific peculiarity of the body as "intimate," or as "mine."

As has already been suggested, it is the phenomenon of *embodiment* which undergirds all these discussions, to which indeed they all point without, however, specifically focusing on it *as such*: in virtue of what is "this" particular body uniquely singled out for "me" in "my experience" as *mine*, prior to all theorizing? In different terms, the circumstance that in Descartes' theory the status of "body" continuously undergoes shifts—between being merely "extended" (or, in contemporary terms, being regarded as a complex of closely interrelated physico-biological parts and systems), and being "intimately unioned" with mind—may itself be indicative not so much of a "category mistake" (*pace* Ryle), as it is expressive of the root, elemental inadequacy of an entire conceptual framework—that ground of conceptions thanks to which thinking is itself at all coherent and possible. It is as if modern thought were no sooner launched, on different bases from that which nurtured medieval thought, than the seeds of its failure were sown; and this, with a remarkably honest and perceptive insight by Descartes himself.

What is required if we would truly grasp the human body—rather, embodiment, the embodying organism—is, as suggested already, some explicit discussion of the following fundamental features (preliminarily expressed, at this point): (1) the senses of "intimacy" and "union"; and (2) the sense of the body as a "wholeness-in-action." I shall mark out some of the prominences on this complex terrain—those which will help to elicit the way in which "intimate union" is constituted within the framework of the body-as-in-action.

EMBODIMENT: THE CORE PHENOMENON

A full genetic-constitutive *Abbau*, the phenomenological explication of the founding-founded stratification of embodiment, is not within the scope of the present study. That is properly the theme of an entire study of its own. All I am concerned to show here are the conditions without which, or in the absence of one or more of which, "this" embodying organism would cease to be what it is, or would be severely impaired—or deeply confusing—in its serving to embody or enact the multiple and complex strivings, efforts, and awarenesses of worldly and other objects. Whether or not it is proper to use the substantival term "consciousness" (*Bewusstsein*), or the participial "becoming-conscious" (*Bewusstwerden*), as Ricoeur seems to prefer (*95*, p. 424), it seems evident that there is a complex of intentive processes (*Erlebnisse*)[15] which, so to speak, "presence" the embodying organism, make it present *as such*, or have it within their ambience. Thanks to the continuous functioning of this complex, this body (*Körper*) becomes uniquely singled out as the embodying organism (*Leibkörper*) experienced as "mine." It it thus vital to delineate the textures of that complex in order to make out the meaning of embodiment. In the following mere sketch, I rely heavily on the abundant literature already cited.

(1) *Orientational Locus of the Sensorium*

Sensory experience is not simply one among many other, equally available and important experiences. Nor is it, save by magical devices invoked in the service of a theory that directly clashes with our actual experience, a dubious, untrustworthy deliverance of affairs (sense quanta) which, to be proper grist for the epistemic mill, must be man-handled (treated, handled, transformed by man's own inveterate, inadvertant tendencies, or conceptual a priori wherewithal) into fitting fodder for knowledge and action—only then able to correspond to the world. The deep-lying suspicion of sensory experience, a suspicion pervading present-day physiology, psychology, and much philosophy, is itself the most suspect of enterprises. It is an inheritance, indeed, in Erwin Straus' phrase, "a heredodegenerative defect" (*115*, p. 149) communicated especially from modern dualism and its subsequent post-dualistic monisms. Sensory experience is, rather, the sole means by which the concretely environing world of things is as such at all disclosed to us. It is, Straus continues,

> the basic form of all experiencing, from which other modes of existing—such as thinking, remembering, imagining—separate off, but always return. Sensory experiencing is of the present. But the Now of the present is always *my* Now, a moment of my becoming. The essence of sensory experience itself, in its besetment at every moment, is to be sensitive to the efficacy—*i.e.*, the reality—of the *Other*. (*115*, pp. 168–69)

Along with the skepticism directed to sensory life, it has been a favorite tactic of traditional approaches to seek the principles of worldly order and organization elsewhere than in sensory experience. Finding "causality" (hence: order, pattern, connection, regularity, spatial location) absent from perception, commonly modeled on vision alone, one *had* to seek out an "elsewhere" from whence to derive it. But, as we already have seen, this (as Jonas terms it) "causal muteness of percepts" (*55*, p. 28), which both Hume and Kant took as an ultimate, is strictly a *function of forgetting the body*. For whatever may be the case concerning the causal origins of sense perception itself,[16] Jonas and Straus are clearly correct:

> Causality is thus [Jonas writes] not an a priori basis of experience, but itself a basic experience. . . . [It] is not the a priori of experience in the understanding but the universal extrapolation from propriobodily prime experience into the whole of reality. . . . [T]here is the plain fact that *without* the body and its elementary self-experience, without this "whence" of our most general, all-encompassing extrapolation into the whole of reality, there could be no idea whatever of force and action in the world and thus of a dynamic connection of all things: no idea, in short, of any "nature" at all. (*55*, pp. 23, 24)

And in Straus' terms:

> All this [i.e., worldly order and unity] is part of the immanent content of sensory experience; it does not stem from empiric knowledge—it is its foundation. The unity of empiric knowledge is not the result of combining things originally separate. . . . In the elemental alteration of [sensory] involvement, the *Other*, the world, shows a physiognomy corresponding to sensory experience. (*115*, pp. 155, 167–68)

This body is uniquely singled out in my experience as "mine" just because it is the locus, the "whereat," for the disclosure of the environing world of things, on the one hand; and, on the other, it is that by virtue of which there is an environing world of things in the first place, in the sense that, failing sensory experience, there would be no correlative milieu of sensorily experienced affairs (as the congenitally blind person has no literal world of colored things). It is solely *in reference to* my body's being the locus of the diverse sensory fields that "there are" diverse objects and qualities in the environing milieu. It is solely *in reference to* my body's being "here" that things are arranged as "close by," "far off," "over there," and the like—for perception as for action.

Yet the diversity of objects and qualities is not simply that. Not only may one and the same thing be experienced differently, but one and the same sensory experience can be had of a diversity of things: I can see, touch, taste, hear the coffee in the cup; but while seeing the coffee, I see also the cup, the desk, the pipes lying nearby, etc. Moreover, by means of only one sensory experience, the coffee is apprehended in only one of its aspects—e.g., taste; other experiences disclose one and the same coffee, but each time only as regards some relatively specific quality or determination. As I experience the coffee in varying aspects (when first poured, when slightly cooler, etc.), in each of them I am affected, seized, beset by it in a specific way. Its "thereness" varies for seeing, touching, hearing, tasting, and the like; and the sense of my own body's "hereness" correlatively varies: what is "here" for the eyes is not the same as the "here" for the fingers, or for the mouth, the lips, the ear.

There is thus a *complex* unity-in-diversity as regards *both* the object experienced *and* the experiences of it, and the variety of "places" which the object occupies all *refer to* the *position* of the one body with its variety of sensory members. *By means of* my membered bodily organism, I apprehend the object now this way, now that, and this object itself *refers to* my bodily placement:

> The relationship [Straus writes] to the *Other* in sensory experience is mutual and reversible. In relation to the *Other* I experience myself in my own existence, determined in a peculiar way. Vis-à-vis a thing, whatever it may be, I feel myself as part and parcel of a relation in which the object is the *Other* for me, and vice versa. In sensory experience I always experience myself *and* the world at the same time, not myself directly and the *Other* by inference, not myself before the *Other*, not myself without the *Other*, nor the *Other* without myself. (*115*, pp. 147–48; cf. *55*, pp. 84–85, 99–107)

As Aron Gurwitsch has convincingly shown (*31*, pp. 30–35; Pt. IV), the object of sensory experience is a self-identical thing, a unity of its *own* kind—a unity that cannot be *derived* from either perceptual or cognitive syntheses. The essential "referencing-to" the bodily organism, then, does not mean that the object's unity is derived from the body's. Rather, that unity is an "autochthonously" organized Gestalt-contexture appearing as such to the multiple modes of experiences possible with respect to it. Nevertheless, though not *derivable* from the unity of the bodily organism, the "one" object is strictly *correlative* to the "one" organism embodying me in the diverse modalities and potentialities of concrete sensory life. My embodying organism is thus constituted as my *orientational locus in the world*, "my place," complexly articulated and membered by means of its ("my") sensorium. In the diversity of my senses I am *oriented to* the Other as one and the same, and the Other is positioned and *oriented by* (referenced to) my bodily placement (body attitudes, stances, place, movements, etc.). Hence the arrangement of the environing milieu of things is functionally correlated with my organism: the latter is the orientational, sensorial *center* for the actional and sensible display of surrounding objects.

(2) Co-Presence of the Own-body

Even supposing the above sketch to be correct, there seems something artificial about such locutions. If I am called to testify in court about what I saw at such and such a place and time, I may say: "I saw X entering the liquor store. . . ." If someone asks whether I like the taste of an apple, I may say: "it tastes 'winey,' or 'tart' . . . ." If someone asks why I am sanding a board vigorously, I may say: "I felt a rough spot there . . . ." In all, it seems, my sensory experiences seem to be *of* objects—of this or that particular quality, determination, or relation pertaining to the thing itself. While no one would deny that these experiences are, as the case may be, visual or tactual, auditory or gustatory, and that these are in turn abiilities or features of the body and its organs, it may seem an artifice to drag along my body in all sensory reports. "I" see (touch, taste, etc.) the coffee itself; and "of course" I must have a body in order thus to see (touch, taste, etc.), but I surely don't have to see or be aware of my eyes in order to see the things around me—even though there are "of course" many times, and many ways, in which I do experience my own body's members.

Most of us, most of the time, pay no or little attention to our own embodying organisms. Our attention is captured, rather, by the things around us. If, as Jonas has urged, Kant and Hume, and the bulk of traditional theories, "forget the body," *so do we all* in a way. What do we make of this curious circumstance? Even if we reflect more carefully on the matter, we must still reckon with this, that we are for the most part directionally attentive to objects and rarely to our own bodies. And even when, say, I see my fingernails, touch my sprained ankle, hear my voice, it seems that little alters: these seem to be sensory experiences little different from those of other objects.

Yet I have already suggested the essential correlativity of the bodily sensorium and the sensed Other. How, then, do we reckon with the usual "forgetting" of the body in daily life? It is, as Sartre emphasized, *precisely as* "forgotten" or as "surpassed" toward the things attended to, that my embodying organism is singularly embodying (*103*, pp. 328–30). As J. H. Van Den Berg expresses it, it is the physiognomy of objects which reveals the embodying organism as such:

> The qualities of the body, its measurements, its ability, its efficiency and vulnerability can only become apparent when the body itself is forgotten, eliminated, passed over in silence for the occupation . . . for whose sake the passing is necessary. (*119*, p. 70)

Without having to accept Sartre's early ontology—which has its problems (see *127*, pp. 106–25)—what he and Van Den Berg here point to is that however much sensory attention is focused on the thereby disclosed affairs proper to it, my body is *essentially co-present* along with and implicit to that very attentiveness.[17] Indeed, there could be no sensory awareness of objects without that co-presence: my body is, as already indicated, essentially referred to by these sensibly perceived affairs. To stress the body as an orientational nexus is to note that while it is not itself an object in the way perceived and actionally correlated affairs are objects, it is the *conditio sine qua non* for such affairs at all to appear. Because of this, Gabriel Marcel quite early called the body-qua-mine the "prototype" of objectivity, that which makes possible the appearing of any other object whatever (*75*, pp. 116, 243, 330–38).

For the body to be such, Marcel also recognized, requires that in some profound way I "feel" my own embodying organism. This mode of *sentir* he found extraordinarily difficult to seize upon, much less to express in language. Variously writing of a "felt kernel" (*noyau senti*) (*76*, I, pp. 107–14), of "coenesthesia" (*75*, p. 243), of a mode of participative and mediative feeling (*mediation sympathique*) (*75*, p. 246), and even of an *Urgefühl* (*75*, p. 247), Marcel held that my body *as embodying* cannot be made the object of a perception (i.e., placed before, or over against, me, whose body it is), or of a cognitive process. Its "being felt" is a matter of the "body's potential action . . . my body is only felt inasmuch as it is me-as-acting: feeling is a function of acting" (*75*, p. 260). Somehow—a difficulty Marcel was to grapple with throughout his career—this "felt kernel" *must* be continuously present and efficacious, for otherwise there could be no "feeling" (in the primordial modes of contact and resistance) of anything else in the world.

Jonas, too, has stressed this ineluctable presence of feeling. First, as regards the source of the crucial concept of causality, he stresses that its primary aspect "is not regular connection, not even necessary connection, but force and influence; . . . the source of this experience is, indeed, not sense perception, but our body exerting itself in action . . . " (*55*, p. 33). If the source of causality is an *actum*, not a *datum*, of perceptual life, so, too, it seems is the sense of the live body which is mine a phenomenon of *action*. But, second, one cannot, the physician Herbert Plügge insists, separate the motor and the sensory spheres—doing so, one can only end up with "artifacts

. . . arrangements in which the original phenomenon has already been denatured . . ." (*90*, p. 295). Similarly, Jonas argues, however it may be termed (feeling, sensitivity, response to stimuli), some degree of "awareness," however faint, is *essential* to the organism, for

> only by being sensitive can life be active. In affection by a foreign agent, the affected feels itself, its selfhood excited, or illuminated as it were, against the otherness without and thus set off in its isolation. At the same time, beyond and "through" this inner state of excitation, the affecting presence is felt, its message of otherness, however obscurely, incorporated within. As felt, the affecting agent obtains a presence of sorts "within" the affected subject. (*55*, p. 85)

Here it would be well to pause: what exactly are these "feelings"? Jonas writes of a "quality of felt selfhood . . . [which] must be there for satisfaction or frustration to make a difference" (*55*, p. 84), and this quality is manifested at once in spontaneous efforts directed to objects, and in being impacted by foreign agents. In both cases, something is felt "there"—in and on the organism which, to "feel," must be "sensitive" to the resistances the outward reaching organism encounters and to the impact on it by other affecting agencies. The germinal "awareness" is an "inwardness" over against the "outwardness" of the striving or efforting organism—a complex "feeling" whose place is, as Straus emphasized, always in relation to the *Other*. It arises in *acting*, in the most elemental forms of impacts, hustlings, clashes, collisions, and jostlings of utterly concrete bodily life.

This complex dimension of feeling can occur, Husserl had early contended, only on condition that the bodily organism is a *Sinnesorgan*. Or, we could say, this is "my" body only if it is *sensitive*; in Husserl's terms, only if this body is not simply a body but an animate organism having *fields of sensations* spread out over and on it (*41*, p. 97). But these "sensations" (*Empfindungen*) are *by no means* what traditional theory labeled "sense-data." The animate organism as a "bearer of localized sensations" (*Sinnesorgan*) is, rather, the place of "live-bodily events" (*Leibesvorkommnisse*):

> I find on it, and I sense "on" and "in" it: warmth on the back of my hand, cold in my foot, touch-sensations on my fingertips. I sense spread out over wider expanses of my organism's flesh the push and pull of clothes. . . . The localized sensations are not properties of the animate organism *as* physical thing, but on the other hand *are* the properties of the thing "animate organism"—more particularly, *actional properties* [*Wirkungseigenschaften*], properties of the organism's activity. They appear *if* the organism is touched, pressed, burned, and so on, and they appear *there where* it is and in the time *when* it is. They continue to occur only under circumstances [*unter Umständen*], so long as the contact lasts. (*47*, pp. 145–46)

Thus within this primordial "if/then" (*unter Umständen*)—*which is precisely what undergirds Jonas' notion of "force" as the source of causality*—"feelings" in the sense of live, localized events *occur*, thanks to which one can *then* term this organism a "sensitive" one. Whether initiated by the uninvited intrusions into or onto the body by "foreign agents," or generated by its own effective venturings (*Wirkungen*), the "feelings" spread out (in various manners) on and in the body constitute a "co-presencing" of the embodying organism in all concrete experience. *My embodying organism is thus a kind of sensitive "readiness," a felt potency*, lending a certain physiognomy to environing things, which are thus inseparably (albeit distinguishably) bound up as "actional poles" to the bodily activities within which they alone appear. The co-presence of the embodying organism in all presencings of "foreign" objects is thus a *strict correlativity* which cannot be denied except by losing the phenomenon at issue.

(3) *Bodily Enactments: Causality and Feeling*

My embodying organism is such by virtue of its continuous functioning as the orientational locus of the sensorium, which is inseparably bound up with the motorium as co-presented in all effectual bodily ventures and adventures, in strict correlativity with the environing world of resistant things. Still, an ambiguity in the crucial phenomenon of "feeling" remains. If I reflect more carefully on even the simplest of bodily effectuating, or being bodily affected—i.e., on the motorium itself—something singularly elusive begins to become more salient.

Kurt Goldstein's acute observations of a variety of brain-injured soldiers help to make this phenomenon prominent (*27*, pp. 61–95, 149–57, 162–67).[18] For with such patients, precisely what usually transpires in many cases of bodily enactments (writing, talking, pointing, showing, saluting, etc.) has become altered, even occluded. To take but one example:

> A patient of mine suffering from visual agnosia could not recognize a single letter visually, yet he could make out the significance of words. We ascertained that he accomplished this by way of kinaesthetic experiences, gained through tracing the letters with movements of his eyes. In this connection, we are interested only in the fact that this patient was not at all conscious of any difference between this method of reading and his previous normal way of reading, and, further, that this substitute method had evolved quite spontaneously, and to a high degree of perfection. (*27*, pp. 78–79; see pp. 149–52)

Without discussing here Goldstein's otherwise important distinction between the "abstract" and the "concrete" attitudes (to which I will return in a later chapter), what the example illustrates in another respect is decisively significant in two ways for understanding the embodying organism as such. First, due to a particular lesion a hitherto normal way of "reading" was vitiated; second, without having to "think about" it, apparently, another way evolved "quite spontaneously." Now although there was this unselfconscious evolving of a different mode of reading, in which the patient's "*will* naturally *has no part*" (*27*,

p. 78), and even though the physicians had great difficulty convincing the patient that this way was not the usual way to read, they were finally able to make this clear to him and then to help him improve by proceeding systematically (27, p. 150). The procedure he used to such success involved the initiation of a set of minute *eye and head movements, kinaesthetic* experiences which compensated for and replaced his previous way of reading. Similar observations were made as regards other patients, especially those with lesions in the motor area. Except for total destruction of structure, "in cases of lesion of a sensory or motor area, the relevant performances do not drop out uniformly. The lesion produces effects according to a characteristic selective process . . . the performances affected undergo modification" (27, pp. 79–80).

This is the crucial point: however little actual "thinking" is necessary for one to raise one's arm (e.g., "to point"), however little actual thought is necessary for a patient to realize the same results in a different way ("reading"), both of these inherently involve not only a kind of *effort-to-do* something, but specific sorts of *bodily activity*, which *enact* certain efforts or strivings. Every execution of a movement involves these *kinaesthetic* feelings; or, better, *each is most directly enacted or embodied by certain patterns of kinaesthetic "flows" (Ablaufe).*[19] At times, these can become more explicitly attended to, as in the case of the instruction of the above patient, or if one pays deliberate attention to the "flow-feelings" intrinsically involved when one raises one's arm. "I" need not, indeed rarely ever, deliberately focus my attention on these; as Goldstein points out, the sometimes severe readaptations which brain-injured patients often go through are rarely self-conscious. Or when the patient is confronted with them, either there is flat disbelief or else, in situations calling for conduct not available to the patient (or at hand only with great difficulty), the patient has a "catastrophic" experience (27, pp. 71–74).

What thus becomes salient is that this elusive sense of "feeling"—the patterns, quickly and in many ways spontaneously habituated, of kinaesthetic "flows"—is what *most fundamentally constitutes this body as my embodiment.* They continuously function in a *double manner*: on the one hand, they enact, concretely "flesh-out," the rudimentary strivings, efforts, wishings, and wantings; on the other, whatever appears in any of the sensory fields is strictly, *functionally correlated* to the actualizing of these kinaesthetic flow-patterns. These, too, reveal an *"if/then" pattern*: "if" I move my arm in specific ways, "then" the glass is knocked off the table. Thus *bodily experience at its roots, and not only in relation to resistant or impacting objects, has this "causal" style.* Indeed, the experience of force and effort Jonas describes turns out to be far more basic and complex than even he indicates. This "force" is first and foremost an enacting by kinaesthetic patterns of elemental strivings—whether they are initiated by the organism towards the world, or whether they are reactions by it to impacting things.

These "flows" are not themselves "experienced" or "felt" in the way objects are, nor yet in the manner of coenesthetic or interoceptive data: neither like the pushes and tugs of tactual life, nor the "inner" sensing of growls, gurgles, pains and satiations, kinaesthetic flows are the *"urgefühlt"* of bodily life, at once embodying mental strivings and positioning or orienting the appearing of other objects. In this, they answer fundamentally to what has been termed "mediation" (*75*, pp. 116, 243–60). They are *essentially "means"*; kinaesthetic patterns are that by virtue of which anything else is able to appear or be experienced. My animate organism, then, is what Husserl calls a "freely-moved and -movable sensorium" (*freibewegtes Sinnesorgan*), most directly that which embodies or enacts the multiple kinds of striving (*Willensorgan*) and enables perceptual life to ensue (*Wahrnehmungsorgan*) (*41*, p. 44; *47*, pp. 151–52).

(4) *The Reflexive Contexture*

With every description of life, Jonas has said, the introduction of "self" is unavoidable. Every outward reach and outward exposure to the Other requires an "inwardness or subjectivity . . . imbuing all the encounters occasioned in its horizon with the quality of felt selfhood, however faint its voice" (*55*, p. 84). Husserl, Marcel, Straus, and most others who have addressed the topic similarly stress what Merleau-Ponty calls a *"complexe inné."* Quite sensitive to the subtle phenomena here, Merleau-Ponty nevertheless leaves a number of puzzles in his effort to uncover the profound reflexivity inherent to my embodiment—my being at once "to-myself" and "to-the-world." Ultimately, even while he obviously understands the complex of bodily engagement, of my being *incarné* in and by my *corps-propre* which is *"toujours-déjà-là"* and engages me in the midst of things, the "central phenomenon," he writes, grounding my subjectivity and my transcendence,

> consists in my being given to myself. *I am given*, that is, I find myself already situated and involved in a physical and social world—*I am given to myself*, which means that this situation is never hidden from me, it is never round about me as an alien necessity, and I am never in effect enclosed in it like an object in a box. (*79*, p. 360)

This presence to myself (*Urpräsenz*) is at the same time a *"dé-présentation"* thrusting me outside myself. And this double root of my life is expressive, on the one hand, of my being bound (*engagé*) to a stratum of *bodily life* ultimately "always-already-there," an *"ambiguïté"* with respect to which it is never possible to draw clear distinctions; and on the other, of my being rooted in *temporality*—the "archetype of the *relationship of self to self*, and it traces out an interiority or ipseity [*Selbstheit*]" (*79*, p. 426). Within the setting of corporeality (which is *always* "already established" and delivered over to me as mine but which nevertheless retains its "anonymity"), it is temporality (at once a sort of "bursting" or "thrust" towards the future) which reveals the fundamental sense of "being-self." It is an "ek-stasis": a splitting-apart (*déhiscence*) toward what is to-come (*Zu-kunft*), yet always enrooted in bodily life.

I find much that is brilliant and acute in this conception. Yet if we wonder, as we must, about this *Urpräsenz* and *dé-présentation* (*Entgegenwartigung*—the terms are, of course, Husserl's), and their embodiment in and by corporeal processes, we are led to wonder whether this corporeal engagement has been dis-engaged with sufficient depth. The various usages he adopts to express *le corps-propre*—anonymity, generality, typicality—while correct in a way, fail to come to grips not only with what has already been delineated above, but also with several prominent and striking features of this embodying organism— features which cast some doubt on his conception of "selfhood" as well as the "own-body."

Without rehearsing the positive and the negative features of Merleau-Ponty's work here,[20] I want to go directly to the issues. Jonas continually stresses the "felt selfhood" in the very sense of the live body; Straus, too, unequivocally endorses this, as does Marcel, and still others. But what is this "felt selfhood" within the frame of bodily life? There is a kind of "awareness" no matter how germinal, says Jonas, an inwardness which "harbors the supreme concern of organism with its own being and continuation in being—that is, it is self- centered . . . " (*55*, p. 84). But what does this tell us?

There are two clues, one from Husserl and one from Goldstein, which should guide us in pursuing this. Husserl points out a singular feature of the embodying organism, namely that it is

> reflexively related to itself. That becomes possible because I "can" perceive one hand "by means of" the other, an eye by means of a hand, and so forth—a procedure in which *the functioning organ must become an Object and the Object a functioning organ*. And it is the same in the case of my generally possible *dealing* with Nature and with my animate organism—which therefore is reflexively related to itself *also in practice*. (*41*, p. 97)

Not only, then, in respect of those awarenesses of one body-part by means of another, but also in all my practical-bodily dealings with the environing world, is there this reflexivity or *self-referentiality of the bodily organism to itself*. This seems clear enough in the former case: touching my own hand, each hand is at once touched and touching, each (as we already saw) is *positionally referenced*, inasmuch as what sensibly appears refers to the position (stance, posture, placement) of the experiencing organism itself. Hence we have here a case of mutual, reciprocal referencing: *reflexive self-referencing*.

But in what way is *this* reflexivity evident in my dealings with the environing milieu? To elicit what seems to be meant here, we must fill in an important gap in the explication thus far. Goldstein points out how there may be modifications of performances by brain-injured patients, "due to the functional modification undergone by *undamaged* substrata as an indirect result of the destruction of *other* substrata." Hence it is "reasonable to assume that in the normal nervous system *all parts function in interrelation with the whole*, or at least with more extensive fields" (*27*, p. 81; *my emphasis*). In fact, careful physiological observation shows that the nervous system is an authentic *system*, i.e., has the character of a figure-ground process, such that a given process (with its correlated performance) in one circumscribed area exhibits a form and intensity differing from that in the rest of the system. Thus

> if one raises an arm vertically, the execution of this movement requires, as one can feel in one's self and observe in others, a quite definite position for the rest of the body. The raised arm is the figure, the rest of the body is the background. . . . Taken from our visual experiences[figure and ground] . . . fit not only visual but all 'configurations . . . in speaking, thinking, feeling, etc. . . . Habitually we ignore the background of a performance and pay attention only to the figure. This is faulty observation; for figure and ground are intimately interconnected. (*27*, pp. 87–88)

To execute any movement—walking, pointing, turning one's head to look behind, etc.—requires a definite background attitude for the rest of the body; indeed, if the latter changes (e.g., if one's arms are impeded while walking), so does the former (one's gait alters). Beyond this, Goldstein shows with marvelous insight how performances are as well interconnected closely with the situations of their occurrence: a patient may in one situation do poorly on a test, but perform with great success on a test which supposedly demands much more sophisticated talents (as in arithmetical calculations). Hence the diagnosis and subsequent treatment of such patients becomes exceedingly difficult, since what has been impaired may appear only in some situations and not in others (even though ostensibly similar). In view of these profound interconnections (a term which will itself have to be submitted to criticism, however), helping a patient to learn words requires that one be cognizant of which situations the words belong to naturally for the patient, what their own intrinsic meaning-relations are for the patient, and what are the occasions of typical usage, for instruction at all to succeed (*27*, pp. 133, 157, 198).

From Goldstein's studies—and others he reports—it is plain, too, that not only the nervous system but the entire organism exhibits this figure-ground relation (as the examples of raising one's arm, or walking, make clear). Thus, we may say, the embodying organism is a *complex whole*—an entire series of differently interrelated sets of members, structures, and patterns of interfunctionings, evincing multiple and multiply connected contextures. As such, every bodily performance—sensory, motoric, emotive, or neural—is *necessarily and intrinsically implicated* with others (however difficult or surprising such functional interconnections may turn out to be). The performance of even an elementary sensory act implicates (as a complex set of "backgrounds") other bodily members and functions, postures, and movements, such that "*in practice*" too is the animate organism reflexively related to itself (Husserl).

When Straus claims, then, that "only what belongs together can be united—

i.e., that which in the very peculiarity of its existence manifests itself as a part comprehended within a whole" (*115*, p. 155), it is necessary to understand this as the claim that bodily existence is or manifests itself most fundamentally as a "part/whole" complex. The embodying organism is a "whole" (or, as I will try to show at a later point, a "contexture") articulated in and by differently and complexly interconnected members, organs, performances, functions, and so on. This, "belonging together," on the one hand, is a matter of a *"part/whole" and not a "form/matter" relation,* and on the other, manifests an equally complex set of reflexive referencings. Finally, when Jonas writes of that quality of "felt selfhood," it is necessary to understand this most fundamentally as the nexus of multiply manifested "self-" references intrinsic to the nature of this particular "whole."

In a word, this animate organism is able to be embodying solely on condition of its functioning as the orientational locus of the sensorium, as the continuously "co-present" in all bodily experience, in strict correlativity to the environing milieu; but these, in turn, are themselves made possible by, or equivalently, reveal the more fundamental sense of being, the complex and self-referential contextures whose wholeness is grounded in the "basic biologic law" of "equalization"—namely, that "processes in the organism have a relative constancy, and that the organism remains essentially the same despite its relative change by stimulus" (*27*, p. 72). Indeed, in different terms whose legitimacy I shall have to secure later, one is able to experience, observe, talk about "one and the same" organism solely in so far as it exhibits what Gurwitsch calls, following Gestalt psychology, the principle of "good continuation"—able to remain a viable nexus of contextures (*31*, pp. 150–53). This principle, too, will prove to have far-reaching consequences and significance for the understanding of the phenomena addressed in this study. As will become clear, the maintaining of this constancy or good continuation requires a highly complex number of affairs: in general, a relatively determinate milieu; mental functioning; and corporeal performances. Only after setting out these full and richly articulated phenomena will it be possible to penetrate the core sense of "self." First, however, the embodying organism reveals still further decisive moments which need explication.

3

The Body Uncanny

BERGSON, it was already indicated, had recognized the privileged status of one's own body. Far from being merely passive and primarily epistemic, body and perception are *actional*, and thus environing objects *are* what is portended in contexts of (actual and possible) actions regarding them:

> . . . the body [is] a kind of center from which the actions that surrounding objects exercise on it is reflected on these same objects: external perception is just this reflection . . . [and] measures our possible action on things and by that, inversely, the possible action of things on us. (*4*, p. 57)

Affirming that what is decisive here is that this "center" is "*my* body" (*4*, p. 11), Bergson nevertheless was deflected from analyzing this. What struck him, rather, was *time*. All action goes on in time; hence the past is brought to bear at every moment of the action's duration. The body itself, acting among and on material things, must also be material. The "union of the soul and the body," seen as posing a central impasse (*4*, p. 247), is now taken as the problem of *continuity*: "union" signifies "continuity," which means "action" within which matter is one pole and memory the other.

As was seen in the last chapter, attending to this "intimate union" is both possible and necessary. The question is how to apprehend and account for "mineness," realized primordially in "my own organism." As Marcel has shown, it is the "having" or "belonging" pertaining to my body which makes possible all other modes of having (*73*, pp. 223–55). So "intimate" and profound is this belonging, indeed, that one seems compelled to say "I *am* my body":

> My body is mine for as much as I do not look at it, as I do not place any interval between it and me, or rather for as much as it is not an *object* for me, but in so far as I *am* my body. (*76*, I, p. 116)

This is not to say, Marcel warns, that I *am* this body taken as *object* by others (or as object even to me); it is only the *"corps-sujet"* which I *am*.

Although from within a different ontology, Sartre also comes to this position. My body as it is *"for-me"* (for-itself) *is* me: there can be no question of a "being-united-to" between consciousness and body (*103*, p. 305). I *am* my body (as for-itself) (*103*, pp. 317–19). Even though there are interpretative difficulties regarding the crucial notion of "ambiguity," insofar as Merleau-Ponty's central idea of *être-au-monde* (*127*, pp. 180–92) expresses *my embodied being*, one must say "I *am* my own-body," even while my lived-temporality (as was pointed out in the last chapter) provides the paradigm for *Selbstheit*.

The "intimacy" of the "union," in such terms as these, then, turns out to be a matter of *being*: the intimacy is one I live, one which I am; hence the impossibility of separating me out from my embodying organism. Had Descartes focused on the *sum* of his *cogito, ergo sum,* instead of the *cogito*, he might well have seen this essential bond to the embodying organism.

THE UNCANNY

Yet however crucial is the phenomenon of "mineness," something else continually creeps in: the *"corp-objet"* (Marcel, Merleau-Ponty), the experience of one's own "thingness" (Sartre), the "material composition" of the organism (Jonas), the body as a "physical thing, *matter*, having its extension" (Husserl), the "ambiguity" of the "own-body" (Merleau-Ponty), as well as the body as a biological affair for medicine and biomedical science. Indeed, viewing and reviewing these works, rethinking the embodying organism, one is persistently reminded of Pascal's caustic remark to "the Cartesians":

> Who would not think, seeing us compose all things of mind and body, but that this mixture would be quite intelligible to us? Yet it is the very thing we least understand. Man is to himself the most wonderful object in nature; for he cannot conceive what the body is, still less what the mind is, and least of all how a body should be united to a mind. This is the consummation of his difficulties, and yet it is his very being. (*87*, pp. 27–28)

However true it is that this live body is mine, my embodied placement in the midst of environing things, it is a biological, physical body, and this status cannot be gainsaid but must rather be directly confronted and understood. Whatever may be the status of certain concepts in biomedicine, my "own-body's" physico-biological nature is *not* just a theoretical construct. Sartre seems to have grasped this in his striking analysis of the way in which we experience our own bodies as "being-for-the-Other": insofar as my body is experienced by someone else *I thereby come to experience myself as a body* (object) *apprehended by the other person* (*103*, pp. 303–59).[1] This experience of myself as an object-for-the-other-person, Sartre contends, is that of *nausea*.

Realizing that I have been "looked-at" by the Other, I realize (become to) myself as a *thing*: as, somehow, physical stuff, caught by the Other's "gaze" (*le regard*) taking me as such. The *realization* (becoming-real-to-myself) of my being as material, physico-biological stuff, is the experience of finding myself (as a pure temporality) caught, literally stuck in materiality: hence, nausea.

There is much more to this, however, especially as regards understanding this as a stratum of the embodying organism. Whether or not it requires another's "gaze" for this to become manifest, the embodying organism is not only experienced as "intimate" or "mine" (in all the ways indicated), *it is just as fundamental that it is experienced as radically other than me.* Coupled with the "intimate union" is a *hiatus*: a strangeness or estrangement at the very heart of what is most familiar and intimate. Hitherto it has been the latter—the "union"—which has both puzzled and mainly occupied those concerned with embodiment. Once again, Sartre has penetrated most closely here. The other person's view on my own body not only succeeds in disclosing my own-body to me as material, it is a point of view on my body which I cannot myself adopt: it is "point-of-view-on-my-own-point-of-view," and this I myself, for Sartre, cannot know (or realize). I am an object for the Other, but cannot do more than grasp myself *as* grasped-as-object-by-the-Other. "The shock of the encounter with the Other is for me a revelation in emptiness of the existence of my body *outside* as an *en-soi* [in-itself, or pure "stuff"] for the Other" (*103*, p. 352).

When, for instance, another person is busied with some task (say, sawing a board), he is, precisely, occupied with the board, the thing being ultimately made, etc. but not at all with his own hand, arms, neck, eyes, in short not at all with his body as "for-itself" (as embodying all these strivings, workings, etc.). I can look at him without his being aware of this, covertly taking his body as "for-others" (namely, for-me , or an object for me). However, if he realizes he is being watched, he apprehends (becomes aware of) *himself* as an "outside," as looked-at in a way which is impossible for him ever to adopt. Or if I am the one doing the sawing, my body as a "point of view" on things (what was earlier termed my body-as-orientational-point) becomes (is realized as) one on which *other* points of view can be brought to bear, but which I can never myself take up as regards my own body-qua-point-of-view. *How* I am considered, viewed, interpreted, etc., by others is thus a crucial dimension of my own embodying organism, even though I can never actually occupy *that* point of view. This standpoint which I cannot actualize for myself nevertheless creeps, so to speak, into the way I live my own-body. I "take account of" how I might appear to others; I may literally, of course, *try* to be another to myself—i.e., "other-ate" myself. This, however futile it may be, is a perspective on myself, a dimension of my own embodiment, for Sartre. The other person thus "haunts" my own being. In other words, my body is *alienated, made other-for-me* without my being capable of actually being-other-for-myself. Alienation in its fundamental meaning, we could say, seems located precisely in this experience.

As will be seen later, not only is Sartre's analysis of the encounter with other persons faulty (a point I cannot pursue here; see *127*, pp. 69–80), it does not do full justice to this peculiarity of embodiment. If in a sense it seems that "I *am* my body," yet become alienated (via "nausea" and the "gaze"), Sartre's analysis fails to grasp a central sense in which I am *not* my body—and this "not" is not itself expressive simply of the "other-ation" realized by the Other's "gaze." Nor is it necessarily the case that my being-as-material essentially escapes my knowledge and experience—it is not fugitive in this sense, even though it may be true that I literally cannot adopt this "point-of-view" on my own "point-of-view"—i.e., be a literal other person to myself (but even this must be understood more carefully, as I will show later).[2] Finally, I can only regard it as a dubious supposition that my body's materiality is encountered solely as an experience of nausea: the entrapment of the pure *pour-soi* of consciousness in the viscousness of material *en-soi*.

The "otherness" of my own bodily organism is nevertheless a basic phenomenon inherent to the sense of embodiment. No sooner does one feel tempted to say "I *am* my body" than one *realizes* that "I am yet *not* my body." That "am" stands in need of qualification: it is not identity, equality, inclusion; but then, even more pressingly: what is being said? (*128*, pp. 73–87).

Freud's analysis of the uncanny (*24*, pp. 122–61) is very revealing in this respect. He was not concerned with the present issue, but instead with the uncanny as the experience of something once hidden (repressed) and familiar, but which suddenly makes its appearance. Still, as Ricoeur has shown in his careful study of Freud (*95*), it is quite possible and often fruitful to give a philosophical interpretation of Freudian analyses. In any case, I venture to suggest that Freud's ways of grappling with what he calls the uncanny (*Unheimliche*) provide a suggestive framework for understanding the sense of the body's otherness. There are four moments: a sense of helplessness and inescapableness, of dread and chilling fear, of hiddenness or concealment, and of the radically strange yet familiar (*Heimliche*). To understand my being embodied, I suggest, requires understanding the senses in which my own-body is experienced by me as "uncanny."

(1) *The Inescapable, the Limitation*

Being embodied is no mere accidental affair. At the very least, the fact *that* being-human requires that one be embodied in some manner is one of the essential conditions, although it is surely contingent *which* specific body (with its particular bio-neurological-anatomical makeup) turns out to be experienced by me as "mine." However, apart from being a *conditio sine qua non*, being embodied is also *inescapable*: whatever may be my desires, wishes, or ideals, these find not only their expression but more specifically their *radical limitation* by this very embodying organism. In critical ways (ways which could well result in various pathological expressions), and whether I like it or not, there are some activities, postures, gestures, sensory encounters, and sensory refinements, etc., which are just not within my bodily scope, thanks to my being embodied by *this* and not some other body.[3] It may happen (and frequently does, to all of us) that the idea of having other bodily parts (face, eyes, hands, sexual members, etc.) will occupy my wishes, but inescapably "this" body is both *mine* and *not* those others. My fingers are perchance too short to allow my becoming an accomplished pianist; a woman's hips and weight may be inappropriate to permit her becoming a fashion model; a man's face may be unattractive to the woman he desires; the pitch of one's laugh may irritate people; the least amount of food intake may quickly result in one's becoming too fat; and so on.[4]

Even with all the marvels of molecular biology, genetic manipulations, intricacies of surgery, cosmetics, psychopharmacological prospects, and the like, still each of us is irrevocably determined in our lives by intrinsic limitations of organic embodiments in whose selection none of us had the least initial choice, and yet which each of us must willy-nilly learn (sometimes relearn) to move about, readjust to wishes (and vice versa), to which we must accommodate, with which in the first instance we each must come to terms and reckon. *How* an individual will so reckon is, of course, quite variable; all that is being pointed to here is *that* our every action, dream, desire, etc., is horizoned by this pervasive reckoning.

Even where organic, anatomical, and even neurological modifications or replacements are possible, in a clear and obvious sense one would then merely exchange one set of limitations for another (what now becomes corporeally possible carries with it other corporeal limitations—for better or worse), and even then such modifications themselves are limited (not only can one not attach wings to fly with, but neither can one, presently at least, foresee implanting a viable womb in the male); there are de facto as well as essential limitations to what can be altered in the embodying organism. Inescapably, the sheer passage of bodily time (*III*, pp. 45–58) results in the establishment of corporeal schemata, habituations (e.g., left- or right-handedness, visual abilities, body-postures, gaits, etc.) and patterns (e.g., speech habits of intonation, inflection and accent, body-tonality, walking habits, etc.) which *at once determine and are determined by* my experiences (of myself, of objects, of others), with all their essential contingencies, and the course or style of my life (as athletic, sedentary, etc). Thus even such taken for granted matters as how one expresses one's feelings and emotions, which of these become typical, and the like, are not simply a matter of cultural or familial determination; they are also, and more basically, a function of the possibilities, limitations and susceptibilities (e.g., to certain diseases, injuries, foods) of the embodying organism I find myself with, which this body itself permits.[5] The *other* side, if you will, of the essentiality of embodiment is its inescapability, its irrevocability, which at once makes possible and impossible (with gradations along a continuum, to be sure, but in any case having the sense of limitations intrinsic to them). Examples could be multiplied almost ad libitum; the point is that "limitedness," hence a sense of "otherness," is essential to embodiment.

(2) *Chill and Implicatedness*

If there is a sense in which my own-body is "intimately mine," there is, furthermore, an equally decisive sense in which *I belong to it*—in which I am at its disposal or mercy, if you will. My body, like the world in which I live, has its own nature, functions, structures, and biological conditions; since it embodies me, I thus *experience myself as implicated* by my body and these various conditions, functions, etc. *I* am exposed to whatever can influence, threaten, inhibit, alter, or benefit my biological organism. Under certain conditions, it can fail me (more or less), not be capable of fulfilling my wants or desires, or even thoughts, forcing me to turn away from what I may want to do and attend to my own body: because of fatigue, hunger, thirst, disease, injury, pain, or even itches, I am forced at times to tend and attend to it, regardless, it may be, of what may well seem more urgent at the moment. Hence despite its evident "intimacy," my own-body is as well the experiential ground for frustration, anguish, pain, fear, dread, as well as joy, satiation, pleasure, well-being ("health," as Kass says), and ultimately of death, my own ceasing-to-be.

What happens to my body perforce entails or *implicates* me. And, it may be, just this entailment, this implicatedness, forms the pre-theoretical ground for the possibility of what at much higher levels of intellection is formal-logical entailment: the "force" of something's irrevocable "following" from something else. One can thus come to a "grasp" (*Begriff, con-cept*) of the way a conclusion is entailed or implied by premises ("if . . . then . . ."), inasmuch as one has *already* (prior to the stage of cognitive development at which logical formations become cognizable) undergone numerous experiences of corporeal implicatedness, bodily "if/then" experiences.[6]

Finding myself thus *implicated* in whatever can and does happen to my embodying organism, not only its contingency but also its tenuousness vis-à-vis the ways in which things can and do impact it, my embodying organism is experienced as a kind of "chill." As Leveton's patient Alice reports:

> I was looking at myself intently [in the mirror]; I suddenly saw myself as others must see me . . . . I wasn't invulnerable; I was mortal. "That person" over there in the mirror might be killed by a car, might perish. (*69*, p. 70)

"That person," that is to say, "me-myself," is embodied by this organism and irrevocably bound to suffer what this body suffers—and thereby I am susceptible to what can happen to material things in general. Nor should it be thought that it is only pathological experiences which disclose this dimension of the *experienced biological* organism, nor that all "chilling" experiences are thereby also pathological. As little Emily in Richard Hughes' novel, *A High Wind In Jamaica* (*39*), says, experiencing her own embodiment, "You can't get out of it now, not for a very long time!" One can think, too, of the time one first experienced a funeral, seeing the solemn faces, the slow movements, the hushed yet charged silence, and the mute face and hands of the dead one. Or think only of moments of being ill, of injury, of the sudden seizing upon my own going-to-die: inescapable, my embodiment is as well dreadfully and chillingly implicative.

(3) *Hidden Presence*

It thus becomes apparent that my experienced biological organism includes events, processes, and structures which simply "go on" quite of their own accord whether or not I am, or even could ever become, "aware" of them, much less "control" them. And even if I am aware of them, they still "go on," observed or not by me or by others. The functioning of many of these processes—from those pertaining to ingestion, digestion and breathing, to the far more subtle, barely detectable neural and glandular processes governing the circadian rhythms of body-temperature, moods, tonality, and the slight shiftings of muscles—in *no way requires* my attentiveness or choice. Deeply familiar (what else is more familiar?), my own-body is thus at the same time curiously *veiled* and obscure. Indeed, in certain clear cases, one can live out one's entire life utterly oblivious even to the most rudimentary biological "facts" of organs, organic functions, or neurological phenomena per se. Even if one happens to study textbooks of anatomy, say, and learns about the "lungs," the "spleen," "metabolism," the "heart," the "autonomic system," and the like, these are rarely if ever themselves directly experienced or experienceable by me in my own case—except for certain possible, though highly unusual circumstances, and even then what I would witness is distinctively different from what I learn about "the" heart, "the" lungs, and so on in a textbook sense. In "my" case, this "knowing" remains distanced from direct encounters in innumerable instances. Yet there is a kind of "knowing" which is always involved in the least bodily gesture or movement—a knowing which may become more explicit in cases of pain, disturbance, disease, etc., when the veiled character of my own-body manifests itself even more.

Beyond this, it is solely by virtue of such automatically "ongoing" processes that I am at all aware of anything else—including the case of an awareness of my own-body's own organs. Yet just these automatically functioning processes escape my efforts to know them, or to know them directly (if one could, for example, suppose a possible awareness of the functioning of the rods and cones of the retina, this awareness could hardly itself be of the same sort as that which these functionally condition). If I should ever succeed in becoming aware, in my own embodying organism, of my own heartbeat or my metabolism, this is itself conditioned by still other processes, thanks to which the first awareness is at all

possible.[7] My embodying organism is thus always a *hidden-presence*, a latency
thanks to which anything else can be or become patent. These hidden "goings-
on," finally, are biologically rhythmed and conditioned with respect to my
awarenesses even of my own body—such that I often find it necessary to adjust
my own wishes, plans, desires, to their tempo. For example, hungry as I may be,
wanting to eat now, I must *wait* until the food is "ready" to be eaten (cooked,
prepared, etc.); wishing to be at work, I must still "first" get in the car, drive
through traffic, and in general "pace" myself to the tempo at which my own
corporeal abilities can fulfill the many steps needed to get me from my house to
my office.

(4) *Alien Presence*

Thus, it can now be recognized, this body is essentially an *alien-presence* as well
as chillingly and inescapably implicating me in biological and material
conditions, many of which are for the most part beyond my ken and control.
My body is at once familiar and strange, intimate and alien: *"mine" most of all
yet "other" most of all*, the ground for both subjective inwardness and objective
outwardness. Whatever I want, wish, or plan for, I irrevocably "grow older,"
"become tired," "feel ill," "am energetic"—and these, at times, whether or not I
plan my life, or my day even, so as to gain some control over my bodily "moods"
(and even then, this "planning" is itself subject to underlying moods which
usually are merely latent, episodic, often unpredictable). *It has its "nature" and*
thereby its complex of biological rhythms within whose compass I must live my
life. I find myself, so to speak, "in charge of" or "responsible for" something
with which I must come to terms (or, perhaps more accurately: find that in
multiple ways it has already been reckoned with, in oddly unselfconscious
ways). I must, in the first instance, "care for" it, see to it that my body's
functions and needs are "looked after" (ingestion, excretion, hygiene,
grooming, and others), within their own "time," on which I must at times "wait"
in order to go about my affairs. In short, this inescapably implicating, hidden,
and chilling (as also familiar, intimate, enabling, and accustomed) embodying
organism is "in my charge" in spite of myself, and this no matter how
inescapable, material, handicapped, chilling, alien, intimate, frustrating, odd,
comfortable, or disquieting it may be to me. Embodiment is thus the ground for
both intimacy and distance, the near and the remote.

Responsible for it—unless, in then obviously pathological cases, one finds
instances of utter symbiotic conduct (*5; 7; 57*)—I am yet *at its disposal*, while at
the same time it expresses and embodies me. Compellingly mine, it is yet
curiously foreign: intimately alien, strangely mine—thus are we continually
flirting with paradoxical expressions in an effort to tell truly the character of
embodiment. Most of all, this embodying organism is experienced by me as my
exposure to things, ultimately as the locus of that most alien of all: my own
death. In some sense, with the cessation of its functioning, I, too, die; with it

intimately (whether in coma, sedation, paralysis, or death) I move bodily into
elemental not-knowing.

* * * * * * * *

Whatever else may be designated by the personal pronoun "I," it turns out, as
Julián Marías says, to be "literally *something other* than *its* organism—so
much *other*, that it is not a thing but a person" (*78*, p. 378). At the same time, so
other is the "person" I am that my own-body is *not me* but is *my own*
embodying biological organism. This means: the basis for *the otherness* (and
thereby the otherness of everything else) *of the embodying organism is its
having a life of its own*, even when the person is most "at home" or "at one" with
it, and hence this body presents itself continually as "having to be reckoned
with" in some way or other, to one degree or other.

The fundamental enigma which appears at the very heart of the
phenomenological disclosure of "intimate union" is the radical "alien-
presence" of that very body, an otherness whose root is its inescapable,
implicative, hidden and strange nature as biological, having its own "life." It is
yet my *Leibkörper*, and thus both *Leib* and *Körper*, an organism and a
material body: it seems that the Cartesian equivocation has its basis in the
embodying organism itself! It is that by which I "realize" my life (plans, goals,
wishes, etc., both immediate and long-range) and which yet has a life of its own
with which I must reckon. I, expressing myself by means of my embodying
organism, shape it, govern through it, animate it, and thus "inform" it. Yet,
conversely, so also does my body limit, resist, and thus mutually define and "inform" me myself. One wants to say, "I *am* my body," yet my body resists this
effort to identify myself with it, just as I can distance myself from it, or find
myself distanced from it (sometimes pathologically, though by no means only
then).

"HEFT" AND "LIFT"

The otherness of my own body thus suffuses its sense of intimacy; what is
intimately mine is yet a heaviness, a mass having its own weight and seemingly
alien nature. With impaired, maimed, or mortally ill persons, it seems that the
latter sense becomes pronounced, almost as if the life of the person were
dissipating, dissolving in the very "look" and peculiar stillness of glance,
gesture, and body attitudes. Even patients suffering from paresis in a limb
undergo a marked change as regards the unfeeling leg or arm: it takes on an
aspect, Plügge remarks, of

> objective thinglikeness, such as an importunate heaviness, burden, weight, with the
> quality of a substance that feels essentially strange, wooden, like plaster of paris, in
> any event as largely space-filling and hence not altogether as a part of ourselves. (*90*, p.
> 296)

Whether it be one's entire body (as in severe pneumonia), or as regards only a paretic limb, the sense of onerousness and burden is pronounced. *Other-than-me*, my body or even one of its members seems somehow to lose its intimacy, and with that my sense of caring for it. In illness, maiming injury, and the like, "I" seem to fade, to be "elsewhere" and markedly negligent and indifferent. "It," this husk, seems already to have become an almost cadaver, a "sensed relic" even to myself; once enlivened corporeal abilities now seem merely a faint, haunting memory of what "used to be."

It would nevertheless be an utter naivety to assume that this otherness becomes salient only in cases of bodily failures—as if, so to speak, it were strictly a function of these failures. To stress the body as uncanny is to stress the continual presence of this "thinglikeness" as ingredient to embodiment itself. As Plügge puts it, "within the reflective experience of a healthy limb, no matter how silent and weightless it may be in action, there is yet, indetectably hidden, a certain 'heft' " (*90*, p. 299). Terming this "heft" the "*phenomenon of the bodily as physical*," Plügge's instructive discussions of paresthesia and the notorious "phantom-limb" phenomenon drive home the critical point that neither medically nor philosophically do we have to do with *two* realities (matter and soul, or the physical and the alive)—nor even, strictly, two *aspects* which arise from two different modes of approach (natural science and phenomenology). Hence Plügge directly denies Jonas' claim that reality itself is at its root dual.

To be sure, in fatigue, exhaustion and their like, as also in pathologic failures (injury, illness), this "bodily physical" becomes more salient, its otherwise silent voice more assertive, bringing about sometimes quite serious alterations in conduct (a person with angina facing a flight of stairs, say) and other times the kind of wasting-away we witness in the terminally ill person. But, Plügge stresses, it cannot be forgotten

> that the first traces of thinglike characteristics in our live bodiness are found *already in the healthy*. . . . At one and the same time as this uncanny emergence there is an experience of intensified *belongingness* of this altered [i.e., paretic] part. What threatens to estrange itself in us communicates to us *all the more* . . . that it is actually our own. (*90*, pp. 304–05)

This doubleness of bodily life, Plügge contends, is expressive, not of dualism or even a duality, but of the fact that the "bodily live" and the "bodily physical" are "in fact mutually enhancing. More than this they form *one* single, inseparable event" (*90*, p. 305). Thus even though it is true that the onerousness and burdensomeness of my own body (or member) is disclosed preponderantly in the sphere of pathology, it is nevertheless present, however faintly, in the healthy body.

Confirming our explication almost point for point,[8] Plügge's analysis bears also on the sense of "having" to which Marcel had already pointed, as was seen in the previous chapter, but with a significant difference of emphasis. Studying

paresthesias and other serious pathologies, but also such otherwise insignifi-
cant phenomena as rashes, itches, and the like, Plügge does show that, for
example, in a case of angina, "this" heaviness in the heart is after all *mine*, this
paretic limb is *my* arm, this eruption is on *my* back. But he also shows that the
experiential "having" here is as well an experience of "*being had*" (*90*, pp.
305–07). Always linked with anxiety, foreboding, and perplexity, my afflicted
members, my body itself, "has" me quite as much as I "have" it.

Again, however, for the point is significant, even within the lively,
spontaneous, easy *lift* of bodily performances there is the body's *heft*. As Plügge
sees it, it is precisely this complex "reciprocal intertwinedness" of heft and lift,
of belongingness-to-me and estrangement-from-me, this one single event of
embodiment, which Merleau-Ponty means by calling the "own-body" an
"ambiguity."[9] My "corps-propre" is precisely this "lived intermingling of
fatalité and *élan*" (*90*, p. 308), this being-together of the physical and the lively.
Whether one agrees with this or not,[10] Plügge's own thesis seems to me incisive.

The embodying organism is an uncanny presence, revealed in its every
functioning and structure, its performances and members, its strangeness and
familiarity, its habituations and novelties. Incredibly complex, it is yet "a single
event"; thoroughly unnoticed, it yet makes itself felt. With Emily, Hughes'
enchanting heroine, we sense the wonder of it all:

> Each time she moved her arm or a leg . . . however, it struck her with fresh
> amazement to find them obeying her so readily. Memory told her, of course, that they
> had always done so before: but before, she had never realised how surprising this was.
> (*39*, p. 190)[11]

Yet, with Robert Russell, we know the agony and chill of being at the mercy of
the happenings of bodily life. Blinded at the age of five, he is lying in the hospital
bed trying to see, to make his way from the bed to the window:

> For the first time in my life I had wanted to do something with all my being. I had
> commanded my flesh, and it had failed me. I was ashamed of my weakness, but, even
> more, I was indignant at the refusal of my body to do what I had insisted. I realized
> then that my body could not perform the imperative commands of my spirit. This
> experience was the door through which I passed out of my childhood. (*100*, p. 14)[12]

It will become necessary to attend very carefully to this experience later on.
At this point, however, even though I have begun to trace out the sense of the
uncanny intrinsic to embodiment, I have still not quite circumscribed its full
terrain.

OF TIME AND EFFORT

Embodiment, it has become clear, is not simply a "fact"; it is at once a complex
event and a *task* accomplished at every moment. This complexity is evident. In
a way still to be delineated clearly, this organism is "one," a "whole" comprised

of "many" interrelated and reciprocally functioning and connected parts (members, components). It is not only that "it" *goes on*, moreover; not only that it is "mine" and "lived" by me. *It reveals its own modalities of temporal flow*; each of its members, indeed, each of its performances, has its own way and time of flowing: the times of illness and healing, of initiation and completion of organic processes (e.g., excretion, inhalation), of physiological performings (heartbeat, blood flow, metabolism), of relaxation and innervation, and so on through a spectrum of barely or rarely felt rhythms, fluctuations, pulsations, episodes, and periodicities. There are, moreover, the times of activation and striving, of carrying out more complex and noticeably felt bodily conducts: picking up, letting go, walking, talking, drinking, reaching, holding, listening, smelling, and so on. And, however closely interlaced with what Husserl called the phases of inner-time consciousness (*48*), as I shall later point out, these physiologic, biologic, and organic time-flows have a distinctive *thickening,* a *literal flesh* giving them a flow and sweep of their own.

If we refocus briefly on the earlier discussion of what Jonas calls the "source" of causality, we can detect a prominent sense of *bodily time-as-lived.* The experiences of "force" and "effort," Jonas argued, are themselves *basic* experiences of embodied life, hence "causality" is *not* an *a priori for* experience, but originates *in* primordial bodily experience. Carrying the analysis further, it seems to me, we come upon the bodily enactments of kinaesthetic flow-patterns as undergirding, or as the core moment of, these experiences of resistance and being impacted. Both, I contended, have the form, "if . . . then . . . "—that is, occur "under circumstances" (*unter Umstände*). The embodying organism, in short, at once positioning or orienting the display of environing things and enacting strivings and willings, *is temporally articulated as effort*—that is, as efficacious or, better, *effectuating. Thus the "if . . . then . . ." style of incorporation of strivings and of orienting the arrangement of environing things is the fundamental temporality of the "live body" as embodying.*

This "purposiveness" or "teleology" is not first of all a metaphysical construct and only later postulated of organisms. Quite to the contrary, purposiveness (understood here as bodily enacted strivings, positioning and readying for performances gearing into the milieu) is an essential condition without which the organism (and, as Jonas suggests, organic life generally) would cease, literally, to be itself: it would in that case de-cease, die (*55*, p. 76). The "if . . . then . . ." temporality of the live body is by that very fact a *potency*: a projecting in bodily action, hence a "purposing" which in Merleau-Ponty's term is a "splitting-apart" (*déhiscence*) toward the "what-is-to-come" (*Zukunft*) while remaining fleshed out with the presence of the unfolding, flowing articulation of the enacting-orienting of embodiment.

This "time," too, has its rhythms. At times charged with urgency (in hunger, fear, excitement), at times relaxed, at times fatigued, *the organism embodies rhythmically and episodically.* In moments of fatigue, clumsiness, or sedation, whatever I may want to do, my body won't respond; seriously ill or maimed, it won't obey me, or I am obliged to find other ways of doing what I want to do. In a clear way, then, embodiment as a temporal flux is a matter of embodying more or less, well or poorly, within specific contexts of performance and within particular surroundings. In this sense, embodiment is not a brute *fact* (once done, forever done), nor yet simply an *event* (Plügge). It is in a way both, but the "fact" is an "eventuating," and this is a fluctuating course of "more or less": embodiment is a *task* accomplished more or less at every moment.

There is an obvious point of difference in these complex "times." The flow of physiologic, biologic, and organic processes, I might say, "go on" whether or not "I" will them. To be sure, they (or some of them) reveal a complexity of "going on": the flow of circadian rhythms, for example. Indeed, there are relatively clear cases where there seems an almost total absence of kinaesthetic enactments, much less explicit willing or deciding, where these biologic flows continue nonetheless: e.g., a comatose person whose bodily organs continue to function, usually with the aid of machines. And it is not at all so clear whether such cases are such as to warrant declarations of death—i.e., whether embodiment itself has ceased. However that may be, the point to be noticed is only that the sense of embodiment as a task being (more or less) accomplished requires, as it were, that these biologic goings-on be marshalled in the service of some concrete performance, be taken up into contexts of movements, attitudes, postures, gestures—with respect to which, of course, there is sometimes failure (more or less): disorientation, incoordination, mis-matches, and the like (*27*, pp. 52, 59).

The point, in a word, is that *effort is decisive to embodiment, and has a predominantly temporal ("if . . . then . . .") form.* This is apparent not merely in pathological cases—the effort, say, required to "sit up," or to "cough," when one is critically ill—but also in daily life, however silent it may be. Thus in every "deciding-to-do" that carries with it the intention actually to execute the performance, there is the necessary efforting or striving to "gear up." Certainly clearer in cases such as we can readily call to mind (e.g., getting up from a cozy chair, running the last ten feet of a race, taking the last bite of a heavy meal), this efforting is by no means ever altogether absent in bodily life. The "heft" of bodily corporeality testifies to the presence of "effort" at every moment of healthy life. The *time of embodiment is the effort, the task, of performances,* even those which are designed to keep one still (itself requiring effort). Only in sleep, or, approaching this, in being comfortably relaxed for a time, does the efforting seem to fade into the background—though I doubt it is totally absent even then. In any case, short of total cessation (death, complete unconsciousness), effort is the temporalized texture of embodiment, requiring equalization (*27*, pp. 72–86), equilibrium,[13] or better, *synchronization* of the multiple and complex times of the body and its various functions, members, and structures.

EFFORT AND UPRIGHT POSTURE

These considerations lead directly to the seminal insights of Erwin Straus, especially to his major essay on "The Upright Posture" (*117*, Ch. 7). Noting elsewhere that the "intrinsic connection between sensation and movement" shows that, "Whatever affects our senses derives its attractiveness solely from the simple fact of our motility" (*117*, p. 45), Straus shows that the upright posture is at once distinctive of man's corporeal endowment and makes possible the specifically human modes of deportment and the specifically human world. To sense, to perceive some affair requires that one be able to be affected by it, and for this

> a motor element must be inherent in experience: directions to or fro, attraction or repulsion, attack or retreat. . . . Men and animals experience and perform their existence as sensing, mobile beings in deporting themselves toward the world—in opposing and yielding, searching and fleeing, accepting and rejecting. They experience in their corporeality; experiencing is related, therefore, to gravity, air, light, space, distance, to incorporating, meeting, and avoiding. In every single one of the fundamental functions, the being-directed-to-the-world is realized in a particular form. (*117*, pp. 247–48; see also p. 244)

But whereas animals, whose organisms are structured for quadrupedal motion, move in the direction of their digestive axis (*117*, p. 162),[14] man in the upright posture[15] moves, not in line with the ground, but in opposition to it, through a space opened and embraced by vision. Human sensing, motility, and experience are all prefigured in the upright posture, and with its accomplishment and continual maintaining is found the seat and abode of all matters human. "We can read man's natural endowment from his physique" (*117*, p. 142). And long before the infant can attempt to stand, the upright posture yet to be won (albeit always to be won again and again) has already made itself felt; the eventual possibility of meeting an Other upright, face-to-face, has shaped the rhythm of intrauterine development.

Indeed, the biologist Adolph Portmann has shown that for the human form of life, its social character—which is not only primary, but essential—extends to its entire structure, even into the fetal stages. Although human fetal development is not prolonged proportionately to human complexity (it is, in fact, he says, a year short, if mammals are taken as the norm), still the "correlation between ontogeny and social life" shows

> that our uterine growth is early accelerated far beyond that of the other primates, and that this early acceleration of growth corresponds to the complexity of our central nervous system, that is realized only much later. It can be shown that in man the proportion of limbs to trunk deviates even in the womb from that found in apes, and that this early peculiarity is connected with our upright posture, acquired only much later. (*91*, pp. 356–57)[16]

Thus Portmann demonstrates that the ontogeny of higher mammals is throughout correlated with the special character of the species—and the distinctive features of the human body (those features which will later evolve into standing, walking, speaking, etc.) are present even fetally. For biology, "the special character of the human species is fully at work in every stage of its development . . . the spirit [*Geist*] does not burst forth only at some late date" (*91*, p. 357), but is present in every phase and aspect of human ontogeny. Hence to be human at all is to be born into the human stance.

Even so, Straus emphasizes, while the "upright posture" is a native endowment, it is not thereby a simple fact: it is rather a *task*, an *accomplishment* of that "year too short" (which Portmann mentions only to show that it is wrongheaded to make such comparisons). "The origin and the beginning of upright posture do not coincide," therefore (*117*, p. 141); *originating* in our biologic endowment, it does not *begin* until later, after birth. This achievement must thus be won, struggled for even though it is "natural." Furthermore, it remains a task throughout the life of the person:

> Before reflection or self-reflection start, but as if they were a prelude to it, work makes its appearance within the realm of the elemental biological functions of man. In getting up, in reaching the upright posture, man must oppose the forces of gravity. It seems to be his nature to oppose nature in its impersonal, fundamental aspects with natural means. However, gravity is never fully overcome; upright posture always maintains its character of counteraction. It calls for our activity and attention. (*117*, p. 141)

With this initial thrust upwards there appears the initiating of self in its most definite, genuine sense—as will appear more clearly later on. For now, it is crucial to note what else happens.

In getting up, standing is achieved; and with it, not only does walking become available, but the distinctive forms of seeing, hearing, reaching, grasping, and holding, as well as the primary forms of spatiality, gesturing, and social deportments. Throughout, however, the central fabric of upright posture remains: "the natural stance of man is . . . 'resistance,' " gaining a stand within the world which essentially "demands endeavor. It is essentially restless. We are committed to an ever renewed exertion" (*117*, p. 143). *To stand, then, is to withstand: effort, force, resistance are intrinsic to our native posture.*[17] Hence risks, the continual chance of falling or losing balance, are part and parcel of this posture: "Human gait is, in fact, a continuously arrested falling. . . . It is motion on credit" (*117*, p. 148).

Within the framework of this always precarious, ever re-won accomplishment, furthermore, there are inscribed the peculiar and immensely significant forms of "distance" and inescapable ambivalence which pervade all human life. Our posture removes us *from the ground*, thus instituting singular forms of human gesturing and other postures: lying down, sinking back, giving in, relaxing, resting, as well as forms of motion of the body or its members. It distances us *from environing things* as well, thus enabling a loosening from immediately present things and a "confronting," "beholding" (*116*, pp. 334–61), or "looking-at," as well as "reaching," "pointing," "grasping," and the many forms of tool-using. Finally, our stance distances us *from fellow-men*, in virtue of which we "face" one another for the first time,[18] and enter into the richly textured and subtle forms of social gestures and expressions (*117*, pp. 144–47).[19]

These forms of distance, given with our stance as upright, mark out the possible modes of lived spatiality, gnostic perception (as in touch), and communication, as well as the mobile body-zones (of touching and being-touched, greeting, welcoming, shunning, repulsing, hiding) and all their correlated modalities and kinds of expression. At the core of these and their correlates is the central mode of organization of the body-scheme itself. Standing upright, with the shoulders, arms, and hands hanging in their distinctive manner, not only is a wide range of performances now available, but a critical kind of organization is instituted, with the accessibility of *lateral space*:

> In this sector, most of the human crafts originated. Hammer and ax, scythe and sickle, the carpenter's saw, the weaver's shuttle, the potter's wheel, the mason's trowel, and the painter's brush all relate to lateral space . . . for lateral space is the matrix of primitive and sophisticated skills. (*117*, p. 156)

By means of this important expansion of the body-scheme, furthermore, there become apparent the remarkable enlargement and unification of the oppositions instituted by the distancings established by upright posture:

> The arms can be stretched and the hands can point in opposite directions, to the right and to the left, at the same time. It is this contrast of directions that divides, articulates, and organizes lateral space, producing heteronymous, unequal parts. These can be reunited into an ordered whole where one half dominates the other. Spatial syntax cannot deviate from the general principle of taxis, which always demands a leading part to which the others are subordinated. The pair, right-left, is the true embodiment of unity, unfolding itself into opposites or, if we begin with the opposites, the unity of a contrasting manifold. Both aspects belong together. (*117*, pp. 158–59)[20]

All the highest skills depend upon this unification of opposites—"the coordination of relatively independent parts that are not bound together by symmetry, homology, or synergy" (*117*, p. 159). Once again, we run up against what must now be regarded as the fundamental feature of embodiment: there is here a "*part/whole*," a "*unity-in-difference*," *phenomenon at every level*. But the embodying organism is a contexture (as I shortly say) which is "living," that is, a living whole characterized by "effort" or "striving," here manifested in "upright posture." This effortfully established contexture is, finally, and in almost every respect, a "gestural" phenomenon.

BODY AS GESTURAL DISPLAY

I deliberately want to avoid using the term "expressive" here. My reasons are two. First, the term is widely used to name quite a spectrum of affairs, only some which seem relevant to the present phenomenon. Thus it is used as synonymous to "meaning," "speech," "representation," "manifestation," "significance," "showing," "stating," "depiction," "communication," and still others. It is also used by Straus and Merleau-Ponty, among others, in connection with embodiment, of course. That, however, seems too burdensome a cargo to specify what is seized upon as regards bodily life. Second, the literal meaning (*ex* = out + *premere* = to press) is deceptive, as it can too easily carry in a concealed way the very dualism we have seen it necessary to reject. Body gesturing, in a word, is not at all—certainly not in its primordial appearances— a matter of some sort of "internal" goings-on being "pressed-outward" by bodily movements and attitudes, an "inside" whose "outward" form or manifestation must then be taken as a kind of hermeneutic clue in order to "read" the meaning thereof.

As Plügge and Straus have shown, embodiment is a *single event*, however complex it surely is. Hence for me, as for the biologist, "all the qualities of [our] object appear as qualities of an order, or system. And it is because we are dealing with a complex order that . . . we do not permit our study of the organism to begin with archaic distinctions of body, soul, spirit" (*91*, p. 344). To use "expression" for what occurs with bodily life, then, would be *ab initio* to invite confusion with speech, language, and the like, or, equally erroneous, to introduce a silent but potent dualism of the "inner" and "outer"—thus creating pseudo-problems which divert attention from the issue while also creating a nest of irrelevancies. Finally, as will become much clearer when the self's relatedness to the other self is specifically taken up, there are no grounds whatsoever for any form of dualism, nor is "expression" (as the "presssing-out" of the "inner" into some "outer") at all the fundamental phenomenon.

Portmann reserves the term for affective states alone. This has its own problems. Portmann's more general term, "representational value of forms," is, however, instructive with respect to the present problem. If we consider the internal organs of the body as opposed to its external features and forms, we quickly note "a little-considered fact": namely, that "the representational function of all the external organs of the higher animals is maximal, that of the internal organs slight" (*91*, pp. 352, 353). Coloration, head-shapes and markings, arms, torso, hair, beards, teeth, and still other outer forms display a wealth of fertile invention among animals which none of their internal organs show. The same is true of man, whose body shows an even greater abundance and subtlety of conspicious, exterior forms.[21]

The point Portmann makes is that these forms are understandable only in respect of their "representational value." These forms themselves are perceptible, encountered "values" possessing a far greater phenomenal power of communication than is often realized. Unhappily, though, Portmann himself falls into the very mistake he so assiduously seeks to avoid: "it is the surface organs of the animal that communicate inwardness, the peculiar essence behind the appearance." (*91*, p. 353). Emphasizing earlier in his essay that "inwardness" is a "scientific symbol" signifying, for biology, "the specific mode of existence of living beings" (*91*, p. 345) and *not* some dualistically conceived "inside," he yet goes on to contend, apparently, that there is an "inside" ("essence") lying "behind the appearance," i.e., the external forms. Indeed, even the term "expression" creeps back in a variety of places where the context clearly indicates that it is not a matter just of "affective states," but the more generic phenomenon otherwise called "representational value of forms."[22] It may well be that the idea of "representation" itself is the crafty villain. Inherent to it, as Cairns makes plain (*13*, pp. 251–62), is a *double* phenomenon: what represents and what is represented; what is, in different terms, depicted and the depicting affair itself. To use such terms, in short, is to invite the very confusion and deflection that Portmann clearly wants to avoid.

Nevertheless, Portmann's essay amply demonstrates that the body itself, in its very stance (posture, attitude), forms (legs, arms, head, markings, torso), and motions, is *essentially a display having "value."* Just as I earlier found it necessary to take the intimacy and uncanniness of the embodying organism as integral textures of the same tapestry (constituents of a contexture, as will be shown), so here it is necessary to seize upon the *embodying organism as a gestural display*—having, in a way, an "inside" and an "outside," but where "inside" is *exactly* as Portmann says: *the internal organs*, etc., which leave little to the imagination about what is meant, and whose structure and function is such as to have little, if any, gestural "value." No more can one posit some "soul" or "mind" or "essence" lying in concealment "behind" the "outer" "appearance"—no "inner" life expressed by "outer" organs and surfaces. There is, as is plain, much in human life which *is* "concealment," "disguise," "dissembling," "cunning," just as there is much which is "openness," "innocence," "truth-telling," and "being unveiled." And, to be sure, bodily gestures play their role in both. *But both are modalities of gestural display*, and it is this more fundamental phenomenon which needs to become plain first of all.

Portmann's point can be put this way: *the very "surface" configuration of the body is itself a gestural display* ("representational value"). Exceedingly subtle configurations (e.g., the glances of enmity or lust, or sly desire; the wily movements of people bidding at auctions; the "look" of a person not feeling well; etc.), as well as more obvious ones (e.g., doubling over with severe pain, exploding with laughter, and others), all bespeak the literal, animate presence of human life. There is here *first of all—as presupposed ground—presence,* *conspicuousness, salience, and display, on, in, and by bodily gestures and* *stances, performances, and movements.* Here, as is implied in Straus' analysis of lateral space, a complexity of "parts" (arms, head, legs, mouth, lips, eyes) are coordinated into an essentially inseparable "whole" of gestural displays. And, following Goldstein's emphasis on the figure-ground structure of the nervous system, we must note that in every such display we have to do with a configuration that achieves prominence over against a background of supporting bodily attitudes and stances. With, accordingly, a shift in one, there is a shift in the other(s), and thereby a shift in the gestural display.

As Straus says,

> The sensory organs cannot change without a corresponding change in the central nervous system. No part could be altered alone. With upright posture, there is a transformation of sensorium and motorium, of periphery and center, of form and function. (*117*, p. 164)

Precisely thereby, he shows, are bodily postures, gaits, movements, and so on, *already* significant (have "value"). Upright posture

> is pregnant with a meaning not exhausted by the physiological tasks of meeting the forces of gravity and maintaining equilibrium.
>
> Language has long since taken cognizance of this fact. The expression "to be upright" has two connotations: first, to rise, to get up, and to stand on one's own feet and, second, the moral implication, not to stoop to anything, to be honest and just, to be true to friends in danger, to stand by one's convictions, and to act accordingly, even at the risk of one's life. We praise an upright man; we admire someone who stands up for his ideas of rectitude. There are good reasons to assume that the term "upright" in its moral connotation is more than a mere allegory. (*117*, p. 137)

It is, in other words, no accident that we find such references and correlations. The effort to achieve and to maintain uprightness is the root for concrete meaning. To "stand up in the face of danger," to "turn tail and run," or to "lie down in the face of things" become understandable just when we recognize that this "facing" of what "confronts" is an *exposing of one's vital body*: the heart, the stomach, the sexual organs, the eyes, the mouth, the head. Similarly, as Straus points out, with the constitution of lateral space, it becomes possible to display the gestures of emptiness: shoulder-shrugging, showing open, empty hands, and the like. A play on words suggests itself: the "mattering" body "matters," i.e., displays itself as "value," as "being worthwhile," hence as "making a difference," *for the living body-sphere is experienced as one's integrity*, one's integral life. A further development of this theme would, I think, yield an important ground for understanding crucial ethical issues—e.g., those arising in medical interventions, the area with which my present concern for the embodying organism began.

Throughout the spectrum of bodily gestures—embracing, holding off, handshaking and fist-waving, nodding and kneeling, yielding and confronting—there simply is no viable way to separate out an "inside" which (by magical means only) would then get "pressed" to the outside. The weeping of a small child, the blushing of an embarrassed person, the sighing of relief— all are gestural displays saliently presenced within specific circumstances which always include and comprehend other embodied beings, other embodied human persons, as well as what comes to be differentiated out as physical entities. *Embodiment, thus, is itself a gestural contexture within a still wider context*: the world of concretely environing other live beings, other persons, social life, and that of "nature." As I will later have to show, the embodying organism is "always-already-there" in the midst of life and worldly affairs, always-already "with" other life. *Intersubjectivity*, accordingly, *is not first of all a problem to be solved, but itself a basic experience of embodied life,* a basic experience of each of us, most fundamentally already present at the inititation of bodily life. Gestural display, therefore, will be seen to be the core of that basic experience. With more complex acquisitions, with physiological and anatomical maturations, ever-richer encounters and differentiations, more subtle modes of display become possible: those connected with sexuality, with working, with possessing and valuing, and with power.

* * * * * * * *

These remain as promises for the moment. Having delineated something, at least, of the rich fields of embodiment, here and in the previous chapter, I have encountered again and again the phenomenon of contexture. To understand what has been said, it is, I believe, imperative to square off with this decisive phenomenon. The *complexity* of the embodying organism is striking: I have said that its components are, while patently *distinguishable, inseparably bound together.* But how is this to be understood? Lest these remain empty words, *pronunciamentos* merely, it is necessary to seek out what is meant by the "part/whole" nexus. What follows in the next two chapters will not only give sense to what has preceded; it will also direct me in my subsequent search for the transcendental conditions of being a self with other selves.

4

Interlude: The Phenomenon of Contexture

IT is necessary to pause in the study, in order at once to make sense of the preceding themes, and to prepare the effort to uncover the core sense of self and the concrete relations among selves. Although not directly considered here, the eventual results of this study should provide a viable response to the "non-egological" conception of self propounded by Jean-Paul Sartre (*104*) and Aron Gurwitsch (*32*, pp. 287–300), and at the same time give the basis for answering their complaints against traditional "substance" theories of self. My concern is not at all to carve up other theories; I am rather anxious to address myself directly to the issues themselves.

From Dilthey's dilemma, through Jonas' deliberations on life, and thence to the elusive strata of embodiment, a constant underlying theme has been "wholeness"—of psychic life (Dilthey), organic life (Jonas, Portmann), and of embodiment (Straus, Plügge, Merleau-Ponty, Marcel). Against the thrust of philosophy, indeed apparently of all knowledge, against the claim to universality and totality has emerged the radical opposition of *Weltanschauugen*; with the rise of historical consciousness there has emerged as well an apparent bedlam of opinions, directly challenging that drive to the universal. By means of his crucially important concept of "nexus" (*Zusammenhang*), Dilthey hoped to be able to make his way through that pluralistic anarchy while recognizing the truth of historicity (*16*, V, pp. 139–240). And the idea of the "nexus" exhibited by psychic life leads directly to Husserl's *Logical Investigations* (*49*), especially "Investigation III: On the Theory of Wholes and Parts," and then to Aron Gurwitsch's seminal work on the phenomena of context and contexture, *The Field of Consciousness* (*31*). Here, as elsewhere, I am concerned to elicit the "things themselves," mainly the phenomenon of contexture, but I will deal with the latter[1] only so far as to be able to show that it can and must be extended beyond that to which Gurwitsch addressed himself: sensory perception, in the main.

A brief rehearsal is in order. I found it necessary to focus attention directly and in a disciplined way on the phenomenon of embodiment. It is at all times essential to find accurate and adequate ways to understand and account for this peculiar complex of intimacy and alienness—this complex of "parts," "functions," "members," "systems," "performances" involving at once the unique interconnection of what Plügge terms the bodily physical and the bodily live, such that they form a "single event," or what I have called a living *integrity*. This unique, highly tensioned and complexly articulated organic system is experienced by me as at once "mine" and yet "not me." It is a "wholeness-in-action" (Kass, Jonas), so integral in its upright posture (Straus) and biologic endowment (Portmann) that even when dead and now a cadaver we yet experience it hauntingly as a "sensed relic" (Ramsey). Our ways of accounting for it cannot, without a too-heavy price, remain just catchwords or enigmatic formulas whose sense forever escapes. Thus far, every theory considered has made an appeal to this "wholeness" without, however, specifying just what is to be understood by that.

What is needed is a way of grasping this complex "whole" without reductively stripping away its very meaning and integrity both *as embodying* and *as biological* ("mine" and "other"), both of which reveal intrinsic temporalities, reflexivities, and, as will hopefully become clear now, contexturalities. We face here as nowhere else a curiously complex and tensioned "unity-in-diversity" or "identify-in-difference," but as well a temporally rhythmed contextural flux: an effortful and uncanny complex realized as gestural display. As has become clear, I hope, a conceptual framework permitting only the "either/or" or the "both/and" is not capable of handling this phenomenon of embodiment.

The demand to stick rigorously to the "things themselves" in their own integrity, and thereby to articulate a viable notion of "wholeness" and "unity-in-diversity" (or "alien-familiarity" or "intimate-otherness"), cannot be shunted aside. Without such a notion, one illicitly *denigrates* the phenomenon either by *reductivism* (effectively losing precisely what is to be accounted for, by taking it as "really" composed of something "lower"), or by a kind of *elevationism* (taking all things as merely approximate realizations of some "higher" reality, and thus sucking away its very integrity). Whether either of these essentially metaphysical stances be ultimately true is neither here nor there as regards the present problem, nor do I see any viable way of affirming one or the other *prior* to the actual effort to meet and resolve this problem, as was stressed earlier when I considered Jonas' "new monism."

In any event, the search for the "wholeness" displayed by the embodying organism is not some sort of metaphysical easter-egg hunt. This wholeness is present and salient in every bodily conduct—whether in normal life, or negatively prominent in illness and injury.

OF WHOLES AND PARTS: EDUCING THE PROBLEM

More than twenty-five years of difficult intellectual labor went into the development of Gurwitsch's *Field of Consciousness*. What emerged was not only a penetrating work of scholarship unraveling what he showed was the central problematic of late 19th and 20th century psychology, but the philosophical uncovering of the roots of that problematic—his concepts of "field," "context," "contexture," and "margin."

Given the uncritically accepted, taken for granted "theory of ideas" and the ideal of mathematization, classical psychology was built on the supposition of a sense-data, stimulus-response theory of perception and its intrinsically connected constancy-hypothesis. Sensations, in themselves unconnected and unrelated, are assumed to be the basic ingredients of experience; percepts grow out of these thanks solely to the operation on them of non-sensory, higher-level processes. Because sense-data are defined strictly by physical stimulation (imprintations produced by causally efficacious and external sources), they *"depend entirely upon, and are determined exclusively by, the corresponding physical stimuli.* It follows that *whenever the same physical events stimulate the same elements of the nervous system, the same sensations cannot fail to appear"* (*31*, p. 90).

With this deeply buried "constancy-hypothesis" operatively at work, legitimating and requiring the assumptions of sense-data and supervenient, non-sensory processes working on them, the fundamental and ultimately insuperable problem is set out: how is the recognizable *organization* of sensory experience to be accounted for? If there are *non*-sensory processes (production, projection, memory, association, etc.) which are responsible for organizing the otherwise utterly unordered data of sensation, how is it possible for these processes ever to gain a grip on the (unorganized) data *in the first place*, much less wrench these totally unconnected data into some sort of stable, continuing patterns? All order *must* on such terms be ephemeral, leaving the bedrock of data literally unchanged. James' famous postulation of radical empiricism, despite his evident achievements in other respects, fares no better. Not only are the units of experience which come to be segregated out from the stream supposed to maintain their identity within any system into which they become integrated—thus creating the problem of how *sameness* in different integrations is even possible—but order itself must also be ephemeral, a mere removable patina on the flowing surface of experience. Beyond this, there is the intractable issue: how in principle is the segregation into units of experience even possible? How is it even possible to single out *anything* from the "data," or from the "stream," such that organization itself is at all possible? (*31*, I). No amount of repeated and accumulated experience can account for this segregation (whether of atomistic sensations, or units of a stream), since segregation and stabilization are *presupposed* by the notions of "repeated" and "accumulated" experience. *Every theory which supposes that the organization of the field of sensory experience is brought about by non-sensory processes (of no matter which kind) is thereby in a vicious circle: it presupposes as accomplished precisely what is supposed to have been accounted for.*

The fundamental objection, whose source is the Gestalt psychology of Köhler and Koffka, is just this: the conception of sensations as chaotic and scattered data, in need of being collected together and organized by extraneous factors, is both inconsistent in itself, and fundamentally wrong. That is, as Köhler for the first time formulated it: the constancy-hypothesis must be rejected, and with it go the theories of traditional psychology, of James, of the School of Graz, and even of Piaget.[2] Whichever non-sensory process is appealed to, the same insuperable issues arise: what clues can there be to guide the organizing process in its work? The difficulty is even more conspicuous when one tries to account for stabilized, actually achieved, organizations: "as there is no clue to guide the organizing activity when a certain organizational form results for the first time, so none exists on further occasions" (*31*, p. 54). Since sense-data are and remain "in themselves" devoid of intrinsic organization, just as James' "units" remain self-identical in no matter which system they happen to be found, "organization" (collection, regularity, unity, system, etc.) can only be ephemeral, i.e., no organization at all.

Thus the issue becomes quite clear: *organization must be an autochthonous feature of the field of experience itself.* This insight, won from the critical inspection of traditional theories, led Gurwitsch to the significant thesis that the temporality of consciousness *cannot* be the sole principle of organization of experience. It is *one* principle, but it pertains solely to the nexus of subjective experiencing; it cannot account for the organization and stabilization of the objective field of experience. For the latter, we are forced to recognize that it is *already organized.* Hence the problem for Gurwitsch is to bring out the *sort* of order which is already intrinsic to the field.

The early logical studies by Husserl, especially that of "wholes and parts" already mentioned, are submitted to scrutiny and found seriously wanting. The crucial point for Gurwitsch is that although Husserl, like von Ehrenfels and Stumpf, does not appeal to "non-sensory" processes to account for the perceptual experience of a plurality as such (a "group," a "melody," or even a "heap" or "swarm" of things), he nevertheless endorses a *dualism* of another sort. No longer "non-sensory" processes, but now *sensory processes of a higher order* are called on to account for the experience of organized wholes. There is a stratification between *inferiora* and *superius*: "on the one hand, sensuous elements which are simply given and which, even without its being explicitly stated, are conceived of according to the constancy hypothesis; on the other hand, a higher stratum, above those elements but founded on them" (*32*, p. 253; see also *31*, pp. 74–78).

Although the discussion of wholes and parts in the *Logical Investigations* does not fully follow this *inferiora/superius* division,[3] it is nevertheless the case that later writings seem fully to confirm Gurwitsch's interpretation, and thus to fall under his critique.[4] For the same reasons given for rejecting the inner dualism of higher/lower sensory qualities, Gurwitsch rejects Husserl's appeal to Stumpf's idea of *Verschmelzung* ("fusion" but in a *static* sense) (*31*, pp. 78–84; *49*, pp. 451–53). The data "fused" are held to be "really" *unmodified* by the fusion, and thus the phenomenal prominence of order among pluralities is reduced to an ephemeral status no less than in sense-data theories.

Gurwitsch notes, of course, that in his *Investigations* Husserl defines whole and part by means of his concept of "foundedness" (*Fundierung*). Surprisingly, however, in view of the emphasis Husserl gives to this concept, Gurwitsch says relatively little about it. He underscores rather Husserl's apparently serious and open endorsement of Stumpf's concept of "fusion" and Husserl's distinction between "self-sufficient" and "nonself-sufficient" parts. As regards the latter, all Gurwitsch finds acceptable, it is clear, is Husserl's argument that certain "parts," in virtue of their "material content," cannot exist except in conjunction with other parts: e.g., "color" and "extension." Only of such nonself-sufficient parts can it be said, for Husserl, that they are inseparable from some "whole" (something colored). Other parts, again solely by virtue of their material content, can be said to exist *both* as "parts of a whole" *and* in isolation—so-called self-sufficient "parts" like musical notes. This is to accept the traditional conception of wholes and parts, as Gurwitsch sees it, and thereby effectively endorses the view which Gurwitsch has amply shown must be rejected (*31*, pp. 144–50; *49*, pp. 456–57). For to account for the peculiar *differences* manifestly evident in the cases of single notes sounded in isolation and notes grouped together into a chord or melody, Husserl, says Gurwitsch, has to rely on an *extraneous*, albeit also sensory, principle: namely, "fusion," or "figural moment." Hence *that* dualism has to be rejected: because of the problems already mentioned, and because (as Gurwitsch subsequently shows) experience of "wholes" and "parts" contradicts the supposition of that dualism.

Thus only the concept of "mutual foundedness" among certain "parts" (nonself-sufficient moments) is acceptable (e.g., "color" and "extension," "pitch" and "intensity");[5] the rest of what Husserl includes under the concept of foundedness is rejected, as it inherently invokes one or another dualism regarding perceptual life. But with the former there is no need for a unification—and this very absence manifests the *intrinsic*, mutual dependency. The self-sufficient parts ("pieces") *require* a unification, but, as Gurwitsch says, "unification between independent elements cannot be established except by means of a new and specific datum, founded by, and dependent upon, the elements" to be unified (*31*, p. 84). Because such unified elements are said to preserve their identity even when thus grouped, it is necessary for Husserl to maintain that the unification be accomplished by a "higher order" sensory quality (*Einheitsmoment*, a "moment of unity") which does *not* affect the *inferioria* in any substantial way. "Order" for such parts is therefore strictly ephemeral, and we are back to the traditional theory, wherein order is not accounted for but presupposed. As Husserl admits, "strictly speaking our approach is positive in the case of what is non-independent, negative in the case of what is independent . . ." (*49*, p. 447).

I need to pause briefly, to clarify the terrain and make it possible to pursue my own problematic. Husserl's inquiry here is intricate. Considering Stumpf's argument (*118*, pp. 112, 113) that quality and extension are "functionally dependent," "inseparable" (*untrennbar*), and thus are "part-contents" (*Teilinhalte*) or "nonself-sufficient" parts not "separable" even in our ideas of them, Husserl asks what it might mean to have an idea of a content "by itself" or "in isolation":

> Does this mean, as regards the actually *experienced* contents of the phenomenological sphere, that such a content can be freed from all blending [*Verschmelzung*] with coexistent contents, can therefore ultimately be torn out [*herausgerissen*] of the unity of consciousness? Obviously not. In *this* sense all contents are inseparable [*unabtrennbar*],[6] and the same holds of the phenomenal *thing*-contents in their relation to the total unity of the phenomenon as such. If we form an independent idea of the content *head of a horse*, we inescapably present it in a context, the content stands out saliently from an objective background that appears with it, it is inescapably given with many other contents, and is also in a way united to them. (*49*, pp. 442–43)[7]

What is striking here is that this emphatic claim could very well have been written by Gurwitsch! But Husserl goes on to maintain that, contrary to Stumpf, considerations such as "functional dependency" and "moments of unity" do not so much *prove* as they *define* the mutual inseparability of "part-contents" (nonself-sufficiency). As such, he contends, such "contents," while *in fact* inseparable, are *in essence* not thus dependent:

> Separability means nothing else than that we can keep this content identical in the presentation despite unlimited variation (arbitrary, not restricted by any law grounded in the *essence* of the content) of the contents connected and somehow co-given; and this means that the content remains unaffected by the removal of any set of co-given contents. (*49*, p. 443)[8]

By the same reasoning, Husserl argues that nonself-sufficiency (*Unselbstän-digkeit*) must be defined by laws of essence, not in reference either to matters of objective fact or to the contingencies of subjective thought. Thus the "can" in the phrases: "cannot be thought" or "can be thought" indicates a reference "not to a subjective necessity, i.e., to the subjective incapacity-to-represent-things-otherwise [*des Sich-nicht-anders-vorstellen-könnens*], but to the objectively ideal necessity of an inability-to-be-otherwise [*des Nicht-anders-sein-könnens*]" (*49*, p. 446).

Now here Gurwitsch interjects two basic protests. First, Husserl has in truth defined *actual separatedness* rather than *separability*. In his discussion, Gurwitsch contends that Husserl has focused on

> the content as already singled out [e.g. "head of a horse"] and made into a theme "in itself," not, however, a phenomenological description of a constituent susceptible of being singled out, though not singled out actually. Failing to differentiate between the two means to overlook the fact that by being actually singled out, the content in question undergoes a qualitative change and is, phenomenally speaking, no longer "the same." (*32*, pp. 261–262)

Here, that is, Husserl erroneously foists into the example (seeing the head of a horse) a distinction which is the *result of a cognitive operation* (freely imagining the head of a horse "in itself"), which he fails to notice is a qualitative modification of the content. "An item," Gurwitsch concludes, "which *can* be singled out must be sharply distinguished from one which *is* singled out actually" (*32*, p. 263).

Thus there are two fundamentally different issues confused by Husserl: whether a certain item (e.g., a straight line) is so integrated into a whole that it comes to our awareness only as being within that whole (e.g., a triangle); or whether that item is in its own right focally attended to as *already* singled out (a straight line given by itself, as opposed to being given as the side of a triangle). Starting with the former (the whole itself), Husserl thematically *alters* the situation, attending now to the latter (the line given by itself), and then concludes that because the line "*can*" be given by itself, it is "*able*" to be given by itself even in the case where all that is given is the whole itself, the triangle. But the "can" glosses over the *already altered* presentational content: the line Husserl focuses on is one already singled out, not the line actually given as the side of the triangle. Thus the idea that there can be "self-sufficient" parts just does not hold up to careful analysis; indeed, it can be argued only by making that confusion.

The second exception Gurwitsch takes to Husserl's account follows directly from the first. Expressed in simple terms, Gurwitsch maintains that the kind of dependence exhibited by the constituents of a Gestalt contexture is a quite different one from that emphasized by Husserl as holding between examples of *species*, or what determines the instances of one species "*as parts of more inclusive wholes of a certain appropriate Species*" (*49*, p. 447). The species "color as such," for Husserl, predestines the color of a particular piece of paper to being a "part-content," such that it can only be the nonself-sufficient moment of a colored, extended thing. So-called self-sufficient parts or pieces (*Stücke*) are those with respect to which such a law of essence is lacking, and thus they *may*, but *need not*, become parts of a more inclusive whole (e.g., notes of a melody). Gurwitsch's objection is just this: what is missed by Husserl's focus on individual parts taken as examples of species is the concrete particularization of individuals in a given case. Since for its concrete particularization, each constituent of a Gestalt-contexture depends essentially upon co-constituents, the unity between the constituents is established by their very existence and consists in their mutual determination and qualification. Experienced in the relationship of Gestalt-coherence, the constituents form a whole which is but the organized co-existence of the parts. (*31*, p. 146)

Hence what Husserl's analysis fails to grasp, *especially* that of so-called "self-sufficient parts," is that where such parts do in fact enter into a more inclusive whole this must, first, fundamentally alter the presentational situation from what it was, and second, this "being-within-a-whole" exhibits a *crucial dependency of its own kind.* Husserl in effect ignores the latter since he is obliged to call on a "unifying factor" (moment of unity, figural factor) in order to account for what is then perceptually apprehended. This *additional* factor, "built on the elements that we primarily distinguish" (*49*, p. 442), effectively obfuscates the *sui generis* dependency Gurwitsch insists upon.

In effect, Gurwitsch stresses that what Husserl says of only *some* wholes must be so for all wholes: *there is no need for a specific moment of unity which binds parts into a whole* (*49*, p. 476). Those wholes which Husserl regards as *able* to be "pieced"—so-called "extensive wholes"—must therefore be reinterpreted, along with the reinterpretation of so-called "independent" parts.

Gurwitsch insists that the proper way to grasp the distinction Husserl attempts in his self-sufficient/nonself-sufficient dichotomy must on principle avoid the confusions and mistakes he marks out. He suggests that way is to be found in the distinction between the two sorts of Gestalt-contextures: those whose items are *given in no other way than* within a specific contexture (and thus are *not* susceptible of being "singled out"), and those whose items *can* become themes on their own (and are thus susceptible of being "singled out"). As he puts it,

we do not contest the difference itself, but only its interpretation. For us it is not the same whether a content *can be made* independent or *is made* independent. . . . [Thus] we deny that an item which is susceptible of being singled out remains phenomenally the same when it is singled out. This is the central point in our divergence from Stumpf and Husserl, who maintain that an item can merely be isolated and otherwise remain what it is, whereas according to our analyses a *materially* different what, a new theme, results from such isolation. (*32*, pp. 264–65)

CONTEXT

The major issue is thus clear: the structure of the "field" of consciousness, and more especially the nature of Gestalt-coherence. It is not necessary to give more than a cursory review of the former, as the latter is the significant conception for my purposes.

Beginning with James' analysis of the field of consciousness as consisting of a "focus" and a "margin"—or the "substantive" and the "transitive" ("fringe") parts of the stream of consciousness (*31*, pp. 21–25, 309–12)—Gurwitsch delineates a type of organization in what James calls the "margin." Utilizing James' important distinction between the "object" and "topic" of thought (*52*, I, pp. 275 ff.), he shows that what is included in the former are not only several different kinds of affairs, but also an essential and necessary "reference" to the topic. Thus if one says, "Napoleon was the victor at the battle of Jena," the *topic* is, say, Napoleon (though in a given case it might instead be "battles" or "Jena"); the *object*, to paraphrase James, is nothing short of what is designated by the entire sentence, "Napoleon-was-the-victor-at-the-battle-of-Jena." In phenomenological terms, while "Napoleon" is the *theme* ("topic"), what is designated by the entire sentence is the *thematic field*, in general. But closer scrutiny will show that "in the fringes" is a host of affairs which, although co-present with the theme, has no relevance or reference to the theme itself, nor much connection with what lies in the thematic field. For example, while paying attention thematically to the affairs designated above, there are other noises in the room, feelings of hunger or thirst, and the whole field of other affairs co-presently experienced with the asserting of the sentence but having no bearing on it (*31*, pp. 312–18).

Thus Gurwitsch distinguishes the *theme* from the *thematic field*, and both from the *margin*. Ignoring the first for the moment, it is clear that whatever may be the theme, it always and necessarily appears or emerges "*from a field* in which the theme is located occupying the center so that the field forms a background with respect to the theme" (*31*, p. 319), and thus the field essentially *refers to* the theme and vice versa. The *thematic field* is the *context* from which a particular theme emerges. Clearly, the sense of "pointing" or "reference" which characterizes the relationship here is one of *material relevancy*: the theme "stands out from" a background to which it refers precisely as the "ground" for the "figure." As such, it is also clear, the background can shift and alter while the theme remains the same (e.g., seeing one and the same person in the front yard, or in his house), and thus the theme has a certain *independence* relative to the thematic field. Nevertheless, that a figure (theme) appears in one field rather than another (the number 2 drawn on white paper, or drawn on a background of green and red spots) is not merely an extraneous matter. "The perspective under which the theme presents itself, its organization along determinate and specific lines of relevancy depend upon the thematic field or context within which it appears" (*31*, p. 359). Inherent to the theme itself is this phenomenon of perspective, orientation, or position: i.e., the theme has a "positional index" thanks to its specific context of appearance, and this index can and will vary as the thematic field itself is more or less structured and articulated (*31*, pp. 360–65). This "position" of the theme, therefore, is strictly a *noematic-objective* one: it concerns *what* is experienced rather than the fact of its being actually experienced. Because, finally, a given theme cannot fit into just any context, "the relationship of relevancy must obtain between the context and the theme" (*31*, p. 364). In the event that relevancy is lost, what was thematic now becomes part of the *margin*—i.e., that part of the field which is, precisely, *irrelevant* (for the moment only, perhaps) to what has in the meantime become thematic.

All such considerations are in a way strictly in the service of delineating the organization of the theme itself. What is *marginal* is marginal *in respect of* some specific theme; what is *field* is field *in respect of* the theme: it is this, the theme (contexture), which constitutes the third and centrally significant mode of organization. Between the theme and the thematic field are *contextual* relationships: there is here a *unity by relevance*, as there is also among the items within the field itself. Between the complex, "theme/field," and the margin, on the other hand, as also among whatever there may be within the margin itself, we have conjunctions which "are of mere temporal nature" (*31*, p. 353). It is necessary to point out that here Gurwitsch confuses the very things he has tried to make so plain, since "temporality" is said to be the organizational principle of consciousness itself, whereas the "field," which necessarily includes the margin,[9] is organized according to "context" relationships—widely enough conceived to be able to take irrelevancy as one of these, of course. However that may be, and whether indeed one could go further, attempting to show that what is "marginal" in Gurwitsch's sense is actually without internal articulation (as he maintains), what concerns me at the moment is only the theme itself.

As I understand it, Husserl's basic error can be pinned down precisely: *he confused "theme/field" relations with intra-thematic ones.* Whereas there is a certain independence of the theme—which can, as James also saw (*31*, p. 22), be considered a kind of "part" as regards the field (a kind of "whole")—the items comprising the theme are strictly bound together as constituents of a Gestalt, the theme itself. *To "context," thus, Gurwitsch opposes and contrasts "contexture": the intra-thematic organization*, within which what is a "part" (constituent) has no independence from what is "whole" (contexture) (*31*, p. 354).

The importance of contextures cannot be overstressed. Not only, as will now be seen, do they display the crucial mode of organization presented by the embodying organism, but in addition, the contexture is foundational for all other modes of order and unity:

Between the theme and its field prevails unity by relevancy so that any independence of the theme is contained within that unity. . . . *Unity by Gestalt-coherence underlies and renders possible unity by relevancy.* For a theme to be a center of reference with respect to which the thematic field is organized, the theme must present itself as a consolidated and intrinsically coherent unit. Only between units of such internal organizational structure may relationships of relevancy exist. (*31*, p. 358)

CONTEXTURE

Although primarily concerned with sense perceptual experience, Gurwitsch does not maintain that his analysis of the principles of organization is restricted to that. Indeed, he suggests that experience of all sorts presents us with the same fundamental structures: e.g., dealing with scientific problems, walking in the street (*31*, p. 1), even logic (*31*, pp. 325–40). "To develop a field-theory of consciousness is to embark upon an analysis of the phenomenon of context in general, as well as upon the eventual disclosure of different types of contexts" (*31*, pp. 2–3). This fully legitimates my ignoring the specific features of sensory experience and focusing on the more general theory—but, again, only so far as it concerns my present problems. After that, it will become necessary to break, in one critical sense, with Gurwitsch's restriction of his theory to the noematic-objective field.

It is the phenomenon of *contexture* (Gestalt-configuration, or intra-thematic organization) which is central. Here four points are necessary: (1) functional significance, (2) functional weight, (3) contexture proper, and (4) good continuation and contextural closure.

(1) *Functional Significance*

Every phenomenon which displays Gestalt-coherency is one which, while being a unitary "whole," is intrinsically articulated and structured, in "varying degrees of richness of detail," by virtue of which it "detaches itself as an organized and closed unit from the surrounding field" (*31*, p. 115). Thus every such "Gestalt" has structures, organizational forms, properties, characters, or features *of its own kind*. Specifically, each "Gestalt" exhibits "parts," *constituents* having their sole placement within that "whole." Hence

> to be a constituent and, in this sense, a part of a Gestalt means to exist at a certain place within the structure of the whole and to occupy a certain locus in the organization of the Gestalt. The locus can be defined only with reference to, and from the point of view of, the topography of the whole. By virtue of its absorption into the structure and organization of a Gestalt-contexture, the constituent in question is endowed with a *functional significance* for that contexture. Each constituent of a Gestalt has a certain function within its structure, for example, being the right member of a pair or the right terminal point of an interval . . . . The functional significance of each constituent derives from the total structure of the Gestalt, and by virtue of its functional significance, each constituent contributes towards this total structure and organization. (*31*, pp. 115–116)

This functional significance, accordingly, strictly determines each constituent. A constituent is what it is solely as integrated along with other constituents into the coherency of the whole. If one should remove a constituent from its Gestalt-placement and place it within another Gestalt, one could no longer speak "of the same constituent being integrated into different contextures" (*31*, p. 121). For instance, if one hears a C-major chord, on the one hand, and a C-minor chord on the other, the note "G" which is a constituent of the first is not "the same as" the note "G" constituent to the second, any more than it is the note "G" sounded by itself or in some other chord. More complex examples make the point even more: e.g., the way a red stop-light phenomenally appears when seen during a leisurely stroll, as opposed to "the same" light when seen during an urgent drive to take one's child to the hospital. Even though both may in some sense be said to have been aroused by "the same" objective conditions, the *functional significance* the light has in the two contextures differs vastly. Thus Gurwitsch stresses that

> it is the *functional significance of any part of a Gestalt-contexture that makes this part that which it is. The part is what it is only as a constituent of the Gestalt-contexture and as integrated into its unity. Any part of a Gestalt may then be said to be determined as to its existence by its functional significance in the sense that the part only exists in, and is defined by, its functional significance.* (*31*, p. 121)

(2) *Functional Weight*

It is obvious, of course, that not every "part" has the precise same significance within the contexture. In our example, while rushing my child to the hospital, the "red light" has greater emphasis or "weight" than does, say, whether my car has radial or belted tires, or even whether my child has been hurt while playing soccer or football. What is "crucial" is to get him to the hospital and the red light stands out as a veritable blockage to the aid I must reach to help him. To be sure, having this functional significance is relative: i.e., whatever the significance may be in one or another case, it is "relative" to that which other constituents have. Each constituent refers to others, equally "parts" of the contexture, but different as regards their *functional weight*. More generally,

> every part has its functional weight within its Gestalt-contexture integration. This import is in proportion to the contribution which, by virtue of its functional significance, the part makes towards the contexture. Whatever the comparative functional weight of a part, that part depends upon other parts since it cannot exist qualified by its functional significance unless other, although subordinate, parts also exist, each qualified by its functional significance. (*31*, p. 133)

Determining this essential reference and weight, indeed, most often appears when there is a change in the reference: when the "weight" shifts, as in the example of the traffic light. Or, in the cases given by Wertheimer, in order to have a continuing contexture, the parts must be such as to retain their "good form qualities" when other parts are added. If the latter "destroy" the form-qualities, then the lines acquire new functional significance and lose what they formerly had (figures 1, 2). In figure 1, the latter occurs; in figure 2, the former (*31*, p. 134).

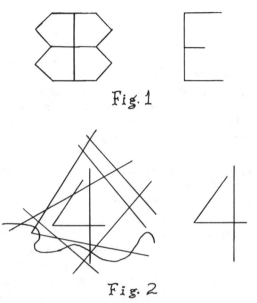

Fig. 1

Fig. 2

We can thus say that there is a thorough interdependence among the constituents of every contexture; the "texture" of any contexture, as it were, is defined by functional significance and functional weight.

(3) *Contexture Proper (Gestalt-coherence)*

Clearly, it is simply impossible in light of such considerations to account for such "whole/part" relations either in an additive way ("both/and") or in a disjunctive way ("either/or"). A "whole" of this kind is neither the "sum" of its parts, nor reducible to its parts, nor somehow "more" than its parts.

A contexture in the proper sense requires

> *no unifying principle or agency over and above the parts or constituents which co- exist in the relationship of mutually demanding and supporting each other. The Gestalt, the whole of Gestalt-character is the system, having internal unification of the functional significances of its constituents; it is the balanced and equilibrated belonging and functioning together of the parts, the functional tissue which the parts form;* more correctly, *in which they exist in their interdependence and interdetermina- tion. The unity of the theme thus proves* [to be] *unity by Gestalt-coherence throughout, entirely and exclusively.* (31, p. 139)

To specify this further, it is necessary to say not only that each refers intrinsically to every other part (and is reciprocally referred to), nor only that each part is a part of a whole. More deeply still, the "whole" itself (contexture) is inherent to every constituent in that each constituent realizes the contexture in its own way, by virtue of its own functional significance. The contexture is intrinsic to every constituent, such that each constituent is what it is, has its own specific locus, by realizing its contexturing whole (*31*, p. 145). Thus the "whole" is neither a "sum," a "more than," nor reducible; it is exactly the *system of mutually interdependent and interdetermined constituents.* It is, literally, formally, materially, and substantively (*31*, pp. 148–49) the totality, the "whole" of such complex references or functional significances. Precisely this "balanced and equilibrated" co-existence of mutual, reciprocal references is what Gurwitsch shows is the "object" of all perceptual experience (*31*, pp. 222–23, 227; IV Ch. 2).

One can thus better appreciate Gurwitsch's strenuous objections to, yet his appreciation of, Husserl's doctrine of whole/part relations. Beyond what was already pointed out, when Husserl proposes that whenever one *can* "freely vary" a content without reference to its factually presented contexture, he in effect commits a version of what James called the "psychologist's fallacy": foisting into the constitution of the experienced object elements extraneous to the object and then trying to account for it in terms of such elements (*31*, pp. 25, 94, 186). "Hence, when a whole is dissolved, actually or mentally, the products of decomposition, the resulting elements must not be mistaken for those very parts contained in the whole previously to its decompositions" (*31*, p. 148). To suppose "independence" of parts on the basis of the possibility (or actuality) of separation or isolation *in imagination* is effectively to have missed, or destroyed, the very presented contexture in question (whether it be a melody, a horse's head, or any other "whole"). Conceptually determined self-sufficiency does not purport self-sufficiency of "parts" actually encountered as "parts of a whole." Similarly, given the essential character of contextures and their constituents, there cannot be a question of priority of part or whole. The question of priority cannot arise except for the contexture itself, hence no dualistic account (whether involving non-sensory, or higher-level sensory processes) can be true. The supposition of "figural factors," "moment of unity," and the like, also commits a version of the psychologist's fallacy, mistaking products of analysis (what the psychologist "knows") for contents of experience (*52*, I, pp. 196 ff.).

(4) *Good Continuation and Contextural Closure*

It was already mentioned that for the field to be a context, the theme must be already formed: *unity by contexture* (theme) *makes possible unity by context* (field) (*31*, pp. 352, 356). But how is the theme itself possible?

One condition is already evident: even though founding and making possible the context-unity of the thematic field, every theme on the other hand appears strictly within and as standing out from that thematic field. In the case of perception, for instance, Gurwitsch (following Husserl) maintains that "*per-cipere* may be characterized as *ex-cipere*" (*31*, pp. 321, 365);[10] it is a "singling out" of the theme from the field. Hence "ground" can never be absent from perceptual "figure" (*31*, p. 113).[11]

In a purely descriptive sense, moreover, the fact is that whatever emerges as possessing Gestalt-coherence, with its characteristic interdependence among constituents, *does* emerge from the field. Not to be absorbed into the field thus *means* that this specific kind of *contextural* interdependence and reciprocal reference does *not* hold among items in the field and the constituents of the contexture: between the theme and its field there are only relevance-relationships. Thus, in general, the segregation of anything from the field follows the lines of organization pertaining to contextures: "Gestalt-coherence is a condition of segregation . . . " (*31*, p. 138).

I earlier stressed the importance of the "positional index"—the perspective, orientation, and position of the theme within the field. For example, a particular proposition may be thematically apprehended as the conclusion of an argument. Its positional index consists of what Gurwitsch calls "contextual characters": e.g., "referring back" as "derived from," and "referring forward" to other propositions, etc., all within the "field" of logical relationships and reasoning. Or, to use another example, although the context does not by itself make a word or sentence meaningful (as if these had no meaning in isolation), it does give to them their *specific* meaning—"that meaning-element or shade of meaning through which the pertinence of the word or sentence to the context is experienced" (*31*, p. 361). Thus the positional index is a determinant, one condition for the theme to be that which it is.

Finally, it has been shown by Gurwitsch that the thematic field is far from a mere undifferentiated mass of data. It, too, has its organization, consisting, in the case of perception, of well-circumscribed and delimited things, already detached from one another. Too, though one may thematize one proposition in an argument, the other propositions do not thereby become an amorphous vagueness: they remain distinct and definite, differentiated from still other propositions, even though not now thematized. In short, each of these already segregated items is thereby a *potential* theme (*31*, p. 361). Precisely insofar as every item in the field refers to other items in the field and to what is now thematic, in relationships of contextual reference, such references imply the possibility of being thematically apprehended. Indeed, as Gurwitsch points out, even items in the margin—though organized as irrelevant—may be thematized, where thematization means possible elucidation of what is "now" indeterminate and indistinct. Briefly, all the evidence points to one central conclusion: *the organization of the field of consciousness into theme/thematic field/margin, cannot be "derived" from anything else; it is, rather, autochthonous* (*31*, pp. 30–36).

Strictly implied from all these considerations are the four factors identified by Wertheimer as determining the organization of constituents into a contexture. These are, in ascending order of import, proximity; equality; closure; and good continuation. Although first established as regards visual wholes, they have significance far beyond that —especially, as Gurwitsch shows, the last two (*31*, p. 150).[12] What is meant here is best seen in cases of incomplete contextures: e.g., a melody broken off before being finished, a sentence which is left dangling incomplete, a face incompletely drawn, a treatise which makes a phenomenon problematic without, however, treating it, or, as I shall presently say, an impaired embodiment. In each case, there is at once an *experienced incompleteness*[13] of the contexture, *and a tendency towards completion* or towards *closure* ("good continuation"). In such cases, the constituents at hand appear as "in need of support and supplementation along the lines of, and in accordance with, their functional significance" (*31*, p. 151). The actually given constituents demand, and set up the lines and manner of, other constituents at certain places and with a certain functional significance in reference to the ones at hand and thus in reference to the (incomplete) contexture itself. Clearly, not everything available at any moment is able to serve as a constituent of a particular contexture: not just any musical note will "fit" the melody now incomplete; not just any words will bring the sentence to completion; etc. The incomplete contexture *itself* "develops strong tendencies of its own towards completing itself. There arise movements of closure along the lines of good continuation" (*31*, p. 151).

Reviewing instances of *incompleteness* helps make clear what the cases of well-formed contextures possess, without this always being easy to detect.[14] *Contextures as such manifest a striking tendency to "continue," "persist," or "maintain" themselves, to preserve their internal "agreement," "concord," or "coherence."* Failing that, what occurs is the characteristic "incongruity," "out-of-tuneness," "clash," "discord," of incomplete, abortive, impaired, or faulty contextures.

THE REFERENTIAL COMPLEXUS

Gurwitsch is content to have specified only that the constituents of any contexture exhibit a kind of "pointing reference" (*31*, pp. 317–35, 368 ff.), or, equivalently, functional significance. The constituents, to use his characteristic phrase, exhibit mutual and reciprocal interdetermination and interdependence. This description is certainly correct, but hardly sufficient to seize upon the profound sense of coherence manifested by contextures. Hence it is necessary to carry out the lines of his analysis further.

Severely to simplify the point here—in order to make the sense of "multiple reference" salient—consider the example of three points placed on a blackboard so as to form the three points of a perceptually obvious triangle. In what sense is there a "whole" made up of three "parts"? There is "both" the triangle "and" the parts; or, there is "either" the whole "or" the parts—or so it might seem. More accurately, however (figure 3), we have to note that, in the first place, point (1) is (as "lower left") placed strictly in reference to points (2) and (3) (as "upper middle" and "lower right", respectively) (figure 4). By the

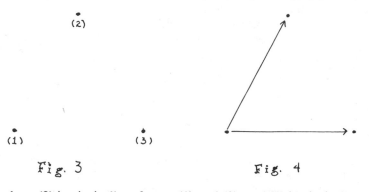

(2)

(1)   (3)

Fig. 3   Fig. 4

same token, (2) intrinsically refers to (1) and (3); and (3) intrinsically refers to (1) and (2)—in respect of which *simple, intrinsic reference* each point is "placed" as such (figure 5).

But this already makes it plain that each point refers as well in a more complex way: (1) refers to (3) both *simply and indirectly*, namely to (3) via (2), which itself refers *simply* to (3). Thus: (1)→(3), and (1)→[(2)→](3) (figure 6). And,

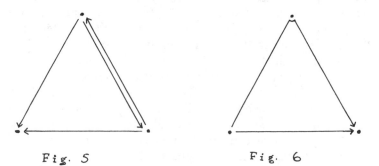

Fig. 5   Fig. 6

of course, the same holds for each of the other points: (1)→[(3)→] (2); (2)→ [(3)→] (1); (2)→[(1)→](3); (3)→[(1)→] (2); and (3)→[(2)→] (1) (figure 7a, b, c, d, e).

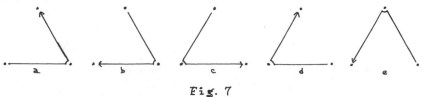

a   b   c   d   e

Fig. 7

Such *complex, intrinsic references* further secure the placement of each point (constituent) vis-à-vis the other points—i.e., is a *second* component of the functional significance intrinsic to and constitutive of each constituent. But, as well, each point is also *doubly referred to*: both (2) and (3) refer to (1), and similarly for each point (figure 8a, b, c).

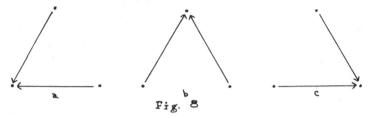

Fig. 8

Since, of course, each point is both simply and complexly referenced, and now obviously doubly referenced, there is also *multiple intrinsic cross-referencing*: for instance, (1) refers to (2) simply: (1)→(2), complexly: (1)→[(3)→] (2), and doubly: [(1)→(2), (1)→[(3)→] (2)]; (2) is therefore multiply cross-referenced: (1)→(2), (1)→[(3)→] (2), (3)→ (2), (3)→[(1)→] (2) (figure 9).

These references holding, it remains only to note that precisely in view of them there is a crucial sense of *self-reference* (simple, complex, and multiple self-reference): (1) refers to (2), and (2) to (1) (simple self-reference), and so for each point; but also, (1) refers to (2), and to (3) which also refers to (2) and back to (1); and (1) refers to (2), (2) to (1), (1) to (3) to (2) to (1); but also (1) refers to (3) which is referred to by (2) and this by (1); and thus (1) is referred to by (3) from (2) from (1) itself (figure 10). And so, too, for each point.

Thus the intrinsic functional significance of a constituent is formed of (a) *simple* reference, (b) *complex* reference, (c) *double* reference, (d) *multiple cross-*reference, and (e) *simple, complex*, and *multiple self*-reference. In these terms, which concern strictly a highly simplified example, *the configuration itself is neither more nor less than this system of intrinsic references*, and each constituent is a "part" of the configuration precisely as a complex of functional significances (references of the sort delineated).

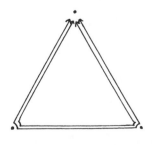

Fig. 9

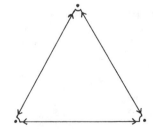

Fig. 10

These different kinds of "reference," finally, constitute a *minimum* system of references for a contexture. While more complicated contextures, and different kinds of contextures, must show at least these references, they may well exhibit still other sorts (or, it may be, the "significance" of these types of references will be systematically enriched). As Gurwitsch shows, the most elementary phenomena apprehended by sensory perception are "configurations" in this sense, and only by *subsequent analysis* is it at all possible to introduce divisions, separations and the like. But in that event, what necessarily occurs is the construction of essentially *different* configurations: to remove a part from a whole is effectively to bring about a different whole and of course a different part. In such a case, one no longer has either "the same" whole or "the same" part (as is evident if one considers any contexture, either the one sketched above, or some other—say, a C-major chord): the complex of mutual references must necessarily alter insofar as one or more "parts" alter, and therefore the *system* of interrelationships (the "whole") itself necessarily alters.

An important caveat is in order here: even in my highly simplified example, it is reasonable to point out that with variation of attention (motivated by whatever it may be) the three points might well be taken perceptually as something different. It might be, for example, that the two bottom points would be seen as end-points of an imagined horizontal line, and the top point as the end-point of a line running vertical to the first and intersecting it at right angles (figure 11). Again, (1) and (3) might be perceived as two points along a line extending beyond themselves, and so, too, for (2) (figure 12).

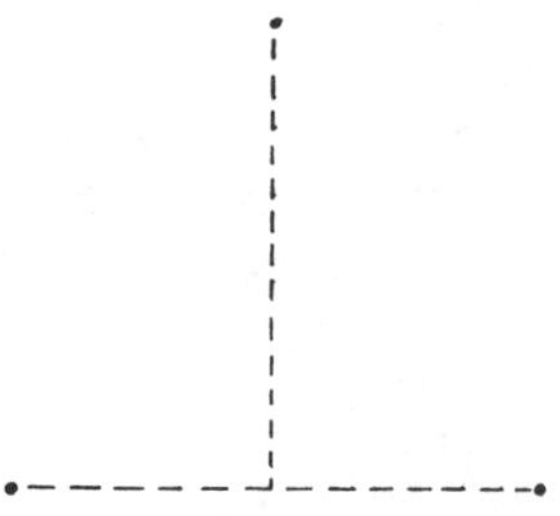

Fig. 11 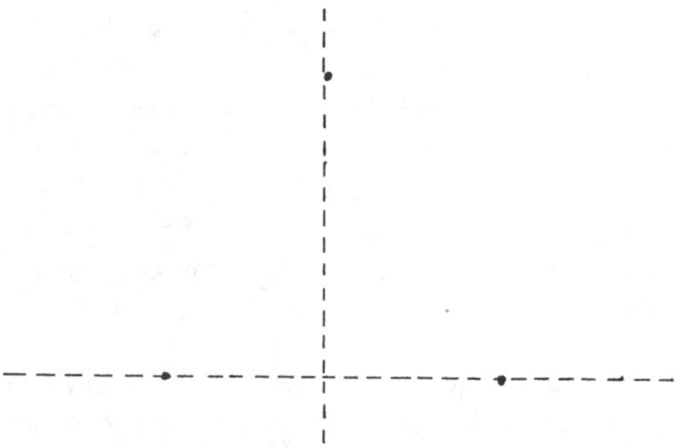   Fig. 12

Other variations are, of course, possible, although it seems clear that such a simplified case considerably limits the range of possible variations. Too, it seems that the specific configuration actually perceived will tend to be only one of the range; one, that is, will tend to be *weighted* for perceptual apprehension. In any event, whichever is perceived, some such system of structures, functional significances, and properties *pertaining to the configuration itself* will be present.

Accordingly, it is a *matter of principle* that (1) contextures have structures, significances, and properties of their own, (2) contextures are the systematic totality of the functional significances of each of the constituents, and (3) constituents are systematically placed within and defined by the contexture formed by the totality of the constituents' functional significances (all of these from Gurwitsch). Beyond these, three further principles have emerged: (4) the *phenomenon of "functional significance" is grounded in the forms of "intrinsic reference"* (delineated above), (5) a *range of different contextures is at least possible as regards a set of constituents* (whose specific significances and "weights" will accordingly also vary), and (6) *the richer or more complex the contexture the greater will be the range of variation of possible contextures apprehendable thereby.* In different terms, the more complex the contexture, the greater the actual and possible functional significances (intrinsic references) constitutive of each constituent, and consequently the greater will be the ways of apprehending or attentionally focusing on one or another configuration, and thus of articulating the kind and functional significances pertaining to the constituents.

CRITIQUE AND EXTENSION

Gurwitsch clearly restricts the phenomenon of contexture (as also "context") to the noematic-objective sphere. The noetic side, i.e., that pertaining to acts and processes of consciousness, has its organizational principle in *temporality* (*31*, pp. 3, 280–305). It will be necessary to address that principle later; for now, I want to return to the embodying organism, which is neither "noetic" nor "noematic," neither "consciousness" nor "world" simpliciter.

But there is a problem with that procedure, and it is this problem with which we need to square off here. In the discussion of Merleau-Ponty's theory of perceptual organization (*31*, pp. 295–305)[15]—which is placed, curiously, within the chapter on "noetic analysis" of perception—Gurwitsch at one point seems ready to acknowledge the very extension of contexture to the *corps-propre* that I am anxious to show. Thus he writes:

Such an organizational form is also realized in our embodied existence. When speaking of the body, Merleau-Ponty has in view . . . the body as experienced by the involved subject, not the organism as a physical object and an object of science. A bodily posture or gesture concerns, if not the whole of the body, at least an extended system of bodily organs. Each organ performs its own specific function in accordance with the total bodily posture on a given occasion. Far from being merely mutually coordinated, the different organs and their functions condition and determine each other in such a way that in the function of any organ, especially those organs with a predominant role in a certain total bodily posture, the functions of other organs are enveloped and implied. . . . Embodied existence exhibits throughout the organizational structure described . . . as Gestalt-coherence. Correspondingly, the same holds for the visual, tactile, and other experiences which we have of our own body. (*31*, pp. 301–02)

Now while it is Gurwitsch who has worked out the details of this "Gestalt-coherence," it is certainly true that this interpretation of Merleau-Ponty is quite correct. And it is a view of embodied existence which seems both congenial to, and agreed to by, Gurwitsch. *Except*: Gurwitsch goes on several pages later to demur at a critical point. This passage, too, should be given fully:

> . . . Merleau-Ponty refers the constitution of perceivable things and the perceptual world in general to embodied existence rather than to consciousness. Of whatever importance and however essential the role of bodily motions and bodily phenomena generally (for example, kinesthetic phenomena) for the constitution of perceivable things, the body . . . cannot be referred to except to the extent to which it is given in experience. Bodily phenomena may be resorted to only as experienced bodily phenomena, that is, phenomena such as they appear and present themselves through our specific awareness of them. . . . Yet, pre-thematic and pre-positional consciousness is still consciousness. . . . [W]e therefore submit that constitutive problems must be formulated and treated exclusively in terms of consciousness, both positional and pre-positional. (*31*, p. 305)[16]

Nothing seems very amiss here, for in emphasizing not the body but the *embodying organism*, it has been clear that the focus of the present study is necessarily on these "awarenesses" of the embodying organism (as well as on the organism *as thereby disclosed*). Of course, one important difference, so I have maintained, is that the reference to the organism "as a physical body" (in the first quotation above) is problematical: the "bodily physical" (to use Plügge's term), I maintained, *is itself an experienced phenomenon*, disclosed especially in the "uncanny" ways mentioned. Thus, too, it should be clear, the organism "as an object of science" is problematical: to avoid rigorously any possibility of a dualism creeping into the analysis, I have urged, it is necessary to rethink this whole issue. At least this much should be said: to the extent that a "scientific conception" of bodily life inherently excludes the body as embodying, that conception must on the face of it be prejudicial and indefensible. Positively, as should become clearer, the contexture displayed by the embodying organism is such as to allow and, indeed, to require a scientific study and analysis, without in the least way thereby introducing a surreptitious dualism between the body as studied in science and the body as experienced.

However that may be, there is surely nothing implicit in that difference that would necessarily run counter to Gurwitsch's point; it is merely a question of giving a deeper explicative analysis of "embodied existence" and, correlatively, of our awarenesses of it.

The difficulty is not there, but rather in a feature of Gurwitsch's understanding of consciousness, embodiment, and the perceptual world. In the general conclusion to his *Field of Consciousness* the problem stands out clearly. He argues throughout his great work (1) that the "margin" is the domain of irrelevancy, (2) that it is not itself organized either contextually or contexturally, but is rather merely the domain of what is simultaneously co-present with the theme and the thematic field (*31*, pp. 343–44), and (3) that as regards the relations between the margin and the theme/thematic field "no effect results from changes occurring in marginal consciousness," or, "the only effect . . . is interference" (*31*, p. 415). As the domain of irrelevancy, it is the *domain of contingency*. Here there are two decisive problems.

(1) Whatever may be the prevailing theme, the margin has an "invariant structure"—namely, "*at every moment, phenomenal time* (or the *stream of consciousness*), *our embodied existence,* and the *perceptual world present themselves to consciousness* through the awareness of data and items pertaining respectively to these orders of existence" (*31*, p. 418). Thus if the theme is a scientific theorem, all three of these orders are strictly marginal, the structure of which is mere co-presence or simultaneity of givenness. There can be no positive effect on the theme, while it is the theme, by anything in the margin—only "interference," "disruption," etc. If something in the perceptual world is the theme, then the stream of consciousness and the embodying organism are strictly marginal; if I am attentive to my body, then the perceptual world and consciousness are marginal, etc. Beyond this continual, marginal co-presence, however, nothing else can be said about the margin: indeed, to say it is already to bring it within the theme or, minimally, within the field.

Now the problem here is that *at least* in the case where something perceptual is thematic, *alterations in the embodying organism, even as marginal, do indeed "have an effect" on that theme.* Thus changes in bodily posture, shifts in movements and attitudes, alterations of bodily position or kinaesthetic flow-patterns (eye, hand, head, torso, etc.), all "have their effect" on the theme, can bring about changes in it, or even force a change in themes ("going upstairs," for instance, after suffering angina; trying "to walk" when one's foot "is asleep"; etc.). These alterations, moreover, may be *either* in positional indices (impacting the ways in which the theme is given, but belonging to the thematic field), *or* in contextual characters (by virtue of which intrinsic relationships between theme and field are established), *or* indeed in the functional significances of the contexture itself (by giving, for example, functional weight to one but not other constituents, as when one seeks to do a right-handed task with one's left hand). In brief: *either the characterization of the margin cannot be wholly correct or the place of the embodying organism has been misconstrued*, and perhaps Gurwitsch has mistaken *both*. For the embodying organism is, within his analysis, simply a misfit: it cannot be simply marginal, but neither is it always within the thematic field, and surely rarely is it thematic! The embodying organism is always already experienced, even marginally, as itself organized, in which case the "margin" is not simply "the domain of irrelevancy and mere co-presence"; yet the "experience" of the embodying organism as such shows that though it is rarely a theme, *its organization is precisely the same as the theme*, i.e., *is a contexture* (as Gurwitsch himself admits in the one passage); yet, again, essentially a contexture, it can and does impact the field and thus, as a contexture, also shows "context" characters and must be (according to Gurwitsch) a unity by material relevancy merely!

In a remarkably apt counterpoint to Jonas' remark about ontology—that the "live body" is the latent crisis of every ontology (including, we say, in reciprocal irony, his own)—here, too, the embodying organism at once fits within and yet fundamentally violates Gurwitsch's conception of organization (margin, field, theme). Everything seems fine, even his agreement with Merleau-Ponty's (in effect) contextural theory of embodiment; but as soon as we focus on the latter, the otherwise neat divisions collapse—in the case of the *embodying organism*, which seems to manifest all the forms of order. Something, then, is indeed amiss here, deeply enigmatic, setting up the task of a much deeper probing of the contexture displayed by the embodying organism. Before that, however, there is a second serious problem in Gurwitsch's analysis.

(2) It is not permitted to talk of the organism except and only insofar as it is experienced by consciousness, Gurwitsch contends in opposition to Merleau-Ponty (as is clear in the second quotation above). How are we to understand this? Insofar as this body is marginal, it lies in the sphere of the contingent and the irrelevant (so far as organization is concerned, but even here I find these claims quite incorrect). From this, and from his many reflective studies of consciousness, Gurwitsch comes to the view that even though awareness of bodily life is interwoven with awarenesses of the perceptual world, even though awareness of bodily life is simultaneous with our acts of consciousness, even though acts of consciousness thus appear as occurring objectively "here and now," *nevertheless:*

> Considered as to its specific nature, consciousness is a domain closed in itself, a domain into which nothing can enter and from which nothing can escape.[17] Still, because acts of consciousness are experienced to occur as accompanied by, and thus as connected with, the awareness of bodily facts and processes, consciousness may be integrated into, and may somehow partake of, mundane reality. Though that participation is merely adventitious and un-essential to consciousness, since its intrinsic specific nature is not affected by such a participation, acts of consciousness may yet be considered as events taking place in connection with, and in dependence upon, organismic and bodily processes provoked, in turn, by occurrences in the external world. (*31*, p. 419)

To take consciousness as thus embodied, connected with, and dependent upon bodily processes, is, Gurwitsch concludes, *to treat it psychologically and not phenomenologically* (*31*, p. 419).[18] This, for him, in no way denigrates the study of embodied life; it merely differentiates the systematic levels of inquiry. Still, while fully admitting that there are such important differences of level, it seems to me wholly wrong to characterize matters this way, and more importantly, wrong to portray "consciousness" and "body" in such terms.

In the first place, Gurwitsch's own phenomenological (and even transcendental) inquiry into perception has amply shown that considerations of perception *necessitate* considerations of embodiment. There could not possibly (i.e., transcendentally) be any perceptual world, any environing milieu, without the various features already delineated pertaining to the embodying organism. Beyond that, there could not possibly (i.e., transcendentally) be any "act of consciousness" at all, especially but not only perceptual awareness, which is not enacted first and foremost by way of specific corporeal and organismic patterns and schemata. Hence Gurwitsch's *own* phenomenology inherently requires *systematic* inquiry into embodiment.

In the second place, even if it is true, as Gurwitsch says against Merleau-Ponty, that one cannot refer "to bodily phenomena *simply* but rather to the experience and awareness of these phenomena" (*31*, p. 305), it nevertheless does not follow that consciousness is in itself a *closed domain*.[19] If nothing else, even supposing that this "closure" is a *methodological* point—the phenomenological reduction does not, as Gurwitsch stresses, too, suppress or obliterate bodily processes or the "awareness" of them—the positive danger of such a stance is that it openly invites what would be expressly denied by Gurwitsch (and Husserl): a rigid *dualism*, and not the "duality" Gurwitsch elsewhere prefers.

Beyond the danger lies an error, however: if it is true (as I think it is) that acts of consciousness are experienced as integrated into and even dependent upon processes within the embodying organism, then these acts of consciousness *cannot be supposed to be merely adventitious, unessential, or extraneous.* Even if it is true (as I think it is) that one can reflectively focus one's attention on the nexus of consciousness itself, "disregarding" for clear and legitimate purposes the actual and possible connections to the embodying organism (and the thereby disclosed "world"), *that reflective possibility in no way requires or implies that those connections are adventitious.* To the contrary, as I hope to make clear later, considering the "stream of consciousness 'in itself' " (*in "Reinheit" betrachtet*) makes it evident that this stream of noetic intendings is inherently and necessarily enacted by means of the kinaesthetic flow-patterns fundamental to the embodying organism. The "connection" between consciousness (the nexus of temporal *Erlebnisse*) and embodying organism turns out to be *essential*; the exact nature of this connection, however, must be left open for the moment.

I therefore conclude, in Gurwitsch's words, that embodied existence exhibits throughout the organizational structure of Gestalt-coherence. The problems I have tried to confront here—namely, Gurwitsch's insistence that embodiment is strictly "marginal" even while exhibiting contextural complexity, and his regarding embodiment as merely unessential—cannot be fully resolved until I have given a fuller explication of that complexity, and then turned my attention to the other, extraordinarily difficult, issue I have raised: namely, accounting for the "connection" between consciousness and its embodying organism.

5

On "Complexure": The Bodily Contexture and the Nexus of Consciousness

THE embodying organism is susceptible of being experienced, viewed, and studied in quite different ways. It has been already seen that it is at once "intimate" and "alien," and has been studied in these respects. It is also able to be viewed with respect to its physiological nexus, its anatomical structures, its neurological functions, or in terms of aesthetic valuations, etc. Each of these ways of attentionally focusing on the embodying organism is clearly possible; yet throughout it remains "one and the same." The key to this complexity, I have suggested, lies in its *contextural* organization. As was seen in the last chapter, it is descriptively possible to take different "points of view" on almost any contexture: the three appropriately placed points I used as a highly simplified example to bring out the full sense of "references," I stressed, could also be perceptually apprehended differently. In such a shift, of course, the functional significances and their relative functional weights also shift qualitatively, and thereby a different contexture emerges. Yet though "different," something seems "the same." I suggested that this is not at all surprising: it is in the very essence of contextures that, especially as they are or become more complex, their constituents have an *intrinsically complex* functional significance, in virtue of which *other possible* contextures can be apprehended without (in one sense) any change occurring, except on the part of the attentive apprehension (one's "attitude"). *This shift in focus would not be possible except on condition that the constituents themselves* (hence the contexture as the systematic totality of intrinsic references) *allowed that shift.* In other words, *this possibility of alternate attentive focus is grounded in the contexture itself.* Expressed simply, one cannot see just anything at all in the three-pointed figure; but one can surely see more than just the triangle. The greater the complexity of a contexture, then, the greater the variety of possibly apprehendable other contextures, for the greater complexity carries with it a richer set of intrinsically complex functional significances. The embodying organism, therefore, one of the most complex and subtly organized of contextures, not surprisingly admits of being apprehended in an enormous variety of ways.

To note this remarkable feature, furthermore, is to give a definitive response to every form of "reductivism" or "elevationism": both are procedures which essentially ignore the specific complexity of embodied life—they are impatient attempts which latch onto merely one possible contextural configuration. As was stressed earlier, they not only lead to absurdities, but are self-defeating as well.

One can begin to see a way by which to respond to Dilthey's hard dilemma—the seemingly unavoidable thrust of philosophy to a singular vision, universal knowledge, and the harsh lessons of historical consciousness. In a word: the phenomenon of *pluralism* (the anarchy of opinions) *is essentially grounded in and made possible by the remarkable singularity of contextures*; indeed, *there could not be "one and the same" contexture except as articulated not only into a plurality of appertaining constituents but also into constituents having intrinsically complex functional significances*, i.e., *as forming a "whole" which is the systematic totality of such significances.* But the fuller sense of this initial insight still must be secured. For the present, two further steps are needed, before I turn to the other features: on the one hand, explicating more fully the body-contexture; on the other, coming to a better understanding of the nexus of consciousness or mental life.

THE EMBODYING ORGANISM AS CONTEXTURE

It is not my intention, nor certainly my competence, to try to detail the precise complex of intrinsic references (functional significances) displayed by the various organs, organic systems, structures, and members of the embodying organism. That task properly falls within biomedicine and associated medical disciplines and sub-disciplines. Rather, I am concerned only to point out certain (by no means all, I am confident) of its principal modes of functional significance, illustrated by a few examples, using what has been learned from the critical exposition of Gurwitsch's theory. I shall terminologically simplify matters, and use "member" to include any distinguishable constituent: structure, organ, etc.

In the first place, it is obvious that some of the body's members are less important or less weighted than others—"less important" in respect of the body's being able to continue to be experienced both as biologically alive and as embodying. Merely to illustrate: the hair on the back of the hands can and does function tactually, but tactual capacities are not lost in the event that this hair is lost. Or: one can grasp some objects, to some extent, without one's thumb being functional; but grasping is far better accomplished when the thumb is present and functioning well. Again: the organism continues to be effectively embodying even if one's teeth are lost, one's appendix is taken out, or one's back gets boils. On the other hand, even though one's embodiment is somewhat limited thereby, how much more curtailed it is if one develops angina, loses a leg, develops ulcers, or has a collapsed lung. Further variations are unnecessary: although highly membered, *not all members are of equal, functionally significant weight for the contexture's continuance or its integrity.* It thus becomes important to know the specific functional significance of each such member, how far each can undergo modification, negative or positive, etc.—a task falling within biomedical science and medicine, both of which are thereby fundamentally contextual/contextural disciplines.

In the second place, there are few if any members of the body which, so to speak, have no functional significance whatever vis-à-vis other members. It is rather the rule that these members function closely in *sets* and overlapping sets or patterns, and that these patterned clusters of functioning members can, or may, alter without necessarily disrupting, or at the least affecting, the life of the organism or its being the embodying organism it is. The cardio-vascular system, for instance, functions in convergent and overlapping ways with other organic "systems"—the pulmonary, the brain, the muscular system, etc. That is, *the membered sets of systems are coordinated, synchronized and inter-organized*, such that disturbances in one can result in disturbances in others, and thus interventions into one require close observance of what occurs with the others.[1] Of course, not all the possible disruptions in any one system are fully understood, much less the correlated disturbances which can crop up in others—nor even *in which* other systems disturbances may appear. The full sense of the functional significances of individual members, the way they function within the organic systems of members, and the actual and possible significances (intrinsic references) they have vis-à-vis still other systems—these issues, crucially important, are far from being fully understood, despite recent advances.

In the third place, *not all members of the embodying organism exist at the same level.* Some systems of members must be well-formed (e.g., cellular structures) in order for other sets to become viable members of the organism (e.g., muscles). Indeed, it is problematic whether certain levels of the structure of the organism, taken by themselves, are constituents at all. Rather, it would seem, some sets are members of a lower level, in the sense of being necessary conditions for higher-level members even to function as members. And these, in turn, are similarly conditions for still higher-level members, whose membered functioning goes on according to their own nature or laws, or in their own ways, even though they would not be able to do so in the absence of, or with the improper functioning of, their lower-level members. Only if certain members are formed in certain ways or into structures—i.e., only so far as they form appropriate sub-textures—can higher-level contextural clustering and pattern-ed functioning go on. Thus body-members and parts are not only multiple and complex, but organized into higher and lower levels, and patterned sets, with their own appropriate systems of intrinsic references.

Fourth, the various sets and levels of contextures and sub-textures are not only *temporal and historical*, but also reveal their own *distinctive maturational character and internal rhythms*. Thus while some organic functions commence quite early (heartbeat, pulse, motoric movement), others do not come into play until later (binocular focusing, muscle coordination), still others develop then recede (sucking reflex), and others continue without significant modification (sneezing, blinking). And even with adults some systems come into play episodically (excretion, ingestion), others are continuously present (pulmo-nary, cardio-vascular, muscular tensions, maintaining upright posture), some can become atrophied (sexual organs, eyes, ears, or limbs), and some for com-plex reasons are simply operative only rarely if at all (the appendix, tonsils; or left-handed grasping for right-handed persons, active running for mainly sedentary persons). In short, body-members are temporal and historical, maturational and rhythmical, though each in step with specific others, and still others differently, etc.

Fifth, as for the issue concerning the *establishment of patterns and corporeal schemata*, it is necessary to note a *range of variations*. (a) Some patterned processes are not at all within the possible awareness, hence experience or control, of the embodied person (e.g., generation of blood cells, the functioning of the spleen), while others are at once automatic yet able to be brought into a kind of control even when there seems no or little explicit initiation and/or "experience" (e.g., the minute eye and head movements of Goldstein's patient with visual agnosia) (*27*, pp. 149–52). Still other schemata function automatically but are not only able to be controlled to an extent through deliberate decision, (as through meditative techniques), but also lie within possible awareness (e.g., breathing, so-called biorhythms, or the heartbeat).

(b) Some patterns seem to require initiation by the subject, hence control, but quickly become habituated (e.g., grasping, writing, "handedness"), while others, even though habituated, require some attentiveness, either regularly (e.g., maintaining upright posture) or episodically (e.g., getting up, pointing, excreting, turning the head in order to see, locomotion). Others function not by direct control or even awareness, but only by the initiation of activities of another sort (e.g., ingestion). (c) Some patterns can break down, requiring explicit, sometimes painful attentiveness, in order to be re-instituted (e.g., walking after leg injury, or after being bedridden), while other patterns cannot be re-initiated or re-instituted, and instead one must establish compensating patterns (walking with crutches) or entirely new patterns (e.g., having to use a prosthesis or a wheelchair).

(d) Finally, some patterns must be activated explicitly each time and thus are essentially within explicit control, even though they doubtless involve patterns of the other sorts (e.g., running, resting, sniffing the air, paying attention auditorily, visually, tactually, etc.). Thus the complex patterns of intrinsic referencings lie on different levels, from purely automatic and outside possible awareness, through partial awareness, partial control, habituation, to explicit control and awareness. Some are subject to innocuous modification, some to more extensive alteration, some to none at all. Through, say, dieting or exercise, global alterations can be brought about; through happenstance, injury, illness, or latent genetic occurrences, other patterns will be modified, lost completely, or reestablished.

In the sixth place, there are crucial patterns of human embodiment which, as it were, seem *capable of organizing* large clusterings of subtextures *into a whole activity*. Thus, as Straus points out, "with upright posture, there is a transformation of sensorium and motorium, of periphery and center, of form and function" (*117*, p. 164), as becomes obvious in walking, reaching, pointing, talking, lying down, and the like. In turning my head to see what made a noise, a complex series of kinaesthesias is activated, but more than that: the sensorium and motorium are transformed into a *different figure-ground relationship* from what was before (e.g., when I was writing at my desk). These more globally enacted postures, gestures, movements, and the like, while involving in highly complex ways a number of body-members, organize them into these larger patterns and thus give different functional significances to them as constituents: what was figural for one activity (feeling the textures of a fabric) becomes a constitutive component, part of the background, for another (e.g., pointing, grasping a pen, etc.).

Seventh, then, for all the variations mentioned, the embodied person not only experiences his own organism *as a whole*, but as well this "whole" becomes *contextured with a variable surrounding sphere or zone*, not at all synonymous with the skin but extending outward into a sort of "three-mile zone" belonging to the central body but not completely, as Straus says (*117*, p. 153). Not static, but susceptible of expanding and contracting, it is "not so much a concept or image that a person has of his own body as it is an ensemble of directions and demarcations . . ." (*117*, p. 154). This is the sphere, the body-spatiality, of meeting and greeting, of holding-off ("at arm's length") and embracing, of circumscribing (or "circumwalling," as Straus says) ourselves in defense or fortification, of closing off the other or welcoming him. In short, it is the *medium of sociality*, or as John O'Neill has put it, of "skin-trade" (*84*) with or among others (in dancing, shaking hands, grouping, marching, etc.).

Still, the central body itself is experienced as a whole, as an *expressive unity* whereat and whereon are displayed and displayable "what I feel," "what I want," etc., in joy, sorrow, worship, fear, disgust, and the like. In these terms, as Merleau-Ponty says, the fact is that

> the normal subject has his body not only as a system of present positions, but besides, and thereby, as an open system of an infinite number of equivalent positions directed to other ends. What we have called the body image is precisely this system of equivalents, this immediately given invariant whereby the different motor tasks are instantaneously transferable. It follows that it is not only an experience of my body, but an experience of my body in the world. . . . (*79*, p. 141)

My embodying organism is thus experienced as always in the midst of environing things, in this or that situation of action, positioned and positioning relative to some task at hand, manifesting a *common style*, a unity with the Other—whether thing, artifact, or person(s)—and in different ways:

> None of the modalities [of sensory experience] plays in only one key. Yet in each one the basic theme of I-and-the-*Other* is varied in a specific way, so that in the visible the persistent dominates, in the audible the actually present, in the tactile sphere the reciprocal, in the area of smell and taste the physiognomic, in pain the power-relation. In their totality the modalities are to be arranged in a broad scale, which extends from the visible to the area of pain. In this spectrum of the senses the aspects vary with respect to temporality, spatiality, direction, boundary, distance, movement, physiognomy, connection, freedom and constraint, contact, objectivity, enumerability, divisibility, measurability, empty forms, and possibility of abstraction, of recollection, and of communicability. At one end of the scale insight predominates, at the other, the impression; *there* is found the communicable and actual communication in shaped wording and writing; *here* is the loneliness of pain, which can finally express itself only in unformed plaints and cries. (*115*, pp. 161–62)

Thus the complexly organized body is an experienced *organism*, unified and unifying in various modes of figure-ground contextures with the surrounding milieu, mainly by means of its zonal spatiality and thus its unified movements. In Merleau-Ponty's words,

> movement, understood not as objective movement and transference in space, but as a project towards movement or "potential movement" forms the basis for the unity of the senses. . . . [M]y body is a ready-made system of equivalents and transpositions from one sense to another. The senses translate each other without any need of an interpreter, and are mutually comprehensible without the intervention of any idea. . . . With the notion of the body image we find that not only is the unity of the body described in a new way, but also, through this, the unity of the senses and of the object. (*79*, pp. 234–35)

Or, as Straus concisely expresses it,

> the muscle, the *motorium*, cannot move by itself, for no world and no open space is at its disposal. Just as little is the *sensorium* capable of moving itself, for, taken by itself,

it lacks a motion apparatus. Neither *motorium* nor *sensorium* can move itself, but I *can* move myself. Spontaneous motion can only be propounded of a living being as a whole, not of any single part of it. . . . In fact, the individual sense does not perceive, the experiencing person does so by means of one or several of his senses. Potentially we are directed toward the *Other* in a variety of ways. The actual is never more than a limited realization of the possible; it is experienced in its limitation—*i.e.*, always pointing to further actualization. (*115*, pp. 151, 154)

The embodying organism as a *complex contexture* is thus always a *gestural display* with and among environing things and other embodied beings and persons. Hence it is obviously not possible to draw *any* sharp lines between these zonally constituted interchanges, no way to section off the body from itself, or the embodied self from its circum-standing world.

Finally, complexly contextured and inseparably bound up with the circumstances, this embodying organism has the significance of *locating* me "here and now." My sense of hicceity and ipseity is fundamentally locused within and by my central body and my surrounding zonal sphere of immediate bodily action and spatiality. *My embodying organism is my complexly contextured "habitus,"* thanks to the continuously ongoing patternings of intrinsic (simple, complex, reciprocal, and self) referencings or significances constitutive of the contexture itself. "I," whatever else this will be seen to signify, am literally "rooted," "grounded," "positioned," and thus embodied.

* * * * * * * *

The impressive feature of contextures, and contexts as well (though less so), is that thanks to their "tending toward good continuation," toward the particular kind of closure or balanced equilibrium pertaining to each sort (a closure which differs for different contextures), they tend to *endure* or maintain themselves, and present a kind of *strength* or connectedness, a striking togetherness and unity. Precisely those features allow, one could say, for *substantival locutions*—which can too easily, however, lead one metaphysically to posit them as substances, another matter entirely. It is a wide, ultimately unbridgeable leap from the substantival locution to the metaphysical substance. For, while presenting its own sort of density and persistence, a contexture is nonetheless not a *res* but rather *a systematic totality of intrinsic references or functional significances: hence every contexture, while "one," is yet an intrinsic diversity.* Yet the constituents of a contexture are "many"; they are, while systematically placed solely within the topography of the whole—the system of interwoven and reciprocal references which *is* the whole—nonetheless *differentiated. They differ from one another*: indeed, only by virtue of this intrinsic differentiation is there the possibility of being placed and referenced. *They differ as well from the total system of references*: each constituent presents the whole from its own specific placement, and this is inherent to its own significance. Yet it is solely by virtue of this whole that each constituent has its specific placement and significance. Each constituent is thus *other-than* every other one and *other-than* the whole; and, conversely, the whole is *other-than* any of its constituents. Here, then, is the fuller importance of Gurwitsch's theory of contexture, as I have tried to elaborate it: *a contexture is necessarily a unity-in-diversity, since it is the systematic significance of each constituent to be at once "itself" and "other-than," and essentially a complex referencing and being-referenced vis-à-vis other constituents.* This feature is *eidetically constitutive* for every contexture as such, of whatever specific kind it may be.

The embodying organism is evidently a contexture. How, in actual development, it becomes specifically shaped and textured will, of course, vary in many ways from case to case. Still, it seems evident as well that throughout the variations persist *genetic invariables*, an intrinsic *order* without which no actual development could occur or which is evidenced and presupposed by such actual development. I have not, to repeat, done more than indicate this genetic constitution and its order. All I have attempted by means of the preceding reflections is to lay out the complex stratification and its contextural principles; that is, my inquiry is largely a "static" phenomenological one.[2]

This kind of inquiry is nevertheless necessary, and helpful to shed further light on the kind of wholeness evidently presented by the embodying organism.

THE COMPLEX OF CONSCIOUSNESS

Paul Ricoeur, as will shortly be seen, came to question the Husserlian usage of "consciousness" (*Bewusstsein*), and suggested the Freudian term of "becoming-conscious" (*Bewusstwerden*) (95, p. 424). Now while the latter is not innocent of problems either (seemingly, it obliges one to use notions like the "unconscious" and the "preconscious," and perhaps even others), there is a point to his concern—though what I have in mind does not seem to have been his point exactly. This *substantival* usage—*Bewusstsein*—might make one think either that everything in mental life (to use a perhaps broader and less loaded term) is "conscious," or that it is itself a substance (*res*) in the manner of Descartes' *res cogitans*, or perhaps both. In any case, there seems little question but that Husserl's usage is neither the one nor the other. The contexts within which the singular substantival occur, it is perfectly clear, show that he has in mind a plurality: i.e., subjectively lived processes of awareness (i.e., *Erlebnisse*, or *Bewusstseinserlebnisse*) either in respect of their own appertaining qualities and properties, or in respect of their being intentive to, "experiences" (*Erfahrungen*) of, something appearing in the field (whatever it may be, and however it may appear in the manner or manners peculiar to whatever it may be). Yet since each of these *Erlebnisse* reveals, universally, certain properties and qualities (e.g., temporality, synthetic flow and connection, intentiveness, and others), it is warranted by the evidence to talk, e.g., of "consciousness" as intentive, and similar expressions.

This circumstance—that "mental life" is composed of a multiplicity of temporally located intendings-to-objects (of all sorts)—should now give us pause: is *this* a "unity-in-diversity," i.e., a contexture of a certain kind? To see that it is, while yet having *its own* distinctive features, it is necessary to consider the nexus of mental life itself.

Consider any particular process—seeing, hearing, recollecting, judging, loving, etc. Whichever it is, it soon becomes obvious that a remarkable complexity is evidenced, one which Husserl began to detail in respect of its own intrinsic features in his well-known lectures on inner-time consciousness (*48*). Suppose, for the purpose strictly of allowing us to detect something of the features of the temporality of mental life, I ignore the obvious and even eidetically true circumstance that every process of awareness is in one way or another an "awareness-of-something" (whether it be "simply going on" while "I" pay attention or not to the objects disclosed thereby, or whether it be one of whose objects "I" am only marginally aware, or whether it be one with whose objects "I" am explicitly occupied at the moment). Let us ignore, too, for the sole sake of getting a manageable problem, the also eidetic fact that each such process of awareness is connected in complex ways with other processes. We can admit all that, and still study but one facet of the matter, so long as we do not forget that this is what we have done. I can thus reflectively focus my attention on this "noetic," as it were the subject or "active," side (ignoring the "object" side), just as any of us can, if we so desired, focus our attention on the color of the wine in the glass in such a way that, though ignoring the glass, the taste, etc., we in *no* way have *thereby* falsified, distorted, or reified anything. The wine remains the wine, the glass, the glass; for that matter, simply focusing attentively on the color does nothing to the color either, except to *thematize* it. So, too, for mental life or any of its distinguishable but inseparable component processes, properties, or qualities.

Consider, then, a touch*ing*, a see*ing*, a hear*ing*, or a valu*ing*, disregarding now any specific objective correlates (particular correlated noemata), and any actual and possible connections one or the other of these may have to other processes. Each shows a certain temporal character, a certain "phasing" or sequencing of "phases," and a certain "flow" or "flux." Indeed, it is immediately clear, the whole concatenation of mental processes forms a temporal flow, highly articulated into complex and interconnected phases, each of which is simultaneously protentive (anticipational), retentive, and impressional (having a "now" character). If one considers any one phase, it becomes immediately clear that, as a phase within a temporal flow of phases, it is constituted as a "now" (impressional) by virtue of its being retentive to past phases of itself as having been phases which then (as then impressional) protended the present phase (among others) as going to occur, and (when occurring) as going to be retentive in this specific sense (retaining the past phase *as* a phase protending the present which will then be retentive to the past phase as . . .). At the same time, the "now" phase is protentive to phases not yet occurring but which, when they occur, will be retentive to the present now-phase *as* having been protentive in this specific sense. In more general terms, because of this complex structure of inner-time consciousness, I can now remember that yesterday I expected to remember yesterday today; and I now expect that tomorrow I shall remember that today I reminded myself to do something tomorrow.

Each phase, therefore, is retended or protended *in all its complexity*, i.e., each phase preserves its impressional/retentive/protentive structure. Thus there occur *syntheses of transition* among the noetic temporal phases. But these transitions from phase to phase are, first, *continuous*; and second, as Husserl emphasizes, they are fundamentally *syntheses of identification*. Each phase of the temporal flow of noeses is what it is thanks to the multiple self-references inherent to these retentive and protentive characters: "now" is constituted as "now" by virtue of the multiple retentive and protentive references. The noetic flow, then, is as well a complex totality of reflexively interconnected temporal references.

It is necessary to make this point in greater detail: on it hangs the very decisive point concerning the principle of organization exhibited by the noetic stream of mental life, that it is a contexture. It should be clear that Gurwitsch, as was seen, would hardly endorse this thesis. Temporality, not contexture or "field," for him, is the form of noetic organization. I do not disagree with that so much as I want to show that this *temporal form is itself a specific kind of contexture*. To help make this point, consider (figure 1) Dorion Cairns' extension of the diagram given by Husserl in his published lectures on inner-time consciousness.

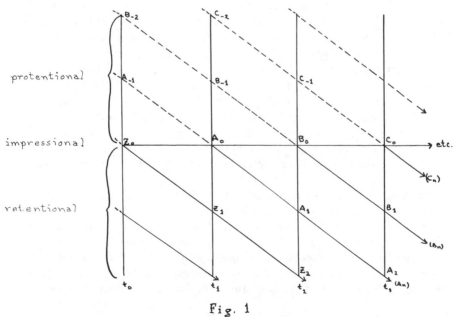

Fig. 1

Considering phase B_o at t_2 as the "now-phase" (say, "hearing the third note in the opening phrase of Beethoven's Fifth Symphony"), B_o is at once "now" ("impressional") and also "retentive" and "protentive." The just-past phase, A at t_1 (say, "hearing the second note . . . "), is forthwith automatically or operatively retended at phase B_o *as* a phase which was itself impressional and with its own complexity: i.e., it is "now" retended as a "then-now-phase" which was complexly retentive and protentive in itself. Among the phases protended at A_o (and, depending on what is at issue, these will be more or less delineated)[3] is the present phase, B_o, which was then protended (B_{-1}) *as* a phase which, when (and if) it occurs, will be retentive, among other phases, of A_o, and also protentive of phases of the same mental life still to come. Similarly, at phase B_o, the just-just-past-phase, Z_o at t_o (say, "hearing the first note . . . ") is now retained directly (Z_2) *as* a phase which was itself similarly complex and which, in addition to being retentive of phases past of itself, protended future phases, among them the present phase, B_o (then at t_o, B_{-2}), as well as the just-past phase, A_o (then at t_o, A_{-1}), which is itself also retended at B (as A_1). Moreover, since phase A is also retained at B_o (A_1), and since phase A is *retained as itself retentive to Z* (Z_1), phase Z is retained at B_0, both *directly* (Z_2) and *indirectly* by way of phase A (Z, through A_1 from A_0).

Clearly, *there are not two "Z's"*; rather, thanks to what Husserl calls the automatic synthesis of continuous identification, phase Z is intentively retended *as temporally modified* (Z_1, Z_2, etc.); it is the *same* phase, and it and *all its own specific complexity* (including, as could be seen if we shifted our attention appropriately, all its specific intended noemata) are retended. As is also clear, however, phases A_0 and Z_0 are retended at B_0, *not* as constituting a uniform whole but precisely as *different phases of one and the same mental life*. In addition, *any one phase is*, while synthetically identified with itself, nevertheless *differentiated in a specific way*: namely, *as modified* within the differing phases of the flux (B_{-n}, B_{-2}, B_{-1}, B_0, B_1, B_2, B_n, etc.). Yet again, thanks to the retention of each phase *with its own complexity*, each phase as retended "collapses" or "telescopes," so to speak, its complexity: A_1, for example, *is* A_0 with all its structure, but now "collapsed" or "modified." To illustrate: when I now recall, say, a part of a conversation this morning, I may also recall that while then listening I "made a mental note to myself" to do something this afternoon, say, telephone the person to remind him of the appointment we had agreed upon last week, to meet tomorrow.

Obviously, matters can be and usually are far more complex than even this. Among other things, not much was said about protentiveness. Similarly complex, future phases are protended as "possibly" or "probably" going to occur (with greater or lesser degrees of likelihood, obviously) and when they occur precisely the same complex qualities and properties already laid out will appertain. Thus: I now expect that my friend and I will meet tomorrow, and inherent to this is as well the expectation that the future phases of our meeting will themselves become "now," "just-past," "just-just-past," as well as their going to be themselves protentive, and so on. With varying degrees of clarity and obscurity, sharpness and fuzziness, every phase of mental life reveals these multiple connections.

Consider now an even more delimited segment of the temporal flux which flows on, of itself, in the complex ways indicated (figure 2):

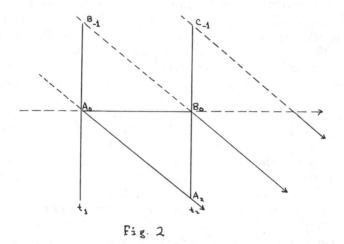

Fig. 2

If we focus on t_1 (A_0 is "now"), B is protended (B_{-1}) and includes its own "going-to-be-retentive," among other phases, of A (A_1). Similarly, A_0 protends B (B_{-1}) as retentive, and thus *protentively intends itself* as such, through other phases as well, of course (A_1, A_2, A_n). Thus what Husserl calls the "synthesis of continuous identification" (and differentiation) is as well *a specific form of self-referencing* inherent to the flowing of mental life. Furthermore, as is clear, B_0 *complexly references* both itself and A (and other phases): B retends A actually (A_1) and potentially (B_{-1}). The other modes of intrinsic referencing delineated before[4] are also present here: A is "prior to" B, and B "comes after" A; A refers to B both as protended and, when actual, as retentive to A; and, simply, A is A in reference to B.

Thus mental life stands out as a continuous "flow," a stream of noetically manifested and noematically directed experiences (*Erlebnisstrom*). It is a "flow" inasmuch as it is comprised of strictly inseparable *phases of a continuum*, each of which is related to others as "earlier" and "later"; each of which progressively undergoes modification of temporal orientation ("to come," "now," "just-past," "just-just-past," "further in the past," "still further," etc.); and each of which strictly maintains its temporal relations with other phases (if A is earlier than B, then it will always be so—mistakes and confusions of this being but confirmations of the point).

The *complex of consciousness*, however, is a clear instance of the *eidos, "system of intrinsic, functionally significant and referential constituents"*: it manifests an evidently *contextural* character, a "whole made up of parts." This becomes apparent even if we "screen off" an essential feature of every phase, that it is intentive to affairs other than itself, and not simply to other phases of the same mental flow of experiences but to these in all their own appertaining complexity. That is, not only is each phase in one way or another an intentive awareness of something not itself an intrinsic constituent of the temporal flow, i.e., to some noematic affair or other (an "object" which is not itself immanent to the temporal stream), but each phase is as well an intentiveness to other phases and thus to *their* own noematic objects as well. Thus we must say (*41*, secs. 17–20, 50–52; *46*, secs. 113, 118, 122–23, 140) *every phase has an intrinsically, necessarily complex multiplicity of "objects"*: those to which it is primarily intentive (which may coincide in particular cases with those of other phases), and those to which it is secondarily, tertiarially, etc., intentive, thanks to its being intrinsically retentive and protentive to other phases of the same mental life and all their own appertaining "objects."

Because of this structure of inner-time consciousness, it is understandable in principle that we are able to "recognize" something (say, a pen) which we recollect having seen "before"; that we are able to anticipate touching what we now only see (and, when and as touched, what appears does so as "the same" as what was first only seen); that something presently experienced can "serve to remind" us of something else; and so on. In brief, what Gurwitsch delineates as a "noematic" phenomenon—the "field" organization of the objects of experience—turns out to be *strictly correlated with an equally complex "noetic" field*. With respect to any particular experience, furthermore, just as the noematic field exhibits the theme/thematic field/margin organization, so does the noetic field exhibit a strictly correlative organization: phases of mental life intrinsically connected to one another *as* experiences of something thematic (with all their appertaining retentive and protentive intentionalities), phases (or components of phases) having only context relations, and phases which are experiences of what is only marginal.[5]

This correlation, moreover, can already be seen to be highly complex on its own, but in specifiable ways.

ON "COMPLEXURE"

The well-known Husserlian formula which speaks of the "correlational a priori" (*42*, pp. 159–60) is, I can now say, critically *elliptical*: it leaves out something which under no circumstances can be left out, namely, the *embodying organism*.[6] Hence the "correlational a priori" must be reexamined.

"Considered as to its specific nature," Gurwitsch maintains, "consciousness is a domain closed in itself," and its "participation" in bodily acts "is merely adventitious and un-essential to consciousness, since its intrinsic specific nature is not affected by such a participation" (*31*, p. 419). Although one can take this participation in bodily life under consideration, such a viewpoint is, for him, that of psychology and not phenomenological philosophy. I have already shown that the latter claim does not hold up under analysis, even within Gurwitsch's own thought, and at that point in the study I promised to take up the first point. I can now do so. Several steps are needed.

(1) In the first place, if "consciousness" is a contexture (of its own kind, as was just shown), then the *linguistic substantival* does not lead to nor demand any "substance." It is a whole, a "one," *solely as the system of intrinsically signifying and referencing constituents* (phases, with their own complexity). Thus the "-ness" of "consciousness" (i.e., the -*sein* of *Bewusstsein*) is strictly a locution of convenience, *not* a covert ontological position. To refer to "its specific nature" can only mean, accordingly, that one must consider "consciousness" as a contexture; the question of this "nature" is a question of the complex of references (functional significances) intrinsic to each phase of mental life, and to their systematic totality. Moreover, if it is essential to any phase as such to be intentive (in the complex way already pointed out), then this eidetic feature must be inherent to and predicated of the system of phases, for otherwise the phase would not be a phase constitutive of and within that total life. The question, then, concerns the "nature" of that complex intentiveness essential to phases of mental life.

The initial point is the crucial one. Every phase of mental life is *complexly intentive*: to its own particular "objects," retentively to earlier phases and their own "objects" *as* "past of itself," and protentively to future phases and their "objects" *as* "future of itself." As was seen, moreover, the "now" phase is constituted *as now* in virtue of its retending (and protending) other phases as themselves protentive (and retentive) of the present phase as . . . , etc. This "intentiveness-to" affairs other than the temporal phases of mental life is, most fundamentally, an "experiencing" or "encountering" (*Erfahren*) (in whatever way it may be) of environing things—i.e., affairs disclosed and disclosable by way of sense perceptual encounters. "Most fundamentally": that is, as has been stressed by most theorists, sense perceptual encounters are at once "first" in point of *developmental* history, "first" as regards the *eidetic genesis* of consciousness, and accordingly "first" as the primordial ground from which conceptual life emerges. Thus even if, while one is engaged with a theoretical problem, it is fortuitous *which* bodily awarenesses are present (they could be quite otherwise),[7] it *cannot* be fortuitous or contingent *that* there are bodily awarenesses *of some sort*. Contingent it may be *which* embodying organism "happens" to be "mine," but it is eidetically necessary *that* "I" be embodied.

In principle, then, to consider "consciousness as to its specific nature" is to find that its "participation in bodily acts" is indeed essential to it, and in no way "adventitious and un-essential." Each intentive phase (constituent) *of mental life is, indeed, "participant" in bodily activities in multiple ways*: impressionally, retentively, and protentively.[8] The question is thus *not whether* but precisely *how* this "participation" is to be understood. The intentiveness of consciousness is *essentially embodied*. This brings me to the second consideration.

(2) The phasial flow of mental life is thus *complexly weighted*. (a) Each phase is intentive-to something environing and appearing within a "field." (b) Each phase manifests intentive relations (i.e., functionally intrinsic references or contextural significances) to other phases (as "thematically constitutive," "contexturally relevant," or "currently irrelevant, more or less") of the same mental life. (c) Each phase itself, and other phases intentively retended and protended, as well intentively "references" and "is referenced by" the specifically appertaining bodily patterns of embodiment.

In simpler terms, beyond the complex temporality of mental life, its intentiveness to environing affairs ("objects") is necessarily oriented and positioned strictly by means of these embodying patterns of the organism. The "correlational a priori" is, as it were, "fleshed out," hence it is *constitutive of the intentiveness-to-objects that it is an intentiveness-to-the-embodying-organism as such.* Merely to touch a piece of paper, see a red light, smell oatmeal, taste the tang of a piece of fruit, hear a noise, are necessarily already complex acts of embodied awareness of environing things—whether any of these be only globally articulated (as in infancy), more clearly structured (as with normal adults), or otherwise organized (confusedly in certain cases of impairment, highly circumscribed in cases of neural lesion, etc.).

(3) Whatever of the environing milieu "appears" does so as itself organized: a "theme" surrounded by a "thematic field" and fringed by a "margin," as Gurwitsch showed. The positioning and orienting of whatever appears occurs by means of *another contexture*, the embodying organism. And the "experiencing" of what appears is now seen to be still *another contexture*, the noetic flowing of temporally phased mental life.

The remarkable phenomenon here thus becomes salient: *"what appears" (the noema), the "experiencing" of it (the noesis), and the "positioning" of both (the embodying organism), turn out to be strictly inseparable from, and functionally significant with respect to, one another.* Each of these "refers," in its own way or ways, to each of the others, intrinsically "references" and "is referenced by" the others, and in complex ways such that the "significance" (placement, locusing) of each is strictly a "function" nested within the "whole" as such. There can be no "awareness" (noesis) which fails to be "of" something or other (noema), no matter how vague it may be; there can be no noema which fails to be correlated to a noesis enacted and embodied kinaesthetically; there can be no kinaesthesias which fail to be animations of a noesis and which functionally orient a noema.

In a word, these complex contextures are woven together as constituents of an even richer contexture (ever-increasing in its richness). In view of the circumstance that each constituent here is itself an already complex contexture, furthermore, I shall refer to this qualitatively richer one as the *complexure of life*. The rationale for this neologism is that, on the one hand, a locution is needed which will serve as a reminder that linguistic substantivals do not necessitate metaphysical substances. On the other hand, environing world, consciousness, and embodying organism, form a unique and complex *"whole" whose "parts" are themselves strictly inseparable* (albeit distinguishable) *contextures: "inseparable" but "distinguishable" in the manner specific to contextures*—a "whole" which is the system of intrinsic, functionally correlated references and significances manifested by the constituents. The theory of contexture, now extended and deepened to an extent, gives a clear way of understanding what must otherwise remain an empty formula: the "whole" of a "life" (and its "parts": body, mind, world).

THE COMPLEXURE OF LIFE

Merleau-Ponty's work was in one respect a series of modulations on a fundamental theme: *être-au-monde*. Expressive of the fundamental dimension of human reality, this "being-at-world" is intended to capture the crucial *Urpräsenz* of embodied life: to be perceptive of a world is to be opened out onto it, to be *at* it and thereby to disclose the world as the contexture of possible ways-to-be of embodied life. My "being-at-world" is, he says,

> a way of access to the world and the object, with a "praktognosia," which has to be recognized as original and perhaps as primary. My body has its world, or understands its world, without having to make use of my "symbolic" or "objectifying function." (*79*, pp. 140–41)

While agreeing with him, I must nevertheless stress the differences. While Merleau-Ponty unquestionably appreciates that the own-body *(corps-propre)* is always the embodiment of consciousness *(conscience-engagée)*, it is nevertheless the own-body which receives the emphasis: the *corps-propre* is my *être-au-monde*. Obviously, the embodying organism is centrally significant, enacting noetic processes of striving and positioning the environing field. Nonetheless, what has emerged from the present study is that the emphasis must be placed on the "whole": *the significance of the own-body is precisely that it is a constituent of the complexure of life.* Thus while Merleau-Ponty's claim to have found in the own-body what Husserl called the "logos of the aesthetic world" (*45*, p. 292) is in a way true; and while it is true that

> at the heart of the subject himself we discovered, then, the presence of the world. . . . We found beneath the intentionality of acts, or thetic intentionality, another kind which is the condition of the former's possibility: namely an operative intentionality already at work before any positing or any judgement, a "Logos of the aesthetic world," an "art hidden in the depths of the human soul," one which, like any art, is known only in its results . . . (*79*, p. 429)

—while that is true, in its way, two points need modification. First, as I have already pointed out, and as Gurwitsch stresses (*31*, p. 305), this "operative intentionality" (*intentionalité operante* = *fungierendes Intentionalität*) is intentionality nonetheless. That is, we have to do with constituents of a contexture (the complexure of life): "world," "body," and "consciousness" are, as it were, *mutually presenced* to one another, so that for *any* of them it must be said that the others are "present at their heart." Second, it is *not* as if the one mode of intentiveness—"operative"—were the *only* one whose functioning would be enacted or embodied, while the other mode—"active" or "thetic"— were *not!* To the contrary, as was stressed, *every* phase of mental life is complexly intentive, among other affairs, to the embodying patterns of the organism: mental life is *essentially embodied*.

Any stress on one constituent of a contexture is necessarily one-sided, and is done at the cost of missing the contextural references composing the whole, and thus of distorting it. Just as I found Gurwitsch's stress on the autonomy of consciousness and the autochthonous nature of the field's organization an exaggeration and consequent mistake, so does Merleau-Ponty's stress on the own-body have a heavy price. In both, the authentic complexure of life is not seized upon.

Straus' studies, moreover, despite their sensitivity, manifest still another mis-emphasis. Insisting that "in sensory experience I always experience myself *and* the world at the same time, not myself directly and the *Other* by inference, not myself before the *Other*, not myself without the *Other*, nor the *Other* without myself" (*115*, p. 148; see also *117*, pp. 144, 153–54), Straus tends to obscure the complexure in another way. When the "I-Other" character of embodied experience is emphasized, what gets forgotten is the *noetic* constituent: the complex of processes of awareness *(Erlebnisse)*. For surely, however deeply am "I" enmeshed in all these contextures, there are many awarenesses which "go on" without "my" actually having to pay attention explicitly to them, many which "go on" and of which "I" am merely marginally aware, and many with whose objects "I" am not and possibly cannot be busied or occupied (for Husserl, the nexus of inner-time consciousness falls here—the sphere of "primary automaticity").

And again, just as in common parlance we find possessive usages with regard to the own-body ("my" leg, "my" heart, etc.), so do we find these with regard to mind, awareness, or consciousness: "my" feelings, "my" thoughts, "my" mind, etc. That is, Straus' insistence on the "I-Other" effectively collapses, or at least tends to obscure, the crucial and common distinction between this "I" and the "mind," a distinction which seems just as evident as that between "I" and "body" (which he clearly appreciates and studies).

Yet not only Straus, but also most of those who have tackled the issues of "self" and "consciousness" invariably seem to conflate that very distinction. Thereby, too, is the essential character of the complexure of life lost, in favor of one or more of its contextural constituents, which also makes it impossible to account for the concrete experience everyone has of *not* being identical with one's own body or with one's own mind. Indeed, in prominent forms of so-called "mental disturbance" one finds that the texture of the anxiety, of the fear, of the sheer awareness, is that this distinction has been somehow breached; the usually harmoniously balanced referencing of the complexure goes awry and one finds oneself, sometimes severely, "at odds" with one's own mind. Even in common life a kind of internal distancing occurs. Thus one can become quite upset that one's mind simply doesn't "work that way," e.g., with facility in mathematical calculations. One can be a kind of "witness" even at what transpires with and among one's awarenesses: Aldous Huxley's intriguing study, *The Doors of Perception*, shows this (*51*), as does the way in which one becomes frustrated or delighted with how a host of memories, yearnings, urgings, desirings, can bubble in and out of awareness—alternately embarrassing, pleasing, or even terrorizing "me." "I" am able, indeed, even to "train my mind" to work in certain ways: acquiring a better memory, learning to meditate, developing emotive or volitional habits (as when one commits oneself to a particular religious sect), etc.

In all, just as something is amiss with the idea that "I *am* my body," so something is wrong if one fails to distinguish "I" and "my mind" ("my" contexturally articulated clusters of awarenesses). What has been made salient thus far, however, as the complexure of life, has no sooner become clear than another issue becomes focally problematic: the "I" or "self" which is "somehow" central to all this, to "my" world, "my" mind, "my" body—in short, to "my" life. In Ortega's formulation, "I am my life and my circumstances" (*86*, pp. 38–39, 42, 48, 58): "my life," i.e., "my" embodied contexture of thinking, willing, striving, sensing, etc.; "my circumstances," i.e., "my" environing milieu, including "my" zonal reach and its modulations; but "I"? If "I" *am* all this, what is this which says "I"? "I," who seem so self-evidently present throughout, yet seem only at best a kind of mysterious presence: is this all that is somehow sayable?

Part II

THE HAZARDS
OF SELF
AND THE WAGER
OF OTHERS

Introduction

IN William Golding's novel, *The Spire*, the good Dean Jocelin reflects, thinking "how the mind touches all things with law, yet deceives itself as easily as a child" (*26*, p. 4). Nowhere does this seem so telling as in efforts to unravel the dimensions, the meanings, the essence of "self." So readily characterizable in language by the substantivization of a linguistic reflexive, but divested of the pronominative it qualifies ("myself," "yourself," "itself," etc.), few phenomena seem so elusive, fugitive and yet so deeply dear and prized, despised and terrorized, intimate and strange. The infelicities of custom and habit may seduce one to believe in the continuous identity and subsistence of "one's self," often with marked passion. Yet efforts to ferret it out just as often end by entrapping themselves in their own belief and passion. It were wiser, perhaps, to leave such matters to those more accustomed to the regions of illusion and sly dexterity: the magical crafts of art, of religion, of poetry, even of psychoanalysis.

Yet the self is often invoked in daily life, in art, in religion, and in both medicine generally and psychiatry and psychoanalysis in particular—not to mention the other occasions of usage: philosophy, psychology, the sciences of human life, and so on. If not presupposed explicitly in all these, and other, engagements, the self lurks importantly in the background of thought about consciousness, politics, history, the body, and in the intriguing talk about the patient as a person, as an individual, as a particular human being. Notions of self and of the significance of the self structure the backdrop of many reflections concerning human deportment, such as references to hallucinations, self-punishing behavior, or obsessive self-reproach. The self is a phenomenon centrally invoked in all talk about man, but in an especially remarkable way in diagnostic and therapeutic contexts. Yet on the whole, even with so outstanding a physician and philosopher as Erwin Straus, references to the self have remained mostly uncritical, merely implicit and unexamined. And the variety of views in philosophy are nothing if not notoriously inconsistent with one another.

What is the "self"? Opinions on that have varied with astonishing difference and tension. There are, for instance, the great affirmers of substance, such as Augustine, Descartes, Locke, Leibniz, or contemporaries such as Macmurray. There are the firmly implanted deniers: the early Sophists and skeptics, the redoubtable Hume, and contemporaries such as Sartre and Gurwitsch. There are those who argue the *tout naturel*—self is "wholly natural" and thus wholly indistinguishable from brain-states, complex neurophysiology, or just plain matter: the early atomists, Lucretius, Hobbes, La Mettrie, and today "identity" theorists such as Armstrong. And there is an array of uncatalogueables, bewitchers of the common tongue: from Herakleitos and his *Logos* forever uttering dark things, a seer seeing darkly into the labyrinthine corridors which is self; Pascal and his tender, tenacious reed with its peculiarly potent "logique de la coeur"; Kierkegaard and his linguistically acrobatic play on relations relating themselves to themselves, and despairingly willing to be otherwise, offended by the "Other"; to present-day persons such as Merleau-Ponty and Marcel trying to recapture the originary, living unity of human *être-au-monde* and *être-en-route*. There is also a most fascinating contemporary effort which directly takes up the issue of self and of reflection: Paul Ricoeur, who, denying immediacy of self to itself, seeks it hermeneutically, "reading" self through its often wispy traces and haunting symbols, a patient textual scholar bent on painful exegesis. It is Ricoeur, indeed, whose careful probing will serve to initiate this part of my study, for here is not only an extraordinary and influential study on its own, deeply appreciative of the guises and disguises of this elusive phenomenon, but also a direct encounter with an important source of much current thinking about the self in medicine with culture—the work of Freud. Before turning to this, however, a few more words of introduction seem advisable, to help focus the kind of problematic which is presented by "self."

A quite considerable cluster of terms is to be found in such discussions, often used to indicate much the same reality: self, spirit, soul, psyche, subjectivity, subject, inner man, person; but also mind, consciousness, mental substance; as well as mental, psychic, subjective, personal, human, spiritual, and conscious life. Beyond these are some by now well-known philosophical expressions: ego, monad, transcendental unity of apperception, *Da-sein, pour-soi, être-au-monde*, agent, transcendental ego, and a few others. Other expressions also crop up, such as the common way of distinguishing among the material self, the empirical self, the social self, and the spiritual self; as well as the classical psychoanalytical ones: id, ego, superego, libido, sub- and unconscious, intra-psychic unity, and the like. In fact, the more one reads in various literatures, the more bewildering becomes the linguistic and conceptual baggage. It seems an embarrassment, but hardly one of riches.

Such a profusion seems inevitably a confusion as well, and we are at a loss not only linguistically and conceptually but as regards the "things themselves." It takes but little effort to begin to appreciate the utter dismay some biomedical scientists, and some philosophers, have felt over the whole affair, ending by regarding all such discussions either as spurious or as mere epiphenomenal fluff quite unnecessary in scientific and philosophic inquiries. There are problems and irritations enough, after all, simply trying to understand the incredible complexities of the body's many systems, not to mention the brain; to introduce such mentalistic vagaries seems merely to practice the deliberate craft of deception in an area where clarity is already at a premium.

Here, as T. S. Eliot elsewhere notes with insight,

> Words strain,
> Crack and sometimes break, under the burden,
> Under the tension, slip, slide, perish,
> Decay with imprecision, will not stay in place,
> Will not stay still. Shrieking voices
> Scolding, mocking, or merely chattering,
> Always assail them. (*19*, pp. 7–8)

For all that, it is no mere idle curiosity that the many urgent questions people of all sorts ask about self—Who am I? What and why am I? What do I live for? What is my destiny? and others—keep cropping up, will not stay silent, not only in spite of but often just because of that very confusion and dismay. We are, it seems, at an historical time when ways of thinking about human life, values, persons—the self—are not readily available, or not on hand at all for us. Yet these very issues seem most pressingly critical for us, as is clear from even casual acquaintance with disturbed persons. Are "disturbed persons" nevertheless persons? Are there disturbances which can cancel out or so grievously affect the "person" as to imply the loss of "self"? Are fetuses *persons?* Are they *selves?* Or is being a self (or person for that matter) merely potential in such a case? And even if the latter, what are we to say of seriously deformed newborns? Are they, even potentially, persons or selves? As is patently clear, medicine raises the questions of "self" in a dramatically pressing way.

What, indeed, are we to think, and in which ways must our thoughts proceed, when we are called upon to think about the "self"? Expressed differently, thinking about, coming to understand, and ultimately being able to account for the specifically human is in the end possible solely to the extent that we can comprehend that most profoundly subtle and elusive phenomenon of "self." The focus of medical science and practice must in some way come to rest just here—whether the concern be for the organism or for mental life, it is always ultimately "my" or "your" body and life which is at stake, and that cannot be avoided or evaded, on pain of losing the very point at issue. All matters human are expressions of self and of interchanges among selves. Thus any discipline focusing on "the human" and "the human world"—social and behavioral sciences, history, theology, as well as the biomedical sciences, medical practice, and legal and educational concerns—finally depends for its sense and justifiability on the elucidation of the phenomenon of "self."

* * * * * * * *

For all that, few phenomena are more baffling, and this phenomenon in particular seems to mock our efforts to "tell" what it is. Embedded always, it seems, as Merleau-Ponty and Ricoeur have it, in "results"—the wonderfully enigmatic works of self—there seems no choice but to take it as a kind of "text," and subject it to exegesis, using all the tools of that particular trade. Only by a kind of entrapment by or through indirection, apparently, will "self" yield its treasures, enabling us to tell self truly: tell what it is, and how, hence be able to tease out the eidetic core of self by following out the pulses of its movements found in its expressions and works.

This way of putting the problem, however, presents numerous problems of its own, methodological as well as substantive ones. It thus seems advisable to assess the matter as carefully as possible before trying to plunge into the intricate regions of self. For this, few efforts are as searching as that of Ricoeur.

6

Ricoeur and the Adventure of Interpretation

IT is characteristic of Ricoeur's later writings that they are in search of a "general hermeneutics." For this effort, the problematic of symbols is central. And in these terms, few ideas are so distinctive of his work as the notion that "the symbol gives rise to thought" (*98*, p. 347). This aphorism, which, as he says, "enchants me" (*98*, p. 348), constitutes "the third way" by which to escape the Scylla of philosophy in its commitment to think things through "to the end," and the Charybdis of symbolic, religious experience in its resistance to such thinking. It is also the "way" Ricoeur will follow in confronting and surmounting the "conflict of interpretations" in hermeneutics—which he attempts especially in his marvelous study of Freud (*95*). Hence the place of symbols in human life cannot be overstated, but by the same token neither can language or speech be overemphasized, for symbols are always *within* these. And, to that extent, hermeneutics is basic, for "there exists nowhere a symbolic language without hermeneutics" (*98*, p. 350). The problem of symbolism, then, is coextensive with that of language, even though the power of symbols is more deeply rooted—in the *verbum* of the "hierophonies," in the oneiric, and in the poetic (*95*, pp. 14, 16). Even so, these roots, especially *desire*, are already turned toward speech; thus the inquiry into these roots is already within language and speech—and is therefore hermeneutical (*95*, pp. 7, 457).

THE APPARENT "SCANDAL" OF HERMENEUTICS

It is essential, then, for "thought to inhabit the fullness of language" (*98*, p. 348; *95*, pp. 30–31), which means the enigmas and double meaning of symbols, and this requires the work of hermeneutics.

> A symbol exists, I shall say, where linguistic expression lends itself by its double or multiple meanings to a work of interpretation. What gives rise to this work is an intentional structure which consists not in the relation of meaning to thing but in an architecture of meaning, in a relation of meaning to meaning, of second meaning to first meaning. . . . This texture is what makes interpretation possible, although the texture itself is made evident only through the actual movement of interpretation. (95, p. 18)

The "thinking" which symbols "give rise to" is hermeneutics, for the "double meaning" inherent to symbols is what "provokes" the understanding to its "work." Symbols carry the mind within their own essential movement of meaning, for "it is the very excess of meaning ["overdetermination"] in comparison to the literal expression that puts the interpretation in motion . . . " (95, p. 19). Thus every *mythos* involves its own peculiar kind of *logos*, which constitutes the *mythos* as demanding "interpretation."

Symbols are fundamentally *bound:* they are bound *to* their literal, sensible meanings (their "opacity"); and they are bound *by* the symbolic meaning residing in them (their "revealing power"). Hence the "way" of hermeneutics can only be the "way" of symbols themselves. However, this requirement means that any pretension to "phenomenological neutrality" must be given up:

> I admit it. I admit that what deeply motivates the interest in full language, in bound language, is this inversion of the movement of thought which now addresses itself to me and makes me a subject that is spoken to. . . . The movement that draws me toward the second meaning assimilates me to what is said, makes me participate in what is announced to me. (95, p. 31)[1]

To demand, however, that philosophy itself must be hermeneutical seems not only circular, but, as Ricoeur says, "scandalous." There are several issues here needing response.

(1)   On the one hand, the very plurality and diversity of the languages within which symbols have their place seems to introduce a radical contingency into philosophy which, for its part, seems committed to universality. Furthermore, while rigorous philosophical science requires univocal significations, symbols are essentially opaque and have an intransigent equivocity.

Without entering into the full texture of these regions, suffice it to say that Ricoeur is content to recognize openly, indeed to insist, that "the philosopher does not speak from nowhere," he is "unavoidably oriented" (95, p. 48; 98, pp. 20–21). Our "cultural memory" not only orients, but gives rise to one's philosophical questions in the first place, and "it is always in the midst of contingency that rational sequences must be detected" (98, pp. 23–24); this "detective work" is the work of interpretation.[2]

The more formidable issue, however, has to do with the very nature of symbols: how can philosophy attend faithfully and rigorously to symbols as nested within natural languages and thus subject to all their notorious infelicities—i.e., verbal *equivocity* and syntactical *amphiboly?* The well known "intolerance of symbolic logic" to these—namely, the insistence on strict *univocity* of meaning—is in truth a discipline by which thought excludes itself from every encounter with the symbols of human life and language. Such a logic nevertheless presents the basic challenge to any hermeneutics: its very intolerance "forces hermeneutics to radically justify its own language" (*95*, p. 50).

As Ricoeur recognizes, only a *transcendental* "logic of double meaning" *can* radically ground hermeneutics. But *this* logic, which cannot be simply juxtaposed to symbolic logic, requires that one seek "in the very nature of reflective thought," or "in the movement of self-appropriation by self which constitutes reflective activity," the a priori function of reflection necessary for "establishing the conditions of possibility of a domain of objectivity in general" (*95*, pp. 48, 52).[3] Hence this logic of double meanings is not bound by the requirement of *univocity*, since this "holds only for discourse that presents itself as *argument*: but reflection does not argue, it draws no conclusion, it neither deduces nor induces; it states the conditions of possibility . . ." (*95*, p. 53).

Since, in a way, the entire *Freud* book purports to be a fulfillment of this task, all that is suggested here is that (a) the "case for interpretation rests entirely on the reflective function of interpretative thought," and (b) "the indirect, symbolic language of reflection *can* be valid, not *because* it is equivocal, but *in spite of* its being equivocal" (*95*, pp. 53–54). "Reflection," then, is the key to understanding the inner sense and justification of hermeneutics.

(2)   But even supposing that those issues can be settled, the very thing which "gives rise to thought"—symbols—gives rise as well to a perplexing embarrassment; "wherever a man dreams or raves, another man arises to give an interpretation" (*98*, p. 350). Not just this, however: for the one who dreams also interprets, and the one who interprets, dreams; and still others interpret, etc.; and rare it is when the resultant cacophony of voices either sings the same tune or ever even harmonizes. Symbols are *invitations to interpretation*, but *which interpretations should be heard*, and why these and not others? Even more, if our age is one marked by "forgetfulness" of symbols (*98*, p. 349), how shall we learn again to "listen" and to what shall we listen? The whole problem of interpretation refers to a certain paradox of symbols, beyond the epistemological question of truth and error, beyond the moral question of honesty and lying: viz., *illusion*. Peculiar to the act of interpreting as such is a "double solicitation and urgency," an internal polarization:

> According to the one pole, hermeneutics is understood as the manifestation and restoration of a meaning addressed to me in the manner of a message, a proclamation, or as is sometimes said, a kerygma; according to the other pole, it is understood as a demystification, as a reduction of illusion. (*95*, p. 27)

Language beguiles us; symbols even more; and beneath the overt, innocent-seeming expressions of the one who speaks, is one or another form of archaic, essentially hidden meaning. Hence for those in the "school of suspicion"—Ricoeur mentions the three great masters of suspicion: Marx, Nietzsche and, of course, Freud—interpretation as a discipline of deciphering is the unmasker, the debunker, the thinking which meets the guile of language with the double guile of practiced suspicion.

The exact opposite of this is what Ricoeur himself has attempted: the attentive restoration of the meaning of symbols whose root is the "postcritical" and rational "faith" of the one who is confident in language, in its power to reveal a "beyond" which "addresses" us in symbols. Care for the object; concernful "listening" to the "sacred" which is "said" in the scattered symbols of the great myths; emphasis on the fullness of language and its symbols; effort to greet *(saluer)* the revealing power of the primal word—these distinguish the other, polar opposite hermeneutics.

The problem here—the one which gave rise to his masterful "reading" of Freud—is that this internal division of hermeneutics is indeed *divisive*. It not only precludes for now the possibility of a general hermeneutics, but, more significantly, highlights that these "ways" of interpreting are rooted *in the nature of language, of symbols themselves*. In short, the bond between symbols and interpretation, between *mythos* and *logos* "furnishes a new motive for suspicion. Any interpretation can be revoked; no myths without exegesis, but no exegesis without contesting" (*95*, p. 42).[4] Thus the "scandal" inherent to philosophy's appeal to symbols is that it turns out to be essential to justify, not simply the recourse to symbols and thus to interpretation, but the *specific* war within hermeneutics itself! (*95*, p. 42).

But once again, the key to the enigmas lies in the problematic of reflection—the crises of culture, of language, of hermeneutics, Ricoeur believes, may well be but surface indications of a still deeper crisis. The crisis, to be exact, is, "in the strong and philosophical sense of the term, an adventure of the Cogito and of the reflective philosophy that proceeds therefrom" (*95*, p. 37). The risks of the undertaking are many, matched only perhaps by its boldness, an undertaking in which hazards are inevitable and not altogether foreseeable: to appeal to reflection, as Ricoeur well knows, is to make necessary the inquiry into the "self" of that reflection. It is just this problematic which centrally concerns Ricoeur. Before turning to it, however, a final piece of the *scandalon* is necessary.

(3) It is this: the "immensity of the wager of this hermeneutics" (*98*, p. 350) is not simply that it is at odds with itself, but that it must somehow transcend that war, surpass its own "circle," overcome the crisis. The "immensity" of the "wager" is that it is, after all, a *wager:* i.e., a hazardous adventure whose task is to follow out the indications of symbols in pursuit of the self and of its reflective character. The bet is that such a "third way," a kind of transcendental deduction

in the manner of Kant, can in its own way demonstrate that the fullness of language and of the human world embodied and expressed therein are made possible by the semantics, the mythics, and the poetics of symbols.

If so, we must have the final courage to accept the consequences of this *scandalon:* " . . . a philosophy instructed by the symbols has for its task a qualitative transformation of reflexive consciousness. Every symbol is finally a hierophony, a manifestation of the bond between man and the sacred" (*98*, p. 356). But before such a philosophy can claim its payoff, it must resolutely adhere to its own problematic: the adventure of the Cogito and the reflection which follows it. The main enterprise is the disciplined reading of Freud, for it is with his monumental works that one finds the radical obstacle in the path of the restorative hearing of the symbols of hierophany.

SYMBOLS AND REFLECTION

I will not attempt to follow in detail Ricoeur's brilliantly executed "reading of Freud." Rather, I want to meditate with him on the central thematic of his work: the self and reflection. That this is indeed central is unmistakeable. In *The Symbolism of Evil*, binding the "know thyself" to the admonition, "Be wise," one must ask: what, who, is this "self"? What "transformation" must occur to it as it pursues "symbols," and *what must it be in order to be able to be* thus transformed from a narrow "knowing" to a richer "being wise"? In terms of the *Freud* book, "what new self-understanding comes out of this interpretation, and what self is it which thus comes to self-understanding?" (*95*, p. xii). And, a little further on, "when we say philosophy is reflection we mean, assuredly, self-reflection . . . [but] what does Reflection signify? What does the Self of self-reflection signify?" (*95*, pp. 42–43). And, after having gone with Freud through the intricate complexus of the psychical apparatus, its topography and economics, Ricoeur focuses on Freud's epistemology:

> First, it must be made clear that it is in reflection and for reflection that psychoanalysis is an archeology; it is an archeology *of the subject*. But of what subject? What must the subject of reflection be if it is likewise to be the subject of psychoanalysis? (*95*, p. 420)

At the heart of his task is the double question: what is reflection? and what is self? The "reading of Freud," too, is in a sense conducted with these issues at the forefront.[5] This is precisely as it must be for a "philosophy of reflection": it must be hermeneutical throughout.

First, we must be clear about Ricoeur's thesis that "symbols give rise to thought." Symbols are *double meanings, opaque signs* (but not every sign is a symbol), are *analogues* (but not analogical reasonings or analogies) and thus *donative*, are *enigmatic evocations* (but not allegories), are *bounded* (and thus not able to be abstracted from their locus in natural languages, and cannot function as "placers" or elements in a logical calculus), and are *spontaneously created meanings* and thus are more radical than myths (myths are a species of symbols, or are symbols fleshed out in narratives) (*98*, pp. 15–18). Here the crucial points are that symbols (e.g., "stain") reveal a double intentionality: a literal one ("stain" = "unclean") which, however, is itself a conventional sign within language, which intentively points to a second meaning which is *like* the first (as "unclean," man is symbolically "like" this, i.e., morally "defiled"). The second meaning is not given otherwise than through the first, literal meaning.[6] In this sense alone is the symbol a "donative movement" of one meaning to another. The second meaning is "given" through the first, hence to achieve the second there is no choice but to be carried there *by* apprehending the intentive movement of the first. In this sense, symbols are *necessarily bound-to* and *bound-by* these ties. Thus, finally, myths, while deeply tied to symbols, are not quite the same. Rather, the symbol (e.g., "exile") makes the narrative elaboration of the symbol in myth possible (e.g., the history of the expulsion of Adam and Eve).

In the *Freud* book, there is only slight advance to this line. The crucial point is this: the "double meaning" is the "semantic structure" of symbols, but this is not sufficient to make the intrinsic need for reflection clear and demanding. It is "the second trait of symbols"—i.e., their *mythical* function—which shows new traits of symbols and thus new hints for hermeneutics. First, myths introduce exemplary personages that generalize human experience in the form of universal paradigms functioning to enable individual persons to "read" their own condition. Second, through the narratives involving such personages in events happening "once upon a time," human experience receives temporal orientation, a beginning and an end. But these myths thereby recount, transhistorically, the "irrational break" which generates the two primitive "ways" of hermeneutics: the innocence of coming-to-be, the guilt of history. This feature gives symbols both an expressive and a heuristic value. Thanks to their semantic and mythic functions, symbols inherently demand reflection, and reflection can only be an interpretation of symbols. Symbols are the "dawn of reflection" (*95*, pp. 38–39).

But, third, every narratively nested symbol also intrinsically refers to still other myths: for example, the myths of evil (e.g., defilement) are the obverse of a greater symbolism, that of salvation. In this sense, every symbol shows not only *semantic opacity* and *mythic structuring*; it also is essentially *systemic*: "each symbol belongs to a meaningful totality which furnishes the first schema of the system" (*95*, p. 40). This characteristic suggests "the architectonic task of reason," which is to articulate the sense of that totality.[7]

Symbols, then, as semantically "doubled" meanings, mythical revelations of the human estate, and systemically locused within a totality, call for reflective interpretation. That much seems clear.

But is the reverse also true? Even if symbols "give rise to reflection,"[8] does philosophy itself demand symbols, myths, equivocity? Is it the case that "the philosophic act, in its innermost nature, not only does not exclude, but requires something like an interpretation"? (*95*, p. 41). The problem Ricoeur here faces in his effort to show that philosophy itself is hermeneutics is that if philosophy is to be hermeneutical, it must "have recourse" to symbols. But, so far as I can tell, this "recourse" means that philosophy must be rooted in an act which is intrinsically divisive: for interpretation yields internally conflicting "ways."[9] Symbols at once "disguise" and "reveal." Hence the task for Ricoeur is to "test" whether these radical alternatives can be "reconciled," "mediated," "surmounted." This is the task of the *Freud* book, and on its completion hangs the very possibility of making sense of self, reflection, philosophy.

THE "DISPOSSESSIONS"

Let me emphasize: we are on extraordinarily slippery terrain—especially after the "reading of Freud," whose work, if nothing else, is an exceptional exhibition of the guises and disguises, the cunning and terror of being a subject. To understand Freud's work as "about the subject" is to find that "the subject is never the subject one thinks it is" (*95*, p. 420). That fact itself forces a change in our notions of self and of reflection. Yet, Ricoeur insists, the whole of Freud's "unmasking" of consciousness and ego, though "perfectly adapted" to the effort to disclose the illusions and lies of consciousness, "prevent psychoanalysis from ever rejoining the primal affirmation" (*95*, p. 428), from posing any problematic concerning the primal and fundamental self.

If one searches for the self in consciousness, all one finds is a surface phenomenon, the representative of the external world (*95*, pp. 181–82). If one seeks more deeply for an "ego," all one finds is the id; if one looks for a governing or dominating function, the superego appears (*95*, pp. 185–186, 212); and, going to the bottom, one finds the great barrier to oneself, narcissism (*95*, pp. 125–27, 213–17). At every point, the most disappointing feature of Freudianism is its flight from the egological foundation (*95*, pp. 117–34), from the "positing of self." Far from being a definitive conclusion about Freud's work, however, this "flight" is, for Ricoeur, a "stage of reflection" expressing an "antiphenomenology" necessary as a discipline for thought in search of the primal, concrete "*I*" and "*am*" of the Cogito, beyond its bare, abstractive self-positing. Moreover, a properly philosophical appropriation of Freud's work is decisive in another way for this project: viz., a recognition of what can only be called a "false Cogito," a false self-knowledge that is necessary to prepare the way toward apprehending the genuinely "full" Cogito. These steps require elaboration.

Three points are central. (1) Even a modest reflection on oneself is sufficient to show that one finds a really striking clamor of voices: images, beliefs, values, ideals of oneself; roles, masks, fronts; pretensions, wishes, hopes, fantasies, dreams; encouragements, urgings and impositions from others and from culture; and a host of feelings, strivings, and wantings, bubbling up from unsuspected depths, which, as I have already mentioned, can surprise, embarrass, delight, and terrorize. What, which, who, am I? More careful reflection shows that the "self-positing" intrinsic to the very act of reflection is hardly sufficient to characterize either "myself" or reflection.

The truth is that if there is anything "immediately present" in self-consciousness, it is at best an empty feeling of self. What is incontestable in the Cartesian doubt is "but a certitude devoid of truth . . . only a feeling . . . that I exist and that I think," which is hardly self-knowledge (*95*, p. 44). The so-called "immediacy of self-consciousness" is a profound *illusion* within consciousness itself. Reflection is not an intuition in the sense of an immediate deliverance of a self-givenness. But what from one viewpoint is an enigmatic, fugitive phenomenon is from a full reflective viewpoint something else: reflection captures, or rather *recaptures*, the "Ego of the Ego Cogito in the mirror of its objects, its works, its acts. . . . The first truth—*I am, I think*— remains as abstract and empty as it is invincible; it has to be 'mediated' by the ideas, actions, works, institutions, and monuments that objectify it" (*95*, p. 43).

Reflection, then, is a re-appropriation:

> I must recover something which has first been lost . . . I make "mine" what I am separated from by space or time, by distraction or "diversion," or because of some culpable forgetfulness. Appropriation signifies that the initial situation from which reflection proceeds is "forgetfulness." I am lost, "led astray" among objects and separated from the center of my existence. . . . Whatever the secret of this "diaspora," of this separation, it signifies that I do not at first possess what I am. (*95*, p. 45)

Hence reflection on oneself is a task (*Aufgabe*); self is not *gegeben* but *aufgegeben*.

Nor is this all. More fundamentally, the prominent data gleaned in clinical settings by psychoanalysis (post-hypnotic suggestion, autism, hysterical phenomena, etc., but especially dreams) compel us to "form the notion of 'thoughts' (*Gedanken*) excluded from consciousness by forces that bar their reception" (*95*, p. 118). Indications, hints, signs of psychical activities, and contents which are in no way "conscious" abound in human experience. As Ricoeur reads this, " . . . consciousness has become the least known, since to become conscious is to become an object of perception under certain conditions" (*95*, p. 120). Accordingly, there is no choice but to recognize the definitive *"dispossession"* of consciousness: "Henceforward there is a question . . . of the process of becoming-conscious (*Bewusstwerden*), in place of the so-called self-evidence of being-conscious (*Bewusstsein*)" (*95*, p. 424). The immediacy of consciousness is an illusion to be dispossessed; its "evidence" is a pretension.

This disclosure, Ricoeur insists, is no stranger to Husserlian phenomenology, for it too "reveals the self-misunderstanding inherent in immediate consciousness" (*95*, p. 377). It was, after all, Husserl who emphatically showed that "apodicticity" and "adequacy" of evidence need not go hand in hand. Indeed, even the "transcendental *I am*" is subject to this, for apodicticity does not automatically extend to that which "determines its being more particularly and is still not itself given, but only presumed, during the living evidence of the I-am" (*41*, p. 23).[10] This presumption, which is co-present with apodicticity, shows even that the "*I am*" can be deceived about itself, to what extent is unclear (though possibly determinable, possibly not).[11]

(2) Nor is this all reflection must learn from psychoanalysis. For with the dispossession of consciousness there goes the dispossession of the *object*. In trying to make sense of the "Unconscious," the notion of "being-conscious" (*Bewusstsein*) is supplanted by that of "becoming-conscious" (*Bewusstwerden*). Precisely inasmuch as one here is dealing with psychical matters which are *barred* from "becoming conscious," the notion of the unconscious lies totally outside of phenomenology (indeed, is a veritable "antiphenomenology"):[12] "the text of consciousness is a lacunary, truncated text; the assumption of the unconscious is equivalent to a work of interpolation that introduces meaning and connection into the text" (*95*, pp. 119–20). It is a systematic, *explanatory* concept and not a *descriptive* one.

It is similarly the case for the fundamental concepts (*Grundbegriffe*) of "instinct" and the "vicissitudes" of instincts. What is crucial for our purposes is that this entire procedure (the *epochē* "in reverse," says Ricoeur) requires that the "object" (wished-for, hated, desired, feared, etc.) no longer has the primacy of "phenomenological clue" (*Leitfaden*), precisely because it is *displaced* by the "aims" of the instincts. It is "the thing in regard to which or through which," Freud says, "the instinct is able to achieve its aim" (cited in *95*, p. 123). The object turns out to be as "false" as immediate consciousness.

(3) The topography and the economics of Freud—constructed as an effort to "read" the truncated text of consciousness—require as well the notion of an "ego-instinct" symmetrical with that of "object-instinct," for just as the "object" can no longer be taken as something immediately presented to an ego endowed with immediate awareness, so must the ego be conceived as "a variable in an economic function. The economic interchange between the ego and objects must be carried to the point where not only is the object a function of the aim of an instinct, but the ego itself is an aim of instinct" (*95*, pp. 126–27). This is the place of *narcissism*: the generic notion of "self-love," conceived as "instinct," effectively *dispossesses the ego itself*. The ego suffers unanchoring no less than consciousness and its objects. It is "no longer the subject of the Cogito but the object of desire . . . which exchanges itself for object values on the market of libidinal investments or cathexes" (*95*, p. 425).

The philosophical "reading" of this critical turn of affairs is, for Ricoeur, clear: it, too, must be taken up into reflection—i.e., radical questioning of the "sense of self" is unavoidable. What then occurs is also plain: narcissism leads to the *reflective* discovery

> that as soon as the apodictic truth *I think, I am* is uttered, it is blocked by a pseudo evidence: an abortive Cogito has already taken the place of the first truth of reflection, *I think, I am.* At the very heart of the Ego Cogito I discover an instinct all of whose derived forms point toward something altogether primitive and primordial, which Freud calls primary narcissism. (*95,* p. 425)

Center of resistance to truth though it is, narcissism has received three profound blows in the history of science for Freud. First of all, the Copernican revolution forced man to give up his view of himself as center and lord of the cosmos; then the work of Darwin and others forced him to give up his view of himself as lord over animals and as distinctively different from them. Now, with Freud, we are forced to a still deeper humiliation: the ego is not even master in its own house, the mind! (*95,* pp. 182–83, 426–27).

What is crucial for Ricoeur is that the tripartite dispossession— consciousness, object, ego—inextricably requires that the "first truth" (*I think, I am*) must be a "forgetfulness," a "wounding," a "vacillation." Man, it must be said, is "essentially a being threatened": from the world, from conscience (source of guilt), and more powerfully from within (the menace of the instincts).

REFLECTIVE REAPPROPRIATION OF SELF

Nevertheless, Ricoeur insists that Freud's topography and economics, though "perfectly adapted to a struggle against illusion," never comes to grips with the primary "positing of the self [as] a truth which posits itself" (*95,* pp. 428, 443). What is the "I" of the "I think"? On this, Freud's work is "very disappointing," but the disappointment itself is significant, having its source in the humiliation and wounding which psychoanalysis inflicts on self-love. That is to say, for Ricoeur, this "disappointment" is not definitive but is rather one of the *stages* which reflection must necessarily "go through" in order to disabuse itself of the multiple, beguiling disguises with which the self masks itself.

As "stages for reflection," however, Freud's work is immensely significant for Ricoeur: the pursuit of that "first truth" is obliged to become equally as cunning in stripping away the disguises of self, as the self is in constructing and remaining fugitive within and among them. And this task has an anchor in Freud's work despite his silence on the vital issue. The root of the metapsychology is the notion of "psychical representatives of instincts" (*95,* pp. 115–16, 134–50). Instincts, unknowable in their biological character, are always designated or "represented" in the psychism by ideas and by affects.[13] Indeed, the *only* way an instinct can enter into the psychism is by way of its ideational representative. Hence there is always a profound *affinity* between the unconscious and the conscious. They are "relative," not "absolute," others (*95*, p. 430).

Accordingly, the *ground* for "restoring" or "recapturing" what was "relinquished" and "dispossessed"—consciousness, object, self—is at hand even in Freud's work. But the more important anchor is that of "*affect.*" The adventure of the metapsychology has yielded a "wounded Cogito . . . a Cogito that posits itself but does not possess itself; a Cogito that sees its original truth only in and through the avowal of the inadequacy, illusion, and lying of actual consciousness" (*95*, p. 439). But this, along with the facts of narcissism, dreams, neurosis, and the like, point to the "positive" side of the dispossession of consciousness: affect, effort, desire. The "positing of self," in short, is not at all an epistemological or perceptual act, nor the result of either. It is rather "the emergence or positing of desire through which I am posited, and find myself already posited" (*95*, p. 439). It is in *effort* and striving that one finds that core sense of self, not in the cool, refractory rays of perceptual awareness.

Pursuing this "regression" (understood philosophically as "archeology"), one continually comes up against something which, if "sayable," is so only via metaphors of *force, energy, potency*—the more "deeply" and "primitively" one goes, the more such language seems unavoidable. This is clearly true of Freud's work which, in its fundamental thrust as "a revelation of the archaic" (*95*, p. 440), is rich in such terms (restraint, discharge, cathexis, barrier, drive, compulsion, etc.). As one plumbs this "ever prior," this "ever more archaic," one comes up against the really remarkable core of psychical depth: the system, "unconscious," consists of instinctual representatives which constantly seek to "discharge their cathexis," processes which are nevertheless "timeless," exempt from any sense of contradiction, heedless of (external) reality. These are later attributed to the id (*das Es*) as well, but what is crucial here is that the "primordial"[14] is "the impersonal and the neuter . . . a neuter that, never being an *I think*, is something like an *It speaks*, which expresses itself in laconisms, displacements of emphasis of meaning, and the rhetoric of dreams and jokes" (*95*, p. 443).

This core—neuter in essence and a sea of tumultuous, instinctual impulses— is expressive of the essentially hidden darkness of self, approachable only by metaphors and the hermeneutics of "double guile" (*95*, pp. 34, 444). And yet, it is in just this "implicit philosophy of our timeless, immortal, indestructible desires" (*95*, p. 453) that Ricoeur finds the roots of self, and with this the basic rationale for conceiving philosophy as hermeneutics. The vital point[15] is this: the problematic of the affective representatives shows that affect (effort, desire) is *primordial*. "That which is represented in affects and which does not pass into ideas is desire qua desire. . . . That which, in the unconscious, is capable of speaking, that which is able to be represented, refers back to a substrate that cannot be symbolized: desire as desire" (*95*, pp. 453–54). As he insists, however, "what this regression designates is precisely the *sum* of the Cogito" (*95*, p. 454).

Taking a clue from Leibniz' notions of "expression" and "appetition" (95, pp. 455–56), one can gain a critical insight into the "double law of representation: as standing for objects or things, representation is pretension to truth; but it is also the expression of life, expression of effort or appetite" (95, p. 456). Freud's originality here is to have pointed to the role played by the *barrier* between these functions, but his stress on this generates a profound paradox in that the reflective grasp of the bond between them (especially as regards affectation, desire) "is not possible in the direct form of mere conscious awareness; here, the prereflective is inability to reflect" (95, p. 456). It is only by the battery of psychoanalytic "techniques" (95, pp. 406–18), which cannot be overstressed, that the psychoanalyst has access to this bond.

Nevertheless, Ricoeur insists, the "homogeneity" between the unconscious and the conscious shows that the affective representative, however "unnameable, . . . is turned from the very outset toward language; [desire] wishes to be expressed; it is in potency to speech . . . [it] is both the nonspoken and the wish-to-speak . . ." (95, p. 457). Thus the twofold law of expressivity shows that there are two possible modes of inquiry: either a gnoseology which takes up the representation in respect of its intentiveness to objects; or an "exegesis" which explores the desires that lie hidden within that intentionality. "Intentionality" is thus opposed to "manifestation" of life (95, p. 457).

Hence it is that "reflection" must be conceived as a "reappropriation," whose "goal is to grasp the Ego in its effort to exist, in its desire to be. . . . Effort and desire are the two sides of this positing of the self in the first truth: I *am*" (95, p. 46). Reflection can accomplish this *task*—which, for such a being, *is* its "truth"—only through the works, often unclear and revocable, which bear witness to that effort and desire. Reflection must be hermeneutical just because "I cannot grasp the act of existing except in signs scattered in the world" (95, p. 46). Hence it is necessary for any philosophy seeking to understand "man," "consciousness," or "self" to learn all it can from the results, methods, and presuppositions of all the sciences that try to decipher and interpret the signs, symbols, and myths of man.[16]

THE SELF ENRICHED

The archeology has discovered, too, that the problematic of consciousness is that of "becoming-conscious" (*Bewusstwerden*) and not of "being-conscious" (*Bewusstsein*)—indeed, that the latter turns out to be a mere truncated text in need of dispossession, of being taken up as "false consciousness." The sense of this "becoming" has, however, remained in the background: bound, to be sure, to the *effort-to-be* of self, but effort to be . . . *what*? "Becoming-conscious," as a "moment" of self, is inherently a *positing of an end*, a *telos*: to have an *archē*, the subject must have a *telos* (and the inquiry, to be an archeology, must be also a teleology).

It is Hegel's phenomenology of *spirit* which has addressed itself most directly to just this teleological thrust of the self of self-consciousness, and Ricoeur unhesitatingly appropriates it, even though he is quick to insist that it cannot be simply taken over today unchanged.[17] In any event, the critical themes are well-known to us. Consciousness only *becomes* self-consciousness through the *progressive* dialectics of figures or moments; the path of repossession must follow that of dispossession.

Here the key is the *"pro*-gression": later moments are the truth of the anterior ones (unsuspected by them), thus the meaning of earlier phases is achieved only by way of the later ones. Spirit, as the ultimate truth of consciousness, of life, progressively *achieves* its *self* (*Selbst*) in the process of "becoming conscious." It is this noncoincidence with its self, then, which is the "restlessness" (*Unruhigkeit*) of consciousness; thus "negation" is already-always presumed and, indeed, at work "other-ating": consciousness, as restless (noncoincident), is thus "not" itself and moves to "the other" of each stage, and this progressively makes it become *"itself."*

Of the several stages, none seems more critical than that of "recognition"—the master-slave dialectics. For here, Ricoeur believes, is found the truth of desire. "Desire is desire only if life manifests itself as another desire; and this certainty in turn has its truth in the double process of reflection, the reduplication of self-consciousness . . . [in] this work of mutual recognition" (*95*, p. 467). Ultimately, desire is specifically human desire solely if it is a desire to be recognized by another man, i.e., is an *unending mutuality* in the sense that each term goes beyond its own limits and becomes the other, continuously.

Yet for all the progression here, it must never be forgotten that the unsurpassable character of desire, life, is not obliterated (Freud's work is within Hegel's), even though life is surpassed by self-consciousness (Hegel's work is within Freud's) (*95*, p. 469). Struggle ("effort" and "desire") is found at all levels, and is, at the critical stage of recognition, "a struggle to tear from the other an avowal, an attestation, a proof that I am an autonomous self-consciousness . . . a struggle in life against life—by life" (*95*, p. 471). Hence "effort" and "desire" are in no way eradicated; they are "mediated"; so, thereby, is the "self" (*95*, p. 472).

The interpretation of self is thus "completed," at least in its core moments, by Ricoeur's insightful study of the "mixed texture" of *feeling* ("spiritedness")—in particular, the trilogy he gets from Kant: having, power, and worth or valuing. The point of his study is to show the way in which the self of self-consciousness comes to maturity by incorporating ever-richer strata of objectivities into the sphere of ever-richer subjective life, mediated by these three prominent modalities of "feeling"—objects constituted within economics (in a non-Freudian sense), politics, and culture. The final, hierophonic stage is that of the disclosure of the sources of speech and art, of the "sacred," and of their expressive manifestation in the great symbols and myths of human creativity, and its manifold relationships to and within religious life.

The crucial stages of "self" are before us, and with them Ricoeur's philosophical understanding of "reflection": the self-positing whose texture is effort and desire, but also their primitive and, eventually, ideational expressions; the unending reduplication of self and other in recognitive mutuality; and the dialectical enrichments of the fuller tapestry of self in the complex relations of having, power, valuing, poetic and artistic creating, and the revelations of the sacred. The path of self via the symbols of the Freudian archaism and the Hegelian teleology is one which reflection, if it is to be authentic, must appropriate and reappropriate. It is the path which *restores* the fullness of language as realized in the "spoken word," "speech simply heard and understood."

METHODOLOGICAL CRITICISM

By virtue of their semantic, mythic, and systematic structures, symbols demand interpretative understanding. So far as self ciphers, it calls for deciphering.

Another way of expressing part of the point here: "methods" of inquiry must take their guides and be grounded in the "things themselves" that are to be investigated (*109*, I, pp. 3–47, 207–59). The principle underlying this canon of method is a *principle of evidence (Evidenz)*. For every objectivity (every thematized or thematizable state-of-affairs), there is an originary mode of evidence pertaining to it, by or through which alone it is "presented originaliter," or by means of which one is at all aware of it as such. Such evidences or encounters of necessity *vary* according as the objectivity itself varies (*45*, Pt. II, Chs. 4, 6; *129*, pp. 209–30). Disclosing the most originary mode of evidential encounter (*"Evidenz est ein Erfahrung,"* as Husserl stresses) (*41*, I) is thus equivalent to the disclosure of the "thing itself." In Ricoeur's own terms, " . . . we must stop dissociating method and doctrine, stop taking the method without the doctrine. Here, the doctrine is method" (*95*, p. 433). A methodological critique is therefore unavoidable.

Yet, though alluded to in several places, and figuring importantly in others, the phenomenological principle is found to be wanting, and in fact is dropped,[18] in the face of the task of interpreting symbols. Their "revealing power" is grounded in their "donative character," and this is to have "already broken the phenomenological neutrality." For here I am not a subject studying some object; I find myself, rather, a being who is "spoken to." The symbol "draws me," "makes me participate in what is announced to me." This is not phenomenology, but "an existential assimilation, according to the movement of analogy, of my being to being" (*95*, p. 31). Remarking on his earlier work, Ricoeur makes the break quite plain: "a hermeneutic method, coupled with reflection, goes much farther than an eidetic method I was then practicing" (*95*, p. 458). So far as I can see, with this step Ricoeur has in effect given up the central principle of evidence which otherwise seems so essential to his own work.

Now, though, two critical issues arise. On the one hand, the claim that "symbols give rise to thought" *is itself a judgment which inherently appeals to some mode of evidence*, on the sole basis of which one could at all understand the claim and ultimately come to either agreement or disagreement with it. *It matters not in the least* whether *this* evidence turns out to be "interpretative" or not—the principle of evidence must still hold, if this is indeed the way by means of which we are at all cognizant of and eventually knowledgeable of symbols. Hence it cannot be the case that "hermeneutics" stands opposed to "phenomenology" and the principle of evidence.[19]

On the other hand, the claim that philosophy itself demands symbols (*95*, p. 41) is quite a different claim, as Ricoeur recognizes. But if philosophy is hermeneutics, we are left with a profound enigma. *What is the status of the claim that* "the philosophical act, in its innermost nature, is hermeneutical?" Either this claim is *itself* a hermeneutical claim, or it is not. If it is, it can only be called (with an awkward stretching of the tongue) *meta*-hermeneutical (a "circle" which, so far as I can see, is not at all the "hermeneutical circle"). If it is not hermeneutical, then philosophy is not and cannot be hermeneutical at its root. However, even if it is itself a hermeneutical claim, its "meta" status must itself be accounted for, and the *difference in systematic levels or status is unavoidably admitted.*

This is no small issue, for on it hangs the problem of how we are to understand the very project Ricoeur embarks upon, not to mention its results. Ricoeur seems aware of the problem in the early pages of the *Freud* book: hermeneutics stands in need of being radically justified, and only a *"transcendental logic"* concerning the "conditions for the very possibility of . . ." can accomplish this crucial task. The difficulty here is that while calling in one sentence for a "radical justification" *of* hermeneutics, he promptly goes on in the next sentence to assert that this logic *"is proper to"* hermeneutics. The text seems clear that this ambiguous phrase is taken to mean that hermeneutics *is itself coextensive with* this logic—a "logic of double meanings." But, again, the "of" is quite ambiguous: it might mean "is proper to" in the sense of "properly falls within" or "belongs to," in which case one could hardly call it "transcendental." Or it might mean, "establishes the conditions for the possibility of" double meanings, in which case it can hardly itself be *at the same level* as what it thereby establishes.

Beyond the ambiguities, however, is the difference in systematic level inherent to Ricoeur's "talk about" symbols, hermeneutics, interpretation. This "talk about" can only be transcendental, and cannot therefore be confused with what it is supposed to justify radically—viz., hermeneutics. It may well be that one must "live in the *aura* of meaning" of the symbols in order to understand them; but this claim as such is not at the same level as that inquiry, since it speaks to what is transcendentally necessary in order to conduct such an inquiry. To confuse these, as I think Ricoeur does, is to *vitiate the very sense of inquiry at both levels.*

THE QUESTION OF "SELF"

These remarks bear directly on the focal issues of self and of reflection. For, Ricoeur stresses, method cannot be separated from doctrine. What is the "question of self"? Ricoeur's early study of *The Voluntary and the Involuntary* puts it this way (*94*, pp. 6–17, 55–59), following a deliberately Husserlian phenomenology. Taking up the "reflexive direction of decision," and agreeing (as does the *Freud* book) with the Cartesian "Cogito," he contends that "a certain presence to myself must covertly accompany all intentional consciousness." Yet "such an immediate self-presence clinging to the very thrust of consciousness" is not found in such explicit judgments as "It is I who . . . ." *This* self-affirmation is a kind of "prereflexive imputation of myself . . . a self-reference which is not yet self-observation. . . ." Now the question here is, "how is this possible?" The quest, in turn, must be a working back "to the conditions which make it possible." That is, *this* problematic is manifestly a transcendentally eidetic one.

But just this kind of inquiry, asserted in the earlier work as necessary to justify hermeneutics itself, is precisely what is found wanting in the *Freud* book. Hermeneutics goes "much farther." At most, what was earlier called "self-presence" is now to be understood merely as a "first tendency [of reflection] to identify itself with immediate consciousness" (*95*, p. 54).

Not surprisingly, the *question* asked in the *Freud* book has also shifted. "What new self-understanding comes out of this interpretation, and what self is it which thus comes to self-understanding?" (*95*, p. xii). The question, in short, has become two-pronged. On the one hand, it concerns the *"meaning"* of self and reflection—"what does Reflection signify? What does the Self of self-reflection signify?" (*95*, p. 43). On the other hand, the question concerns what *The Symbolism of Evil* called "a qualitative transformation of reflexive consciousness," a "participation" in the "revealing power" of symbols. (*98*, p. 356). The *Freud* book, too, exhibits both lines, expressly advancing the idea that authentic reflection "itself undergoes change by incorporating into itself the discourse of its own archeology; instead of abstract reflection, it starts to become concrete reflection" (*95*, p. 342). The polar opposite of this is not merely "abstract" reflection, but rather the *pretension* to reflect "neutrally," which is "to speak from nowhere." It is thus no surprise that Ricoeur "breaks" with his former "phenomenology": *the very questions he poses are no longer the same, they are not transcendental but rather the hermeneutical questions of interpreting "meaning."* This fact renders the very sense of his appeal to "transcendental conditions for the possibility of . . ." highly dubious at the least. To repeat: the *statements about* the hermeneutical task, and the *practice of* hermeneutics, are *not* at the same level.

Yet the appeal to the transcendental, as I understand it, can only be perfectly right. And, in fact, there are haunting reminders sprinkled throughout the *Freud* book that give one pause. In one passage, writing about the dispossession of the object, Ricoeur points out that the true genesis of the notion of the object, within Freud's work, is merely an "ostensible antiphenomenology."[20] It is "merely the long detour at the end of which the object will again become the transcendental guide, but for a highly mediated reflection. . . ." Husserl's "passive genesis" indicates the area of research here, but Freud remains original in his linking of this genesis with that of love and hate—the desires (*95*, p. 425).

Earlier, too, Ricoeur suggests that "what is economically reconstructed at the end of this process [narcissism] is precisely 'the object' in the phenomenological sense" (*95*, p. 126). Thus the history of the object is the history of the object-function, and this is the history of desire. The so-called "antiphenomenology" is "ostensible" just because, as I see it, the "object-function" in psychoanalysis is indeed *not* incommensurate with "the object" in the phenomenological sense, which, as in Freud, is a "sedimentation" resulting from the complex functions of *Passivität*. While Freud has stressed desire far more than did Husserl, this difference surely makes no difference *in principle*. Indeed, in many ways, Ricoeur's own philosophical reflection on desire seems quite capable of being understood as an *eidetics of desire*, using (here) Freud's work as a clue.

More important is the notion of "dispossession." Consider that of "the object." To what does this refer? If (as Ricoeur has suggested) "the object-function" is really the "object" in the phenomenological sense, then this can hardly be what is "dispossessed" (i.e., the machinery of the primary process and of narcissism can hardly be said to be dispossessed). And, phenomenologically, when one engages the epochē and reduction at all seriously, one's thematization can hardly be said to "dispossess" the object as it is taken (intended) by the natural consciousness whose "object" it is. What, then, does this "dispossession" signify? I can only skim a few surfaces here, but these are important indices, suggestive of a deeply troubling matter. As Ricoeur nicely shows (*95*, pp. 375–90), there are some alluring similarities between Husserl and Freud. Notwithstanding these, phenomenology is not only not psychoanalysis, but can give only an approximate understanding of it. The first is certainly true; the latter is problematical. In any case, the point here is that *the entire issue of "dispossession" falls within the clinical discipline of psychoanalysis.*

Nor could it be otherwise, as Ricoeur shows. "Psychoanalysis is not a reflexive discipline; the off-centering it brings about is fundamentally different from the 'reduction' in that *it is very strictly constituted by* what Freud calls the 'analytic technique' . . . " (*95*, p. 390; *my emphasis*). Here, two things. First, this being so, it seems most gratuitous to interpret Freud's "dispossession" as a "reduction *of*" consciousness *in contrast to* Husserl's "reduction *to*" consciousness; to write of an "epochē in reverse"; and to characterize psychoanalysis as an "antiphenomenology." The stress must be on the "fundamental difference": we have here a *non*-phenomenology, not an *anti*-phenomenology; nor is there a "reduction" in Husserl's sense. Thus the second point: the "technique" simply has no counterpart in a "reflexive discipline" *of any kind.* The terms of that technique, similarly, have their sense strictly within their appropriate clinical context: object, intersubjectivity, ego, unconscious, conscious, transference, resistance, etc., have no "conceivable phenomenological equivalents" (*95*, p. 414).

Nor could that be otherwise—not only for phenomenology, but for any reflexive discipline, *hermeneutics included.* The problematic of "dispossession" has its place solely within that psychoanalytic praxis. Thus the effort to "reappropriate" Freud's work within hermeneutics seems suspect to begin with. But, more, what could such "reappropriation" actually signify? That is, in what ways can reflective philosophy "relate" to Freudian analysis?

So far as I can see, philosophical discourse with analysis (or other clinical disciplines) is possible on two counts (realizing that this is itself an immense topic). First, one must be able to explore the "conditions for the very possibility of" that analysis itself. Where Freud, for example, treats intersubjectivity within his notion of "technique," Husserl explores the conditions for the possibility of "relating to another person" as such (however well or badly this may be done). Where Freud takes his work as science, phenomenology explores the conditions for the possibility of science as such. Hence, as even Ricoeur insists, the sense of "primacy" differs vastly for psychoanalysis and for transcendental philosophy.[21]

Second, philosophical engagement with analysis is possible wherever Freud's claims exceed the limits of his own praxis. Thus when he maintains not only that the neurotic is not master in his own house, but "also and above all the man of morality, the ethical man" (*95*, p. 183), then surely this claim is *properly philosophical* and assessable *only* as such. On both counts, furthermore, there is certainly no way—*beyond actual demonstration*—to say that only hermeneutics can properly "relate" to analysis. That demonstration is not forthcoming; furthermore, the reasons Ricoeur gives are quite inadequate (indeed, seem to me to involve him necessarily in phenomenological "evidencing"), and where relevant apply no less to a hermeneutics than to phenomenology: they apply to *any* reflexive discipline.

But Ricoeur formulates the question of self in *quite another way*:

> First, it must be made clear that it is in reflection and for reflection that psychoanalysis is an archeology; it is an archeology *of the subject.* But of what subject? What must the subject of reflection be if it is likewise to be the subject of psychoanalysis? (*95*, p. 420)

The first point here clearly concerns the project of philosophically *assessing the status of psychoanalysis itself*: its claims, sources, evidences, etc., which show that it is an "archeology." This is "Freudianism" taken, if you will, as an "acceptance-phenomenon."[22] As such, *this* issue must be kept rigorously distinct (however closely related) from the very *different* issue concerning the self (and reflection).

That other issue is the concern of the second part of the passage. But here it is necessary to notice that there is at once a mixing of different issues, and a posing of the proper question. To ask, "of what subject?" is to *remain within* the problematic pertaining to the explication of the sense of "Freudianism" itself. But to ask, "what must the subject of reflection be˙if it is likewise to be the subject of psychoanalysis?" is *to pose a radically different question,* for this concerns *the transcendental conditions for the possibility of being-as-self* (subject), such that to be this is likewise to be-able-to-be both reflectively apprehended ("of reflection") and neurotic ("of psychoanalysis"). What this question sets out as problematical is not at all "Freudianism"-qua-acceptance-phenomenon, but the "self"-qua-phenomenon.

This transcendental question, however, does not seem to be the one Ricoeur explicitly pursues. What concerns him, to the contrary, is the effort to take "Freudianism" as a "stage of reflection," as a necessary "way" for transforming the self, to work through the metapsychology, reflectively attempting to find in it (to reappropriate) the "subject *of*" the "archeology,"[23] and *not the conditions for the possibility of being-as-subject within* that archeology.

Clarifying these questions helps in another way. Namely, it seems to me that the force and epistemic status of Freud's vaunted "antiphenomenology" is hardly that. In one sense, as we already saw, so long as it remains within the particular clinical settings of therapy, it is "*non-*", or better, "*a*-phenomenological"—for the very reasons Ricoeur states. But to the extent that analysis either does, or can be shown to, engage in speculation which exceeds that context, then it is unabashedly *philosophical.* Here, however, there is a subtlety: whether explicitly or implicitly philosophical (maintaining, for example, that human subjectivity *as such and without exception* reveals the sort of archaism Freud has postulated and claimed to find clinically), does not the very possibility of clinically encountered phenomena—hysteria, autism, dreams, etc.—however they may be specifically and therapeutically interpreted, point to the transcendental? I mean: independently, for example, of whether dreams are taken as the disguised discourse of desire, as revelations of occult phenomena beyond the ken of normal awareness, or whatever, there is a significant transcendental problematic concerning the "conditions" without which that occurrence would not be possible; i.e., what dreaming signifies for "being-a-self." It is the same as regards illusion, deception, and the like: how is it possible for me to be deceived (or is it to "deceive myself"?), to mask myself to myself . . . ? This kind of issue is, it seems to me, not at all the one Ricoeur engages in, even though he raises the question.

THE EIDETIC CORE OF SELF

These considerations bring me almost full circle. Many of Ricoeur's results about the self—effort, desire, mutuality, feeling, and the like—seem *either to suppose the truth* of Freud's analytic (as an "archaism"); *or* they must be understood as *phenomenologically "verifying"* the properly philosophical content of Freudian analysis. Judging from the text, it would seem that the latter is closer to the case. For if one asks of Freud's analytics, what is the rationale, the ground, for at all introducing such notions as the "unconscious," it seems clear that it is done as a way of *making sense of* or *accounting for* what must otherwise remain utterly incomprehensible, though plainly there in experience—the clinically discovered phenomena such as hysteria, autism, etc. Ricoeur points the way here:

> . . . the justification of the unconscious takes on an aspect of scientific necessity: the text of consciousness is a lacunary, truncated text; the assumption of the unconscious is equivalent to a work of interpolation that introduces meaning and connection into the text. (*95*, pp. 119–20)

The rationale is found in what is regarded by Freud as an assumption necessary to be able to account for the clinical phenomena. The "interpolation" seems little short of a *transcendental* supposition: the facts of the "dream-work" are not possible, not accountable for, *except on condition that* the one-who-dreams continually undergoes processes of imagining, feigning, fantasying—of which, however, he must be continually *unaware* in any explicit manner. And this is eventually said to be so *for us all, and not simply for the patients actually encountered.* In order for each of us to be able to be the dreamer (at least, so far as Freud is concerned), it is thus *essential* that there be the system "Unconscious." But this, as Ricoeur reminds us, is not merely a supposition: the "realism" of the unconscious is a positing of the Unconscious as "real," efficacious. As such, it must somehow *be accessible*, make itself felt, give signs, for otherwise it would be on a par with instincts in their biological character: utterly unknowable, and thereby would collapse the edifice of *psycho*analysis.

The "instinctual representatives," in the end, Ricoeur points out, are on the side of the psychical. Hence there is indeed *a mode of access to, and therefore a mode of evidence for* (these are strictly correlative) the unconscious. This mode of access is available *to the patient* only by way of difficult, tortuous "work"; and it is available (almost beforehand, one might even say) *to the psychoanalyst*, but again, with his or her "work."[24] Thus numerous clinically encountered and now reflectively considered examples of these "representatives" show rather ample grounds for the "interpolation." To the extent, of course, that these examples come from *actual* encounters, all that the "evidence" here can warrant is a conclusion pertaining to the region of actuality *(Wirklichkeit).* To make out grounds for the ostensibly transcendental status of the interpolation, evidence concerning the "possibility" (any possible subject whatever) must be found—namely, by way of reflective philosophical inquiry of the kind Ricoeur himself often practices, or which, by attempting to "appropriate" the "work" of Freud, seems to be yielded by that mode of reflection. *Ricoeur's conclusions, after all, concern any possible "self"*; hence it seems not unreasonable to understand them as *transcendental*. Being-a-self is *essentially* (among other things) to exhibit oneself as a desire-to-be.

That is, in the course of being guided by Freud's analysis, Ricoeur comes up with what must be called the *eidetic core of being-a-self:* the effort-to-be, an effort which, as profound desire to be acknowledged as such by others, would (if further delineated) show how it is even possible for a "self" to be deluded or genuine, masked or open, split or whole, terrorized or acknowledged. This self-positing as desire-to-be, however, seems to me precisely what *The Voluntary and the Involuntary* had already begun to uncover under the name of the pre-reflective "imputation of myself" locused and implicitly affirmed in my actions, deeds, and works. Thus although the *Freud* book has surely *advanced* this considerably, it can hardly be seen as a *repudiation;* the "much farther" which Ricoeur has now gone is not at all due to a dropping of his earlier "eidetics." Just the opposite.

I thus see no reason whatever for a supposed move "from" phenomenology "to" hermeneutics, even in the case of studying a "text" in the usual sense. After all, the principle of evidence, taken rigorously, *requires* that one's "method" have its source and grounds in the "things themselves," in the modes of evidence strictly proper to them (and thus, in his terms, inseparable from "doctrine"). *If these "things" ("texts") are such as must be "interpreted"*—that being the originary mode of evidence through which alone they would be accessible to us, and on the basis of which judgments about them could alone be made—*then surely the phenomenological principle of evidence leaves one no choice but to "interpret." Hence "interpretation" can only be understood as at once the mode of evidence for, the way by which we come to experience, and the method for phenomenological inquiry into, these "texts."*

Ricoeur *need not* differ on that point. Nor need he be at odds with the real demand for grounding hermeneutics in transcendental logic. In this sense and to this extent, there can hardly be a question of a *choice* between methods, or between supposedly less adequate and more adequate methods: the very thing demanded by Ricoeur is inherent to the principle of evidence, hence is phenomenological.

But on the questions of self and reflection, it seems to me that Ricoeur would sharply diverge from my suggestions. For he holds that his inquiry into "self" has discovered a being that is at root a "being-hidden," a "being-in-disguise": "as a man of desires I go forth in disguise—*larvatus prodeo*" (*95*, p. 7). While the self is rooted within the intentionality of consciousness (the one side of the law of expressivity), it is also, and more fundamentally, rooted in "life, desire and effort" (the other side of that law). And this more basic status of self is not only the discovery of "the unsurpassable nature of life, but the interference of desire with intentionality, upon which desire inflicts an invincible obscurity, an ineluctable partiality" (*95*, p. 458).

But here matters grow very elusive. I agree with Ricoeur: reflection and self are critical issues, closely intertwined and contextured by desire and effort. We both agree with Husserl: "I, the meditating phenomenologist, set myself the all-embracing task of *uncovering myself*, in my full concreteness—that is, with all the intentional correlates that are included therein" (*41*, p. 38). But Ricoeur would insist that "desire" *interferes* with, inflicts an "invincible obscurity" on, intentionality. This is quite questionable.

Desire itself is surely "intentive" just as much as other psychical processes *(Erlebnisse)*. And, indeed, *it must be so even for Ricoeur:* desire does, after all, "tend to" or "wish for" speech, utterance, or manifestation. Whatever the mode of expression, the "desire-to-be" is *intentive in its own way* (but, then, so is every process, *in its own way*). Though it *may* well be "hidden," "distorted," and the like, still this *does not in the least belie but precisely reveals its manifestly intentive character*. But even though some modes of desiring are disguised, surely not all are; some, indeed, are strikingly clear and unmistakable, even very subtle desirings—whether or not some particular persons are capable of recognizing the gestures of desire. Even so, however, these too are no less *intentive in their own manner* than are the disguised desirings. Hence it is most improper to *oppose* desire to intentionality; this succeeds only in obfuscating their nature.

On the other hand, pointing this out helps us to see that the real opposition Ricoeur is urging is not so much that, but rather the opposition between what Husserl had called the "doxic" and "non-doxic," between what Ricoeur wishes to call "acts of knowing" and the desire-to-be. (cf. *95*, p. 458). Here several further issues crop up.

To speak of acts of knowing at the level in question here (the ground sense of "self") is not at all proper. Just prior to this, though, Ricoeur draws the opposition more clearly: between the *"intentionality"* which is "ruled by the objects that manifest themselves in that intentionality," and the "manifestation" of effort and desire "hidden in that intentionality" (*95*, pp. 457, 458). Now as was already emphasized, what is wrong here is that *even if true*, the latter claim simply fails to grasp the very sense of desire Ricoeur himself claims it has: that it is "turned toward language." But here there is a subtlety Ricoeur seems to me to have overlooked. To adopt Ricoeur's mode of expression, desire not only "wishes" to be spoken; it seeks to be locused in *"speech-about"* and in two crucial senses. There is the effort to *manifest self*, to express self (speech "about" myself); but this speech is, as Ricoeur knows well, speech desiring the other. The speech-about is "about" myself as ineluctably *in the world with others*, hence it is "about" my circum-stances: what stands around me and helps to constitute in some way what I am. We must recall the prime feature of desire for Ricoeur: that it is "desire of *another* desire," i.e., a "demand," and is thus essentially set within the world of others, in such a way that this "being-set-within" can only be the peculiar mode of intentiveness characteristic of "desire."

That such "speaking-as-manifesting-myself" and "-as-about-the-world" is multivalently signifying is not only not surprising in light of this complex intentiveness, but probably quite essential. We must ask, though, why does the effort-to-be manifest itself in enigmas? Why is it that being-self is, among other things, able-to-be deceived, able-to-be neurotic, able-to-be even uniformly obscured to itself (as in autism)? If truth is a task, and I agree, then surely so also is deception, illusion, fraud, feigning. These latter are no less than the former always a "having-to-be-maintained," they are "tasks" or "projects." And these tasks, no less than that of "truth," are *intentive*. Hence even desire and effort "relate" to the circumstances of life, quite as much as "believings," "perceivings," "knowings"; they relate to the environing world, and intentively shape it as well as manifest a particular "self" expressing itself. The distinguishable but inseparable complexus of intentive life is matched by its strict correlate, the surrounding milieu, and that milieu, however distinguishable, is strictly inseparable from that life. The supposed dualism of intentionality and manifestation of desire turns out, then, to be itself a kind of "false consciousness."

Furthermore, however a particular self may particularly express itself, whatever it may "strive to be," it is clear on the one hand that this "striving" cannot be opposed to "believing" (in Husserl's broad sense), for the latter itself is a "striving-to-believe," a "striving-to-know" what and how to reckon with things, how to orient oneself within the milieu, and ultimately, I suppose, a wanting to know what is "real." For the self, the "real" is precisely what it must, or believes it must, "reckon with," with respect to which the self "needs to know" what to hold by. This "needing to know," which is a telling exhibiting of one's "effort-to-be," is thus not so much "hidden disguisedly" in the intentiveness-to-objects as *it is* that intentiveness in its core form.[25]

But, on the other hand, given this, it is then necessary to ask what the notion of "indirect discourse" amounts to. "Indirect" in relation to what? "Direct" discourse? But what might that be? Surely not logical calculus, for Ricoeur has already shown that its urge to univocity is severely limited, and appropriate only for highly specific purposes and problems. It represents, if you will, an abstraction (indeed, a complex of abstractions) *away* from natural language, so far away that while it may be written it can in no way be "spoken": hence it cannot be "discourse" at all. Then what is "indirect" discourse?

It may be, as Ricoeur suggests, that the "disguised," "laconic," or "fantasy" discourses—the fabric of the speech of dreams, hysterics, neurotics, and in a clear way the rest of us—may well be the *only discourse* of self in its eidetic core: the discourses of desire. Metaphor, metonomy, laconism, as well as analogy, allegory, myth, symbol, story and even colloquialism, joke, irony, satire—all these may well be the only, or at least the primary, discourses for that being whose *eidos* is striving, efforting, needing, desiring . . . *at once* to make itself known or present to others *and* to disclose or know that selfsame world of others.[26] *The self's "talk," that is, is not so much "indirect" as opposed to some so-called "direct" discourse; it is rather that this "talk" is what it is*—self-revealing/other-encountering—*precisely because the self which strives is what it is.*

What thus becomes prominent is not some sort of contrast between that mode of discourse and, say, symbolic logic—which is not even a discourse. Rather, what is at issue is the discourse of self, its modalities of utterance (at once intentive-to, and intentive-manifestations-of) and their *philosophical articulation.* The issue concerns the marked contrast between the upsurge of self and the language of reflective philosophical inquiry seeking to understand the (and "its") self in the fairest and most rigorous way possible.

REFLECTION

I thus complete the circle of this inquiry: the problematic of reflection on self cannot signify the collapse of this reflection into what is reflected-upon; nor can its language be literally (or uncritically) the language of the reflected-upon. Philosophy must obviously reflect upon the self, its manifestations, discourses, and the like. But, whether these be "symbolic" or not, philosophy loses itself if it is taken to be *also* symbolic *in the same sense.* To the "equivocity" of symbols, it is necessary to contrast, not the "univocity" of formal calculus, but the *univocity of philosophical discourse.*

To this point, there is no better witness than Ricoeur himself. It is *perfectly clear*, indeed *univocally* clear, what Ricoeur means by, e.g., "symbol," "speech," "language," "hermeneutics," and the like. Whether he is explicating Freud's texts or the textures of self, he is again clear, or at a minimum is *striving to be univocally clear*—however difficult and complex a task that surely is. If, then, he means by "reappropriation" of self a strict effort to *repeat* philosophically what the self as reflected-upon shows itself to be, then this is just wrong. His philosophical discourse *is not itself* equivocal, ambiguous, cunning, disguised, a repetition of the laconisms of the subterranean self; nor, properly speaking, was Freud's *theoretical* discourse. Philosophical language is not that of logical calculus; but *neither is it that of the self reflected-upon.*

Husserl put this point exactly:

> Owing to the instability and ambiguity of common language and its much too great complacency about completeness of expression, *we require, even where we use its means of expression, a new legitimation of significations* by orienting them according to accrued insights, and a fixing of words as expressing the significations thus legitimated. *That too we account as part of our normative principle of evidence. . . .* (*41*, pp. 13–14; *my emphasis*)

It is just this that Ricoeur in fact tries to *practice*, but his professed *aim* seems sometimes quite different. What he does not recognize is that this effort to "fix" expressions, when and only as legitimated by "accrued insights," is part of the normative principle of evidence already emphasized above. Thus although he believes that reflective philosophy must "have recourse to symbols," it is quite evident that this "recourse" is not itself a "doing again" of what is "done" in the discourses of self, nor is it a collapse of that reflection into that discourse. Where the self metaphors, philosophy *reflectively apprehends* and then expresses in judgments which are *about* these metaphors. Or, at the very least, philosophy has an intrinsic requirement to reach the clarity proper to the "things themselves" being studied, and proper to its own nature and tasks as philosophy—guided at every step by the full principle of evidence (*11*, pp. 224–27).

The claim that reflection is a "reappropriation" of self is thus in one clear sense false. But there is a sense in which, even though misleading, it might well be true. Insofar as reflection is itself a *mode of "experiencing"*—experiencing, precisely, what is reflected-upon in its own integrity and context—insofar as reflection *thematizes* the self, then I suppose one might take this as an "appropriation." And since what is now reflectively thematized was not before thematized, there is a sense in which something is "altered": from being hitherto not reflected-upon to being reflected-upon. But this alteration in modality surely does not alter the "thing" thus apprehended: it could hardly be part of Ricoeur's claim that *his own reflection on desire of itself indelibly changes desire* in its own proper character. Thus if "appropriation" means a "transformation of reflexive consciousness" in this sense, it strikes me as plainly false in Ricoeur's own terms; either that, or else a confusion of the tasks of philosophy with those of therapy.

Such considerations, however, make it much clearer just where Ricoeur seems radically to diverge. Distinguishing between "straightforward" awareness of something, and "reflective" awareness of that straightforward awareness, Husserl points out:

> The proper task of reflection, however, is not to repeat the original process, but to consider it and explicate what can be found in it. . . . Precisely thereby an experiential knowing (which at first is descriptive) becomes possible, that experiential knowing [*Erfahrungswissen*] to which we owe all conceivable cognizance [*Kenntnis*] and cognition [*Erkenntnis*] of our intentional living. . . . The reflecting Ego's non-participation in the "positing" (believing, taking a position as to being) that is part of the straightforward house-perception in no wise alters the fact that his *reflecting* experiencing is precisely an *experiencing* experiencing of the house-perception with all its moments, which belonged to it before and are continuing to take shape. . . .
> The non-participating, the abstaining, of the Ego who has the phenomenological attitude is *his* affair, not that of the perceiving [desiring, etc.] he considers reflectively, nor that of the naturally perceiving [desiring, etc.] Ego. We may add that it is itself accessible to an appropriate reflection; and only by means of this do we know anything about it. (*41*, pp. 34–35)

Because of what he takes to be the "overdetermination of meaning" of symbols, Ricoeur contends that *reflection must be precisely a "participation"* in the movements of symbols themselves; reflection on self must be an "existential assimilation" of the reflecting self with the self reflected-upon, and thereby a "qualitative transformation" of both. Still, it is solely because of that stance on reflection's task that his effort to take Freud's analytics as "stages of reflection" makes any sense; only thereby, too, is the turn to Hegelian dialectics even possible; only thereby is the urge to "mediate" sensible.

But this stance is fateful for Ricoeur's own enterprise: its consequence is that it vitiates the sense of this enterprise. Reflection in its philosophical guise is a "reappropriation" in the sense of a doing for the "self" of the reflecting philosopher what Freud's analytics at least purports to do for the "self" of the afflicted patient: *the philosopher turns out to be his own therapist.* And, so far as the philosopher talks and writes, his "texts" must, one must suppose, become therapeutic for his readers and auditors—those who authentically "hear" his "speech."

That I am on the other side of this gulf should be clear. Unquestionably, at one level Ricoeur is right: the self confronted with authentic symbols (let alone myths) cannot hope to understand them except by going whither they lead, and how; the overdetermination of symbols determines the definite path of that inquiry. Still, it must be recognized that *conducting that inquiry* and *stating what is necessary in order for that inquiry to be possible* are evidently different matters.

Thus it *may* be that the *task of the emerging self* is hermeneutical, having all of its pitfalls and guile to contend with along that way. But when the self becomes reflective upon itself, seeking to unravel the *"that by virtue of which it is at all,"* it takes on for itself *another kind of task*, the task of understanding itself in its own *eidos*. This task can hardly denigrate the hermeneutics of emergence, since that is precisely what it must now come to understand; yet neither can it collapse the tasks, since that serves neither, and disserves both.

ADDENDUM: PHENOMENOLOGY AND HERMENEUTICS

In a recent essay, Ricoeur has clearly tried to redress a number of the problems I have raised (*97*). At the same time, he has made it much clearer just what are the complaints he has against Husserl's phenomenology.

As for the latter, what he finds objectionable is by no means the whole of Husserlian phenomenology; nor has the sort of "eidetics" Ricoeur earlier practiced really been rejected. In this, then, Ricoeur agrees with my criticism, and seems to reject the view advanced in the *Freud* book. As for Husserl, Ricoeur's objections center on two points: (1) the "idealistic" interpretation Husserl gives to his own work is said to be both wrong and unnecessary to the central insights of his phenomenology; and (2) the "intuitively" secured "primacy" of "subjectivity"—the main thesis of the "idealism"—is found deeply erroneous.

As for the former point, Ricoeur appears to be in substantial agreement with the criticisms I have advanced here—save for one basic point.[27] While he now fully agrees that *"phenomenology remains the indispensible presupposition of hermeneutics,"* he insists that "phenomenology is not able to establish itself without a *hermeneutical presupposition"* (97, p. 85). Hence the two are in a relation of "mutual belonging," or "mutual foundedness," as Husserl might have expressed it.

This is not the place to tackle many of the problems here. Still, some discussion is clearly called for, especially in view of one key notion Ricoeur uses to contrast his understanding of Husserl with his own hermeneutics.

Ricoeur's major objection to Husserlian idealism (or that part of Husserl's work which seems most "idealistic") is that

> it has expressed its immense and unexceedable discovery of intentionality in terms of a conceptuality which weakens its scope, namely, in terms of the subject-object relationship. From this conceptuality proceeds the exigency of finding what makes the object's unity of meaning and of basing this unity in a constituting subjectivity. (97, p. 88)

This point, as has already been pointed out earlier, was already made trenchantly by Gurwitsch: one cannot account for the organization of the experiential field by reference to what the subject brings to experience. Rather, that field is "autochthonously" organized into a "field."[28] Here one can only agree with Ricoeur, even though he does not seem to have either Gurwitsch or the problem of organization ("field") in mind. Rather, Ricoeur wants to say

> that the problematic of objectivity presupposes, prior to itself, a relationship of inclusion which unites the allegedly autonomous subject and the allegedly adverse object. This inclusive relationship I call belonging-to [*appartenance, Zugehörigkeit*]. (97, p. 89)

Taking this "belonging-to" to be an "ontological condition of comprehension" or inclusion, Ricoeur contends that this constitutes a "foundation" for all thinking, and thus that the question of "foundation" (so crucial to phenomenology) cannot coincide with that of "justification" (also fundamental to phenomenology). What must be recognized, for him, is that the core truth of intentionality itself requires a non-idealistic interpretation: "no consciousness is self-consciousness before being consciousness *of* something *toward which* it overcomes itself . . ." (97, p. 96). Hence every effort to think through (whatever it may be) is of necessity *in medias res*, and thereby is essentially *mediated* by the *"hermeneutical experience itself,"* i.e., *appartenance* (97, p.

89). Explicating the "world" into which the thrust of consciousness ineluctably places the thinker is thus the hermeneutical task *par excellence*, and is therefore the presupposition for phenomenology. More accurately, as Ricoeur suggests in concluding this article, what Husserl himself came to call "explication" (*Auslegung*) turns out to be nothing other than hermeneutics itself (*97*, pp. 100–01). For such explication, as Husserl came to view it, is not only sense-explication of the world existing prior to all thinking about it—an uncovering of the sense of world, which never alters it but precisely makes it explicit—but is also one requiring critical *distancing* (distantiation), the Husserlian epochē non-idealistically interpreted, which is the "dialectical counterpart" (*97*, p. 92) of the hermeneutical "belonging-to." Finding the paradigm of this interplay of belonging-to/distancing-from in the "text," i.e., in the interpretative experience *par excellence*, Ricoeur is then able to argue that hermeneutics is not only deeply akin to phenomenology, not only presupposes phenomenology, but also forms the critical presupposition for phenomenology. Every question about "being" is a question about the "meaning" of being; but every "asking" about the meaning of being is comprehended by the inclusive belonging-to (history, culture, society) which is the very frame for thinking itself.

This rethinking of the relationship between phenomenology and hermeneutics is most fruitful, it seems to me, and a far more accurate way of conceiving both of these tasks. Nevertheless, it is hard to resist the observation that, aside from the flaws in Husserl's study of the organization of experience—flaws clearly marked out by Gurwitsch—most of what Ricoeur has to say about hermeneutics was already central to Husserl's thought throughout his career. Thus, aside from variations in terminology, it seems perfectly clear that what Ricoeur calls "appartenance" was precisely what Husserl included in what he called the "general thesis of the natural attitude" (*46*, secs. 27–31). Moreover, since Husserl nowhere seems to me to advocate what Ricoeur criticizes as "intuitionism," the latter's complaints seem to involve a straw man (and the same might well be said of his attack on Husserl's so-called "idealism").

Still, quite independently of that (admittedly a point of apparent divergence between us, and one which would require far more analysis than is here possible), and independently even of Ricoeur's insistence that "appartenance" is an "ontological" condition, the interplay between *appartenance* and *distantiation* effectively sets up the crucial issues pertaining to self and its experience of the other self. As will hopefully become clear as the study proceeds into these elusive regions, the experience of finding oneself "always-already-there" (*toujours-déjà-là*) in the midst of things (*in medias res*) will be a central theme for beginning to unravel the sense of "self." And in a similar vein, the phenomenon of "distancing," or as I shall call it (for reasons which will become clear later) "possibilizing," will be seen to be a critical moment in the emergence of "self." The sense or status of the claims which will be made regarding these phenomena, however, is that they are *phenomenological*—

specifically, that *appartenance* and *distantiation* are phenomena disclosed precisely by phenomenological explication, carried out consistently by means of free-phantasy variation.

7

On Self:
Reflexivity and Wonder

EVEN though I have found Ricoeur's hermeneutics either wanting (as in the *Freud* book) or in effect a return to the core of Husserlian phenomenology (as in the more recent writing), much of what he says about "self" is sound and important. Still, the transcendental question remains: what are the conditions for the very possibility of being-self? In this and the following chapter, I want to give at least an initial response to that issue; it will then be necessary to assess the results of this study in respect of the relation of self to other selves.

As for the present task, one can put the transcendental question in several ways. Even granting, as Ricoeur insists, that for all the force of Freud's topography and economics, the central phenomenon of "self-positing" in effort and desire is not itself addressed, still, one might ask: how is it even possible for there to be narcissism or self-love? Alternatively, to use Ricoeur's philosophical reformulation: how can there even possibly be an "abortive Cogito," an "instinct" which points to a "primordial" desire seeking to be "told" in "speech," yet "masking" itself in the discourses of metaphor, laconism, allegory, and other disguises? How is it possible for self, *my* self, to be thus cunning, wounded, forgotten, passed over, so threatened as to conceal itself in clever guises and ruses even from . . . *me*, who am that very self? "I" reflect on "myself": yet what I find is an essential fugitive, i.e., *I* do not find *me*. Is it, as Sartre once insisted, that every reflection *I* engage is essentially abortive, since that "I" which I seek is, precisely, the one reflect*ing* and never itself capturable as reflect*ed-on*? Or is it that reflection (as Ricoeur says, in connection with the hermeneutics of suspicion) must be a "double guile"? But if it is *I* who practice reflective "double guile," this can only be a practice having the same "I" as its "object." How is that possible? Or *is* it possible for the self who reflects to unmask itself, to "dis-guise" its own disguises? Is the *desire-to-know* myself sufficiently strong and true to be able to overcome the "desire-qua-desire" posited by the fundamental Cogito (Ricoeur)? And if I do succeed, is what I find that utterly strange and alien "neuter" (*das Es*) which Freud posits? If so, whether its "manifestation" be "desire" or something else, how shall I recognize it as myself? What would it mean, in Ricoeur's terms, to "appropriate" it at all for the *first* time, much less "reappropriate" the utterly foreign, the neuter and impersonal, into *my* life?

As Jonas pointed out, showing the crucial differences between Gnostic and Cartesian dualisms, where the former conceived Nature as antagonist (and hence in some way at least humanly familiar and comprehensible—as is any enemy), the Cartesian notion is the most rigorously alien of all: the uncaring, impersonal, indifferent matter which "matters" not at all, but is merely extended particles in motion. Am I to believe, then, that what is most intimate—even while terrorized and threatened (Freud)—is yet the most radical of all: myself as at core a neuter? *Can* the consummately non-personal also "wish," "strive," "desire," "speak"? Let us grant straightaway: few things seem quite so capable of surprising, shocking, disturbing, or upsetting as me-myself. Is this signal experience of self with itself, this veritable uncanny, an experience with the altogether *other*?

At issue here is the sense of the "archeology" which Ricoeur stressed, the critical lesson reflection learns from Freud's move to the archaic. What Ricoeur believes we glean from Freud here is the primordiality of desire (affect, effort), the essential darkness of self-to-itself: the elemental urge-to-be-itself which *is* myself in its archeological root, and is approachable only with the sly indirections of metaphor and "full" speech.

Transcendentally understood—and this, it must be recalled, is at Ricoeur's own insistence—the claim of the archeology is that the uncovering (with Freud's help) of this primordial "urge-to-be" and "self-caring" (narcissism) are conditions without which "self" would not be *self*. What might be called the rudimentary shock of self-recognition, furthermore, likewise points to a transcendental status of self: namely, that self encounters itself, and that this critical experience of self is an astonishment, an inner vertigo. But if we ask, as we must, about the very possibility of that self-encounter, that deeply set concern-for-self and that urgency-to-be, we are left without much response from Ricoeur. Yet his uncovering of self's textures ring true, so far as I can see. What becomes salient are three initial, crucial directions for inquiry, for gentle probing, as I shall try show, and to show why and how, and possibly what.

REFLEXIVITY

To pose the transcendental questions about self properly, it is helpful to call to mind the working out of the fuller reach of Gurwitsch's theory of contexture, especially the fuller meaning of "intrinsic references" or "functional significances." These were found to be exhibited by the embodying organism, and by the temporally phased nexus of mental life, as well as by the perceptual field. Indeed, considering the field organization of the environing milieu along with the contextures of mental life and the organism, I was led to the *complexure* of human life: a "whole" which is the totality of ever-unfolding, intrinsically interreferenced and mutually significant constituents—"world," "mental life," and "embodiment."

The constituents of any contexture are *strictly inseparable but distinguishable*. This principle, clearly, has its *raison d'être* "in the things themselves": viz., in the system of intrinsic references. Most particularly here, however, the fundamental kind of "referencing" is *self-reference*: by it, constituents are *at once bound mutually together yet tensioned in reciprocal difference* from one another and from the system itself. Recognizing that the different sorts of references delineated are but a way of explicating what is in truth an intrinsically *complex* "pointing" among constituents, it is nevertheless necessary to underscore *self-referentiality, for this in effect comprehends all, or is the fullest expression of, the set of references intrinsic to the constituents, hence to the sense of the contexture itself.*

This self-referentiality, of course, is present in even the simplest of contextures: e.g., the figure I examined earlier, or to take Gurwitsch's even more simple example, of two dots placed proximately on a homogeneous background (figure 1):

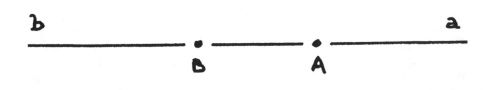

Fig. 2

Even here, Gurwitsch emphasizes, one does not see "one point *plus* the other located a short distance away. Rather one point appears as the *right member*, the other as the *left member* of the pair" (*31*, p. 106). Such perceptual characters can be perceived only if the one is seen *with reference to* the other, and *reciprocally*. This can be made even more plain. One can note that the interval between them has special features of its own, quite different from the field beyond the points (to the right and to the left of the respective dots). The interval is perceived as "closed, delimited, encompassed by the terminal points" (*31*, p. 106). If the figure is modified somewhat, the phenomenally perceived interval stands out more clearly (figure 2):

Fig. 1

Here one can alternately perceive point *A* as the *termination* of line segment *a*, or as *one of a dyad, A/B*. In the first case, the interval is perceived as a gap, an interruption of the continuity of the line; in the second, however, it is perceived as the separation and correlation, the conjoining of the pair. A *break* in the one, the interval is the *bond* in the second.

One could obviously extend the analysis with still further modifications. The point is already at hand, however: in order for even this elementary perception of a pair to occur in the way it does, the *interval itself is apprehended perceptually* as, if you will, the "in-between" of a pair (a "between" which can vary, but only within narrow limits, due to its very simplicity). The dots are the right and left members of a pair only in so far as they *mutually refer* to one another: they are bound, that is, by their *self-referentiality*.

As was said earlier, the greater the complexity of constituents, the greater is the range of variation in possible functional significances of each constituent. In figure 2, thus, adding the line segments opened up the possibility of perceptually apprehending the interval as either "gap" or "link," and that by virtue of the perceptually apprehended contexture with its constituents. The more detail given to such figures, the more detail will be the self-referentiality of the system of constituents. Thus, too, will the variational range of constituents increase, or become increasingly complex, and thereby also the increase in ways of *good continuation*: hence, conversely, the increase in ways by which a contexture can be modified, altered, even destroyed. For where in highly simplified contextures there is little possible variation in functional weight, with more complex ones *a qualitative enrichment* is exhibited in this phenomenal feature—a complexity which may (and the likelihood of this also increases) make the functional weight more difficult to determine.

However that may be, it is now plain that self-referentiality is the critical constitutive feature of contextures. Since, however, it has been necessary to distinguish among at least *three kinds* of contexture—noematic, noetic, and that of the embodying organism—it becomes necessary to distinguish as well among the kinds of reference and especially self-reference displayed by them. In a way, terminology is up for grabs, dependent on one's stylistic predilections. Thus one might note the intrinsic "reciprocity" or "complementarity" of a noematic contexture; the temporal "interrelationships" or "connections" of the noetic flow; and the "interdetermination," "bearing," or "affiliation," of the own-body. Other terms could be found, though obviously within limits, the important point being to be clear. My usage of "self-referentiality," "cross-references," and the like, was guided solely by my concern to lay out the common or invariant features of contextures as such, and I used other terms ad libidum merely to help mark out their in principle understandable complexity.

But when we moved to the *complexure* of life, things seemed to be markedly different, enough indeed to motivate the neologism. Here, in the embracing ensemble of complex contextures which are themselves (and whose constituents thus have the significance of being) complex constituents, the interlacing of "references" seems distinctively different. First, of course, the constituents are themselves contextures. Second, both mental life and the embodying organism are essentially weighted: the experiencing of an apple is positionally oriented. More specifically, every phase of mental life inherently includes intendings to a multiplicity of noemata (primary, secondary, tertiary, etc.), intendings to a multiplicity of temporal phases of the same mental life, and intendings to its own embodying corporeal patterns (kinaesthesias). The embodying organism, too, not only kinaesthetically enacts phases of mental life (strivings, wishings, perceivings, etc.), but functionally orients and positions the appearing state of affairs and its milieu ("field"). The meaning of their specific contextural character is that they tend to be focal points of the complexure of life; they are the counterpoised loci for life. It is this feature, I think, which is suggested by the biologist's usage of "inwardness" (*Innerlichkeit*).[1] As Portman expresses this,

> biology leads us into the realm of the spiritual if only by its concern with the study of that special mode of existence which is best known to us from our own existence, and which the biologist designates by a word of his own, a scientific symbol, "inwardness." . . . What we call inwardness is the specific mode of existence of living beings [*die besondere Seinsweise des Lebendigen*]. (*91*, p. 345)

Noting that one initial path to this, for the biologist, is the study of the "directive mechanism," he emphasizes that one can through careful observation find evidences of it even in creatures somewhat remote from ourselves (where our evidence is clearest) (*91*, pp. 346–49). And, just as the organism is here underscored, so is the mind—as in the classic expression: consciousness is *self*-consciousness.

Thus it is inherent to the complexure of life that it exhibits an experiential weight or "inwardness," focused on both mental life and the own-body. In view of this and the fact that all its constituents are contextures, there is a unique and decisive kind of "referencing" exhibited here: namely, what I shall call *reflexivity*.

SELF AS SITUATED REFLEXIVITY

As was seen in Chapter 1, Jonas fastens onto a remarkable phenomenon evidenced in the merest of living forms. The problems raised there concerning his "new monism" are here of little consequence. For whether one attempts rigorously to explore the "evidence of our own organic awareness" (as I have tried to do throughout), or extrapolates from it to other organic beings (as both Portmann and Jonas do), the point Jonas makes is crucial here:

> With the first dawn of subjective reflex, the most germinal "experience" of touching, a crack as it were opens in the opacity of divided being, unlocking a dimension where things may exist once more in the mode of object: it is the dimension of inwardness . . . Thus, in facing outward, internal identity becomes the subject-pole of a communication with things more intimate than that between mere physical units. . . . (*55*, p. 85)

Whether or not this "quality of felt selfhood" can be posited of all living forms (as Jonas believes), it surely is dramatically presenced in "the evidence of our own organic awareness." So, too, is it clearly true that with greater complexity of the bodily contexture—Jonas calls this "an increase of the mediacy . . . peculiar to organic existence" (*55*, p. 107)—a "more pronounced self is set over against a more pronounced world" (*55*, p. 107). An "enhancement of selfhood" is strictly realized as there is enhancement of organic capacity: toward sentience, emotiveness, and motility especially, to which correspondingly there develops an enhancement of world.

But not only does Jonas tend to conflate the contexture of mental life with that of "organic existence," he completely misses the *contexturality* of both, hence the complexure of life. To be sure, "consciousness" is essentially embodied consciousness; just as surely, however, the "inwardness" seized upon by Jonas is not just a phenomenon of "organic existence" but is rather, as Portmann emphasized, a "phenomenon of the spiritual" (*Geistliche*). Neither, therefore, are "organic existence" and "world" in a relation of mere "correspondence," nor is it a "dialectical" relation of mediation. Rather, as has been shown, we are confronted here with a *complexure*: a "whole" which is the system of functional significances intrinsic to its constituents (each of which is a complex contexture on its own). *The "inwardness," thus, is precisely the weighted reflexivity displayed by the complexure.*

In what must be one of the most profound insights in Western philosophy, precisely this radically "spiritual" phenomenon was grasped by Kierkegaard. In a passage which must otherwise appear as a most unfortunate, tongue-twisting piece of linguistic legerdemain, he wrote:

> Man is spirit. But what is spirit? Spirit is the self. But what is the self? The self is a relation which relates itself to its own self, or it is that in the relation that the relation relates itself to its own self; the self is not the relation but that the relation relates itself to its own self. Man is a synthesis of the infinite and the finite, of the temporal and the eternal, of freedom and necessity, in short it is a synthesis. A synthesis is a relation between two factors. So regarded, man is not yet a self.
>
> In the relation between two, the relation is the third term as a negative unity, and the two relate themselves to the relation, and in the relation to the relation; such a relation is that between soul and body, when man is regarded as soul. If on the contrary the relation relates itself to its own self, the relation is then the positive third term, and this is the self. (*61*, p. 146)

To this, three points initially. First, what Kierkegaard here calls "a negative unity" is precisely what Gurwitsch analyzed as the multiplicity of functional significances whose totality is the whole or contexture. All that should be added is that Kierkegaard's usage of "negative" is too prejudicial, if we think clearly about Gurwitsch's analysis, e.g., of the two dots.[2] While it is true that "the two relate themselves to the relation and in the relation to the relation," we face what is rather a *positive* (perceptual) phenomenon. More importantly, second, what Kierkegaard seizes upon with astonishing insight is the *reflexivity* inherent to the complexure of human life: the peculiarity of the "self-referentiality" of *this* highly complex "contexture" is precisely that it takes on as it were a *life of its own*. It is "*that* in the relation, *that* the relation relates itself to its own self." The double "that" expresses what I have called the "weightedness" or "inwardness" of the complexure.

However, third, and going beyond[3] Kierkegaard here, reflection forces the recognition that this *reflexivity is embodied*: it is weighted, positioned; the double "that" is a *situated reflexivity. Self is thus precisely that by virtue of which the contexture of temporally flowing mental life and embodying corporeal patterns are oriented, positioned with respect to and in the midst of the environing world. The body as habitus, mental life as inhabiting, and world as home, the inhabited*—these achieve their specific significances thanks to their being *reflexively situated* by the inwardly potent relatedness of the complex contextural self-references. What is true of any contexture—the multiple self-references of the constituents whose totality is that contexture—becomes with the full complexure of human life the potent inwardness of the self-relating itself.

Hence one can now say, *transcendentally*, that the condition by virtue of which I am *able* to reflect on (or: love, desire, hate, be disgusted with, be pleased with, remind, correct, etc.) myself is that self is situated reflexivity. By the same token, I am *able* to be obscured, disguised, lost, deceived: the condition without which these would not be even possible is the same. *Narcissism no less than reflection, self-positing in desire no less than in thinking, therefore, are transcendentally grounded in situated reflexivity.*

GENEALOGY OF SELF

Clearly enough, the reflexivity delineated thus far is hardly the whole story. Ricoeur, Portmann, Jonas, and others are quite right: effort is a fundamental moment of self. But before this can be grasped properly, it is important to attend carefully to how it happens that self at all comes about, how self at all emerges or makes its appearance. Whether, and in what sense, it "appears" as "efforting" (desiring, striving) must be a question decided in the light of how self becomes "apparent" *at all*. Transcendentally, "efforting" is conditioned by "awakening," the genesis of self, as both of these phenomena are conditioned by being situated reflexively. There are a number of moments to this genealogy which must now be made more explicit.

(1) *"Aloneliness" and "Alterity"*

What I seek to understand here, James Agee expressed with masterful simplicity:

> We are talking now of summer evenings in Knoxville, Tennessee in the time that I lived there so successfully disguised to myself as a child. (*1*, p. 11)

There is for every self that by which it is itself and is utterly alone. Subtle, elusive and often disguised, this can only be discovered *to* the self; it can never be chosen nor can it be created. For it is that whereby all choosing and creating are accomplished. The self can and does build screens for itself and before others—masks, fronts, images—but that within the self which accomplishes this is not itself constructed. On this, accordingly, what Ricoeur sees as Freud's "silence" on the self—the "self-positing" in desire—is clearly correct. The question is always: *whose* disguises are they, and thus *who* is behind their making and being lived? It is this, which I shall call "aloneliness"—as distinct from "loneliness," an essentially *social* phenomenon—that must be seized upon here.

Although self is thus an aloneliness and elusive thereby, it is not secret, not an essential hiddenness; for *it seeks to be manifest*, to be a presence, an inwardness seeking to become outwardly revealed. This appears in many and varying modalities, among them what Ricoeur designates as "desire for another desire," whose central moment is the "desire seeking to be 'told' or 'said,' " i.e., desire toward "speech." That whereby the self is itself and alone is experienced by the self as an urgency to be itself in explicitness, ultimately in fullness, as an urge for meaning, clarity, and order (and as dread over their constantly possible distortion, failure, or absence). The self seeks to be this manifestly, to utter overtly and share openly with that within the actual other self whereby he or she, too, is himself or herself, alone, and has an urgency to be with the other, this self.[4]

Inwardly, each self shows itself as a situated reflexivity, habited and inhabiting what is for it "its own" (*sein Eigenes*)—i.e., its own sphere and zone of embodied subjective life. It has, thus, two foundational moments: its own "whereby it is itself and alone," and its urgency to let itself be manifested outwardly, to "ek-sist" in the environing milieu for and along with other selves. As for the former, it is not chosen or decided or created, nor yet simply a product of its milieu and tradition. Neither is it given as already overtly full-bodied and explicitly ready-made at birth. Hence "growth," "maturation," "emergence," "awakening," are *constitutive moments of self*. As regards self, these indicate something other than movement from potency to act, organic increment of abilities and reactions, or a process of assimilation and accommodation. All the latter occur in their own way, but not as regards this foundational moment of self, its emergence. Nothing assures *in advance* that the emergence or growth of self shall or must occur; it is only a possibility for the self. However, it is an essential one. Thus, growth, if it occurs, is an unfolding, a focusing into progressively explicit shape and detail of what is always-already-present but only as implicit, as possible, though not recognized as such. It therefore indicates the happening of self-awakening, of self-recognition (encounter, disclosure, emergence, discovery). That whereby the self is itself and alone is already-present from the outset, but is not already-awakened *to itself*. Nor does the fact of being one's self mean that the maturation of self happens automatically. The organism may develop into adulthood, its physical activities mature and function effectively, even its mental life (its abilities in cognition, perception, etc.) may be efficacious, and still that whereby the self is itself and alone may remain implicit, covert, immature, infantile.

This happening or focusing does not occur, if and when it does, all at once, but rather *in time and slowly*; nor is it something which is "once done, forever done," but is rather an *adventure*, a torturous and precarious task whose outcome is never assured in advance, and whose risks are not given beforehand. The happening of self may be lost, betrayed, ignored, curtailed, ridiculed (by the self no less than by others). Ultimately, only the self in its essential aloneliness and urgency to be itself can "tell"; but it can become so encrusted, hardened, embittered, opaque to itself that even it can no longer "tell" itself its own condition. Its "urge-to-be," its "effort-to-be" itself is an essential openness to all these eventualities. Self may, indeed, become merely a faint memory of itself, a recollection of authenticity no longer possessed, a nostalgia for itself. It may never happen that a self will come into focus for and to itself, as that whereby it is itself. All of these are essentially possible, and indicate the character of this moment of self.

Self is also an urgency *to be itself outwardly*, to reveal itself to other inwardly realized selves, that are alone and urge to be outwardly. This urgency to reveal or show itself—essential to being-self—though most often nested in actual speech, talk, and utterance, need not always be so manifested; for it may appear (and does appear) in gesture, glance, physiognomy, and movement, as well as in speaking. Too, this moment of self may mature or remain naive, curtailed, betrayed, distorted, infantile. Since this is an urgency felt inwardly but before and to the other self, its maturation is intimately bound to the reception given by the other to the self's urgency. Hence the self is not accidentally or contingently, but *essentially* responsive to this reception; this, it will become clearer, is as well *constitutive* for being-self. The self may so reveal itself (at every stage of its emergence) that it brings ridicule to itself (justly or injustly). It may show itself before another (whether the other be the infant's mother, sibling, father, or teacher, friend, colleague, etc., later in life) who is either unable or unwilling to receive it as what it is.[5] In any case, the self's urgency to be itself outwardly (in the world, along with other inwardly alone and urgent selves) may become short-circuited or blunted (as will be seen in greater detail later), and may revert to mere posturing, or to one or another chosen mode of disguise or deception, as well as of pity, concern, or indifference.

The self experiences (but not always with self-cognizant awareness) the urgency to be itself manifestly with others, to be recognized in its inward aloneliness, to be awakened to others (and for them to be awakened to the self), to be *affirmed* and *affirming*, giving and given. It undergoes thus the agony of *singling itself out before others* whose receptiveness (or lack of it) to this showing inevitably has an impact on the self and its maturation, its emergence (in respect of its being itself, and its urgency to reveal itself).

Clearly, then, there is no simple relation between the two foundational moments of self; it is artificial even to speak of them separately. To speak of the ways in which self experiences the other self presupposes already emerged selves, as will be seen later; yet without the essentially reflexive inwardness, the aloneliness of self, there could be no emergence in the first place, there being nothing to strive or make the effort to emerge. Self is an essentially contextural phenomenon, essentially situated and embodied within concretely environing things and other live persons and creatures. Hence explicit self-awakening (self-presence) and explicit alterity (presence-to-other) are always happenings which occur within concrete circumstances. Still, there are several kinds of experiences which seem decisive for the explication of self-presence and presence-to-other-self.

On the one hand, regarding explicit alterity, there is what Alfred Schutz calls the "We-relation" (*109*, II, pp. 159–78; *130*, pp. 71–93). This will have to be studied in depth later; for now, I note only that the sorts of experiences included here vary widely, but their essential meaning is that there is what Schutz calls a "mutual tuning-in" relation. In explicit alterity I and the Other experience one another *and* our "We" (whatever its specific character); each of us experiences the other as "available" (*disponible*) (*74*, pp. 26, 49–50).

Before moving into these experiences—those, as I will call them, following Schutz again, of vivid presence and co-presence—it is important to be as clear as possible about the emergence of self, even though, as I hope to show, this emergence is essentially bound to the presence of the other self. Presupposing this for the moment, there are nevertheless certain critical kinds of experience which uniquely manifest the self's aloneliness to itself, experiences which the self frequently undergoes and which it itself feels to be of decisive significance for itself—its moments of self-encounter, the sudden lucidity of self-awakening. Such experiences are of several kinds, and may happen at various times in the life of self (especially in childhood), but that whereby the self is itself and alone is manifested in each, and each type may therefore be explored for what it reveals of self. One such type is what Herbert Spiegelberg has called the "I-am-me" experience (*114*, pp. 3–21), but there are others. Van Cleve Morris and Clark Moustakas, for instance, write more generally of "the existential moment" wherein self encounters itself as existing and as responsible for itself. "It is," Morris writes, "the abrupt onset, the charged beginning, of awareness of the phenomenon of one's own presence in the world as a person" (*80*, p. 112).[6] Other types of experiences may be delineated—the encounter with one's own being-able-to-die or one's going-to-die; the disclosure that one is alive; the confrontation by self with its own contingency, its own having-been-born without prior knowledge or purpose and without a sense of its having chosen or been chosen; and others—but all of these are manifestations of that whereby the self is itself and alone, and may be designated as experiences of self-awakening.

(2) *Obstacles*

Experiences of self-awakening involve a number of difficult obstacles—not only as regards their examination, but barriers which are intrinsic to the experiences themselves and thus are lived-through by the self. Three in particular need to be emphasized.

Any experience of self-awakening is strangely compelling, not to say intricate and fascinating. Yet at the same time, only in rare instances does the intense immediacy of the experience retain its impact and vividness. And even in such cases the person in question must rely on his recollection of the experience—a circumstance which inevitably introduces the real possibility of distortion, over- or under- interpretation, mistake, etc. For most persons, indeed, however lucid and compelling things seem to be during the course of such an experience (and often all that is recalled is *that* it was felt to be crucial, somehow), the fading of immediacy and the return to the usual frequently includes not only a kind of *bewilderment* and even dubiousness, but also a tendency by self to belittle what happened, to disarm its sting and regard it within the category of the "mere" (as being "merely" one of those things which occur to children, or which happen during moments of reverie to adults). Even when a sense of its significance remains, however, distance and other concerns enter in and further obscure the "what" of the happening.

A second barrier seems more serious. Not only are such experiences felt to be compelling and important, but the self feels compelled to "say" what has happened, to articulate the experience; as Ricoeur put it, the "effort-to-be" seems somehow to want to be "spoken," it tends towards speech. *Yet language resists just this effort.* Seeking to give voice to what is felt to be decisive, to grasp and hold it in words and thereby give it presence and order, and attain an understanding of it, the self finds that the available language for "saying" seems incapable of just this burden. Not only is it difficult to break out into words capable of retaining the true sense of what happened, but when the self does make the effort it encounters the *incongruity* of having to use an already constituted and public language. Thus in the descriptions and reports of these experiences, one commonly finds linguistic devices which must themselves be submitted to careful inspection: underscores, double exclamation points, sentences and phrases written in capital letters, unusual and contrived grammatical structure, and similar devices. Beyond this, when it is a case of children (and childhood is the time when such experiences seem frequently to happen, sometimes never to happen again), there are the obvious difficulties regarding language. Capturing (and one gets the positive sense that for the self in the grips of such an experience, language is itself experienced as a "capturing" or literal seizing upon) such experiences as they occur in childhood does seem possible, but only, it seems, by persons having extraordinary sensitivity to the dimensions and subtleties of childhood.

A third, equally serious, barrier deserves mention. The *effort to "say" is also the effort to "tell,"* i.e., to communicate not only in an already public language, but to tell it to others, to communicate the sense and decisiveness of the experience. And here the self encounters a further incongruity—between one's experience and the context of concerns prevailing in the world of daily life (within which the individual often learns to "keep to oneself" such experiences). Self-concern generally, much less experiences of self-awakening, may typically be taken for granted in daily life as either evidence of immaturity or psychosis, or as sentimentalistic, maudlin, even morbid. Peter Berger's remarks concerning a similar incongruity are apposite here:

There are some cultures in which the metaphysical dimensions of human existence (such as death, evil, passion in all its forms) are recognized and maintained in consciousness. There are others in which these dimensions are suppressed as much as possible. Within western civilization, Spain might be taken as an example of the former—in that respect a polar opposite of America. For, if human existence could be said to have a day side and a night side, then American values strongly emphasize the former against the latter. . . . Such a cultural "way of the middle" (to use a Confucianist term) will attempt to avoid any experiences of ecstasy, that is, any experiences where men may step outside the routine of everyday life and confront the terrors of their condition. This characteristic of our culture is expressed very clearly in our funeral customs. The procedures, terminology, and professional ideology of the mortician's trade in this country all revolve around one fundamental aim—the camouflage of the reality of death. . . . Both passion and evil then become forms of pathology. (3, pp. 47–48)[7]

Experiences of self-awakening, which so characteristically vault the self out of the usual style and mood of daily life, meet precisely this incongruity. But such "day side" thinking about self-concern and its fundamental dimensions has its expression at the philosophical level as well, in the common disrepute into which "subjectivity" has fallen—due in no small part to the very history which initiated this study. Not only must any study of self and self-awakening take note of such difficulties as these, but it must also reckon with the very real ordeals inherent in the effort to articulate the subtle and complex dimensions of subjectivity. Here, indeed, the "discourses of desire" run up against not only the cultural stress on "daytime" thinking, but also, as Ricoeur has rightly stressed, the theoretical "intolerance" toward metaphor and analogy, colloquialism and ironic counterpoint—in short, of verbal equivocity (better: polysemy) and syntactical amphiboly, as theoretical specters to be exorcised.[8]

Such barriers notwithstanding, the study of these experiences and disclosures of self is not only possible but positively necessary for the understanding of what it is to be human. Herbert Spiegelberg's observation on the "I-am-me" experience is to the point:

. . . the phenomenon itself is far from simple and transparent. In fact, the formula "I-am-me" . . . is more than ambiguous. At first sight it appears to be a downright tautology. Yet for anyone who has been in the throes of the original experience the formula expresses anything but a truism. A careful phenomenological investigation of the experience behind the puzzling expression is clearly the primary need; its ontological and metaphysical interpretation will have to wait. (114, p. 20)

Such an analysis must involve a direct inspection of such experiences, an examination which appeals neither to prior theoretical commitments nor to explanatory principles lying outside them and their own intrinsic structures and rhythms. What must in particular be focused upon are the ways in which the self who has gone through such experiences sees itself, what these experiences themselves mean to the self whose experiences they are. Perhaps the best means for this study would be to turn to certain reports of such experiences, some in literary form and some directly autobiographical.[9]

(3) *The Language of Awakening*

The case of C. L.[10] is good to begin with:

> The I-am-me experience first came to me when I was very young, perhaps five or six. I remember that I was standing in an upstairs porch of my parents' house. I was quite suddenly filled with wonder over the fact that I was me. I remember asking my mother, who was in the same room, what made me *me* and not someone else; I'm not sure if she understood, although the reply was such that perhaps she did. Of course, it was a very hard thing to put into words, since it did not come to me in a verbal way, but rather as an overwhelming feeling of wonder. There was really no vocabulary for it. This feeling came to me a number of times during childhood; I became used to it. It would come quite suddenly, for no apparent reason. It is impossible to say how often or when, since they all blend into each other and seem, in a way, outside of time. I wondered what made my body so radically different from everyone else's. How did I wind up inside it? When I think of them even now the same feeling comes over me, but it is nothing in intensity compared to those sudden unexpected moments in my childhood.

Then, Maria Le Hardouin reported the following:[11]

> Several weeks before becoming ill at the age of 5 I was invaded by a strange impression. An odor from the paneling of the staircase, a beam of sunlight heightened by a yellow stained glass pane had immobilized me on the treads as if a hand had touched my shoulder. "I am ME" I murmured to my mother, who was astonished at my disturbance. . . . A voice spoke up distinctly: "Fancy this somebody who feels and who looks—why, this is me."

Duke, in Warren Miller's *The Cool World* reflects:[12]

> Some times back home when I was back home in Harlem I laid there on the beat up sofa with the chitterin springs and I used to think about who am I. But I give it up. It dont get you Know where.
>
> You start figurin out who am I why I am I and why am I here in Harlem—and, Man, they aint no end to it. You end up askin your self whut is the world an whut was the world before it was the world. . . .
>
> Man—you ask why should I be me—how I get to be me—why am I me here and not someplace else—and you just end up scared like you was walking down a empty street at night. So scared it running out you ears. Or you end up thumping out a hymn.

Spiegelberg has recorded his own experiences:[13]

> As far as I can tell, I must have been younger than eight years old when I began having what I now call I-am-me experiences. On such occasions I would tell myself insistently "This is me, me . . . " (or rather in my native German: "Das bin ich, ich . . . "). The

inner pronouncing of these words and especially the repetition of the personal pronoun were accompanied with the feeling of a cave-in, a dropping down from a surface level of self-awareness to a more and more personal me—myself. Along with it went a feeling of being sucked down as by a whirlpool into a bottomless depth. As I repeated the pronoun "me" I felt as if one mask after another fell off until the actor behind these masks was stripped to his naked core. This experience of dissociation from my previous roles went together with a fascinated horror at the inevitable and almost incredible fact that this being in this particular place and at this particular time was really, really me, and that nothing at all could be done about it: "This is deeply serious" ("Dies ist tief ernst") would be phrases that went with the near-terror of the full realization of the inescapableness of this my existence.

There are, as mentioned, other kinds of experiences. Several very revealing types are found in Ray Bradbury's splendid novel, *Dandelion Wine* (8)—the encounter with one's own *being alive*, the undergoing of "the essential impact of life's loneliness," and still others. All these, however, can show us something of the inner textures of reflexivity—the self's being itself and alone—whether a self becomes explicit in such experiences as these, or whether it remains for the most part only implicit, unawakened.

(4) *Self as Wonder*

In such moments as these, that whereby the self is itself, and is alone, appears; it becomes manifest to the self. Something is discovered *to* the self, namely, itself. But what appears, what stands out through such experiences, is precisely "what-I-am": *"I am me-myself!"* Third-person descriptions are most inappropriate. We need to think here, Marcel advises, of the situation in which a child, say, picks up a flower (does a drawing, kicks a ball, etc.), races up to a parent and exclaims, "Look, *I* (i.e., "I myself and no one else") picked these for you!" (*74*, pp. 13–14). This "exclamatory consciousness" of *being alive*, or as William E. Hocking called it, this "hearth-fire" and "passion-filled presence" (*37*, p. 444) is exactly what must be seized upon here.

I am *to* myself. But this expression is elliptical, for what occurs is my *self-presentedness* to myself. I am present to myself, given to myself, but not in a passive manner, for I *participate in my own self-givenness*, and in this sense am not so much "given" as "gift" and "task" (*aufgegeben*)[14] to myself: *I "receive" myself*. The "I-am-me" and related experiences are moments in which I *become phenomenon to myself*; I encounter myself *as and solely as* that whereby I am myself, but in a double sense. On the one hand, I am *discovered to* myself—i.e., I "stand out" to myself singularly. At the same time, this "I-am-me" experience is felt to be profoundly *decisive*—i.e., *what "stands out" is also "outstanding,"* charged with a sense of importance and urgency; "emergence" is often experienced as "emergency." What has happened is not merely unusual but remarkable ("marked out" and hence to-be-taken-note-of) and astonishing. It is me-myself which stands out, and thus it stands out as requiring my notice, my attention; it is not only *able* to be noticed (re-markable), but it *must* be noticed, for I who take note *am* that which *is to be* noted.

This complex phenomenon is peculiar in a unique sense: "I-am-me," that whereby I am myself, utterly, is manifested to me, who am "gifted" to myself *as* that very "whereby." That is, the phenomenon is *reflexive: the self stands out decisively* (is out-standing) *for and to itself*, and this reflexivity *itself* stands out—it is not merely implicit in the experience, as I shall have to say presently.

That whereby the self is itself "stands out decisively"; but there is another dimension as regards both senses of the phenomenon. The self "stands out" to itself, but the experience does not have the sense of "*making* (the self) stand out" or appear. The self suddenly "*happens*" to itself "for no apparent reason," that is, *without having been asked-for or requested*. At least in its initial occurrence, and commonly even in subsequent ones,[15] it is characteristic that these experiences are both *sudden*, or unexpected, and *unrequested* happenings, and just these qualities contribute to the sense of strangeness and decisiveness. The self feels that what happens is authentic precisely because it did not itself bring about its own self; what manifests itself to self without its having had a hand in it seems somehow less liable to error and deception. Indeed, one might venture to say, the "decisiveness" of the dis-closure is that the grip of narcissistic closure seems somehow breached: in a way, self's "giftedness" is a crucial break with "self-love," and hence seems more authentic, less (or not at all) "self-serving," *to the self undergoing the experience*. Yet what happens here, the standing-out of self to itself, is noteworthy, surprising, startling, and thus outstanding or decisive precisely because it is me-myself.

Thus far only a few features of the phenomenon have emerged. The self happens suddenly to itself, it stands before itself as being in need of notice by that self which it is. The self is led to its own discovery. This self-discovery inherent in the phenomenon is, again, unique: it is not a case merely of "finding again what has been lost," nor of "bringing to light what was hidden." The self is at once the discoverer, the discovered, and the discovering, and *it experiences itself as such*. What happens is the unfolding of the self in its reflexive moment. The self, in short, *recognizes itself*. What is disclosed, brought to light, or found, is experienced by the self as "what I am." I recognize me as myself, as having been me all along (although, as is often reported, "I did not notice it before now!").

This *discovery-as-recognition* has several aspects. I am able to "tell" that it is me-myself who has been discovered and disclosed to me (it is me, I realize, and no one else). On the other hand, I experience myself *as what I have been* all along, even though I did not realize this before. I discover myself *as myself* and *as* previously unrecognized (not noticed and now noticed as not hitherto noticed). I happen (stand out decisively) to myself without having asked for this; I am suddenly and unexpectedly put before myself, *gifted to myself* as "what I am" and experience myself as such.

Hence the prevailing mood of such experiences is that of *wonder* or astonishment—a feeling which, in the words of C. L., is "overwhelming." The sudden happening of self to itself astonishes the self. Recognizing itself as such, the self experiences an *astonishment-over* the startling circumstance *that it is* this self in all its richly dimensioned, but barely "tellable," strata and complexity, in all its amazing and inexhaustible sources, features, tendencies, thoughts—some pleasant, likeable and worthwhile, others disagreeable and disgusting, but inescapably inherent to this self. This *astonishment-over* the "what" of that whereby the self is itself, is highly *contextural*: what is experienced is apprehended as at once *clear* and *singular, opaque and multiple, lucid* yet *dense*. The self having the experience is confronted with precisely itself, unmistakably; yet just this is strangely impenetrable, inexpressible. As Duke remarks, "You start figurin out who am I why I am I and why am I here in Harlem—and, Man, they aint no end to it." Again, the self is disclosed to itself as *distinct yet ambiguous*: it is itself and no one else, but it is not clear why this should be so, nor even what this all includes (another common report is the feeling of wonder *over* being this self, out of all the selves one might have been). The self is itself and yet it *overflows* itself; however intimate and familiar, it does not know itself at every moment (much less fully); it surprises, confounds, puzzles, pleases, disgusts, judges itself continually. The self is itself, yet awakens to find itself treating itself as if it were another. The experience of awakening, in short, is a highly stratified and contextural wonder-over that whereby it is itself: clear, lucid, distinct, and singular; yet opaque, confused, ambiguous, and multiple.

Being-in-wonder is not only astonishment-over, but also *astonishment-at*: the self is astonished *at the very happening, that* it could even *happen* ("to *me*, of all people!"). It is astonishing *that I am myself*; it is equally, if not more, astonishing *that I could be astonished in the first place, that I could be myself and not realize it, and then be disclosed to myself as not disclosed to myself before now!* What is so characteristic of the experience, in other words, is that it is not simply a discovery of one affair among others, all at the same level and of the same import, but is *doubly-reflexive* and *stratified*: the reflexive disclosure of the self as itself (astonishment-over) and the reflexive apprehension of that very self-disclosure (astonishment-at). The self is disclosed to itself, but even more radically it reflexively apprehends that reflexive disclosure.[16]

The doubly reflexive astonishment (being-in-wonder) has its ground in a more fundamental contextural feature of the experience. The *self is itself*, and nothing could be less surprising, less obvious or more familiar and accustomed (who else might it be?). But if the self were *only* this, it would not only be incapable of discovering itself, but would be eminently unsurprised by itself. If self were only that, it would not be capable of puzzling, reminding, deceiving, pleasing or disgusting itself—it would, in short, fully coincide with itself and hence be either a total ignorance (total non-reflexivity) or a total knowledge (total reflexivity) with respect to itself. But it is neither, if we are to take seriously the sense such experiences have for the self undergoing them. Indeed, the ground for what happens in self-encounter (the doubly reflexive being-in-wonder) is that it is not only intimately familiar (*heimliche*) with itself but at the same time utterly strange and alien (*unheimliche*) to itself.[17]

This experience, then, is potent and compelling precisely because it is an experience of that whereby the self is itself and alone, utterly, a "whereby" which is disclosed as a *situated* reflexivity. What is discovered is not simply the discovery, but more fundamentally and fully, the doubly reflexive encounter itself—which *is experienced as* that whereby the self is itself and alone.

Just this, I suggested earlier, is what Kierkegaard had come upon when he wrote of the "self-relatedness" of the "relation" between soul and body (and, I want to add, the world). Precisely the same complexity was found, it is not surprising, regarding the embodying organism—if at that point I wanted to underscore the embodying *organism*, it is necessary here to underscore the *embodying* organism. Self, as situated, is embodied; and as doubly, reflexively related to itself, the embodied self stands out as uncannily *itself*, its embodying organism as uncannily *its own*, its environing world as uncannily *its own*.

What constitutes the selfhood of self is this complex, situated, contextural reflexivity. And it is precisely this which stands out decisively in the experiences of self-awakening. These experiences are decisive for the self, for the self is *no longer the same* thereby. The experiences are transforming, and in several ways. The inner move of self is at once a self-locating, an inward spiralling which focuses the self as center,[18] and a progressively insistent contrasting of the self with "everything else." The surrounding milieu is set off from the self and frequently experienced as startlingly lucid. Sometimes only an aspect of an object is thus set off and seen in a strange and new perspective, often fascinating the self; sometimes it is the entire surrounding milieu.[19] Things, and especially one's own body, seem at once strange and new, yet familiar and well-known; not only the self but its surroundings gain depths and textures hitherto unsuspected.

Thus self-encounter is essentially *self-awakening* and *self-transforming*. The experience is "awakening": (1) it "wakens" the self to its milieu in a novel, sometimes shocking way; (2) it "wakens" the self to other selves, as beings able to be similarly awakened (and thus able to be wakened to me: to love, suffer, be alone, and be with me); and (3) the experience "wakens" the self to itself, and not only as being itself and alone, but as inextricably bound to its world, things, others, its own body, in the setting of wonder-over and wonder-at. But this "wakening" may well be only momentary, episodic, thus remembered but faintly, a mere nostalgia; and with the fading of the disclosures, go the fadings of what was "wakened."

Such hints and clues, however, have still not unraveled the phenomenon at its roots. The awakening of self to itself fills the self with awe, reluctance, resistance, anguish.[20] The experience is fascinating, almost hypnotic, yet tends to "get out of hand" and the self feels that it "had better not go any further."

Reluctance and fascination are at the heart of the self's astonishment-at (a vertigo, an inner bafflement of self). It feels as if it were being stripped away, as if its supports were crumbling and its ground collapsing: abyss appears. An early poem by Paul Tillich captures this dimension lucidly:[21]

> Bin ich denn ich,
> wer sagt mir, dass ich's bin?
> Wer sagt mir was ich bin,
> was ich soll werden?
> Was ist des Werdens,
> was des Lebens Sinn?
> Was ist das Sein
> und das Vergehen auf Erden?
> O Abgrund ohne Grund,
> des Wahnsinns finstre Tiefe!
> Ach, dass ich nimmer Dich geschaut
> und Kindlich schliefe!

There is here a kind of actual unfolding of the experience of self-disclosure. Having recognized that "I am I," the self seems struck with astonishment-at its very occurrence: "If I am I, who tells me that I am? Who tells me what I am . . .?" The disclosure of self as at once familiar and strange emerges as an inner dialogue; it is in wonder-over itself and in wonder-at its very being disclosed. But insofar as there is the very question, what I am seems a matter of what I shall, or might, become. But who tells me that? And even if an "answer" were forthcoming, how shall I be able to tell whether it is genuine or not, for me or for another?

What, after all, is Becoming itself? With this, the inward spiral becomes outward. It opens out onto new terrain, immediately becoming more sweeping: what is the meaning, the point, of living or being alive? To ask this, though, opens up the range of the experience even deeper and wider: what is Being (to-be), and what is dying?

Here the experience strikes the fundamental dimension of that whereby the self is itself and alone, utterly: "O abyss, without Ground, obscurest depths of madness!" Viewing this abyss, the final stripping-away of support ("grounds"), the self recoils from its chilling encounter and laments its vision, longing now for the restful sleep of children. The self yearns for "rest," "sleep." To "rest" is to relax or lay back, not to "face" what it has encountered.[22] But to "rest" is as well to lay back on (as: to lay on top of . . .), to be supported by, or to be underpinned; that is, the opposite of "doing something on one's own," "being self-sufficient." The self seeks rest, then, support, something to "ground" itself. But the experience is one in which "groundlessness" or "abyss" is displayed; the yearning for grounds, for reasons (by extension, justice and justification), is exactly the fundamental meaning of this nostalgia. Regarding the experience itself, then, what is discovered is that the reflexiveness of the relation which is that whereby the self is itself and alone (that the relation relates itself to its own self) *is not self-grounding, but is precisely a seeking-for-grounding* (i.e., a radical contingency): the self is a vertigo in quest of grounds in the face of the fundamental lack of grounds displayed in its own self-awakening. It is just this phenomenon which underlies Ricoeur's delineation of "desire," which I suggested must be understood as clearly including a profound "striving-to-know," to know what to reckon with and how, what to hold by: a seeking for "footing," hence the prominence and urgency of "efforting."[23]

This disclosure is "radical:" all "closures" are ultimately efforts by the self to "close" itself, to close the essential rift of self from itself. Not only, then, is there the disclosure of groundlessness, but there is as well the self's own reflexive awareness of itself *as* being confronted with this focal abyss, and wondering-at this disclosure, seeking its own grounding. That whereby self is itself and alone is its own radical open-endedness, its non-coincidence with itself—which is doubly reflexive in the sense indicated. As Tillich put it in his youth, there is this finding of "abyss without ground"; and, as Marcel expressed the other side, to be-human (to be-self) is to be "*en route*," "*en marche*": man is *homo viator* (including in this the dimensions implicit in radical self-awakening), and the formula "*homo rationale*" expresses but *one of the ways* in and through which man "seeks," as self, for grounding.[24]

The experiences of self-awakening reveal the self as the being *whereby what is possible is able to be actualized*—whichever specific mundane possibility is to be made actual by the self, it is precisely the very *task* of self-actualization which the self experiences itself *to be* in its deepest dimensions. Whether there are "grounds" or not, whether or not an underlying potential does essentially justify the self, it is the fundamental project of the self to determine; it "wakens" to this task in the doubly reflexive wonder of self-encounter and self-awakening. This task may even be called the self's ontological vocation (the setting and the being of self). Coming to a decision on such ontological questions is not, however, a proper part of the present study. The ontology of self can come (if at all) only after a more complete phenomenology of self has been accomplished.

It is nevertheless in these terms that "effort" and the other foundational moments of self will have to be comprehended. Now, however, it is possible to appreciate more readily the unique kind of "experience" involved in the encounter with oneself. It is not, it seems to me, an encounter with a sort of radical *neuter*, with an unconsciously broiling sea of radically non-personal urgings and feelings; the non-personal "feels" not at all. It is rather the disclosure of myself in wonder-at and wonder-over. What is awakened in such critical moments is what Marcel calls "*a highly sensitive enclosure*," which cannot properly be termed "self-*love*"; it bears, on the contrary, the burden of anxiety evoked by the groundlessness pouring through the wound of my "I" (*74*, p. 16).

This anguish and wound, discovered *to* me in wonder, is that just because it emerges as, in Ricoeur's term, an *urge-to-be*: to be itself, most profoundly to be recognized *as* "itself" by others, to be authenticated by others whose reception of this "offering" which *I am* (my self) is just as often a cutting and keen denial of my urge-to-be as it is an affirming-receiving. In the critical moments of self-awakening I have tried to mark out here, what appears (what forces itself on the self undergoing the experience) is the radical astonishment: for all the self's "wanting to be," often all the self experiences itself to be is an empty void. Marcel's analysis focuses on the inability of the self to fill the void alone,

> for, still, I can affirm nothing about myself which would be really myself; nothing, either, which would be permanent; nothing which would be secure against criticism and the passage of time. Hence the craving to be confirmed from outside, by another; this paradox, by virtue of which even the most self-centred among us looks to others and only to others for his final investiture. (*74*, p. 16)

It may be that Marcel has exaggerated the situation; it may be that he is describing another level of the critical phenomenon whose roots I am seeking here. Nevertheless, his point about the "craving" must be carefully investigated before it is possible to understand the relating to others that Kierkegaard articulated:

> Such a relation which relates itself to its own self (that is to say, a self) must either have constituted itself or have been constituted by another. . . . Such a derived, constituted, relation is the human self, a relation which relates itself to its own self, and in relating itself to its own self relates itself to another. (*61*, p. 146)

Whether this "other" be transcendent or mundane—a question yet to be posed here—the self-relating is in its very self-relating a relating-to-another: awakened reflexivity. Prior to posing the question of the "other," therefore, this "referencing-to" or "craving" must itself be explicated. It is to this task that I now turn.

8
Self as Effortful Possibilizing

THE emergence of self as desire is an emergence of a "desire for another desire" (Ricoeur), a striving to be acknowledged or affirmed by the other desiring self as autonomous as *me-myself*. Much earlier, Gabriel Marcel made the point that already in the early development of a person there is a positive "urge to make ourselves *recognized*" by another person, whether it be someone who helps or someone who opposes. This other person functions to integrate the self, although how this occurs in each case can vary almost indefinitely (cf. *74*, p. 15).

Thus the reflexive presence emergent within the complexure of life is "fleshed," embodied as a kind of *emphasis* before the other self who is also an embodied, reflexive presence emphasized before the first. This *mutuality*, as I will designate it later, is profoundly constitutive for the self. This was already suggested in the last chapter. There, however, I found it necessary to focus attention first of all on the conditions, for the self, of the very possibility of that mutuality: reflexivity and emergent wonder. As these were explicated, several further conditions appeared on the horizon, the attending to which had to be postponed until the primal conditions were more fully grasped. Now, too, the understanding of mutuality must be further prepared, for the self-emphasis before and along with the other self presupposes not only reflexivity and self-awakening in wonder, but also what I shall call *effortful possibilizing*. I mean: to encounter or meet the other self as also a genuinely reflexive presence involves as conditions both the presence of striving (effort, desire) and the awareness, however minimal, of "other possible" ways of being aware, principally that mode of awareness of self uniquely had by the other—the *Allon*, as Straus calls it:

> In sensory experience, the world is opened to us. As experiencing beings we are related to the Other as the Other. The term "the Other" is used in the broadest sense signifying

earth and sky, inanimate and living things, man and animal. . . . Whenever I consider an object, I find myself confronted with something else—the Allon—that exists apart from me. I may leave it to itself and return to it, see it again. Nevertheless, this something, characterized as being-not-me, presents itself to me. . . . That something is at the same time mine and not mine, so that I can establish a relationship with the Allon and yet leave it as it is. . . . (*117*, p. 279)

Unlike sensory stimuli, which are incorporated within the own body, the Allon can at once be witnessed as it is, and left as it is to its own integrity. How is it that there can be this "leaving it as it is"? Constitutive of authentic mutuality, this essential tension itself has its constitutive conditions which must now be explicated: effort and possibilizing.

MOTION AND EMOTION: THE SENTIENT SELF

By means of embodiment, the flow of temporal phases becomes fleshed, achieves presence, lift and heft. *The "now" is my bodily "here"*—the ambiguity of "presence" is no accident. Straus writes:

> As an experiencing being, I am at the center of my environment. My position here and now is the hub of my spatiotemporal orientation. The actual moment, my now, is the divide between future and past. Future and past are personal tenses of time that are always related to the present of an experiencing being. From this center, the surroundings are opened to me as a field of action and observation. (*117*, p. 212)

But my embodiment, as was seen, is essentially actional, a *proprius motum*: "self"-moving and feeling, hence orienting and organizing of the environing milieu. Thus time and space become corporeally presenced through the motility of the embodying organism. Herewith, Jonas emphasizes, emerge the crucial connections between motility, sentience and emotion:

> Locomotion is toward or away from an object, i.e., pursuit or flight. A protracted pursuit . . . bespeaks not only developed motor and sensor faculties but also distinct powers of emotion. . . . The appearance of directed long-range motility (as exhibited by the vertebrates) thus signifies the emergence of emotional life . . . [but] it is motility which makes the difference [between sheer maintaining of metabolism and genuine appetition]: it consists in the interposition of *distance* between urge and attainment, i.e., in the possibility of a distant goal. Its apprehension requires distant perception: thus development of sentience is involved. Its attainment requires controlled locomotion: thus development of motility is involved. But to experience the distantly perceived *as* a goal and to keep its goal quality alive, so as to carry the motion over the necessary span of effort and time, desire is required. Fulfillment not yet at hand is the essential condition of desire, and deferred fulfillment is what desire in turn makes possible. Thus desire represents the time-aspect of the same situation of which perception represents the space-aspect. (*55*, p. 101)

Just these central correlations—what I now term *contextural* references—are manifested in the sensori-motor stages of childhood, as Piaget has meticulously demonstrated (*89*). What Portmann terms "appetence" [*Appetenz*]—to make clear the tie between appetite and appeasement—is, he suggests, that peculiar "state of expectancy" which is able to be detected so markedly in animal life thanks to "discoveries in our own inwardness" (*91*, p. 348). This *motively articulated appetence is the fundamental presencing of time and space, requiring effort, thus emoting—desire and sentience*. Richard Griffith's evocative terms make this clear:

> Through motion, place is placed in *space*.
> In transiting from place to place I pick up space-and-time, hitchhikers. Start to move and they appear from nowhere, I could not travel without them. Space and time co-sprout from motion. Space and time, so different, are in some way the same, at least in source—Anthropodology would say so. There are con-structive constructs. Another way to view it: from *my* motion from place to place—*via the simple footstep*—from motion, I fractionate space as stable timelessness, and time as moving spacelessness; then forget in my high-flown intellect that it is *body*, me, who is walking. How could we put a foot on such things as these? How *far* it is is how long it takes to get there; how *long* it's been is how far I've come to get here. (*29*, p. 289)

As embodied contexturally, space gets mobilized, too, put in motion with "heres," "theres," "way beyonds," and "yonders": *lived spatiality places time*. And, time, fleshed corporeally in kinaesthetic patterns and flows, requires a *heft and placement*, a habitus localized: *temporality gives flow to space*. The measuring of distances by "how long," the counting of time-spans by "how far," these are no inventions of modern, technologized culture but *concrete entanglements* of every moment and placing of the embodied self.

To carry out the seeking of distant things—whether distant from my hand, or from my corporeal place—motion is requisite, and for that desire and sentience: effort and feeling/striving. There is no desire without this sentient directing-to-something felt as "goal." Thus the presencing of temporality and the placing of spatiality are manifested in effortful sentience.

But this is only a part of the story. For, as Straus insists, to "feel" oneself as mobile is to "view the objects in my surroundings as alterable, contingent on a shift from an actual condition to one anticipated in imagination." In this, he continues, "the actual situation is but a limitation of possibilities. The goal to be reached thereafter, the possibilities to be realized, inhabit the present potentially" (*117*, p. 212). More generally, Straus elsewhere suggests the series of connections at issue here:

> Experiencing is synonymous with experiencing-the-world and with experiencing-oneself-in-the-world. . . . Experience is of the I-world relation. This relation, which is not a compound of two parts—I and the world—but exists only as a whole, cannot

be translated into or replaced by the sequence "stimulus and response." Experiencing beings do not merely occur. In sleep—or to be more correct, in coma—they resemble inanimate things, which are simply present or at hand. Experiencing beings, while awake, always find themselves in a situation. . . . Therefore, a motor element must be inherent in experience: directions to or fro, attraction or repulsion, attack or retreat. The fundamental functions delineate the possible situations. (*117*, p. 247)[1]

What was said earlier on contexture and the complexure of life, however, makes Straus' point far more exact: there is here not "a compound" but a "whole," that is, there is here a complexure which is precisely the system of complex referencings and self-referencings (reflexivity) situated within and displayed by the contextures of mental life, embodying organism, and environing world.

Now, however, we come across, again and again, two further component dimensions of the sense of self: effort (desire, striving), and the situatedness within the actual which yet harbors the possible. The former stands out more clearly than the latter, though; I must, then, after pulling out the significance of "effort," dwell more carefully on the latter.

EFFORTING

As was found so often before, such matters as concern me in this study are so deeply familiar that they are thereby devilishly difficult to fasten onto; their very familiarity breeds a unique forgetfulness—which Schutz studied so profoundly as "taken for grantedness" (*109*, I, pp. 3–47; *111*). My efforts to make "effort" thematic, to see it as problematical, are inhibited, rendered trivial almost by that incredibly potent device of daily life: "of course" and its invariable accompaniment, "so what!" It is because of this by no means trivial fact that it is useful, perhaps even necessary, to begin at those points where the "usual" breaks down; "the observation of failures," Straus remarks, as has Goldstein, "makes us wonder about the normal performance" (*117*, p. 260). We need not turn to the kinds of "failures" with which medicine, generally, is concerned; one could as well note even the more modest breaks, upsets, disturbances and interruptions in the usual course of any life—which, though commonly taken as usually smooth, is to the contrary riddled and textured by just such as these.

Still, illness, impairment, and injury are special cases of circumstances which block one's usual path, call out for attention to be brought to bear upon the situation, one's prospects, and the like, and are thus uniquely illustrative of what otherwise seems so quickly forgotten or taken for granted. In illness, whether it be a mild case of influenza or a more seriously incapacitating pneumonia, one's *bodily enactment* fails. It becomes, as is said, "an effort" even to get up, to go about the daily round of chores; "chores," indeed, become *chores*—wearying, toilsome, burdensome, however needful. Or to take another case, the man with angina tries to climb the stairs, yet his dull substernal pain prevents him. He is forced to rest. His project of climbing to the top of the stairs for the time is arrested, and the stairs themselves assume a very different coloration and aspect from what they were when he could run up the whole flight. Strictly correlated to the bodily alterations are other contexturally-referenced modifications in the modes and sorts of "strivings" and "desirings" as well as in the aspects of the environing world. Wishes not wished before bubble up; the stairs now "loom" over him as "forbidding." The man thus has his usual train of thoughts interrupted and replaced, as Heberden says, with "a sense of strangling and anxiety" (*33*, p. 293). Angina is thus not for the man an external force, nor even just an internal event within the neurophysiology of his body, but a significant (contexturally referential) constituent of the complexure of his life, within which and with a constant view to which he defines himself.

When he first developed angina, what had hitherto *not* been called into focus and question now is, with a vengeance. Stairs take on their new proportion; new desires, feelings, emotions, aims, crop up; what was a lark becomes a troubling burden. New things become relevant—e.g., having an elevator installed in his house, walking up only so many steps at a time or at a certain pace, placing a nitroglycerin tablet sublingually, etc. Illness, injury, and the like call into question components of the complexure hitherto present only as taken for granted and passed over in silence. Indeed, what gives such examples their peculiarly dramatic force—the hush, anxiety, and awe engendered when the "normal" person encounters the ailing or the maimed—is precisely that illness and impairment affect us directly in what seems our unique humanity, our selfhood: our autonomy in choosing and deciding, our wanting to be free from critical dependency on others (often utter strangers), our sense of ourselves in our own "urge to be."

Forced to undergo sometimes severe modifications and redirections, the self is obliged to maintain itself *differently*, and always with *effort*. The self as a contextural achievement is thus always *precarious*: a hazard and a risk having to be secured in the face of always impinging threat, whether trivial or serious, noticed or not. This precariousness is suggestively elicited, too, in cases of illness or impairment: consider only what must transpire for the quadriplegic and his radically truncated embodiment; or, for that matter, the commonplace weakness and strain attendant to a cold. In each of these the crucial phenomenon is educed here: the effort to maintain self, which gets called out uniquely by the hindrances of life, evoked by illness and injury which re-define, re-delimit, and curtail the sense of self—which at the same time calls attention precisely to this sense of self.

In such times, of course, the efforting and emphasizing of self tends to be suppressed, subdued. As Plügge points out, considering a mortally ill or wounded person,

> across the appearance presented by such a patient lies a peculiar stillness, often in fact an apparent lifelessness. His skin shows folds, is dull, and lacks luster. Play of gesture

and expression, all live bodily orientations outward have become sparse, often even extinguished. These patients question less and less; the intentional character of all healthy live bodiness is on the wane. Just as they withdraw from their own living and live human body, they withdraw too from their world. . . . With this not merely does their world fade but their live bodiness becomes husk. Voice and echo become softer and softer. (*90*, p. 297)

With this waning, the suffusion of stillness gradually replaces the unique vividness, the quickening and animating liveliness so characteristic of the fully efforting (thus apparently so effortless!) self.

Hence to *witness* this fading and slow dulling is in a way—as Ramsey remarked even of the cadaver—to be alerted to what is otherwise so prominent in the alive, efforting self: its buoyancy and presence. By means of its suppression we are brought to notice that "something is wrong"—whether it be a mother concerned for the subtly manifested listlessness of her child, or a physician noting the lackluster "look" or the sluggish "feel" of a patient. *The very absence of effort marks out its essential character for being-self.*

But what is subdued by injury or illness is on the other hand markedly salient in the context of upsets or disturbances in the life of the healthy person. It can readily be seen that having this effortfulness elicited explicitly helps to seize it more clearly. Every situation of disturbance is an upset in the balanced system of contextural references which is the complexure of life. Whichever example one chooses, certain common features stand out. Suppose an interruption in the usual course of affairs occurs; something crops up as an obstacle (a *problēma*), i.e., an impasse, in view of which I am obliged to pay attention, become alert. I can no longer, at least for the time being, simply proceed in the usual way. I must "stop and think": "stop" doing what I had been doing, and "think" to see if I can somehow get out of the difficulty, solve the impasse, settle the upset, and once again return to the daily routine.

This allows others things to become salient: such upsets have special ways of *referring*. Suppose I am in a traffic jam, anxious to be on my way. (1) The traffic jam refers *to me*: *I* am obliged to "do something," for *I* am blocked. (2) It refers more specifically to *my prevailing concerns*, to "what I am doing" and "where I am going," and is more or less serious in view of these (going to the hospital, taking an idle stroll or drive, going to work, etc.). In one or another way, my "way" is blocked and this will be "bothersome," a "damned nuisance," or an "urgent crisis." As well (3), the upset includes multiple references to the *concrete circumstances*: other cars, pedestrians, streets at hand, time of day, mores and codes of driving, laws, etc.; and still further references to the surrounding world of city life, to "the times we live in," the world at large—everything going to constitute this scene as that which it is, each with its own functional weight.

Obviously, these multiple referrals mutually determine and delimit each other and "what can be done": what I am here and now ("busy," "late," "irritated," etc.), what my concerns are ("going to work," "idly driving," etc.), and the textures of the scene itself ("heavily trafficked," "real jam," etc.) At the same time, other persons are ingredient to the scene and cross-referenced and referencing in complex but explicable ways. Clearly, too, in obvious as well as subtle ways I must reckon with these sometimes conflicting networks (someone else may also "be in a hurry," and block "my way out"; I must be on the alert for a pedestrian; etc.).

Thus what I do at the time is functionally co-determined and reciprocally significant with reference to the actual circumstances, to the where and when of the upset, to others present there, to what I have been accustomed to doing before, to what I now want or need to do, etc. Hence *being-in-a-situation is essentially being-contexturally-placed*. Whatever I do, whatever occurs there, whatever is done to me directly or indirectly, all these are constituents of this context, and have their own determinable significance and weight. In every case, there is a contexturally defined and delimited range of possible actions which I and others can do.

Another feature thus appears: the occurring of the upset *solicits attention. I am alerted, called on to "think and do."* Within the determinable range of variations, I must at once cease doing what I was doing and do something else: *effort* is called forth by the upset. To be capable (transcendentally) of "being interrupted" or "being upset" (whether by traffic jams or bodily impairments) signifies a *kind of alertness, a being-solicited into focal attending and tending to some obstacle* (in a broad sense), hence an *effortful seeking to note and resolve it*. For this, as was already seen, self must be the situated reflexivity noted. We can as well note that self is "awakened," "explicited" by the disturbing circumstances. To "put an effort into" is in the first instance to be reflexively awakened, alerted, called forth as "having (needing) to do . . . ." Such awakened effort, of course, evokes modes of bodily enactment (in the traffic jam no less than in affliction). Hence the self is contexturally bound up with bodily movements, postures, gestures, attitudes, actions, and sensory fields whereby something is experienced.

What becomes prominent in this reflexively awakened effort is, moreover, that the emergence of self is deeply textured by a *sense of import*, a concern for "having" to regain its poise or what Goldstein calls "equalization"—i.e., that "relative constancy" by which changes are "equalized" with other bodily components and, as he stresses, with the milieu (*27*, p. 72). Again, cases of illness and injury uniquely mark out this critical correlation between the time of effort (reestablishing equalization) and alterations or disturbances due to the affliction. "In place of a circumscribed response—corresponding to the circumscribed stimulus—we note a more extensive and diffused response" (*27*, p. 86). Within the grips of a disturbance, self is charged with a kind of diffused, globally presenced emphasis or exigency—which may well be manifested by frustration, fidgeting, or by a variety of anxious gestures, as well as by more normal action designed to resolve the difficulty. Effort thus involves a kind of alertness, and this in turn is manifested as striving, desiring, preferring, decisioning, acting. The disturbing situation solicits, calls out that which is self: alertful effort and striving, a concern for settling the now unsettled.

Self's emergence, then, is a pronounced effort, in no way simply as a sort of "in-itself" (as a "desire-qua-desire," in Ricoeur's usage), but always as an alertful attending and tending-to, in contextures of disturbance and upset, hence as a kind of *care* or *needfulness*. In other words, the efforting is always *concretely* contextural and focused on regaining its *self*, re-equalizing its *self*: for it *is* precisely that weighted self-referentiality. Self is fundamentally a situated or positioned reflexivity oriented towards the environing milieu, which is itself displayed and arranged strictly in complex reference to this reflexively oriented habitus. As such, disturbances to *any* constituent of the complexure of necessity have the significance (intrinsic self-reference) of being an upset to and in the self. Whether something appears in the field discordant with expectations, or a bodily process undergoes changes and may thus fail to embody, or the noetic flow (mental life) alters and finds no adequate enactments in bodily schemata—the prevailing equilibrium is upset. *With this modification in the constitutive reflexive orientations of the complexure, there is a consequent alertness which is provoked, which emerges as "effort" to reestablish the contextural balance of situated reflexivity—i.e., "self" is alerted to itself and "strives" to maintain or*, as the case may be, *"find" itself.* Self is thus of necessity *an alertness which strives: "effort."*

This, it seems to me, is exactly what Jonas means:

> Motile existence is fitful and anxious. . . . [But] if mere assurance of permanence were the point that mattered, life should not have started out in the first place. It is essentially precarious and corruptible being, an adventure in mortality, and in no possible form as assured of enduring as an inorganic body can be. Not duration as such, but "duration of what?" is the question. This is to say that such "means" of survival as perception and emotion are never to be judged as means merely, but also as qualities of the life to be preserved and therefore as aspects of the end. It is one of the paradoxes of life that it employs means which modify the end and themselves become part of it. The feeling animal strives to preserve itself as a feeling, not just as a metabolizing entity, i.e., it strives to continue the very activity of feeling: the perceiving animal strives to preserve itself as a perceiving entity. . . . (*55*, p. 106)

And, it is necessary to add, the "entity" here is no *entity* at all, but rather the contextural, reflexively situated self striving to maintain itself *as such: therefore* the critical and dramatic character of cases where that is breached, in illness, injury, or the many ways of psychical threat and disturbance, as well as the myriads of daily upsets. And therefore, too, the continuous presence of effort is necessary to the "fitful and anxious" nature of embodied life. Indeed, as was said earlier, embodying matter *matters* to the embodied self, and it is this sense of *import* which is displayed in every efforting. Were there none such, there would be no self; *self is what "matters,"* within its mattering body turned always to the Allon.

GOLDSTEIN'S CONCEPT OF "ABSTRACT ATTITUDE"

We are always "in an actual situation," and as Straus said, this actual situation "is but a limitation of possibilities . . . to be realized, [and which] inhabit the present potentially" (*117*, p. 212). How is this to be understood? It has been noted that self is essentially a "craving for the Other," and both Marcel and Ricoeur remark the way the desiring self is a desiring for the Other's desire to affirm the self and thus authenticate it. Yet, Straus insists, genuinely to relate to the Allon—especially, it seems to me, when the Allon is the other *self*—requires a being-able to "leave it as it is" while yet, precisely, *relating* to it "as it is," whether as witness, helper, rival, or adversary. Effort, it is clear, is requisite for self to be self; but how is it possible at all to establish that crucial mutuality-relation, or what Schutz calls the "Thou-orientation" (*Du-Einstellung*)? (*111*, pp. 61–63). More generally, whatever may be the concreteness of the Allon, the "relating-to-it" (or "to-thou") is *necessarily conditioned by a constitutive moment of self*, thanks to which something "other" can at all "appear" in the first place: what I shall call "possibilizing," a phenomenon hinted at by Husserl's concepts of "analogical pairing" (*Paarung*) and "associative sense transfer" (*41*, V). I do not intend to take up his attempt to explicate intersubjectivity here, for this is not the proper context. I want merely to note what seems to me a kind of *Ungedachte* in his analysis, a moment intrinsic to the self and presupposed by the mutuality of selves. To get at this critical phenomenon, I propose again to proceed, first, by way of observing prominent failures, and then to find cases of its clear presence.

I have already cited Kurt Goldstein's lifelong studies of and work with brain-injured patients. Recognizing the genuine variations among them, due to specific injury, circumstance, past history, native abilities, and the like, still he came to the conclusion that the structural disintegration—what he prefers to call "dedifferentiation"—of systemic neurological functioning invariably involves an impairment of the "abstract attitude." As opposed to the "concrete attitude," within which "we are given over passively and bound to the immediate experience of unique objects or situations" (*28*, p. 6), the abstract attitude, Goldstein maintains, is basic for the following abilities:

1. Assuming a mental set voluntarily, taking initiative, even beginning a performance on demand.
2. Shifting voluntarily from one aspect of a situation to another, making a choice.
3. Keeping in mind simultaneously various aspects of a situation; reacting to two stimuli which do not belong intrinsically together.

4. Grasping the essential of a given whole, breaking up a given whole into parts, isolating them voluntarily, and combining them to wholes.
5. Abstracting common properties, planning ahead ideationally, assuming an attitude toward the "merely possible," and thinking or performing symbolically.
6. Detaching the ego from the outer world. (*28*, p. 6)

Not only is it the case, Goldstein notes, that there are various degrees of the abstract attitude, as of the concrete attitude, but it is also clearly the case that what is clustered under the former is quite a variety of abilities. Indeed, an impairment in this attitude has an impact even on the *concrete* one: normally fluid and accomplished with relative ease, concrete activities now "show a more *passive, compulsive character; they are more stereotyped and rigid*" (*28*, p. 7).

Goldstein notes, for example, that a patient suffering from central motor aphasia displayed, after careful examination and observation, apparently perfectly normal performances in many instances, yet in others markedly different behavior. If a particular request was made in a concrete situation, he was able to perform well, although slowly and sometimes with difficulty. Though he was able to some extent to carry on a conversation, if asked for a specific word whose usage was not particularly demanded within the concrete situation, he failed totally—but if the word was a natural part of the actual situation, it was used with no difficulty. Thus careful examination revealed that "he *was disturbed when the execution of a performance demanded the abstract attitude*, while he might perform well if it could be done in a concrete way" (*28*, p. 209). He spoke spontaneously very little; he could not recite series on demand, and was unable to say any of them backwards (e.g., 1 to 10, 10 to 1); he had great difficulty when asked to name objects; he could do simple repetitions only with similar difficulty; though he moved his lips when reading, he was often unable to read the same passage aloud; he did not write anything spontaneously; he understood simple stories if they involved words and actions within his concrete "reach," but not otherwise; he had difficulty recalling affairs unrelated to present, actual conditions; his attentive span was variable and often weak, easily distracted; he had no idea what spatial directions meant, and similarly regarding time; and he showed a striking absence of emotive expression except in concretely demanding situations, as well as a lack of interest in other people, even in immediate family and friends (*28*, pp. 209–15).

Given a series of tests, such patients (always taking into account, of course, the variations among them) typically reveal certain invariant behaviors. For instance, whether it be a Color Form Sorting Test, an Object Sorting Test, or the Stick Test, it becomes clear that brain-injured patients, to one degree or another, are unable to collect and sort in ways demanding conceptual, imaginative, or abstract principles. Objects may be grouped by the patient, for instance, according to color in which congruent colors cohere and obtrude; but if asked to sort out the objects in a *different* way, he is unable to shift to, say, those shaped alike. Only if the examiner places chips of the same color in front of him will there be a chance for the patient to collect according to congruent and obtruding shapes, but if the same chips are turned over to show their differently colored sides, the patient cannot sort out the shapes as he had just moments before done (*28*, pp. 170–71; see also 154–69). Goldstein refers to cases in which a person sorts out things according to immediately congruent characters (color, shape; or, use, pairs, material of which they are composed, etc.) as a functioning within the concrete attitude. But such cases "can be considered as pathologic only if the subject proves unable to *shift voluntarily* within the concrete realm and from that to a conceptual frame of reference" (*28*, p. 175). Hence he emphasizes that it is this *shifting* which is crucial for these tests, which is the telling point regarding the impairment of the "abstract attitude"—as regards not only language and abilities to collect and sort, but also bodily gestures and emotive expressions (*28*, pp. 57–59, 74, 136–37, 212, 214). In all of these patients, finally, one observes a fascinating variety of ways by which "the basic motive of organismic life" is accomplished—through modified performances, opening up of different pathways, and retraining. That principle Goldstein identifies as "the *trend of the organism to actualize itself*, its 'nature,' its capacities, *as well as possible*." In these terms, "*pathologic behavior is behavior of functions of parts of the organism isolated from the whole*" (*28*, pp. 19–20). A breach in any of the contextural constituents of the complexure of life, more generally, is thus the basic meaning of pathology.

POSSIBILIZING

What has become salient here by its very absence or impairment is the "abstract attitude," and the basic motif of embodied life: viz., its tendency to maintain itself in the best possible way. However, it seems to me that Goldstein includes far too much under the "abstract attitude"; by including so many different abilities, the concept becomes unnecessarily loose, unwieldy. This is not in the least to fault his observations, nor even to deny that these abilities are indeed clearly impaired to one or another degree in the patients he has clinically studied, tested, and treated.

I rather want to suggest that these cases exhibit a far more critical and specific "ability" (a "being-able-to . . . "), one which underlies those he includes within the "abstract attitude." Equivalently, whether it be a question of voluntary shifting, building wholes or delineating parts, etc., the "abstract attitude" itself involves and is grounded on a more fundamental phenomenon.

This may be illustrated with any of the cases he presents. For instance, one patient showed that only one way of collecting objects was "natural," namely that in which these things could be used in an immediately practical way in the actual situation of testing or action; other modes of sorting were not possible, even those regarding use in other situations not presently at hand. Thus she could not shift from one to another pattern of sorting and collecting (not even the making of "heaps" of colors) (*28*, pp. 266–69). At every point in the testing, what proved to be impossible (or extraordinarily difficult) was, negatively expressed, the patient's *inability to disentangle herself from* the concretely demanding situation. Or, in different terms, the patient exhibited a conspicuous *inability to "realize"* (i.e., "make-real-for-herself") *any situation other than the actual one*—namely, one within which *different* ways of sorting *might* be called for.

If, in other words, one focuses carefully on these "concrete" behaviors, what is so striking about them is that the patient (to one degree or another) seems *more claimed by* the situation demanding them than he is able to *make claims on* the situation, varying the objects at hand "at will." Such patients seem *singularly unable to feign, to simulate affairs other than what lies actually at hand.* "Nothing was more illuminating than the wardrobes of these men and the meticulous way in which the innumerable odds and ends, the accumulation of ten years' residence, were always disposed. Everything had its appointed place, and, moreover, had to occupy that place in a very definite way" (*28*, p. 14). With this, Goldstein regularly observed an inability to handle new situations, in certain cases leading to catastrophic results for the patients: severe anxiety, disordered behavior, even complete self–exclusion from the world and loss of consciousness (*28*, pp. 11–12).

As Goldstein remarks, a patient of this type

> may be able to orient himself in a complicated building which has become familiar to him but cannot say anything about even the simplest relations of rooms or floors to each other. He has the greatest difficulty in pretending. He fails on performances which are meaningful only with relation to future expectations or occurrences. If the patient . . . acquires certain materials by rote-learning, these new acquisitions lack stability. Only repeated experience of the usefulness of these connections in concrete situations will stabilize them. (*28*, p. 8)

Having now given a rather full description of the behaviors and abilities of such patients, the point toward which I am driving becomes quite plain. As thus (more or less) locked into the immediate zone of actuality, captured and claimed by the here and now of demanding action, such patients alert us forcefully to the manifest difference, the conspicuous absence of the *core form of human freedom: being able to free-oneself-from the actual, and thus being able to free-oneself-for the possibly-otherwise.* For such patients, it is no longer true (or, only with the greatest difficulty is it true) that the possibilities of action, the sentience for goals, inhabit the present as potentialities, for they no longer are able to "realize" or think what is *possible*, what is other than the actual, or move to the "*possibly-otherwise.*" In short, such patients are fundamentally impaired in respect of the essential ability to *possibilize*, and *because of that* exhibit the prominent inability "to abstract" in the modes Goldstein delineates.

Being thus impaired—unable to "take initiative," to "choose voluntarily," to "keep multiple aspects in mind simultaneously," to "grasp wholes" or "break them into parts" or "compose new wholes," to "plan ahead," and thus to "detach themselves from the world"—such patients are affected in what precisely constitutes a core moment of their humanity, their essential *sense of self*. Just this, it should be stressed, constitutes at once the drama and the tragedy of all illness, injury, or defect: that these focally impact the very texture of self, disrupting the precariously balanced reflexive presencing of the complexure of the human life affected. For this reason, too, do such impairments *of themselves* present the observer (whether friend or physician, family or relative stranger) with a sense of *import, a sensitivity toward damaged selfhood; impairment solicits alertness, sentience to "worth" or "import" in and with the affected other*. Thus one *ground for ethics in medicine* is found in the embodiment of self confronting the impaired other self.

The phenomenon of possibilizing stands out clearly in other ways, ways which are helpful for eliciting it more fully. Suppose we consider again the example used earlier, coming up against a traffic jam. As already emphasized, this, as every other situation, is contextural; hence in any of its many variations, the specific case is one constituted by and as a system of mutually referring constituents, each of which receives its particular significance, weight, and placement by reference to every other one. Thus the range of available courses of action a person may take—getting out of the car, honking the horn, turning left or right, swearing, etc.—are possibilities having their strict placement within and delimited by the prevailing network of intrinsic references. Other possibilities—swimming, playing tennis, typing, sleeping, etc.—are not at hand just because the complexure in question does not permit them (principle of good continuation and appropriateness), or makes them more or less likely or unlikely—e.g., reading the newspaper, smoking, talking.

Suppose the situation is one in which I am late to work—hence I "need" to get through the snarl of cars. The interruption, then, is one which, commonly enough, is "irritating," possibly even "exasperating." What occurs, as was noted, is the experience of "being blocked." Confronting the scene as a frustrating obstacle, what is on other occasions not noticed (or noticed only marginally) now specifically calls attention to itself. I am forced to *cease* doing what I was more or less automatically doing (driving along in the usual, habitual ways), and now to do something else: I must "stop and think." What is this "thinking"? •

It is necessary to review the special ways of referring such scenes as this have. Something "blocks *my* path" solely inasmuch as it calls, not just for attention, but for *my* attention: *I* must be "on the alert." So long as I "want" or "need" to continue on my way, the blockage refers to me, who must go that way. If I decide it is not worth the effort, obviously, the complexure has critically altered; hence the blockage refers to *my prevailing course of action and plans*. The problematic situation thus has a kind of *dramatic force*: it crops up in my life as an interruption in "what I need to do," and thus has the force (so long as I continue to maintain my plans) of *calling for resolution*.

I can no longer simply do what I was doing. I am called on to *assess* whether I should, and if so how I can, continue. The scene has the force of *making me call into question* what I have not been questioning up to now. Obviously, I shall do so only to the extent necessary to allow me to be on my way again. I may, for example, find an opening in the traffic, turn off the crowded avenue to a side-street, and be off: I shall have "thought" only so far as necessary.

Even so, this "thinking," this "being alerted," etc., even when momentary, exhibits the characteristics indicated: the referrals, the dramatic force, the calling into question in order to seek resolution. Clearly, too, the more "serious" the obstacle, the more of an impasse it presents; and the more it is needful for me to get through or beyond it, the more radical is the force of the scene and the more deeply am I obliged to seek in order to reestablish ultimately my very self, my life, my "who I am."

Viewed somewhat differently, even such common upsets, however episodic and momentary they may be, show a *common structure*. In the nature of the case, I *cannot ignore* the actually present situation: indeed, the occurrence of interruption is precisely the necessity *to become alerted to it as such*. I literally am "in" it, I "live" it; yet to be able to be alerted to the actually present scene requires at the same time that I "keep it at a distance." Only thereby is it possible to be aware of it, to assess it, much less to resolve it. I must keep it actually before me in order for me to get beyond it: the upset is thus an essentially *dramatic tension* requiring effortful "thinking."

It is noteworthy here that it is just this dramatic tension which produces the catastrophic anxiety in the patients Goldstein studied. Those tasks which are performable only with great difficulty, or not at all, produce distress and thereby sometimes make medical examination, much less efforts to help them, impossible or exceedingly difficult. Hence Goldstein's strong advice: where the pathology cannot be removed, the physician's task must be

> to *secure the best possible milieu for the patient and to decide how much of his defect a patient may be able to bear without being too much disturbed in general.* . . . This result is of *greatest significance for any examination.* The more we take it into consideration, i.e., the more we avoid the entrance of distress, the longer we are able to examine a patient in one session and thus to reveal the modifications of his behavior due to his damage. (*28*, pp. 16, 18)

Just this "distress," which is closely correlated with the fatigue observed in patients confronting such difficult or impossible tasks, is on the other hand the sense of urgency which is prominent in the common experience of interruptions. But, unlike the situation with pathological patients, who "perseverate" (i.e., utilize any means at hand to void and avoid such situations), in normal life the complex act of distancing-while-remaining-within the unsettling situation is clearly manifested. This act is a kind of *de-actualizing*: i.e., *I "look for other ways out"* of it. This "thinking-for-the-possibly-otherwise," then, is a sort of *freeing-from* and *freeing-for:from* what is actually at hand as an obstacle demanding alertness, and *for* what might otherwise be realized. It thus intrinsically involves the *reflexive apprehension of self* (as "blocked") and the *effortful feigning* or simulating of self (as "otherwise," i.e., "no longer blocked"). The complex "freeing" (being-able, that is) is thus a freeing-for the possibly-otherwise ("alternatives"), *strictly within the prevailing, concrete, and actually confronted situation.*

Depending on one's own ingenuity and inventiveness, on what is appropriately (i.e., contexturally) at hand within the given complexure, and on possible available "futures" to it, one will have at hand a greater or lesser number of alternatives ("possibly-otherwise") to draw on. The "thinking" is therefore a seeking within the limits at hand for ways to resolve the interruption—to rearrange the deranged course of affairs, to settle the unsettled—in light of the "possibles" de-actualizably at hand. The act here, then, is *a leap into the "as-if"* ("other possible ways"), but a leap which is concretely, contexturally bound to the interruptive situation. The "actual" is pregnant with the "possible," but solely on the grounds of this act of *circumstantial possibilizing (a de-actualizing in order to actualize another possible than the actual).*

It can now be noticed that there can on principle be no apprehension of what is actual *as actual without thereby its being apprehended as one among other possibles* (which either could have been actual or might become actual if so chosen, and if circumstances permit). Circumstantial possibilizing is essential to the being of self; correlatively, so far as it is essential to contextures, and beyond that to the qualitatively enriched complexure of life, that self exhibit reflexive effort and thus possibilizing, *self is the eidos of life*—however faint its voice (as Jonas remarked)—the transcendental condition for there being life in the first place. *The quest for the transcendental conditions of self has thus discovered that self is that without which there could not be life: embodied, sentient, motile and emotive presence within the midst of environing things.*[2]

Such disturbances as have been mentioned—whether due to illness or injury, or upsets due to circumstances—have a unique way of making self conspicuous. Indeed, unless there were the specific kinds of mutual and reflexive referencings intrinsic to contextures—i.e., if there were merely relations *partes extra partes*—no amount of alteration or modification would prompt such alertness, effort, possibilizing. Having to do with contextures—indeed, the complexure of life—such modifications and alterations within any of the constituents necessarily have the significance of being genuine disturbances, disruptions of the profound tendency toward self-maintaining, self-equilibrating, or self-actualizing "as well as possible" (Goldstein). They therefore solicit and provoke reflexive alertness, effort, tending and attending, and circumstantial possibilizing.

Awakened, situationally called forth, as this effortful freeing-from and freeing-for, self thus becomes increasingly enriched and differentiated, along with the thereby enhanced bodily patterns, surrounding milieu, and modes of awareness: emotions, volitions, and passions. As Jonas noted, enhanced "self" *means* enhanced milieu—but also, it must be added, enhanced embodiment and subjective life. Thus, more generally, *self is in essence a problematic to itself*, precisely to the extent that disruptions occur within any of the contextures composing the complexure of life. The "problem of self" is that self is a foundational problem to itself, always and essentially contexturally bound to *its* body, *its* mind, *its* milieu—*its life*, in short.

Its emergence and continuously enriched modes of embodied and situated life are thus strictly dependent upon the occurrence of the unexpected, the unsettling of constituents and their mutual referencings, with respect to which the striving to maintain or to reestablish contextural balance (equilibrium, equalization) emerges by possibilizing efforts resulting in increasing differentiations within "mind," "embodying organism," and "milieu" (barring the occurrence of irreparable neurological dedifferentiation, psychic upset, or severe disruptions of the milieu). The genealogy of self thus signifies the emergence of heterogeneity, complexity, enriched reflexivity, from relative homogeneity.

As pointed out earlier, it is not in my present purposes to take up the fuller genetic-constitutive explication of self. That task, which from this study thus far is seen to be closely tied up with reflexivity, effort, and possibilizing, will form the main theme of a future study. For the present, it is hopefully enough to have gone this far. It now remains to pursue the conditions of self a final step: everything delineated up to now receives its completion and proper sense only within the experience of mutuality and vivid presence: the other self.

Seeking and Finding:
The Other Self

CONVINCED that only a concerted searching for the fullness of "personhood" could counter what he called "*egolatry*"—the idolatry of the solitary self (*solus ipse*)—Marcel came to develop a notion not only basic to understanding his own work, but one of the great ideas of our times: *disponibilité* (openness, availability).[1] It is in the very essence of "subjectivity" to be "intersubjectivity"; no explication of "self" can in principle be complete, balanced, or ultimately true to the nature of self if it does not see the profound place within the self of the other self. Preferring to think of this richly real presence as "person"—"self" seemed to conjure up the egolatry he fought against—Marcel wrote at the conclusion of his fine essay on the "ego" that one's own establishment as a person is strictly correlative to one's own realization or acknowledgement of the existence of other persons (cf. *74*, p. 22).

This "being-with" (*être-chez*) the Other as an effective, efficacious presence is for Marcel (to use different terms) a *constitutive moment of being-myself* ("person"). If, as he says elsewhere in the same collection of essays, *sum est sursum* for human reality, this *sursum* is always and essentially a "growing older together" or "making music together," a being "tuned-in" to the Other, in Schutz's closely parallel terms (*109*, pp. 159-78; *130*, pp. 89-93). Thus, as Marcel believes, so long as one's self remains shut up in itself, unattuned to the other self, it remains unawakened to reality. Precisely because of this, he went on to argue, the "essential characteristic of the person" is openness or availability (*disponibilité*) (*74*, pp. 22-23).

Given this—an insight which has yet to be given its due—it is no wonder, one might say, that, as Ricoeur points out, the Freudian analytic is so deeply "disappointing" on the central theme of reflective philosophy (*95*, p. 428). Although Ricoeur does not express it quite this way, the point is that Freud's focus on the disguises of desire (his "hermeneutics of suspicion") is essentially, perhaps properly, on the *pathological* "self"—the *ego* and *its* understandably "neuter" core. Ricoeur's insistence that "desire" is essentially "desire for another desire" is far better, but I suspect that Marcel would still have demurred: a desire that is focused on objects or others taken as "mirrors" can only be a kind of *"poseur"* (*74*, pp. 17–20) at once terrorized, victimized and wounded. *Here*, it seems clear, is the genuine "false Cogito," not at all a disclosure of appropriative reflection but the condition of the self seen solely as "desire": *egolatry*. In these terms, Ricoeur's focus on the "hermeneutics of revelation," on the self as intrinsically "rising above" itself, is far closer to the nub of things, especially for Marcel.

Thus the two fundamental moments of self I delineated earlier turn out to be profoundly bound up together: that whereby the self is itself and alone *is* the centering urgency to be-with the other self. "Awakening" and "alterity" express the axial "urge-to-be"; alterity, one should say, is the fulfillment of and in a way the condition of awakening. An always precarious *task* of self, its opening-out to the other self is never "once done, forever done," but rather is an always-ongoing and internally rhythmed accomplishment. This *disponibilité, however, is, as Marcel says, a "highly sensitive enclosure," a producing or placing of self before the other, a "gift"*—and thus is essentially a sensitive responsiveness to the other's reception of self's gift of itself. It will be necessary to focus careful attention on this "being-at-hand" for the other self. Before that, however, it is necessary to be clearer on the crucial dimension of self, its alterity, or what Schutz calls the "Thou-orientation." Whatever may transpire subsequent to the "opening-out" for the other self, how are we to understand that very alterity, that "turning-toward" the Other *as* other-self-turned-toward-self? How is this *mutuality* itself possible?

THE PHENOMENON OF AUTISM

As before, the procedure of focusing on the *absence* of a phenomenon will help in eliciting what must be understood. The phenomenon of autism is especially remarkable for this purpose—beyond its intrinsic fascination; beyond, too, the deep and baffling tragedy these children present. The tantalizing riddle of autism was well expressed by Bruno Bettelheim, whose life was devoted to comprehending and treating such children (5). Autistic children, he wrote in an introduction to the splendidly sensitive study by Gerhard Bosch,

> suffer from the consequences of having lost themselves, or of never having been able to discover themselves, since they were unable to establish contact with others. Only when they respond favorably to therapy do they slowly emerge out of their deepest autistic position; then they desperately begin to seek for a feeling of self. (7, p. iv)

If the child ever does come to the point of attempting to interact with others, it is both agonizing and fascinating to witness the enduring fear he has that at any moment he may disintegrate, disappear literally. One can observe how such a child may need continuously to touch himself, as if to authenticate his own reality, that he has not evaporated; he may resist sleep for weeks, convinced that if he lets go of the tenuous grip on the real, it will disintegrate entirely and never be reestablished; he may need to "tell" the parts of his body as if to insure their continual presence. Thus, as is quickly clear even to the clinical neophyte—or even to the merest layman who chances upon such a child—their very mode of life is in a way a continual, pitiable posing to themselves of the deepest philosophical questions—who, what, am I? More pointedly, *am* I? And what, who, or is, the Other?—and thus do they elicit these questions to the rest of us, and do so with vital urgency.[2]

Autism was first singled out as a distinct clinical phenomenon by Leo Kanner, in 1938; he first reported his observations in 1943 (*57*, pp. 217-50; *17*; *18*). Dr. Kanner followed up his earliest findings with numerous observations of autistic children, and later did studies of their parents as well. Using common clinical language, Kanner and others argued for the uniqueness of this "syndrome." In brief terms, what is observably common are these characteristics ("symptoms"): primarily, what Kanner calls "isolation" or "aloneness," and a powerful *"desire for the preservation of sameness"* (*59*, pp. 378-79). All the other "symptoms," he believes, can be explained on that basis: linguistic peculiarities such as echolalia, pronomial reversal, inappropriate talk, rote enumerations, and others; also the peculiar way in which the child's relation to other persons is disrupted, and his unusual way of relating to objects. Diagnosable as early as six months in some cases, these children show little of the progressively differentiated contact with other persons that the normal child shows quite early in life. So unresponsive to verbal address are they that one often finds them diagnosed as deaf, or even as severe mental defectives. Yet close exmination belies these diagnoses; indeed, it is not unusual to find that such children show little apparent significant neurological or physiological damage. Investigations of families often disclose normal siblings, and a "remarkable paucity of psychoses and handicapping neuroses"—fewer than 5%—and reveal instead that they come from "intelligent, sophisticated stock" (*59*, p. 384).

There are some disagreements about Kanner's interpretations—especially by Bosch and Bettelheim—but all agree about the observational findings, when these are cleaned of theoretical blurrings and bias.[3] Every clinician notes the strange, staring look of even very young babies, the behavioral oddities (not stretching out the arms when picked up or being dressed, etc., and the markedly peculiar language, when it is found at all). Of particular interest, however, is the description given by Bosch. It is just with such clinical descriptions, Bosch remarks, that "we do indeed see the patients described . . . clearly before us and remember similar cases. . . ." But, he goes on, we are usually left in the dark concerning "just what is autistic about them, just what characterizes the development of their existence as autistic . . ." (7, p. 50). Precisely this important task is what Bosch sets himself in his monograph—recognizing that one never finds a purely autistic person.[4]

Perhaps the most striking features of the autistic mode of life are what Bosch prefers to call "positive peculiarities," i.e., those which clearly mark out "what it is to be autistic."

> Once one has trained oneself to see these "positive peculiarities" of autistic children, it will be clear that they are extraordinarily attached to certain family situations, to being looked after by a certain person, and to a rigidly followed daily routine within which tenderness [although they do not actively show it to others], such as a going-to-bed ritual with a good-night kiss and certain morning greetings, all have their place. These children are thus not just dependent and incapable of looking after themselves, but their whole behavior shows that they rely on and are adjusted to being cared for, dressed, fed, and looked after. Their behavior presupposes the continued presence of someone to look after them, just like the small baby calling hungrily and searching with its mouth for the mother's breast. (7, p. 59)

Focusing upon this reliance shows that autistic life is a kind of "*symbiosis*," a close mutual dependence or "bond from which the individual partners [e.g., mother and child] cannot freely dissociate themselves and to which they cannot return without renouncing some or all of their freedom" (7, p. 60). Hence symbiosis is a *way of life*, exhibited clearly in the case of the very young infant and its mother, which in the case of the autistic child *has not been overcome or outgrown*. In fact, such children show a marked *failure of efforts* to initiate that overcoming even in its first steps: looking at other people, reaching for things, crying out for something, being angry, etc. Thus the words so often used by observers, family, and clinicians, concerning such children: "glass wall," "looking right through me," "looking at me as if I were a thing," "a chasm," an "abyss" as regards their apparent unaffectedness and unresponsiveness. A child will pound a nail into a wall and keep right on pounding even though the nail is in and the wall is being damaged; another will keep drawing lines even though the sheet is full, and other children romp about him, teasing and pulling his hair—yet the child remains unresponsive.

Even though one finds some mode of behavior which does not so much *relate* to other persons as it symbiotically links to someone reliantly, the encounter with the autistic child is invariably "strange," "eerie," "another world entirely," "uneasy," and "disturbing," as is regularly reported. Such terms spring to mind, Bosch points out, precisely when one "attempts to *meet* the child as a human partner and is struck by the lack of replies and the impossibility of making contact with the child" (7, p. 52). Precisely here does strangeness emerge. It can be approximately understood if one calls to mind when one has felt strange in the company of others: when one encounters foreigners, for example, whose language, gestures, and facial expressions are not immediately recognizable. Not sharing their common world, with all its typifications and taken for granted customs, we are excluded, alienated, we experience ourselves as "foreign." All, or some at least, of these can be overcome, but even initially some primitive gestures are shared: not only such possibilities as pointing to the mouth, lying down, and feigning tiredness, but, more importantly, a mutual recognition even here of one another as persons of some sort—precisely as "foreigners." As Bosch remarks, "the aim in any human meeting is not simply the actual fact of appearing before the other person, but with this meeting a common world is constituted between those involved" (7, p. 53).

The attempt to "meet" an autistic child, however, is most often an utter failure. There thus arises the question: what is this "common world" and how does it come into being along with the various "own worlds" of each person who nevertheless shares that "common" world? What autism presents, more clearly than any other concrete experience, is an extreme case of the failure of that development of "own" and "common." Hence, according to Bosch, we begin to see, as a kind of *limiting* concept, "that in the new-born child both realms are still at first fully un-separated" (7, p. 56). The terms "for me," "for you," "for others," have no grip; all these are still to come, and the course of normal human development progressively unfolds into this richer tapestry of multiple realms and a common world. The autistic child, however, never surmounts more than the first, meager beginnings of that differentiation—if even that.

Carefully probing the linguistic usages of such children, Bosch is able to show that the autistic child *"fails to find a way into the realm of encounter, to the constitution of an own and common world"* (7, p. 115). With respect to the primary modes of meaning (acting, having, being) and their correlative modes of linguistic expression, one finds that especially the forms of acting and having (and the underlying experiences which are given expression by them) are markedly absent (7, pp. 76–92)—with respect not only to persons, but also to things, a point many other clinicians have failed to see clearly. Forms expressive of "belonging" (e.g., not only toys, but the child's own-body), of activity, of the future, of imperative calling on others (cf. the inappropriate use of personal pronouns)—these are at most inadequate. All these correlate, too, with observations of their behaviors. Only fragmentary relationships are formed with other persons; even more, only fragmentary parts of others seem even focused upon: "the child does not address a complete person . . . but it relates to a part of the body (the mouth), to a demand (doing up own laces, coming, questioning) without addressing the originator of the demand. The part of the body and the command are, as it were, substituted for the complete person encountered" (7, p. 94). But it is not very different as regards the child's relation to inanimate things, as can be seen especially in the ritualistic handling of objects, the odd fascination with specific parts of objects (e.g., in circular shapes), or the lack of any experimentation with objects. In general, the distinction between "animate" and "inanimate," like that between "own" and "common," is not yet at hand or is acquired only very slowly (and then, not fully). Thus it becomes clear that "things" seem no different from "people," and vice versa: these distinctions simply have not yet been made, and

> actual compulsive experience of the strange and the obtrusive is completely lacking. Things do not have a double face . . . they do not have one face that is fixed and confirmed intersubjectively in all its various aspects, and a second face that obtrudes strangely on the children and contradicts reason; instead, things are clearly experienced as being accessible through incantation, through magical practices. . . . [These children] do not really become involved with the things. They do not destroy, do not work on things, do not investigate them, but leave them exactly as they find them or repeatedly perform on or with them the same actions once these have been learnt . . . revelatory discovery is missing. (7, p. 105)

Failing ever to grow out of symbiotic reliance into the differentiated environs of self and other, animate and inanimate, own-world and common world, "haunted" things and "normal" things, the autistic child's links with the surroundings—whether "person," "animal," or "material thing" (artifact or not)—are severely disrupted. It is accordingly not possible to characterize such children as either "selved" or "othered." Or, as Bettelheim shows so well, autistic children, faced with at least what they apparently take as an overpowering, immensely threatening and radically unalterable world, seem to put up a defense—a retreat into non-action or rigidly ritualized and repeated actions (Bosch's "incantations"). But, Bettelheim emphasizes,

> unfortunately for those who use this defense [whether schizophrenics who "withdraw" or autistics who ritualize], its nature is such that it debilitates the self till at one moment what was still utter defiance, may in the next moment turn out to be suicidal. Thus in a child's last-ditch efforts at assertion he defies his parents by doing nothing. But in doing so he gives up the very being he tried to protect. Or, to put it differently, the self he tried to protect by not acting becomes even weaker, until it disintegrates through nonuse. (5, pp. 55–56)

When communication with others is stopped, or never initiated, and when the very presence of the world is blocked in crucial ways, not only is world impoverished, but so is self—and, as Bosch and Bettelheim both observe, the embodying organism is curtailed as well. With the autistic child's failure to develop links with the world of things and others, there is a strictly correlated (contextural) impoverishment and debilitation of mental life. In fact, these children's lives seem rigorously embedded in a very limited subjective life: feelings are for the most part extinguished, cognition is markedly missing, passion is apparently diminished or distorted, and there is little apparent volitional or valuational life. What is observed, instead, is but a few such processes, made all the more prominent and even outlandish by their very singular presence: sometimes there is rampant anxiety and dread; thought seems almost exhausted by rote calculation and memory; all passional/ volitional energy seems funneled into the single aim of blocking out the world; they often seem to feel little or no pain at all, but reveal on the other hand incredible strength.[5]

The self, Bettelheim insists, is not an "isolated entity. It is a totality of inner processes that develops slowly" (5, p. 56). This idea is quite congruent with what I have tried to show as the being of self; still, there are clear differences, mainly connected to the understanding of contextures. Nevertheless, Bettelheim's point is, it seems to me, perfectly (indeed, much more clearly) accountable within this conception. As he later says, for example,

> the more communication is interfered with, the less contact there is with others and the more the person must fall back on his inner experience to interpret reality. . . . [But] the less contact with reality he has, the less he can test his inner experience against something permitting a balanced judgment about it. . . . An inner life that is not validated against outer experiences and then organized through such validation, remains chaotic. If this is so, then the more attention we pay to the inner life alone, the greater its chaos. (5, pp. 78–79)

Precisely thereby does the autistic child's ritualized conduct, his penchant for sameness and unaltering order in his "world," become understandable. But, as has been maintained throughout, *any disruption within any of the contextural constituents of the complexure of life must of necessity breach its contextural balance, hence awaken or solicit reflexive effort and possibilizing in order to restore, reorganize or reestablish "as well as possible"* (Goldstein). The more serious the disruption, the deeper the breach, the more radical the solicitation and effort. But how must it be when from earliest childhood there is a determined effort to close off what threatens? That is, not only do the rudimentary differentiations fail to occur with the autistic child, but there develop instead *defenses against differentiatedness*: mainly, as most clinicians have observed, *against time* and the "*otherness*" of things and the surrounding milieu.

But their observations also show, convincingly it seems to me (even if not expressed as such), that there are clear disruptions in the sense and experience of *space*. Living spatiality (as the context of "ways" and "byways," of "enchanting" and "haunting," as well as "friendly," *places*) is weakened or never develops. Similarly, as Bosch emphasizes, there are no "double faces" to things; autistic children rather show a literalistic reliance on incantation, a kind of magic. Thus one finds a marked *absence of "possibilizing."* In short, *the whole complexure is radically altered, as are its intrinsic constituents: body, mental life, and milieu, and thereby the qualitative set of "self"-referencings, or what I have delineated as the sense of self, is fundamentally circumscribed and narrowed.* Bettelheim's view, then, seems quite correct: the more autistic the infant is, or as may also happen, the more a schizophrenic person withdraws into autism,

> the emptier, the more repetitious and stereotyped becomes his fantasy life, though this is all he has left: the vaguer then become even his sensations, the less content and structure [i.e., contextural balance] has his self.
>
> Among the reasons for this is that a self, if it is not to wither away,[6] must forever be testing itself against the nonself in a process of active assertion. . . .[7] Testing implies both respect and consideration for what we test ourselves against. Otherwise it becomes not a test of self, but of something entirely different, perhaps of brute force.[8]
>
> As a matter of fact, what a person selects as a testing ground is most indicative of the nature and quality of the self. A passive yielding to certain experiences can be a much more subtle testing of the self against the nonself than meeting it aggressively. Success is then not a question of how unchanged the self emerges from the test nor how much it has bent the nonself to its will, but how enriched it became in the process. (5, p. 81)

Clear and exact, Bettelheim's analysis suggests as well that precisely to the extent that the nonself is ignored or shut out, there are obvious and profound reverberations for the quality of self: it then becomes "vague, nondifferentiated" (5, p. 81). Hence the *"enrichment" of self* must be understood not as a mere playful metaphor, but a *rigorously descriptive concept*: all I add to Bettelheim's remarkable observations, at this point, is that such enrichment is not only "a continuous, simultaneous process in which one enhances the other" but is in the clearest way a main feature of the *living complexure.*

Even this brief exposition of the phenomenon of autism makes it dramatically clear that the failure of autistic children to emerge out of the symbiotic stage of life radically curtails the otherwise possible enrichments of bodily conducts, mental or subjective life, and milieu—hence of self and other self. Precisely through its marked absence, the sense of the *Du-Einstellung* (Schutz) comes clearly before us. As observers or clinicians, we note that its absence is manifested as the strange and uncanny inability to "meet" in human interchanges (eye-contact, clasping, or talking); philosophically, we note that what is at stake is a continually ongoing, internally rhythmed and always precarious mutuality. I can now turn my attention directly to this phenomenon.

MAKING A DIFFERENCE

Jonas pointed out how different is Cartesian from Gnostic dualism: the latter posited a world, a cosmos, as antagonistic, decidedly unfriendly; the former posited a "Nature" utterly barren of anything recognizably human, an utterly uncaring indifference. Marcel, too, fastened onto the latter: the "object" is what in no way "takes me into account." Conversely, as Ortega emphasized (86), only what I must reckon with, what I must account for as taking me into account, is in the end what counts as "real."

How is it, then, if the other person is, or is taken to be, impervious to self no matter how well or strongly self "produces" itself before the other? A child asks a question of its mother, but mother fails to respond; the child grows insistent, jabbing mother with louder words and finger pokes, but mother, too busy for the nonce, ignores the child; the child flails, jabs, eventually kicks and screams; mother notices—the notice, however, being to reprimand child for being so noisy and pesky. How does it stand with self and other self? R. D. Laing has brilliantly delimited the nexus of relations between self and the many others (imagined, dreamed, fantasied, or real). In one place, he wrote:

> The unresponsive or impervious other induces a sense of emptiness and impotence in self. Destruction in phantasy of the other sets off a vicious circle. Self receives and gives. Other is needed to give and to receive. The more self receives, the more self needs to give. The more the other cannot *receive*, the more the self needs to destroy. The more self destroys other, the more empty self becomes. The more empty the more envious, the more envious the more destructive.
> A prototype of the other as giver but not receiver, unresponsive or impervious, tends to generate in self a sense of failure. . . . [Thus here] to make a difference to the other is victory. To allow the other to make a difference to him is defeat. Incapable of genuine reciprocity, he never finds it. (*68*, p. 68)

Nothing is so frustrating as sensing oneself as *not making a difference* to the other, as feeling as if no one else "cares" or that one's presence means nothing to others. But the "complementarity" relation, Laing shows, is no simple matter: there are multiple ways, and subtle they can be, for the other to be "giver" and to be "receiver," as for self to be "giver" and to be "receiver." Moreover, recognizing the multiple others with whom the self is in a relationship, one recognizes, too, the multiple modes of giving and receiving which are at hand at every moment. Self-other relations, even in one of the modes, turn out to be immensely complex. Thus self achieves its "sense of identity," its "that by which it is identified" for itself, only in respect of its identity for others. This is already complex:

> His identity-for-himself; the identity others ascribe to him; the identities he attributes to them; the identity or identities he thinks they attribute to him; what he thinks they think he thinks they think. . . . Other people become a sort of identity kit, whereby one can piece together a picture of *oneself*. One recognizes *oneself* in that old smile of recognition from that old friend. (*68*, p. 70)

But one can find oneself identified, too, and often in embarrassing, disgusting, or shameful ways, quite as much in warm, endorsing ways. One may find quite incompatible definitions of oneself from others, even from others whom one respects or loves. The other, indeed, may define or take self in simultaneously incompatible ways; the other may endorse a consistent view of self inconsistent with the self's view of itself; the other may define self in a way which conflicts with the self's view of the other, hence the other's view of self as self sees it. The variations are endless.[9]

But all these make it all the more salient just what is *invariant*: all these modalities of relating would be utterly senseless, were one to suppose that what is "other" is only that, i.e., were one to suppose that these incredibly complex, convoluted, subtly reciprocal modes of relating were done in connection solely with what fails to take self into account, i.e., "natural" things, inanimate things. We are all familiar with the marvelously comic dance we do when, walking down a street while deep in thought, we bump up against another person and try to get out of each other's way; consider only what would have to be said were one to come across a person doing this before a telephone pole. The only condition on which that "dance," much less the modes Laing delineates, are even possible is that they are intended, at the least, to "make a difference." They are essentially *modes of reckoning, of taking into account what is taken as taking the self into account, as reckoning with the self.* Rightly or wrongly, none of us would try to infer how natural things experience our study of them, our interventions into the natural process (*68*, pp. 12–14). We walk on concrete and dirt, mow our lawns, throw rocks, kick sticks and stumps, not to say study, experiment, and dissect, never once having in view whether these affairs "experience" these actions on and with them by us.

Our actions toward what is taken as taking us into account thus reveal a fundamental moment of self, and beyond that of human life and, still further, of animate life generally. What is invariantly made to stand out throughout all these examples, and the actual and possible variations on them, is this: *self*, that reflexively locused and solicited effort and possibilizing *is essentially an orientation to an other whose otherness is disclosed precisely as "experiencing" the self*, is an orienting to and of the self. Even more, I shall try to show, without that "making a difference to" (Laing) or "testing" (Bettelheim), it would not be possible for self to be "awakened"—and, failing that awakening, that emerging into explicitness as reflexive alterity, what would have been a self can only be described as an impoverishment (minimally), or an utterly failed potentiality (maximally). Without that "testing," self must lapse, even though the presence of significant testing can never guarantee what self then will be or become, nor how enriched, nor yet how long it will continue to be. "Testing" in order to "make a difference," in any event, is a condition without which "self" could not be self.

SEEKING AND FINDING

There is a heap of clutter in our conceptual yard, much of which I have tried to clear away by laying out, as far as presently possible (and I am cognizant of how much further work there is yet to do), a theory of contexture. That yielded an insight, among other things, into this: that every interruption to the balance of intrinsically referring constituents reverberates throughout—how deeply, how lastingly, and whether serious reorganizing of the contexture occurs, will depend on when, how long, where, which, that is, on specific circumstances wholly particular and concrete. But, it was also noted, following Gurwitsch's analysis, that since "the acquisition of a schema purports a modification of the psycho-physiological system, every future perceptual process will be co-determined by the new internal conditions established by the acquisition of the schema" (*31*, p. 100). Thus mental growth and development, Gurwitsch insists, must be conceived as brought about by *actual* achievements, hence as reorganization or transformation of experience. "By virtue of achievements in the course of mental development, the *stream of experience is substantially transformed* so as to exhibit features varying according to the stages of mental development" (*31*, pp. 103–04),[10] and, it was necessary for me to add, according to the specific circumstances of embodiment and the environing milieu.

For a temporal being, then, time is not only itself a lived contexture and fleshed out bodily (hence co-originative with spatiality), it is also *continuously enriched*, augmented, transformed, reorganized, by means of continuously achieved placements with respect to the milieu. Thus is the remarkable feature of autistic children—their resistance to time and space—made understandable, as also their deep anxiety and frustration (Bettelheim). Beyond this, perhaps another conceptual clutter can be cleaned up, keeping this feature of contextures before us.

It has become almost an article of faith that, to use but one formulation (in this case, that of Laing, who unfortunately confuses matters), one person

> cannot have direct awareness of the other's experience of the "same" world. He cannot see through the other's eyes and cannot hear through the other's ears. . . . All one "feels," "senses," "intuits," etc. of the other entails inference from one's own experience of the other to the other's experience of one's self. This presupposes that the other's actions are in some way a function of the other's experience, as I know mine to be. (*68*, p. 14)

Now there is here something at once patently obvious, yet insidious. I have in mind, not so much the notion of "inference" correctly and definitively criticized by Max Scheler (*107*, pp. 239–41), but something else. In one obvious sense, *of course* I cannot literally use your eyes, ears, etc.; if I could, I would just as literally *be* you. The question of others does not crop up there, but rather on the issue of "*direct* awareness of the other's experience."

First, one must be clear. In certain ways, I do indeed "infer" and even "impute" various attitudes, beliefs, etc. to the other. For example, encountering a particularly irritable clerk, I may infer that he is having a bad time of it with his boss, or his family, or that he has had a bad day generally. All these, however, proceed on the assumption that the clerk is already experienced by me *as* another person; "inferring" in this sense presupposes the live presence of the other. Seeking the other is finding that the other is already present. The question, then, is how to understand this *already delivered presence of the other*—and to call attention to the impossibility of literally seeing with the other's eyes, etc., is just diversion.[11]

But this is the case as regards even *non-empirical* senses of "inference"—it being problematic at just what level, and in just what sense, the passage from Laing is to be taken. As Scheler has shown, all theories which seek to *argue for* the "existence of Others"—whether by empathy or by inference—involve internal inconsistencies. Although he elaborates this in greater detail, the essential points are these. (1) The necessary premise for any such argument to yield "others"—namely, that the other's bodily expressions are "like" my own—is simply missing: the ways I know and experience myself are radically different from the way I experience others, thus every such argument is a *petitio principii*. (2) We have little difficulty recognizing that there are non-human, but nonetheless animate, creatures (fowls, fishes, etc.), but one could hardly maintain any "gestural similarity" here. (3) To suppose that others are "inferred" involves the logical fallacy of *quaternio terminorum*: the only logically correct inference would be that where I find bodily gestures analogous to my own, my self would perforce exist over there. All that such an argument could yield is myself all over again—that being solely what the premises concern (*107*, pp. 240, 242–48). And so, too, for empathy. As Schutz remarks to this point, "interpretation of the Other's gesture as expression can only be the consequence of and not the proof for his existence" (*109*, I, p. 160).

At the root of such theories are the two presumptions: (1) that the self is essentially a kind of *insularity*, capable only of thinking its own thoughts, feeling its own feelings, etc.; (2) that the only "direct experience" the self has of the other is of the other's body, and the other's self is only "expressed" by that body. Both involve *under*estimating the obstacles to self-perception and *over*estimating the difficulties in perceiving the other person (*107*, p. 251; *108*, pp. 3–97). There are, Scheler contends, any number of experiences we are all familiar with where it is not at all clear whether a particular feeling or thought, value or belief, is "mine" or someone else's: e.g., being caught up in a crowd's frenzy. Moreover, if we consider the phenomenon of parents grieving over their lost child, it is absurd to say that there are *two* griefs, any more than that there are two children (the mother's and the father's): rather, it is necessary to say that they share the grief, they grieve together over their child. The commonplace that the mother "lives" her own and the father "lives" his own grief—each with his/her own mental life and organism—is neither here nor there as regards the *common* grief (*107*, pp. 12–13, 24–25, 258).

Indeed, Scheler goes further, maintaining that the "we" precedes the "I"; it is the "social" from within which the "self" emerges (*107*, pp. 245–47). Perhaps, as Schutz suggests, Scheler's analysis is much keener on its critical side, whereas his positive theory of the perception of the alter ego (*Wahrnehmungstheorie des fremden Ich*) is weak (*109*, I, pp. 164-79). Be that as it may for the moment (I will return to this later), his acute observations and significant examples are quite as telling as his critique of traditional theories. For just as the traditional theories inherently invoke illicit metaphysical distinctions of inner/ outer, mind/body, spirit/nature, etc., so his own observations present insuperable problems for the traditional approaches. Thus, as any parent, lover, or clinician knows well, the suffering of a person is apprehended with as much immediacy as is possible for human beings, in his tears, his visage, his voice; the child's joy is there in her smile, her wildly waving arms, her jumping about; a friend's exasperation is there in his sigh (*117*, pp. 234-51), his shrugged shoulders, his upward-turned eyes. Reasoning, trying to figure out another person, wondering what is on her mind—these all come into play only when there is an upset in one's expectations, when one is provoked into distrusting one's perceptions—precisely as one undergoes profound shock when one "meets," or rather attempts to "meet," an autistic child. For what fails there is precisely what is manifestly present otherwise: even if I mistake another's look I nevertheless see not merely his eyes but his *looking-at-me* (indeed, if all I saw were his eyes, I should doubtless sense the oddity of confronting an autistic kind of behavior!).

Schutz's objections to Scheler's theory are fundamentally two—and it is useful to lay these out so as to elicit what is truly at issue in the question concerning the experience of the other and the other's place within the life of the self. On the one hand, while maintaining that his theory meets the transcendental problem of intersubjectivity, Scheler consistently calls on merely *empirical* facts taken from developmental psychology and anthropology. On the other hand, Scheler's thesis that the "we" antedates the "I," though true developmentally and empirically, confuses that sort of primacy with the kind that reflection delivers: Scheler's thesis is therefore wrong. These objections need to be reviewed, for thereby it will become possible to clean up still further cluttering items.

(1) What is the status of references to "empirical facts" so-called? This, as must be clear, is a serious problem, not only for Scheler, but for my own study. After all, if Schutz is right my own study must fall with Scheler's, for I have made copious references of just this kind throughout.

Here I shall only indicate where I think Schutz's point fails—indeed, it fails here in just the way his own delineation of the structures of the lifeworld succeeds (so far as it does). Let me take the latter point first. Schutz's philosophical works are replete with very much the sort of thing he complains about in Scheler: references to concrete people, concrete animate creatures (dogs, fishes, etc.), concrete situations, particular artifacts, etc.[12] Indeed, one of Schutz's more important essays concerns Goldstein's inquiry into language and language disturbances in brain-injured patients (*109*, I, pp. 260-86), to which he gives a fine philosophical analysis—remarking how Goldstein's findings ("empirical" ones, be it noted) are important "for the clarification of certain fundamental problems of philosophy" (*109*, I, p. 286).

Schutz himself, then, "refers" to presumably "empirical" particulars. Thus the question is not *whether* these are referred to, but rather what is to be understood by that "reference." Now although neither Schutz nor Scheler (*107*, pp. 245–46) specifically mentions it, especially *in this connection*, it is perfectly clear in Schutz's case that his "references" to empirical data by no means have the meaning of drawing conclusions of an empirically general sort from them; he is not in the least pretending to be an empirical observer or scientist. How, then, can one make use of such empirical data to clarify *philosophical* problems?

This question opens up a significant set of issues, fully deserving of a complete study on their own: the phenomenological method of free-phantasy variation.[13] In a word, what Schutz does (as practically every other philosopher does) is to take such "empirical" (*actual*) data *as examples*, freely-varied through a range of variations of these and other *possible* examples, in order to determine whether and which characteristics intrinsic to the range of variations are *invariant*, i.e., "*eidetic*." It is never a matter of trying to generalize, not even when Schutz is trying to delineate the "*eidos*" of generalized types; it is rather a question of trying to determine what is invariantly common to (exemplified by) every actual and possible example of the kind in question. Hence "reference" has the meaning of "*ideation*," not "generalization"—the seizing upon the "invariant," i.e., the *eidos*, as exemplified in every actual and possible example.

For now, the question concerns whether Scheler's "references" to the data of developmental psychology, anthropology, and still other empirical sciences, purport to be empirical generalizations or variational ideations. Putting the question this way makes it immediately clear, I am convinced, that Scheler is doing precisely what is called for in phenomenological philosophy—practicing a (modest, to be sure) kind of free-phantasy variation, precisely as is Schutz. While the range of his "examples" for the most part comes from *actual* cases, this is of *no consequence* for what he at least purports to find, or for assessing the status of his claims. Thus when he refers to works of psychologists such as Ghinn, Koffka and Erdmann (*107*, p. 239), and maintains that "from these facts and others like them, we conclude that 'expression' is indeed the very *first* thing that man apprehends of what lies outside him [as, i.e., an infant], and that he only goes on to apprehend sensory appearances of any kind, inasmuch and insofar as they can be construed as *expressions* of mind" (*107*, p. 239), we should understand by this "concluding" that Scheler's *claim* is that "infants" studied by child psychologists serve at once as (actual) *clues* and *examples* for clarifying the philosophical problem concerning the perception of other selves. It is the same in others of his references to "empirical" (i.e., actual) affairs. Finally, the fact that he does not practice his phenomenological method very self-consciously, that he does not give an analysis which would show its legitimacy, should in no way divert our attention. Few, indeed, including

Schutz and Husserl, have given such an analysis—and not even the latter gave it the rigorous explicative study needed to legitimate its place. In these terms, considering that Scheler's work here was done *before* even Husserl had begun to pay explicit attention to this method, and considering Scheler's remarkable insights into these issues, one can only be amazed at his prescience and even brilliance. I will return to the substance of his work on the issues in the next chapter.

(2) But Schutz believes that Scheler is wrong in several important respects. First, Schutz dissociates himself from what he understands by "transcendental" phenomenology: whatever may be said at that level, Schutz claims no more than to be giving a "mundane" phenomenological analysis (*109*, I, pp. 164–67). If Scheler purports to be transcendental, Schutz's objection is as much a confession of not understanding the sense of such claims as it is a substantive one: the Husserlian (and presumably Schelerian) effort to isolate the "ownness-sphere" (*Eigensphäre*) belonging to "me" and radically distinct from what pertains to others, and the curious difficulties of determining whether there is *one* transcendental ego or a *plurality* of them—these Schutz sees as simply insuperable.

Whether he is right or wrong on that cannot be determined here; many a good person and true has tread on those grounds only to find himself stuck in the quicksand of that bog.[14] All that I can remark upon here is this: *all* talk of "the" transcendental ego (or, for that matter, "many") is on the face of it spurious, for the very same reason as is talk about conscious*ness*. That is, the *substantival locution* in no way signifies either that Husserl *claims*, or that phenomenological evidence delivers, any "substance" of the sort which would have to be claimed or delivered if Schutz's critique is to hold up. And, indeed, precisely such substantial entities have been found to be lacking when one reflects carefully on the "things themselves": but by no means does this "lack" suggest a non-egological theory. For, as has been found here, "self" is no *thing* but the situated reflexivity inherent to the complexure of life. At the very least, this finding seriously reopens the question of the transcendental status of "self," and gives the lie to all discussions asking or seeking whether there is "one" or "many" transcendental egos!

Schutz, in any case, has other reservations about Scheler's theory, objections which do not hang on whether the latter be interpreted as giving a transcendental theory or not. His second point of interest here is that Scheler has confused the *genetic primacy* of the "we" with what the act of reflection discloses as appertaining to the "I-We" complex. Even if it is the case, naively, that so long as babies are born of mothers and not concocted in retorts, the "we" is pregiven to the sphere of the "I," nevertheless this should not conceal the fact that

only in reference to "me," the individual who acts and thinks, do Others obtain the specific meaning which I designate with the pronoun "we"; and only in reference to "us," whose center I am, do Others stand out as "you"; and in reference to you, who refer back to me, third parties stand out as "they." (*109*, I, p. 168)

Hence from the fact that children and primitives only slowly become aware of themselves as such (as "I"), one can only conclude "that the technique of reflection is acquired very late," not that the "we" is primary (*109*, I, p. 171). Too, the fact that you and I share thoughts, feelings, goals, etc., should not in the least obscure the character of these, as belonging to my and to your respective spheres: "thoughts" we do share, but by no means the "thinking" thereof, and the fact that the origin of the thought may be uncertain does not destroy its character of now being my thinking of the thought. Much of the difficulty, Schutz believes, derives from Scheler's broader theory of the Person and the distinction he draws between Person and Self, as well as what seems to be deep inconsistencies in Scheler's understanding of self-consciousness.

The central difficulty, however, quite apart from those broader ones, Schutz focuses quite properly, but does not adequately show why Scheler's theory in this respect is inadequate. Scheler argues against the notion that the self, in order to arrive at the other, must build up a picture of the latter by means of sensory data located in the former. Not only do such "data" have no intrinsic marks of "foreignness" about them—rather, they *must* be "mine"—but these sorts of theories (inference and empathy) misconstrue the nature of experience itself:

> What occurs, rather, is an immediate flow of experiences, *undifferentiated as between mine and thine*, which actually contains both our own and others' experiences intermingled and without distinction from one another. Within this flow there is a gradual formation of ever more stable vortices, which slowly attract further elements of the stream into their orbits and thereby become successively and very gradually identified with distinct individuals. (*107*, p. 246)

We here meet head-on an already familiar doctrine, precisely the one definitely criticized by Gurwitsch and advocated by James: the stream of pure experience is "in itself" undifferentiated and only gradually becomes differentiated and organized around "centers" (*31*, pp. 25–36). As Gurwitsch shows, however, what is unaccountable within such a theory is precisely how that *initial segregation* and differentiation can occur, and then how any *stability* of this organization can be maintained. For if experience is in itself undifferentiated, then, as there could be *no clue to guide the organization* into "vortices" or units *in the first formation* (no matter how "gradual"), so there is none on future occasions—and thus stability of organization is as impossible as is the initial one (*31*, p. 54). It is furthermore not sufficient merely to argue that experience is *somehow able* to be formed into the experience of a specific self; the conditions necessary to this achievement must not be confused with the very process of its *actually being achieved* (*31*, p. 32).

As if somehow sensing these difficulties, Scheler goes on immediately after to argue that "every experience belongs *in general to a self*, so that wherever an experience is given a self is also given, in a general sense" (*107*, p. 246). But, to this, I offer three points (none seen by Schutz). (1) Either this "*general* self" is a plain *hoax*, since (as Scheler goes right on to say) every self is an *individual*; or (2) this "general self" is to be understood as a *supervenient principle of organization*, in which case it falls under Gurwitsch's criticism; or (3) it is a flat *contradiction* with Scheler's claims that experience is *undifferentiated*. Whichever it may be, none is acceptable.

But it should be noted that the *reasons* for rejecting this point do not at all rely on Schutz's argument concerning what reflection delivers. The reasons rather derive from our understanding of the nature of the *organization of experience*: that organization, as Gurwitsch says, is autochthonous, and *must* be so. More directly here, it is the *contextural character of "experience"* which shows that Scheler's thesis is wrong.

In general, what seems to have gone awry in Scheler's still fascinating account of intersubjectivity is that he *confuses two very different problems*: on the one hand, the *genetic* problem, phenomenologically understood, conceiving the conditions for the very possibility of the development of a sense of self and other; on the other hand, the very different issue concerning the already developed self's *experience* of the other self, the ways by which the other is actually experienced (Scheler's perceptual theory of the alter ego having its place here). Schutz's complaint that Scheler refers to psychology thus has a point, but not the one he thought it had. Scheler in one sense was attempting to uncover what I have called the awakening of self and other self, and for this such free-variational references are completely justified. Schutz's other complaint concerns the way Scheler sees the experiencing of the other self, assuming that the self and the other have *already emerged* into explicitness. And here, Schutz's complaint is rightly felt, though his argument misses the real flaw in Scheler's theory.

More importantly, the contextural character of organization of the complexure of life shows that Scheler's thesis is wrong. In an already constituted social world, what is the nature of our experiences of one another? That is one crucial issue, to which Schutz (as will be seen) has given us important insights. In an already constituted social world, how does it happen on principle that the self manifestly grows, emerges out into explicit alterity? That is another crucial issue, which Scheler has importantly analyzed. If Scheler tends to confuse these issues, on the one hand, Schutz on the other does so as well in his criticism of Scheler.

In a word: *"seeking" the other self presents distinctively different questions from those made salient by "finding." In my earlier formulation, "seeking" the other is "finding" that the other is already present: i.e., the developing self finds others always-already-"there," and having so found the other, continues* (barring the impairments noted here) *to experience the other in distinctive modes.* As I have tried to make plain by bringing up the case of the autistic child, however, "seeking" itself may never occur, and thus neither self nor other become explicit in that case. Noting this helps make it clear just what is involved in the two crucial issues delineated here. It remains now to trace out in greater depth what happens with "seeking" and "finding"—or, in Bettelheim's simple term, "testing."

10

Mutuality and the "Test"

TWO central issues regarding the self and the other self have been distinguished. First, there is the question of self's emergence, its awakening into explicit alterity—a phenomenon made prominent in the especially poignant and tragic cases of infantile autism and brain-injured patients. What among other things is plain from such cases, in a word, is that the "self" requires for its elicitation the complex and subtle modes of "testing"—whether initially in infancy, or after severe cerebral damage, or for that matter as the mode of emergence from severe mental disturbance. To become self—for self is essentially a precarious and always hazardous task,[1] an adventure—there must be seeking and finding.

Second, there is the question—parallel to what Gurwitsch calls the *phase of actual achievement*—concerning the modes of awareness whereby self experiences the other self. The other self, then, figures in two ways: as a *constitutive moment* in the explicitation of self, and as itself *experienced by* the self as precisely another self. With respect to both, as I hope will become clear, the theory of contexture is the fundamental clue and key. As regards the first issue the phenomenon of *mutuality* is prominent; for the second, that of *vivid presence*, and both are modulations of contextural relationships.

THE DISRELATIONSHIP IN SELF-RELATEDNESS: MUTUALITY

I return for the moment to Kierkegaard—not without much hesitancy and trepidation, if not fear and trembling. I return for one small point—small, in relation to what his search was all about. But, before the return, a caveat and an acknowledgement. The latter first: it is from his labors that the critical moment of self can be apprehended, as already stressed. The caveat: to glean this is to take it up without the rest. That has its dangers: the small thread I think I find there may not only be so woven into the fabric of his thought that yanking it out unravels the whole cloth; but also, it may not even be possible to seize upon it at all without also taking on the whole of it. Of course, it may also be that this crucial moment is indeed in Kierkegaard's work, whatever else is also there. In any event, my acknowledgement involves that claim, as my caveat implies that my claim may prove wrong, but only so far as it relates to Kierkegaard. The insight may stand by itself, and perhaps even Kierkegaard would have come to acknowledge it; perhaps not. That said, to the test.

Recall: self is not a synthesis (relation) between two (soul and body), but "that the relation relates itself to its own self." Now of such a relation two possibilities appertain: either it constitutes itself, or it is constituted by another. If it were the first, then it would be impossible for the self in its relatedness to itself to be more than itself. Self would be *solus ipse*, perhaps capable of pretending otherwise, but the sheerest of pretense it would be: an utter and windowless monad incapable even of reflecting the world interiorly, since it would of necessity lack any sense, even the merest glimmering, of "other." This can be seen as well if one considers that, as self-constituted, the self-relatedness of the relation between soul and body would necessarily not be related to any milieu (any "other"), and because of that would not be related to body—which is always a placement of and within the environing milieu—and therefore would not be "soul," for it would not be embodied, and thus the relation itself would completely collapse, hence there could not be any self-relatedness of a relation: no self. Indeed, it could not ever have been in the first place, thus "self-constitution" of itself is an *essential absurdity*.

If, on the other hand this relation which relates itself to its own self is constituted by another, then in so "relating to its own self, [it] relates itself to another." As such, self is not *merely* the reflexivity holding between soul and body, but is as well the self-relatedness holding between soul/body and, *minimally*, milieu. Or, better expressed, so as to be finally rid of naivety, there are not *two* relations (soul/body → milieu), nor *three* relations (soul → body → milieu), but a *single* one, complexly displayed by the total complexure: "self" is then the reflexivity exhibited by that complexure *as such* (soul/body/milieu). But even this is incomplete, for that reflexivity would be only a mode of self-referentiality if the sole intrinsically self-referring constituents were mind (soul), body (embodying organism), and world (milieu). This would be to suppose a kind of radical version of Robinson Crusoe: a creature somehow placed down full-bodied like Athena from some unknown and unknowable Zeus, in a milieu void of any creatures like itself, nor having any notion thereof.

For such a creature, could there be a *self*-presence? I think not, unless by a piece of double-think one illicitly supposes far more than is stated—e.g., having been born and raised within a social milieu, but then plunked down in some "elsewhere" with neither memory nor unconscious hold on *anything* prior. One might approximate such a supposal, by extrapolatively supposing a "purely" autistic child—but this, unlike the radical Crusoe, is a *limiting* notion, whereas that Crusoe would perforce have to fall *on the other side* of the limit. Which means, when you think of it, that such a supposal is quite literally *senseless*, non-supposable: an eidetic self-contradiction. But even if one were to broaden the supposal and say that such a Crusoe should be endowed with "self," the supposal is nowhere near what one began by trying to suppose. For in such a case, the crucial giveaway is made:

> such a Robinson Crusoe would never think: "There is no community and I belong to none: I am alone in the world". He would not only possess the notion and idea of community, but would also think: "I know that there is a community, and that I belong to one (or several such); but I am unacquainted with the individuals comprising them, and with the empirical groups of such individuals which constitute the community as it actually exists." (*107*, p. 234)

Such a Crusoe, then, though having no others like himself around, would necessarily—being posited as "enselved"—have a "specific and well-defined consciousness of *emptiness* or absence" (*107*, p. 235) with respect to emotive, perceptual, volitional, and valuational acts—acts, that is, which by essence, even if currently unfulfillable, are possible only in conjunction with the possibility of a social response. And, I suppose, given what has been learned from the last chapter, if one seriously posits this Crusoe, one would perforce *have* to follow out the consequences for that "self" of the regular and radical failure of such acts to find their mark: the inevitable failure and final collapse of "self." As a corollary to Bettelheim's and Bosch's observations of autistic children, if there is no *other self* against which to "test" the self, then not only will there be a fading of self, but of the other, and of the milieu as well. And with that withering and decline of self and nonself, there must go the *disappearance of both*, there then being no "self" into which to "withdraw." Hence if "milieu" means *only* a world of environing *things*, utterly unlike because unresponsive to and taking no account of the self, then there could not possibly be self at all—eventually, surely, but also from the outset, if one tries to make (*per impossible*) the first supposal.

Accordingly, *the fundamental condition for the very possibility of self is the other self.* Without the other self, the self cannot emerge in the first place; and, if one supposes a Crusoe-like creature already endowed with "self," then without the other self, self eventually must wither—and in both cases, without self, there can be no nonself, no milieu, hence no body: an utter and complete nought. This, I want to say, is the core sense of Kierkegaard's "another"; or in different words, that "the self cannot of itself attain and remain in equilibrium and rest by itself, but only by relating itself to that Power which constituted the whole relation" (*61*, p. 147). I am cognizant of the capital "P" there; I do not see, however, any good reason to suppose that it is essential to equate "Power" with "God"—as Kierkegaard of course believes. *At the very least*, in any case, *another self* is necessary, but this self is not necessarily "the" or "a" God. There may well be such, but even if there were not, "*another*" is intrinsically necessary for there to be self, a relation which relates itself to itself and in relating itself to its own self relates to another self. The same would, moreover, have to hold even if there were the "Power" with the capital "P" (God): i.e., even if one were forced to suppose a sort of ultimate Ground for the self-relating relation, in order for the self-relating to be *self-relating* it must at the same time be *other-relating*—and it is that moment of other-relating (alterity) which is here crucial.

Even so, this complex self-relatedness reveals on still closer scrutiny a curious disproportion, a disrelationship. Consider: self is no entity or substance; it is the delicate, precarious, yet tenacious reflexive fabric of the complexure of life. Yet this *self*-relatedness cannot be "itself" without the presence within its very self-relatedness of *another* self-relatedness—which, in turn, *is not* "itself" without the first self-relatedness. The self as self-relatedness is *as such* related to the other self *as* itself a self-relatedness to itself, and *as such* to the self. Thus self-relatedness requires the presence of the other self. The "power" of the other self is precisely the "empowering" of self in its self-relatedness, and is thereby also a "*self*-empowering." Seeking the other is finding that the other self is already present.

Precisely thereby, however, is the delicate fabric of self a *disrelationship*: it is forever reflected to itself while reflecting to the other, and is not at all without that *mutuality*. *What constitutes self yet distances self from itself is precisely "other" self.* This, I take it, is what Kierkegaard means:

> The disrelationship of despair is not a simple disrelationship but a disrelationship in a relation which relates itself to its own self and is constituted by another, so that the disrelationship in that self-relation reflects itself infinitely in the relation to the Power which constituted it. (*61*, p. 147)

Yet this self-distancing which characterizes both self and other self—which, when it is present, is that by virtue of which the infant *is at all able* to grow out of its initial symbiotic relation to the mother—this self-distancing, while it is in the very distancing a dis-*relationship* of a sort, is also and more keenly a *dis*-relationship. For the forms of despair Kierkegaard lays out must, as he emphasizes, be

> viewed under the category of consciousness. . . . Generally speaking, consciousness, i.e. consciousness of self, is the decisive criterion of the self. The more consciousness, the more self; the more consciousness, the more will, and the more will the more self. A man who has no will at all has no self; the more will he has, the more consciousness of self he has also. (*61*, p. 162)

As the conscious, willing, reflexive relation, self is a task—the task, "is to become itself . . . to become concrete." However, he goes on, a self, every instant it exists, is in process of becoming, for the self [potentially] does not actually exist, it is only that which it is to become. In so far as the self does not become itself, it is not its own self; but not to be one's own self is despair. (*61*, p. 163)

For (to continue picking my way carefully through these words) to be thus continually in the *dynamic tension of mutual distancing yet affiliating with the other self* is to be continually *on the way* (*en-route, journeying*), not only becoming oneself, but becoming oneself-along-with-the-other-self. Hence self is a willing—a willing or desiring (Ricoeur) to be itself grounded in and along with the other self—and as such, self is *aware, alerted, efforting*. Being aware ("consciousness"), alerted to oneself along with and by means of the other, however, is being aware of oneself as *not* oneself; the more cognizant of not being oneself, the more "testing" with the other self. But the other can, as also willing, give and receive, give only, receive only, or neither give nor receive (and with degrees for each). For self to emerge the other self is requisite; but its modes of being requisite can vary, as also may the self's willing with the other vary, and all these in numerous modes of combination, degree, and in time and rhythms vary still more.

The *dis*-relationship is thus made present in and by the very mutuality of self/other self relationships: the initial discord of and in the self is its very being aware of itself and therefore willing to be itself, hence its awareness of not being itself. Continually reflected back to itself by the other while at the same time reflecting the other to itself—in the embrace of the contextural networks of selving and being enselved—self can come to see itself *there, in the other* (again, in multiple ways); or *there, in images*, causes, goals, beliefs, etc.; or *there, in itself* as reflected by this or that other, now and then, and then again at another time. The *dis*-relationship in the self is its being the complex relatedness it is. Hence the modes of despair—willing to be itself, willing to be rid of itself, not willing to be itself—are the direct consequence of "that in the relation, that the relation relates itself to its own self and in so relating to its own self relates itself to another."

This is the further texture of self, that *in its self-relating to the other self-relating self, it is enmeshed within the giving and receiving of self* (selving and being enselved). Whether, if ever, the self ever can come to will to be that self it truly is (*61*, p. 153) in its relating to the other—i.e., whether the "rising fever in the sickness of the self" can ever be healed by other selves—is a question to which Kierkegaard has a clear response. "The self is in sound health and free from despair only when, precisely by having been in despair, it is grounded transparently in God" (*61*, p. 163). Whether that be so, the implications of his words for the present problem seem clear and evidently to the point—even if, to make that point, it is necessary to wrench these implications from his main concern. The major point in going through this somewhat acrobatic, if not eerie path of words, is just this: the self is precisely that eerie acrobat, and attending carefully to its moves and turns makes plain that the presence of the other self at the heart of self, and vice versa, is no mere rope of words. *The decisive condition without which self could not possibly be itself is the tensioned, affiliated presence of the other self, for whose emergence and maintaining self is likewise necessary as a constitutive moment.* Precisely this is the significance of *mutuality*: the myriad-formed reflexivities present in self's relationship to other self, and other self's relationship to self, and both to the relationship. Hence *mutuality is the contextural mode of the complexure of life.* Self, I earlier said, is the *eidos* of life; but, as self is *essentially affiliated*, that *eidos* can now be seen in its fuller textures, as mutuality.

THE ACHIEVEMENT OF MUTUALITY

Schutz, it was seen, agreed with Scheler's idea that the "we" is primordial for the "I" only in one respect: within everyday life, the existence of other persons is taken for granted, just insofar as each of us lives naively directed mainly toward the life-world. I simply live amidst other human beings, other animate beings, and a world of things, without questioning very much or very deeply, and even when I do question, it is usually "this" or "that," rarely the life-world itself and as such. But herein, too, I am for the most part not much aware of myself; and nothing of what systematic reflection discloses is at all apparent so long as I remain naively occupied with my life-worldly concerns. Indeed, it takes a critical shift of attention, an epochē of the epochē inherent to daily life (*109*, I, pp. 229, 233) (a refraining from the refraining-from-questioning, which is the mark of everydayness), to bring out any of the distinctions, even to make the structures and textures of daily life itself stand out.

In that respect, the "we" is indeed pregiven to the "I." If Scheler, however, were saying only that, Schutz would be perfectly correct in his criticism. It seems to me, though, that Scheler is onto quite a *different* issue: precisely the present one, namely the question concerning what is essential to the *emergence* of self, and Scheler's thesis here is quite *independent* of whether in reflection "I" find "my" thoughts and thinking as "mine." Keeping firmly in mind the reflexivities just elicited from Kierkegaard's writing will make this phenomenon evident.

In the course of discussing the analogical argument *as a theory of origins*— which he quickly rejects—Scheler notes some findings from anthropology and child psychology. Miss Ghinn and W. Stern are cited as observing how the very young infant (about 25 days old) already seems to show signs of interest in human faces, voices, and gestures; the child responds with "a gentle smile" (Stern). This, Scheler claims, shows that "it is the inflections of the human voice and not just the simple auditory stimuli thereof, which first arouse attention and interest" (*107*, p. 239). From such observations, from Koffka's great study (*63*, p. 134),[2] and from studies of primitives, Scheler concludes that what is *first* apprehended are "*expressions* of mind." This shows no analogical inferences. Rather, he then maintains in a most important passage,

The rags and tatters of sensation from which associationism endeavors to piece together our picture of the world are just pure fictions. In the case of the primitive, so well described by Lévy-Brühl, we might perhaps go further and say that everything whatsoever is given, for him, as "expression" and that what we call development through learning is not a subsequent addition of mental elements to an already-given inanimate world of material objects, but a continuous process of disenchantment, in that only a proportion of sensory appearances retain their function as vehicles of expression, while others do not. Learning, in this sense, is not *animation*, but a continual "*de-animation*". One should not impute to children or primitives the world-view of a civilized adult, and then go on to postulate real processes in order to transform this picture back into that of the child or the primitive. (*107*, pp. 239–40)

Now although Scheler seems (it is difficult to tell precisely) to return to this point by insisting on the "undifferentiated" flow of experiences, and on his notion of the "self in a general sense"—both of which must be rejected for the reasons already given—this passage nevertheless strikes me as absolutely fundamental for understanding the emergence of self within the embrace of mutuality.

It is first necessary to emphasize that the above passage in *no* way implies, requires or presupposes that primordial experience be "undifferentiated as between mine and thine." Indeed, the passage can well be taken as exhibiting precisely the rudimentary and autochthonously developing mode of organization of the mutuality of selves. The claim about undifferentiatedness seems to me sheerly gratuitous, and wrong in any case.

Nevertheless, Scheler here has one of those flashes of genius for which he was so well known. To see it, it is necessary to consider his formulation and critical rejection of the undergirding assumptions of so much traditional and current theory. Descartes' claim in a way initiates the tradition, when he maintained that it is easier to know one's own mind than anything else, even one's own body. Scheler's formulation is apposite: "(1) that it is always *our own self, merely, that is primarily given to us*; (2) that what is primarily given in the case of others is merely the *appearance of the body*" (*107*, p. 244), and on the basis of whose movements and alterations we somehow come to accept it as animate and embodying another self. Whether the former be argued in the service of "self" or "mind" or "soul," and whether the second be argued by inference or analogy, or even the Husserlian appresentational pairing (*41*, V; *47*, pp. 44–47, 50, 51)—Scheler strenuously objects to and rejects both. It is crucial to see how and why, even though some of this is doubtless already familiar terrain to many.

(1) The first presumption is this: that the subject (mind or self) is *primarily* a *cognitive subject*, and is *a self-subsistent and self-existent entity* (*res*) which is *ontologically on a par* with other entities (extended things). The cognitive relation between these ontologically coordinate and mutually independent entities is such that, if there is a cognizing, the *sole immediately presented "object"* of the cognizing is something that is internal to, an immanent

component of, the cognitive subject itself (i.e., "impressions," "stimuli," "data," or "ideas"). Hence the prime epistemic question: given (by presumption, of course) that there is no cognitive subject immediately acquainted with anything except what is immanent to and an internal determination of its own interiority (mind, self), how is it possible for it to know anything else? The typical move was to the mind's own immediately presented object, the "idea," and its sources, sensory "impressions." These are taken as causally delivered; they essentially "come from" an "elsewhere" than the mind (except for the products of imagination, but even these are ultimately traceable to sensory bases), hence the philosophical task is doubled: (a) to trace out the "origins" of ideas (which led to its causally efficacious sources, and left this "causality" utterly presumed), and (b) to find out how it could happen that, though interiorly resident in the closed room of the mind, "ideas" were yet (magically, one must think) "of" things other than the cognitive subject or its activities. This *theory of ideas* (*132*, pp. 51–71), so deeply entrenched in modern thought, supported and reinforced by an either explicit or implicit dualism, comes to be the frame for posing and attempting to resolve the question of "other minds." Scheler, having formulated the presumption, finds absolutely no evidence for it, and mountains of evidence against it. With its rejection goes the rejection as well of its way of putting the question of other minds.

The only thing "self-evident" about the assumption is this:

> that if once we postulate a *real substratum* for the experiences, of whatever kind, which I may happen to have, then all the thoughts and feelings which occur in me will in fact belong to this real substratum. And that is a tautology. (*107*, p. 245)

And, it is a tautology by simple *fiat*, a covert definitional trick which hoodwinks us into thinking then that nothing is more certain than that "I know myself best and most immediately of all!" We have already seen how damaging is that postulate. Scheler's response is basically to mark out the incredible optimism of it, and to show positively that its equally incredible pessimism is completely false.

The optimism of it is (as already mentioned) this: that it radically *under*estimates the enormities of self-knowledge. The pessimism is this: that by consistently building in a radical suspicion toward concrete embodied life and sensory perception, it seriously *over*estimates the difficulties of knowing other persons. Honest and careful scrutiny shows how often it is that one knows oneself least of all: one's motives for doing this or that, one's own feelings at the moment, where one's ideas come from, and the numerous urges and notions which, I have stressed, continually bubble up to surprise, embarrass, even terrorize oneself. And the same honesty shows ever so clearly just how well we know other persons, their doubts and faiths, their lying and lust, their care and collusions: the subtle glint in that fellow's eye, the way that man averts his glance from me, the openly embracing look and aspect of one's lover, and the myriad ways of touching, walking, holding the head, shrugging the shoulders, lifts of lips and grimaces.

From all this, Scheler is convinced that if there is anything to the idea of "inner perception," it can only be that the other self is perceptually apprehended *within* myself. As distinct from the "sphere of 'inner sense' "—which is that wherein I experience my own embodying organism and which *is* closed to all save myself—is the "sphere of internal intuition (or those of internal perception, representation, feeling and the like)." However the details of such "spheres" be worked out—and Scheler does work out the rudiments of an intriguing theory—his point here is, I think, sound and noteworthy:

> The only thing we can never perceive in our observation of others is their experience of their own *bodily states*, especially their organic sensations, and the sensory feelings attached thereto. It is these things which account for that particular *kind* of separateness among men which the above-mentioned theories attribute to the *whole* of mental life. (*107*, p. 255)

This exclusiveness of the experiences of one's own organic states and feelings derives from the fact that the embodying organism is the *condition* for the occurrence of perception (inner and outer): "the brain and the nervous system and all the events occurring in them merely determine what is *perceived*, but not the occurrence and content of mental processes. . . . [T]he body and its changes merely condition the appearance or aspect that our experience presents to inner sense, but never the experience itself" (*107*, p. 254). Thus, in view of this *functional dependence and orientation* (as I earlier called it) which is a crucial dimension of embodiment, *my own feeling of my own body is my own entirely* (even though I may be quite confused and uncertain, vague and the like, about, for example, where a "pain" lies, etc.), and so for the other self. *But that is all* that can with evidence be called "private," "closed" to anyone else's experience, for Scheler.

We are thus free to recognize how much indeed of the other's emotions, thoughts, feelings, we can and do share in common. The signal difference, as I get Scheler's point here, between the noetic-noematic correlation pertaining to the awareness of the own-body, as distinct from what pertains to the awarenesses of other affairs (whether worldly things, other persons, goals, etc.) is just this: that, whereas in the first what is experienced (kinaesthetically, coenesthetically, etc.) is my own embodying organism and never my body as apprehended by the other (for to apprehend my own body I must activate and rely on its organic processes, whereas the other self activates and relies on his own embodying organism), in the second there is not this dependence, even though for me to be aware of the tree there must be the embodying processes already mentioned. In the latter case, my own embodying processes are not themselves "objects," but rather functional orientations which alone allow the object (the tree over there) ever to appear as such. Thus *simply because my own experience of my own body is my own entirely, it in no way follows that everything I experience is also my own entirely.* The mutuality of selves shows that matters are quite different.

In any case, to return again briefly to Kierkegaard, it is precisely with regard to this signal difference that it is necessary to stress the *"dis*-relationship" in the "relation that relates itself to itself and thereby to another": *while bound to one another, we yet are distanced precisely by our respective embodiments, which on the other hand are the primal conditions for our ever being able to "experience" anything, including one another.* And *that* is a true "dis-relationship" at the heart of mutuality, of our reflexively intertwined self-relatedness.

If mental life—or what Scheler at times, and I at all times, must call "self"— were utterly imprisoned and private, he remarks, we should be condemned to a "solipsism of the moment." Nature itself would perforce *have* to be equally "private"—and just this follows with strict necessity from the dualistic theory of ideas. It is thus no accident that Hume, for example, came along; "the only incorrigible certainty would be," Scheler remarks, "the existence of the solipsist's own momentary self" (*107*, p. 259). The only thing which saves Hume—though not his theory—is his appeal to that quite incredible, because so potent, "inadvertence" of daily life. It makes no difference what Hume wrote, for his skepticism is quickly overcome because we all believe in the world anyway. But what Hume the philosopher completely failed to see is just that: that Hume the person (and the rest of us) do indeed, by custom and habit, go right on taking for granted the existence of the world, other people, and ourselves as well. What the first Hume should have done is to have made the second Hume thematic; doing that would have landed him in the thematic arms of Simmel, Weber, Husserl and Schutz: the "life-world" as a fundamental theme for inquiry, precisely in the form of that "inadvertence," as the "taken-for-granted."

Scheler's comment to that solipsism of the passing moment is suggestive:

Nor is it without interest to observe how in the history of philosophy the existence of a real external world has been far more frequently denied than the existence of other selves; and this though no one has denied our ability to perceive Nature, while practically everyone has disputed our powers of perceiving mental life in others. The reason for this is that *our conviction of the existence of other minds is earlier and deeper than our belief in the existence of Nature.* (*107*, p. 259)

Nor is that the only irony: for disputing our ability to know others always and ironically finds its way into speech and writing—books and speeches—whose nature and goal of address is other persons. Nor is Scheler's the only reason: it is understandable, if still resoundingly comic, that nonliving Nature should be so regarded, as also living beings, when we recall what Jonas has emphasized, that not "life" but "death" is what is left as unproblematic through dualism and its errant offspring, hence it is not "death" but "life" that is the great incomprehensible. Scheler represents, in these terms, the first radical break with the very core of philosophy since Descartes.

(2) Our conviction of the existence of other selves is more primordial than our belief in Nature. Learning, becoming an adult, is a "continuous process of disenchantment," a "de-animation" and not an "animation." Here Scheler sounds the substantive note.

> For we certainly believe ourselves to be directly acquainted with another person's joy in his laughter, with his sorrow and pain in his tears, with his shame in his blushing, with his entreaty in his outstretched hands, with his love in his look of affection, with his rage in the gnashing of his teeth, with his threats in the clenching of his fist, and with the tenor of his thoughts in the sound of his words. (*107*, p. 260)

What is it, then, that I know of the other self? And is it only thanks to my perception of his bodily movements and changes that I then, as a second, subtle, and unrealized step, go on to infer "pain," "love," "anger," etc.? When, in fact, do I come to doubt the other, and what is it I doubt? Surely I may have "second thoughts" about someone, say an old friend, when in contradiction to the sorts of things I have long known him to believe, I learn that he has asserted something entirely otherwise, with all seriousness. Just so may I come to "disbelieve my own eyes" when I witness a well-dressed and lively-looking fellow of a sudden go to his knees and begin a ritual chant in a public restaurant. And I may well clearly infer from a stranger's demeanor and visage that he has evil intentions on my person. All these clearly go on, but they occur only when I find my usual expectations checked, upset, unsettled, in discrepancy with what I otherwise know. But just as clearly, all these doubtings and surmisings, inferrings and wonderings, *presuppose* that these others are directly delivered "in person" to me.

> Thus I do not merely see the other person's eyes, for example; I also see that "he is looking at me" and even that "he is looking at me as though he wished to avoid my seeing that he is looking at me". So too do I perceive that he is only pretending to feel what he does not feel at all, that he is severing the familiar bond between his experience and its natural expression, and is substituting another expressive movement in place of the particular phenomenon implied by his experience. (*107*, p. 261)

It is obvious: I know when my old friend is trying to hide the fact of his great pain; even more, any medical interview displays with remarkable openness the subtle shifts and plays, the ploys and dodges, on the part of patients or physicians. I say to a student, or he to me: "that isn't really what you want to say . . . ." Hence Scheler insists that

> our immediate perceptions of our fellow-men do not relate to their bodies (unless we happen to be engaged in a medical examination),[3] nor yet to their "selves" or "souls."

> What we perceive are *integral wholes*, whose intuitive content is not immediately resolved in terms of external and internal perception. (*107*, p. 261)

Apprehending the other's body as such can be, and is, done, of course, but always within specific contexts having their own specific perceptual and other demands: a medical exam, learning to dance, etc. So, too, do we apprehend the other self, as when we witness his nervousness in the face of being caught in the act of cheating, etc. In whichever way, it is always a question of integral wholes apprehended within specific contexts of action and concern.

> The primary awareness, in ourselves, in animals and in primitives, invariably consists of *patterns of wholeness*; sensory appearances are only given in so far as they function as the basis of these patterns, or can take on the further office of signifying or representing such wholes. (*107*, p. 264)

Simply because my own body must be "stimulated" from another body in no way implies that I have to be aware solely of that body, or that I must "first of all" be aware of colors, feels, smells, etc. "before" I can recognize a friendly or threatening gesture. I *can* become aware of these, e.g., of flesh-tones, as when I try to paint a portrait; but this always comes *after* and as a resolution of or abstraction from the concretely given "patterns of wholeness." As "wholes," however, as we have learned, these are *contextures*; hence these "patterns" are those of reflexive mutuality.

"TESTING": THE EMERGENCE OF SELF WITH OTHER

It is necessary to secure Scheler's insight: learning, i.e., emerging as self among other also emerging and emerged selves, is not *animation but de-animation*, a process of "disenchantment." Our conviction of the existence of other selves is *deeper and earlier* than that of natural things.[4]

"Animism" or "pan-vitalism," it could be said, are not first of all or primarily *theories* or even myths; *they are first of all concrete stages of human life*. Hence "emergence" or "awakening" of self and other self signifies their becoming explicit by way of "disenchantment" or "de-animation." That "way" is *the way of "testing"*: becoming oneself is an ongoing *task*, but this means *strictly* that it is a *work*, an unfolding drama, sometimes a battle and always a hazardous endeavor, an *adventure whose outcome is never sure and whose achievement is always a risk and threatened in unsuspected* (perhaps even unsuspectable) *ways*. This path of becoming unfolds by enfolding the other in continual "tests,"[5] but the path shows *stages*, some critical and some less so, and most of them are astonishingly early in the life of self. The way of disenchantment is set for richer enchantments, it may be, but *the disengaging of self from these initiating encounters with other selves is requisite*. Nothing shows this so clearly as the phenomenon of autism; but understanding that remarkable failure, as

Bettelheim stresses, requires an understanding of the earliest stages of life. It is to this, guided by him, that I turn as a way of showing what I take to be the significance of Scheler's insight, which I believe is best understood in light of the suggested interpretation of Kierkegaard.

The world of the newborn infant is no mere time of passivity: taking in milk and nourishment, contentedly sleeping for long periods, relieving itself unconcernedly anywhere and anytime. Initial helplessness does not purport passive acceptance. Bettelheim, basing his view not only on his own observations but on those of many others, emphasizes that this is an "age when the human being just born takes important steps in trying actively to master his fate" (*5*, p. 14). However small these may seem to an adult, they are not only critically significant for the whole future of the infant, but are steps requiring comparatively enormous expenditures of energy: we may too easily overlook that "the infant sleeps long perhaps just because the learning is so intense and exhausting" (*5*, p. 14), and it is a process of learning reflexively locked in with other persons from the outset.

Thus the myth that infancy is a kind of golden age, a paradise lost too soon, sponsored even formally in psychiatry and psychoanalysis (*5*, p. 15), is simply wrong. Just as Scheler had earlier maintained, so Bettelheim warns against projecting our view of world into the infant (i.e., a version of the "psychologist's fallacy"). However much we know how helpless is the infant, the infant knows this not at all. Even in the merest incident of nursing the infant is "eminently active," his "efforts are monumental." Kohut, for instance, says that the state of the healthy newborn in the act of nursing

> should be compared with the emotional state of an adult who is totally absorbed in an activity of the utmost importance to him as, for example, the sprinter at the last few yards of the 100-yard dash, the virtuoso at the height of the cadenza, or the lover at the peak of sexual union. (*64*; *5*, p. 15)

Still, however central is the act of nursing for the infant, Bettelheim emphasizes that even the newborn takes note of the world, pays deliberate attention—indeed, were there no "quiet alertness" to the surroundings, it is hard to imagine how "development" could occur.[6] Despite the "passive satisfactions" given to the autistic children he treated, none of the children moved out of their autism because of these. Rather, "they came to life only when we were able to create the conditions, or otherwise be the catalysts, that induced them to take action in their own behalf" (*5*, p. 17). "Self" is then *empowered* or enabled to be itself (the human equivalent, I have suggested, of Kierkegaard's theological "Power").

The act of nursing, just because it *is* so focal for the infant, must be studied for what else occurs around it—as also the rest of the infant's early activities. What surrounds nursing makes a difference—whether the child is held gently or stiffly, securely or anxiously, whether his noises are heeded or ignored, whether his efforts are fostered or squelched. The infant not only *nurses*, he *is being nursed*, and this initiating *mutuality* is highly significant:

> Because while the infant can make it clear, through the way he holds his body, whether or not he feels comfortably held, he cannot ensure that this active expression of his feelings will meet with a positive response. That will depend on how the mother reacts. While he can and does act in his own behalf, his view of himself and the world will depend on the failure or success of his efforts. Consistent nonreward for being active may even lead to his giving up trying to shape his interactions and yield to passivity. The same is true for the way he adjusts to being picked up or diapered or bathed. When he is active, be it in nursing, or in watching the world, he is at the height of his encounter with life. But how his activity succeeds, and the response it receives, will significantly color all his later attempts at self-motivated actions. (5, p. 17)

The infant can be as active as his milieu and his embodying organism allow—initially, and at every moment (barring disaster) *testing* and thereby *receiving* his *self* in turn. Things may go wrong, go from there to bad to worse—always depending upon the multiple modes of *receptivity and kinds of enabling* with which the infant's "tests" are received and returned (welcomed, snubbed, or brutalized). At each stage, what is thus of critical importance is "this initial experience of having acted on one's own within a context of mutuality, of having known what it is to be fully active, of having shaped the experience in spite of one's otherwise dependent state" (5, p. 19). Just this mutuality, this give-and-take and literal push-and-shove of the act of nursing, constitutes its "essence." All the other components of it—the pleasure given and received, the tactile sensations, etc.—are, while enriching, only ancillary to the central mutuality. Already the "self-relating" relation which is "self" is manifestly *being empowered*, i.e., is *in itself* related to the other self and *both are intrinsically related* as well *to their relationship*.

It would clearly be erroneous—indeed, contrary to the very point being urged—to suppose that we have to do with a clearly communicating and receiving self in the case of the infant. At the outset, it is probably true that there is no two-way communicating—or at the most, only minimally: vague hustlings and shovings, ambivalently articulated feelings and strivings. Still, these become explicited, displayed, empowered gradually and in their own time and rhythms, through the holdings and suckings, graspings and cooings, movings and cryings, of the infant. A feel of discomfort when being held a certain way elicits crying, and (say) the mother's responding by moving makes the discomfort lessen: as this goes on and the pain is located "by which part of the body senses it most keenly, the feeling of self (or the body ego) begins to develop" (5, p. 23). Not all at once, but gradually and in rhythms with clusterings of other such experiences. And along with that the rudiments of communicating begin: the sharing with the other of what is proper to oneself. Then further, through the course of continuous and increasingly diverse testings and respondings, mutual playing and so on, a further differentiation of body-awareness and other-awareness begins to grow.

> By now the infant has repeatedly experienced that his needs are not always or immediately met. And the manageable frustration that follows is what makes him aware that an outer world even exists.[7] The emphasis here is on the *manageable*. Because otherwise the child is so flooded by unpleasant emotions that nothing else seems to exist. . . . Thus the child's expectation that something outside of him will satisfy his needs is what powerfully increases his interest in the world and his impulse to learn more about it. (5, p. 24)

What follows is the critical point of learning: that the infant can, through his own efforts, influence the others and the things in his milieu: by noises, by gestures, by glances, etc. This "coming to terms" with what is other than the infant "requires a liminal notion of self evoking, manipulating, influencing a nonself" (5, p. 24). Thus continually enriched through *efficacious efforts* and responsive enabling, an enrichment of self grows, always, however, as precarious. For it can be eroded in many ways: through artificial routinizing of feeding, by ignoring his cries and coos, through the various forms of brutalizing him, as also by the many forms of being *over*-responsive.

What is of such import is that the child *feels that he makes a difference*, that *his* efforts are efficacious, according to his own demands and rhythms: the *testings* must meet with *responsiveness*, else self can but wither, eventually. But the testing is not merely an "appeal"; it is rather more akin to a literal producing of self. If the effort meets vacancy, inattentiveness, inappropriate response, there is no way to tell whether there has even been effort expended: hence *resistance* is deeply akin to *response*, and both are tied in with testing. *To be empowered, self must be enabled to be active, to test*—which is the other side of empowering.

Further stages become increasingly apparent: testing for specific results, testing for independence, etc. Once having grasped the principle, however, working out the subsequent stages and their many variations becomes more readily ascertainable. What I am driving toward is already at hand: what was earlier identified as *effortful possibilizing turns out to be ineluctably bound up with other selves*, whatever may be the particular ways these efforts are responded to. A final point must still be elicited, however, before the conditions for the possibility of awakening (mutuality) can be seized.

It is this: the emergence of self within the contextual embrace of other selves (or its curtailment, as the case may be) goes through *critical* stages. Presenting the idea very tentatively—for although it seems to have been well-established in animals, it is perhaps as yet only suggestive for human beings—Bettelheim nevertheless regards it as immensely significant. Referring to those who have studied animal and bird life, these "critical periods" are those special times in life "when a small amount of experience will produce a great effect on later behavior." A "relative rather than an absolute concept," the difference between the amount of effort needed to produce an effect at different periods depends on how critical the period is. It may be that the failure to develop an ability at a critical period will result in its essential loss, for it may not be duplicatable at all (*112*; *5*, p. 40). Similarly, disruptions which occur during such periods will (in general) tend to be far more crucial than if they occur at another, less critical period.

In the case of the human infant, however, matters are far more complicated, uncertain, and variably flexible. What is one period in the dog, for example, seems covered in at least two of the human, and is spread out over a longer time. In general, it appears, there are at least two such critical periods in early human development of especial sensitivity and intense learning. The nature of the critical period varies, moreover, depending on what has preceded, on its length (the longer, it seems, the greater the chances of later reversal of impact) and on the infant's inherent capacity to learn (some may learn in a short time what it takes others much longer to learn, if at all).

(1) At about six to nine months, the infant "is more definite about recognizing familiar persons" (*5*, p. 41). As well, unfamiliar and even threatening others are perceived, and real object relations begin. "Strangers" are thus separated out from the infant's earlier positive relations to those who earlier mothered and nurtured him, and with this the child's first "rudimentary awareness of self becomes extended to others" (*5*, p. 42). What seems crucial to the emerging sense of self is the initiating of differentiations between "familiars" and "strangers"—and, coordinately, the self's testing results in the initiating within self of the sense of "familiar" and "strange."

(2) At about eighteen months, upright posture becomes firmly attained, hence the beginnings of genuine distancings—with the beginning, too, of language and locomotion, thus of initial freeing from the ground: getting up, independence, fending for oneself, being on one's own, but still within the limits allowed by the parental (or guardian) milieu and the abilities of his embodying organism. "Approach" and "avoid" are thus opened up, and with them the crucial dimensions of intersections of spatiality interwoven with that of others. And with encounters with others, there develops the sense of the zonal space of the body-sphere (the "three-mile" zone of Straus), and the other dimensions of embodiment already mentioned, especially the greater explicitness of "having-an-effect" on the environing milieu (shoving, pulling, grasping, moving) and the senses of "if-then" (i.e., "causality"). Thereby opens up, too, the dimensions of the heft of time noted: "if" the child turns the knob, "then" the radio comes on. "Aiming-at" thus opens up along with "approach" and "avoid," and the presence of self becomes more fully manifested.

If there are critical periods, their sense as critical is found in these stages of embodied life (and there are probably other such stages after these early years), thanks to the functioning of which uprightness, locomotion, distancing, having-an-effect, etc., become articulated. What is "critical" about such periods, then, is that they are stages of explicitness of the reflexive mutuality among selves, some or at least one of which, it seems necessary, *must be an already developed*, full-fledged *person*. This seems necessary, for inspecting the range of cases of the awakening self, it seems that the "year too early" out of the womb which Portmann stressed is indeed just that: not only does the infant exhibit the distinctive helplessness mentioned, but, as has been seen here, for there to be *an emerging self* there must be testing, and this is bound up with the multiple forms of encouragement, responsiveness, and enabling which alone at once permit testing to be successful, hence give it its sense, and are abilities (beings-able) solely of already-developed selves.

It seems plain that the critical periods are deeply tied to the presence of such full selves, for these periods of unusual sensitivity and intensity of alertness are likewise those in which the child seems most susceptible to frustration, anxiety, becoming aware of having *no* effect on things or persons. The essential *Anlage* of autism, Bettelheim believes, stems from "the conviction that one's efforts have no power to influence the world, because of the earlier conviction that the world is insensitive to one's reactions" (5, p. 46). The emergence of "that in the relation that the relation relates itself to its own self," therefore, is contexturally bound to the other self's relatedness to the self, and the ways both relate themselves to their relationship.

Testing, as the mode by which this mutuality establishes the emergence of self, is thus contexturally bound to the responsiveness of the adult self to the emerging self: resistances, expectations, enablings, encouragements, or conversely at the other extreme, inappropriate expectation, failures to recognize, over-attentiveness, inconstant resistance, presenting obstacles and frustrations. Thus the "Power" (Kierkegaard) of the other, which grounds the relation that relates itself to its own self, is no meager affair, but *most real and efficacious for the very possibility of self's emergence at all*, much less the emergence as this or that aspect or talent. Indeed, without the initiating and enabling other, self can never develop, or must shrivel away, cutting off even the potentialities of profound despair. It thus seems justifiable to have taken Kierkegaard as seriously as I did, risky matter though it may be to have read him in the way I did.

The milieu of human life is, of necessity, itself "alive" in its initiating phases: life meeting budding life. But it is also clear that there is *already* a rich differentiation of the milieu, even for the newborn, although in a way Scheler's notion (the "general self," the "undifferentiated as between mine and thine") seems most closely approximated when we try to put ourselves in the place of the infant. But this is only an approaching of what falls beyond any intelligible limit, as was seen.

The course of the emergence of self seems indeed a process of "de-animation," or of empowering the reflexive presence of self. As Bettelheim remarks at one point, for the separation of friend and stranger to occur it is essential that "the baby's prior experience must have enabled him to single out some as friends; that is he must have had the experience that the world is essentially good" (5, p. 47). If it were otherwise, the infant could never have come to emerge to the first critical period in the first place, but would rather have lapsed already into autism (as some do). But the "good" and "friendly" here have their sense, it seems to me, within the relation of mutuality: testing and responding, enabling the activity of the infant to come to some resistant, efficacious grip on his milieu, hence on his self and the other self. What alone can effectuate this is not merely another self, but another already explicited self. *Care is thus a primordial experience* for the enabling self and for the enabled self, although the latter cannot be said to experience it in the way the former does.

On the ground of caring by that responsively alive selfhood, the emerging self thus is able to come to the experience of other parts of the milieu as unfriendly, i.e., as not caring (whether really so or not, from the perspective of the other, is neither here nor there: thus, like it or not, intend it or not, a father may well be grasped by the infant, as it were, as "menacing," etc.).

From among the others in the milieu, some become singled out as "strange," "unfriendly," i.e., as *un*enabling or *un*responsive (perhaps as inappropriately responsive) or, normally, as unknown. That is, the infant undergoes the process of "disenchantment": not all others are able or willing to nurse or care, and among the willing and able, not all proceed in a familiar way. Further disenchantments await the self; the experiences of frustration, anxiety, and the like—that is, of disturbance in the course of testing—are disclosures of these, and thus are the grounds for continuous differentiations, i.e., disenchantments.

Inasmuch, however, as the present study is not at all concerned to ascertain the full genetic constitution of self—as I have said before—but only the critical place of others for the emergence of self, it is not possible to probe these disenchantments or differentiations further. Nor, it must be added, is it possible to try and unlayer more concretely the way in which "de-animation" proceeds. Both, most important topics, are the themes for a future study. For my present purposes, after having delineated what I have set out to do, and having at least marked out the issue for that fuller genetic study, it is necessary to pass on to the final issue of the study, and thereby to secure more firmly the essential yet precarious reflexivity of self as intrinsically related to itself, but as a self-relatedness whose texture is woven within and by the self-relatedness pertaining to the other self—whereby both are reflexively related to the relationship which binds and constitutes them as mutually enabling and enabled selves.

11

The Vivid Presence

IN the previous chapter, it was maintained that an important insight can be extracted from Kierkegaard's portrayal of self: the emergence of self presupposes, as one of its essential conditions, the *presencing to one another of reflexivities*, which phenomenon was termed *mutuality*. For understanding the peculiarities intrinsic to the interrelatings of *two complexures*, his insight, however bizarre on the surface, is, I believe, accurate, and is articulated with care. To excise that account, however, required an equally careful piece of surgery; but even so, Kierkegaard's analysis—dialectical and restorative—is on the way to the idea of the "theological self," the self before God (*61*, p. 210). On the other hand, it is a telling comment on his conception of self that there is hardly a word about the emergence of self with other human selves—despite the forceful irony that he is nonetheless immensely sensitive to the play and interplay of self-to-self relations.[1] Even though one finds in Kierkegaard the central concern for "my reader," the "Singular Individual," and "indirect communication," about all he says about the other self in its relations to the self is that, so considered, the self has a merely finite "measure" thereby; with either parent, culture, or the state, there is only "the self whose measure is man" (*61*, p. 210; cf. *14*, p. 30). My excising of the reflexive core of mutuality from his conception of self-relatedness was in no way intended to be a critique of it, but rather intended as an aid in explicating the complexities of that mutuality. Nevertheless, one clear implication of this explication of Kierkegaard is that the irony is doubled: not only is he silent on the issue of emergence of selfhood while yet being most sensitive; but, reconsidered, his display of the reflexivity of self *can* be seen to illumine the presence of the other self for the emerging self. "Power," interpreted this way, I suggested, is a very real force in the life of self— whatever else its place and significance. So interpreted, however, another thing becomes apparent.

In *The Concept of Dread*, this "Power" is said to be "Spirit":

Man is a synthesis of the soulish and the bodily. But a synthesis is unthinkable if the two are not united in a third factor. This third factor is the spirit. (*62*, p. 39)

Spirit is said to be present in that synthesis "in a state of immediacy, a dreaming state," and is both a "friendly" and a "hostile" power (*62*, p. 39), since it at once constantly *disturbs* the innocence of the synthesis, and yet is precisely what *empowers* the self-relatedness of the relation, *makes it be "that* the relation relates itself to its own self," *by* making the "self-relatedness" be at the same time a "self-relatedness" to the other—*in the same relationship.* So long as man is unawakened as self, Spirit "dreams" only, but the dream is an urge for man to be cognizant of himself: this is the despair that does not know itself as despair, the condition of most persons, says Kierkegaard.

In these terms, if it is possible to interpret him as I have, then that "*spirit*"— perhaps only as a sort of manifestation of "something greater," perhaps not—*is the "power" of enabling, empowering the self to emerge.* But, and this is the main point, *precisely inasmuch as we have to do with the emerged self's enabling of the emerging self, this presence of "spirit" is a fundamentally intersubjective phenomenon.* Spirit is not, then, a possession of the alone self, nor a sort of "breath" within it, nor yet solely its "higher" dimension if what is meant is a phenomenon with which self is *actually* endowed from the outset. To the contrary, precisely because of the *contextural* (i.e., complexural) relatedness among selves, *selves are immanently* (i.e., *reflexively*) *presenced to one another* by way of their mutuality, their enabling/enabled relationships— i.e., *"spirit" as "empowering" of self by the other self is the very texture of the "self-relatedness" of the relation that relates itself to its own self and by so relating relates itself to the empowering other self,* and, of course, conversely.

Accordingly, the other self is, for the emerging self, always-already delivered, intrinsic to its own "being-as-self." *Precisely this immanent presence of others is the first and the last, the initial and the fundamental, disclosure when the self reflectively apprehends itself*—at whatever level, that of social roles and images, or that of its own reflexivity. The "*Eigensphäre*" *is quite as much the sphere of the empowering other as it is that of self*—precisely because it does not appear at all except by way of the empowering other self, the one enabling the emergence of the self. Hence the reason why reflection is not an "immediacy" (Ricoeur), why in reflection "I" am not "immediately given" to myself, is just that *what is in truth "given" is the "giftedness" of self,* the voices and presences of others, embedded since childhood and interwoven from the myriads of contacts and "meetings" with the others in any complexured life. It is not alone, then, as Ricoeur maintains, that self is found only in "works" (actions, deeds, symbols, institutions, etc.). In a clear way, that has its truth, but it is after all only partial, and not fundamental. Others—haunting, delightful, loved, feared, vague, starkly clear, important, merely felt, anonymous, close—are in-separably woven into the tapestry of each of our lives. It is unthinkable for there to be self without the immanent, reflexive presence of other self, for there is no self except as enabled to be by the receiving/giving other self—by the "tested/responsive" other self, who in turn is gifted continually with *its* self by these "meetings."

Thus it is understandable as well how "the social" exercises a continual attraction on so many theorists of self—G. H. Mead, Charles Cooley, or others. But arguing the priority of the social over the self, conceiving the self as emergent from the social process, is, like Ricoeur's, a merely partial view. Moreover, what is partial can be specified: reflection on self is an encounter with the presences of multiple others (of all sorts); emerging as self is a mutuality, an empowering and enabling of self by the emerged other self. But this social thesis says too much and too little: *too much*, for the "social" is not at all the inter-individual sphere (e.g., mother/child) even though it is the *context*, the field, for the *contextural* relationships between self and other; *too much* as well, for it fails to recognize that even the very newborn is by no means a non-self, nor yet simply potential. The newborn is already a self of sorts, precisely evidenced in its beginning-to-act, its initiating of quiet alertness and effort. The social thesis also says *too little*: for the complex interweaving of contextures is constantly fringed and "fielded" ("worlded") by an immense context of sociality, subtly but effectively made present in bodily gestures of holding, cuddling, voicing, glancing, touching, within a positive milieu of artifactual things and doings.

Finally, Schutz's complaint against Scheler can be understood better: reflection *does*, after all, disclose *my* life, *my* actions, *my* thoughts, *my* feelings. But it can also be seen that this has its (phenomenological) naivety: the "my," while apparent, is able to be *denied* by me, and this in several ways. In a sense, I can deny that a particular feeling is "mine," where the denial is a kind of self-deception, dishonesty, unwillingness to admit to myself even that "I'm that sort of person," and this again in many ways. But that is not the important point. I can and do deny feeling that an action, for example, is "mine," where this means, in all honesty, I don't know where it originated, and the sense of the experience is *not* "it's mine but is overtly denied while covertly recognized," but rather, "I find it *in* me but do not know whose it is." Thus do those urgings and emotings bubble up in my life only to embarrass, perchance delight, but always to surprise and pose enigmas.

In a still different sense, reflection uncovers, not merely the "my," but something else which seems to force itself as happening "in me" but neither authorship nor (necessarily, or not always) responsibility for it seem honestly possible (even though there may be a *dis*honest claiming of authorship!). I mean here what Rilke said in his advice to the young poet:

Therefore, my dear sir, I know no advice for you save this: to go into yourself and test the deeps in which your life takes rise; at its source you will find the answer to the question whether you *must* create. Accept it, just as it sounds, without inquiring into it. (*99*, pp. 20–21)

"Going into one's deeps": one finds figures, symbols, ideas, which, far from having the sense of being "mine," are simply found, perhaps (as with poets, artists, but also the rest of us) with an urgency to be said, but always with a sense of astonishment, delight, or anxiety, embarrassment, even terror. I will have to return to the significance of these "deeps." For now, my only point is that while in a way reflection does disclose that these and those feelings, strivings, thinkings, etc., are "mine," in another way there are within my reflectively disclosed self hosts of feelings, thinkings, urgings, etc., which I can only wonder at as being or as occurring "in me," only enigmatically "mine" if at all— sometimes as a kind of "deception," but not always. In part, surely, these are the haunting voices and touches, the smells and visages, of countless others met, read, heard about, imagined, and dreamed. Reflection discloses the inner presence of others, clearly and unequivocally. What alone is a sphere of privacy, as Scheler says, is that remarkable, contextual experiencing of my own embodying organism—*but even here*, it must be emphasized, my experiencing of my own body is shaped, figured, fringed with myriads of "contacts" with others. The relating to others is the *primordial* experience— that whereby the bodily sense of self itself emerges—and, for the emerging self, this continuously voiced presence of others is at once decisive and never to be lost, save for the impacted times of severe retreat (e.g., catatonia). But even these "mental disturbances" must be understood as one or another form of disruption of the self-relatedness to other selves, and to their mutual relatedness.

THE EXPERIENCE OF OTHERS: SETTING THE ISSUE

Thus it is that mutuality—as the texture of self's emergence—must *inevitably shape the question concerning the modes of experience of the other self.* The question is never *whether* the other is experienced; even to raise the question is already to presume the other. That question can never be authentically raised— i.e., without a kind of double-think—by anyone capable of framing it; although it may well be a significant question *we* must ask about autistic children, catatonics, the severely retarded or damaged, among others. Bosch, as was seen, noted the difficulty in attempting to *meet* an autistic child; Goldstein, too, observed the way in which some of his brain-injured patients seemed to be seriously disturbed in their cognizance of even close family members, uncon- cerned, even estranged. We know, too, that some persons can become so deeply, explicitly cognizant of others as to be constantly on the alert from them, and literally undergo the vertigo of madness thereby (*68*).

Considering all these variations, we note two things that begin to stand out clearly: on the one hand, as Scheler maintained, the "problem of other selves" turns out to be a *plurality of problems* (*107*, pp. 213–33); and on the other hand, the nature of the incredibly complex mutuality of selves is such that it *most rapidly becomes so deeply sedimented* in the life of the (normally developing) self as to become buried, radically unnoticed, and *taken for granted.* For the most part, even when motivated to doubt this or that feature, gesture, word, etc., of the other, we never in the course of our usual daily lives question or even come to a clear cognizance of the *other as such.* Even doubting whether someone "really means what he says," wondering whether a particular gesture is to be taken as threatening, etc., never raises up in our minds the idea that the other self may not be at all. Indeed, one can hardly imagine a more foundationally shattering experience than one in which what is taken to be another self (however familiar or alien) turns out to be instead an automaton, a sheer mirage, a creature of utter fancy.

Thus while Scheler's claim is true—that our conviction that other human beings exist is deeper and earlier than our belief in material things—we must, as Schutz points out, recognize that this "conviction" has the form, not at all of a clearly or even vaguely formulated belief or judgment, but rather of a *taken for granted assumption*—one which, as has been seen, is already beginning to be present in the earliest stages of actual life.

If we thus ask what it is to experience the other self, we have to realize that the question is elliptical in two ways. First, there is what I have delineated as the question pertaining to emergence through mutuality; second, there is the question concerning the experience of the other within the contexture of already-emerged selves, *whose mutuality signifies that others are "always-already" constitutive moments of self, as self is a constitutive moment of the other self.* Here, as I have suggested, Schutz is quite right: the question, shaped by already present mutuality, must be focused on the taken for grantedness of others—on what Schutz calls the "general thesis of the alter ego's existence," or what I have called "explicit alterity." Each self reflexively experiences itself and the other *as* experiencing itself and the first self; and thereby each experiences the relationship itself; and each self will variously interpret the other as well as their relationship.

THE SOCIALITY OF ALTERITY

Schutz's work, after years of being mostly unnoticed, has become both well-known and influential during the past decade. It is a body of work, rich in detail, focused on the structure of everyday sociality—the life-world (*Lebenswelt*).[2] I here presuppose the bulk of Schutz's work (and with him, much of the seminally exploratory work of Husserl), as I am concerned neither with his total theory, nor with criticisms of it.[3] What does concern me is the substantive core of his theory of the alter ego (intersubjectivity). Only a few indications of the place of this theory within the body of his general theory are necessary.

Schutz is concerned, in general, to defend three major theses. First, the individual person's commonsense knowledge of the world is an open, relatively well-defined, but not logically precise and closed, system of constructs of its *typicality*. Second, the world of daily, social life is "from the outset" a *shared, common world*, literally peopled with others (past, future, present; also, one must add, dreamed, imagined, etc.) and their products and traces (cultural objects, mores, folkways, laws, institutions, etc.). Third, and in a way most remarkably, the life-world's fundamental character is at the same time the most obvious and seemingly trivial one: each of us in our normal, adult, wide-awake living *takes it quite for granted* that "there is the world which is 'our' world," not in the least private to "me" but shared (*109*, I, pp. 7–19; *111*, pp. 8–14).

These theses are obviously closely related and developed. Of main interest here, however, is the second, and within that what Schutz delineates as the "central dimension" of the social world: the "face-to-face relationship" (*109*, I, p. 318). All the other dimensions of sociality presuppose and take their rise from that. Thus is derived the sense and presence of those "others" who, although living at the same historical time as I, are merely contemporaries whom I do not actually meet in interactions (the *Mitwelt*); of those "others" who existed before me and whose actions impact my own world but on whose world I cannot act (the *Vorwelt*); and of those "others" who will live after my time and whose world is shaped in complex ways by my own (the *Folgewelt*). All these are only *mediately, indirectly experienced* by me, principally by means of a complex set of typifications concerning their lives, actions, motives, plans, etc. (*111*, pp. 68–92). The core of the social world, the fundamental presence and problem of intersubjectivity, is the sphere of "consociates" (the *Umwelt*).

Even within the *Umwelt*, however, the experience of others is not only highly complex and stratified, but also marked by taken for grantedness. Man, in the embrace of daily, life-worldly concerns is not only principally occupied with the everyday, practical concerns of life (the "pragmatic motive") (*111*, pp. 10–14), but is governed by a wholly implicit "attitude" simply accepted and unquestioned (even though always open to question), namely the rudimentary belief that there is *the*, or *our*, world. Thus, as Schutz puts it, to contrast the attitude of daily life with that of reflection on its structures, man in the everyday attitude suspends "the doubt that the world and its objects might be otherwise than it appears to him. We propose to call this *epoché* the *epoché of the natural attitude*" (*109*, I, p. 229). Hence the experience of the *other*, already-emerged self by the now (for all practical purposes) also already-emerged self is a specific *social* relationship: the "face-to-face relationship," or the "pure We-relation" (*109*, II, p. 110). *This* is the theme for the present study.

THE SOCIALITY OF EXPERIENCING SOMEONE ELSE

What concerns Schutz in delineating the We-relation is its purely formal characteristics. He thus makes a crucial distinction which many theorists have obscured: namely, between this "face-to-face relation" and relationships of *intimacy*.[4] They are emphatically not the same. "A face-to-face relationship presupposes that those who participate in it have space and time in common as long as the relation lasts" (*109*, II, p. 109). Hence the face-to-face relationship (We-relationship) may show different degrees of intimacy and familiarity, or of anonymity. In this sense, the intimate relation with a loved one, for example, is merely a face-to-face relation *of a certain kind*, not different structurally from meeting a stranger, whether the stranger be a patient in a clinic or a mere face in the night. I shall have to consider this thesis more carefully as I proceed; for the moment, what concerns me is Schutz's theory of the We-relationship.

Recalling all that has been suggested earlier about embodiment, spatiality and temporality, the fuller significance of Schutz's basic claim is understandable:

> I immediately perceive another man only when he shares a sector of the life-world's space and of world time in common with me. Only under these conditions does the Other appear to me in his live corporeality: his body is for me a perceivable and explicable field of expression which makes his conscious life accessible to me. It is possible only then for my stream of consciousness and his to flow in true simultaneity: he and I grow older together. (*111*, p. 62)[5]

Schutz contends that this "immediacy," however, is, viewed internally and strictly speaking, *mediate*, for the fellow-man's lived experience is in truth grasped and explicited only as "indicated" by his corporeal movements, expressions, gestures, and communication (*111*, pp. 63–64). Still, the encounter with the other self in the We-relation is the *least* mediated of all my encounters with fellow-men—and for this reason, Schutz goes on to speak of it as "immediate."

At the core of the concrete We-relation, furthermore, is what he terms the "thou-orientation" (*Du-Einstellung*): the face-to-face relation is founded on my "turning-to" the other and his or her "turning-to" me, i.e., a "*reciprocal thou-orientation*." For even though I turn to the other, he or she may ignore me. Only if the other self and I *take each other into account* is there the reciprocity of orientations—and this, for Schutz, is the " 'pure' We-relation."

> The essential feature of the Thou-orientation is the recognition that a fellow-man *is* before me; the orientation does not presuppose that I know what are precisely the particular characteristics of that fellow-man. . . . Of course, I never have such a "pure" experience of another Self. I always confront a particular fellow-man, living his particular life and having his own particular thoughts. . . . [Similarly,] a We-relation is always filled with "content," that is . . . the "pure" We-relation, in analogy to the "pure" Thou-orientation, is actualized in different degrees of concreteness and specificity. (*109*, II, pp. 24–25)[6]

Two points are central here. On the one hand, the other and I share a common sector of life-wordly space; on the other hand, we meet not only during a common segment of "world-time," but we meet in the context of "genuine simultaneity," an interweaving of our objectively manifested subjective/temporal streams of experience.

(1) *The Placement of Intersubjective Meeting*

Each embodied self, as was already stressed, thanks to his upright posture and "handedness" (Straus), experiences the environing milieu as spatially organized. Not only are things in general placed "here" and "there," "next to" or "beside," "over there" or "yonder," etc., but the milieu is structured in terms of "what is within *actual reach*," and what is (for now) "out of reach." The latter, Schutz shows (*111*, pp. 36–41), is further structured into a zone "within *restorable reach*" and a zone "within *attainable reach*." For example, having set aside a book and now adverting to my lunch, I tacitly assume that the book (unless someone moves it) is still on my desk (unless someone has moved it, too). I simply assume that "until further notice"—i.e., until forced to think otherwise—what was in my reach can again be brought within reach (restorably); and, I know, too, in an everyday (typifying) way, that in order to bring it again within reach, certain steps must be taken, certain movements must be actualized (getting up, walking, reaching out, etc.). Thus the zone within restorable reach is founded upon two fundamental assumptions intrinsic to daily life: what Husserl analyzes as the "and so forth" idealization, and the idealization, "I can always do it again" (*44*, secs. 24, 51b, 58, 61; *45*, sec. 74). The specific range of the zone within attainable reach, on the other hand, pertains to what, until now, was never within my reach but can be brought within it: riding a bicycle for a young child, expecting to graduate from college for a student, etc. Clearly, this zone is as well founded on the two idealizations, though as regards attainability, my expectations are always framed within degrees of subjective probability and various forms of ability—i.e., experienced limitations related to my circumstances and my embodied abilities.[7]

Clearly, too, there are few sharp lines of demarcation between these zones. It may even be useful to distinguish two sorts of zones falling within that in actual reach: the *zone of operation*, or that which I can influence by direct action (*111*, pp. 41–45);[8] and a broader notion, the *province of the practicable* (*111*, pp. 50–51), or that which, within limits imposed by the world, my milieu, my past experience, and my body, can be done here and now.

Thus every "meeting" of another—whether loved one or stranger, a partner in social action (sawing trees, playing music, playing sports, working together in an office, etc.) or an autistic child—always and essentially occurs within concrete circumstances, in particular places, and between already emerged (to some extent, at least) selves having their own respective stocks of knowledge, typifications, expectations, motivations, values, beliefs, even life-plans. Hence what is within my actual, attainable, and restorable reaches will differ (to various degrees, of course) from what is within the other's reaches. Thanks to these, we each experience different sectors of the world, have different perspectives on things, experience different things as intimate or anonymous, available or not, etc.

It is from the experience of these structures that I know that "the same" Object must necessarily show different aspects to each of us. First, because the world in my reach cannot be identical with the world in your reach, his reach, etc.; because my here is your there; and because my zone of operation is not the same as yours. And, second, because my biographical situation with its relevance systems, hierarchies of plans, etc., is not yours and, consequently, the explications of the horizon of objects in my case and yours could take entirely different directions. . . . (*111*, p. 59)

All these differences are, within the context of daily life, typified and set aside, for all practical purposes, as irrelevant "until further notice"—i.e., until and unless they prove to be of some import (e.g., in giving testimony at a trial). This crucial "setting-aside" involves two further idealizations: that, practically speaking, we can exchange viewpoints (*interchangeability of standpoints*); and that, despite the differences noted, we take it for granted that we understand one another, can and do act in concert, assume that what is important to me can be appreciated at least by you, etc. (*congruence of relevance systems*). Together, these constitute what Schutz calls the "general thesis of the reciprocity of perspectives" (*111*, p. 60; *109*, I, pp. 10–13).

The spatial arrangement of intersubjective meeting is thus highly contexturalized into partially overlapping zones of reach and operation (practicability) whose "overlap" is set within the multiple idealizations inherent to daily life. To "meet" another is perforce to experience one another within specific complexures of plans and actions, within a specific milieu, in terms of varying stocks of knowledge and experience, and within certain limitations of perspective, experience, ability, and circumstance.

(2) *The Time of Face-to-face Meeting*

As was earlier pointed out, whatever else can and must be said of time and space, within concrete embodied life they are deeply and mutually interwoven: at bottom, they have the same source (Griffith, Plügge). This continues into the encounter with the Other self: *the spatially arranged zones of reach and operations are at the same time temporal.* They are fundamentally matters of "turning away and turning toward: the world previously in actual reach (the book on the table at home), from which I have turned away (as I went away), transcends the world in actual reach (the street I'm walking on) to which I've turned (I look at the showcases)" (*111*, p. 45). I can always (within limits) "return," where this "re-turning" is at once spatial (going back to the house) and temporal (going back takes time).

Furthermore, the time wherein we meet is always "at some (objectively determinable) time" (now or then), a time we share in common. I go to sleep, or become engrossed in a book, and mean*time* the time has changed; when I awake or put down the book, the world has become older. "My" time, the inner time of my experience, has its *locus* within "world" time, within which at every moment I myself grow older.

The time of life-worldly experience

is built up where the subjective time of the stream of consciousness (of inner duration) intersects with the rhythm of the body as "biological time" in general, and with the seasons as world time in general, or as calendar or "social time." We live in all these dimensions simultaneously. But since there exists no absolute congruence . . . between events in these dimensions, we have as an inevitable consequence of this congruence the phenomenon of waiting. (*111*, p. 47)[9]

To have my morning coffee, I must wait until it is brewed; if I am ill, I wait for the medicine to take effect; if I plant grass, I must wait upon its time of growth; etc. I can do only so much "at a time"; if I want to go to a movie, I must first do this, then that, and coordinate all these with the time the movie is to be shown. My plans must be ordered, arranged hierarchically according to their relative urgency and the "time it takes" to bring about any goal. Thus, Schutz points out, life-worldly experience is structured by the phenomenon of *waiting*: the principle of "first things first" is fundamental for all social action (*111*, pp. 48–49).

This interlocking of times, of sequenced "waitings," is moreover set within crucial limits. World time is irreversible: I become older, never younger; an assassination cannot be undone; an abortion is decisive for a fetus; even a "rewrite" of a book is a *re*-write; etc. Life-worldly time is thus essentially experienced as *historical*, as is my own time of living. My father came before me, and after his father, and both lived "at another time" than I; I was myself born into "this" time and no other, without having had a choice in the matter. "My time" is as contingently necessary (I had to be born at some time, though *when* was contingent) as is my own embodying organism. Thus, too, the immanent structurization of "my own temporal flow" into contextural phases and units becomes biographically articulated and interwoven biologically: within the rhythms of my embodying organism, the social time of my particular circumstances ("I can only go so fast") and that of my social environs (the "pace of life" in the city, the suburbs, in the country; on vacation or at work; etc.).

The meeting with the other self, accordingly, is not only an interweaving of zones of reach and operation, of ability and circumstance, but is as well contexturalized by these modalities and variations of time (each with its own appertaining limitations and modes of "waiting" and "first things first"). "How I do things" must reckon with "how you do things"; my "pace" must gear with "yours"; as I "grow older," so do you, and "we" together. To experience the other emerged and wide-awake self is necessarily to meet him within this remarkably complex, ever-changing complexure of partially overlapping and interlocking spatial and temporal orders, zones, and arrangements.

THE HEFT OF TIME, THE FLOW OF SPACE

One can imaginatively project: what would it be like for there to be merely a "one-sided" thou-orientation (i.e., a species of the "Robinson Crusoe" example already used)? Clearly, in the case of the emerging self, consistent ignoring of its orientation to, its turning-to, the other, can only signify the constriction or eventual withering of its self (as was seen). In the case of the already-emerged self, were it consistently the case that these thou-orientations, these turnings-to others, were ignored or treated as other than what they are (e.g., treating the self as a thing merely; or as a modification, as a "lower" grade of living being), it is easy to see that something similar to autism is at least a real possibility. It must have taken an extraordinarily resilient and strong sense of self to have gone through the rigorous de-humanization, say, of the Nazi concentration camps—systematically practicing the effort to make the inmates see themselves as degraded and bestial—for one to have endured the experience with any self left intact. Some surely did; but, it is clear, the authentic experience of another self requires far more than a mere one-sided orientation, where "authenticity" does *not in the least* necessarily signify any degree of "intimacy"—and thus is precisely the presupposition for moral or immoral conduct.

The principal phenomenon for understanding the core experience of the other self is thus the "reciprocal thou-orientation": the turning-to each other and taking account of or reckoning with one another *as* selves reckoning with one another and with their relationship itself. What is the structure of this? Although rarely going into the matter with much depth, Schutz's response is important, though not without its difficulties.

While he admits that the stream of my own inner life bears a strong resemblance to that which "fills" the We-relation, Schutz persisted in maintaining that "a fundamental difference, though, remains: my flow of lived experiences is a flow within the inner time of my own stream of consciousness" (*111*, p. 63). In order for that flow to become in any way known or experienced by the other, it is necessary that it be manifested bodily. By means of that "field of expression," or "indications," I make myself experienced by and known to the other. Conversely, so is the other known and experienced by me solely via *his* field of expressional indications. Thus Schutz is compelled to the curious locution: an "immediate" which is, *strictly*, a "mediated," but the "mediacy" here is so close, is indeed "simultaneous," that "we will continue to speak, even though it is not completely accurate, of an immediate experience of the fellow-man" (*111*, p. 64). However "maximally abundant" are the "symptoms" indicating the life of the other through his body, and even though "my fellow-man is in a certain sense presented to me as more 'alive' and more 'immediate' than I am to myself" (*111*, p. 66), indeed, even though I "apprehend the fact that he experiences me as someone who experiences his conduct as an expression of his subjectivity" (*111*, p. 67)—all this notwithstanding, the other self is *strictly mediated* by way of his embodying organism.

That, of course, is a whole lot of "immediacy" to load on the back of any "mediation," and I shall have to consider this more carefully as I proceed. In any event, Schutz's complaint to Scheler's thesis that the "we" is prior to the "I" is now fully understandable, given his views on this "mediation." While it is true that the We-relation forms the basis for the individual's experience of the world in general, reflection on self discloses, for Schutz, *my own* inner stream of experience *as* mine, and not yours (which only you can apprehend). Thus, as he often said in seminars,[10] for all the profound sociality of our lives we each remain ultimately alone in our own respective inwardnesses.

Schutz's view here, nevertheless, seems to me to have confused several issues, and beyond this seems in conflict with what he takes to be the genuine core of the experience of the other self. I begin with the latter, give my interpretation of it, and then turn to the former.

(1) *Vivid Present*

The "reciprocal thou-orientation" is, Schutz says elsewhere, "what might be called the 'mutual tuning-in relationship' " (*109*, II, p. 161). In this We-relation,

> our experiences are not only coordinated with one another, but are also reciprocally determined and related to one another. I experience myself through my consociate, and he experiences himself through me. The mirroring of self in the experience of the stranger (more exactly, in my grasp of the Other's experience of me) is a constitutive element of the we-relation. . . . My experience of my own course of lived experience and of the coordinated course of the lived experience of my fellow-man is unitary: experiences in the we-relation are common experiences. (*111*, p. 67)

What is thus manifestly evident is that this "unity" is *constitutively different* from my experiencing you, or you experiencing me. Dimensionally beyond the already complex interweavings of times and spaces inherent to such one-sided thou-orientations is the distinctive constitution of a space-time nexus peculiar to the "tuning-in" relationship: the *vivid present*. If we think of any concrete example—Mead's "conversation of gestures," e.g., between two wrestlers, or the experience of playing tennis together, or the relation between a singer and her accompanist—the structure becomes clear: in the latter case, for example,

> two series of events in inner time, one belonging to the stream of consciousness of [the one], the other to the stream of consciousness of the [other], are lived through in simultaneity, which simultaneity is created by the ongoing flux of the musical process. . . . [T]his sharing of the other's flux of experiences in inner time, this living through a vivid present in common, constitutes . . . the mutual tuning-in relationship, the experience of the "We," which is at the foundation of all possible communication. (*109*, II, p. 173)

Thus performer and listener, speaker and auditor, lover and beloved, etc., "are 'tuned-in' to one another, are living together through *the same* flux, are growing older together while the . . . process lasts" (*109*, II, p. 175; *my emphasis*).

Indeed, this is *quite precise*: the "time" of intersubjective meeting is "the same flux." This "time," however, is not accurately described as simply "two" somehow joined together. Rather, from the perspective of either of the partners, the vivid present is *actually experienced as the bodily display of the other*, the only way in which consociates are at all experienced. "*Inner time*," I tried to show earlier, however true it is that it is able to be reflectively (methodologically) focused upon and explicated, *is essentially embodied*, "fleshed" out corporeally and is always "filled" with this or that specific intentive "content" displayed by means of this or that specific bodily gesture, attitude, or movement. *Methodological isolability, therefore, does not of itself purport separability in any sense. The time of meeting is a time "in common," a time which is "the same," and it is a time with "heft"*: embodied and thereby *displayed*, with whatever specific and concrete striving, wanting, etc. Rather than call this a "synchronization" (*109*, II, p. 177) (without denying that there is a clear place for this in various forms of meeting), which *presupposes* our having already "tuned-in" to one another, it is necessary to understand this "vivid present" as a kind of *isochronism*, a coalescence or concurrence. The time of consociate meeting is *sui generis*, having its own character, demands, and limits, and emerges strictly within and as the core moment of the "tuning-in" relation.

(2) *Vivid Presence*

However, the tuning-in relation is, as is now clear, hardly "merely" *temporal*. Time as "hefty" is *spatially locused*: the concurrence of "nows," thanks to which alone are *we* able to have a "now" *in common*, "*our* now," signifies at the same time a concurrence of "heres," thanks to which *we* together are *here in common*. Since this is strictly a *contexture, each of us is able to divide our "my" and "your" places only by shifting attention to a different contexture or set of them* (as Gurwitsch had criticized Husserl for doing in his theory of wholes and parts). Within the setting of *our* engagement, our meeting, there is a spatial "here" no less than the temporal "now": as I have had to say many times, *it is wholly artificial to try and segregate out the time from the place of intersubjective meeting*.

It is thus necessary to recognize as *perfectly clear* what in other respects might seem ambiguous: "*presence*," which is *at once spatial and temporal*, and which is the very texture of the tuning-in contexture. It is within this vivid presence of time with heft and space which flows that we at once "make music together" and thereby "grow older together"; and on its base all other modalities of experiencing one another, and each of our experiences of still other selves, are founded (*111*, pp. 68–98).

REFLECTION AND MUTUAL REFLEXIVITY

With the emergence of self within the enabling/enabled phenomenon noted in the last chapter, what emerges is, of course, "self"; but this "self" is (from the outset) emergent within the ever more complex *vivid presence* just pointed out. To emerge as self is to come increasingly within the embrace of that presence with the other (who is mutually presenced with me). This, from the reading of Kierkegaard.

Schutz, I have suggested, tended to make two mistakes. On the one hand, he seemed to have *under*played the genuinely *sui generis* character of the vivid present: its "heft," its spatial locus, as also its embodied placements. On the other, he often failed to see the significance of his own usages, "vivid present" and "vivid presence," *under*playing the latter (and thus space) and *over*playing the former (and thus time).

Still, he has a point when he stresses that the simultaneity of the tuning-in relationship is a matter of "two series of events," yours and mine. Reflection, after all, does disclose that my experiences are *mine*, however vague or confused this may be. The point I see in this, however, is not Schutz's: going his way inevitably is to reintroduce a subtle dualism, whose inner logic must insinuate itself in everything else; or it effectively makes the mistake of confusing different contextures. And, indeed, Schutz's own descriptions of "the same flux" which is presenced in the tuning-in relation (tuning-in-to-another-who-tunes-in-to-me) turn out to be *inconsistent* with the idea of "synchronization," when this is taken as the *core* of the experience of others. The point I see in Schutz's analysis is, rather, this: *that each partner in a tuning-in relationship has his own "perspective" on the relationship, each experiences not only the other self but the very relationship itself* (as was learned from the interpretation of Kierkegaard), *and in the relation each relates himself to his own self and to the enabled/enabling* (empowered/empowering) *other self. Reflection thus does disclose "my own" experiences as "mine," but with equal force does it disclose the other self of the relationship!* Hence there can be no question of a strict mediacy, though the relationship has striking analogues to other relationships which are clearly mediational. Rather, this is a *strict immediacy*, precisely because, in Schutz's own words (quoted above), "I experience myself through my consociate, and he experiences himself through me." *And both of these constitutive moments of the tuning-in relationship are experiences which we each have*: I experience the other experiencing himself in me, and, conversely, he experiences me experiencing myself in him; but also, I experience (as do you) your experiencing of yourself as experienced by me, etc. Think only of a concrete case: when I try to "fake out" the other (e.g., in an athletic contest, or in a business meeting; or, feigningly, in love play, child play; etc.), I am able to know if and when I've succeeded, precisely because I experience his "being taken in" by my feigning! I also, of course, can experience myself as "being had" by the other—whether in fun or as enemies or competitors. All these are possible solely because, within the *sui generis immediacy of the vivid presence*, the other and I form (as Schutz says) a "unitary" or "common" stream of experience. But *this experience*, no less than that prominent in the emergence of self, is *potently reflexive* ("potentiated," in

Kierkegaard's term), and correspondingly enriched and complex. *We*, you and I, each in our own ways, *experience our relationship itself* ("we have a good marriage," or "we are really having fun," etc.), *as well as one another* ("aren't you having a good time?"), *and in the relationship each relates himself to himself* ("I'm having a good time!" "So am I!"), *and to the other* ("You didn't act like you were having a good time!" "Neither did you!").

In these terms, it is by no means trivial, as Schutz in effect charges against Scheler, that "the technique of reflection is acquired very late by the child . . ." (*109*, I, p. 171). Reflection, in the sense of the explicit and deliberate act of focusing on "my own" stream of experiences, is not only acquired late but can be undertaken only by an already-emerged self. More than that, *reflection itself emerges from within the complexure of life, of vivid presence*; it is motivated by elements within it, and is thus conditioned by it. And, as already stressed, *reflection discovers precisely this complexure, as historicized biographically* (all the others whom I have met), and it is only within that contexture that there is or can possibly be an apprehension of "me" myself as opposed to (i.e., as abstracted from) "you" yourself. *Reflection on one's own self is thus made possible by vivid presence*, and what among other things is disclosed thereby are not only "my" feelings, thoughts, etc., but the intrinsic presence of others.[11] What is discovered as "mine" or "pertaining to me," then, is not at all an insularity, closed on itself; rather, I discover my own "perspective," and "point of view"—my own relatedness to the other and to our relationship, as the other discovers his own relatedness to the relationship and to me—and this always in contrast to what I also discover, namely not only that the other has his own perspective, but I also discover this perspective itself (viewed from my own relatedness to the relationship to which he is also self-related). Thus is it sensible and accountable that I *can* understand the other's "point of view," "put myself in his shoes," sometimes "know" him far better than he knows himself (and conversely)—for this perspectival viewing is itself intrinsically locused within our vivid presence. I know—for the most part, but not always—typically, what it's like to be a stranger, an alien, seen as odd and non-conformist, just as I know what it is like to be in love, have friends, be familiar with, get mad at. . . . This in no way signifies that I always know, or know with utter clarity and precision; but neither can it be said that I only know myself, or know myself with utter clarity or precision. *Reflection*, thanks to the complexural reflexivity (vivid presence) which makes it possible, *might thus better be termed "co-reflection"*—this is ultimately a terminological issue, and could be recommended solely to avoid the temptations to regard the self as a pure "in itself" and insulated.

AVAILABILITY

Only within the vivid presence, however fugitive or even superficial it may be in a particular case, is the other self encountered as a unique individual, and correlatively am I made present to myself as unique. Even so, "intimacy," while possible in its core sense only within the vivid presence, is not, as was seen, the same as the vivid present. Obviously, a kind of intimacy can be felt between selves not sharing vivid presence—as between a performer and a long-dead composer, a reader and the author of a novel or poem, a child with his forebears, etc. This modality, however, as Schutz remarks, is a "derived form of the vivid present [sic] shared by the partners in a genuine face-to-face relation such as prevails between speaker and listener" (109, II, pp. 171–72). Clearly, too, in the bulk of our face-to-face relations, we are most often merely "facing" one another as relative strangers, as relatively typified (and, of course, self-typified) and anonymous. The fact of such relative typifications and anonymity, however, in no way belies the structure of the vivid presence; even the glances of strangers establish a momentary vivid presence with all its complexity. (The "visage" of a person in the airline terminal can be just as "enticing," "lustful," "curious," "friendly," etc. as that of someone known better—whether one's taking these gestures as such be correct or not, though we are more often typically correct than not.)

It is solely within the actual vivid presence of selves that they are at all "*available*" to one another, open to each other in the most immediate way, at hand for one another in all the myriad ways of concrete action and interaction. I may, of course, make clear my readiness to help another without actually "facing him": I write a letter, for example, or tell a third party about my willingness. These modalities, however, are again forms of a derived vivid presence, as telephoning is a mode of partial presence (it is an extension of the zone of operation, one of the most profound impacts of modern technology on modern life, as Schutz points out). In view of all these variations, it seems preferable to *divest* Marcel's term (*disponibilité*) of its invoking of "intimacy." Whether or not intimacy, or even familiarity, with another ensues will depend, and may not even be desirable or desired by either partner (one thinks of the situation of the physician and his patient, the teacher and his student, the lawyer and his client). But if it occurs, it is at all possible only within the vivid presence of selves, or some derived form of it.

Nevertheless, to "be-with" the other in vivid presence is *to be able to be of avail*, for whatever it may be, whether it be of greater or lesser import, and whether it be actualized or not. Conversely, to be at hand for the other, or he for me, is possible only within vivid presence. In these terms, the emergence of self from within the enabling/enabled mutuality already presupposes having experienced the "avail" of the emerged self, his responsiveness to the "testings" of the emerging self. As the recent etymology of "avail" suggests, indeed,[12] the mutuality of selves in the vivid presence of "growing up" (and, later, "growing older") together is *already* to have undergone the "avail" of the other. Thus the vivid presence of selves in the we-relation is experienced by each as a being-available-to one another.

This description is not, clearly, a covert piece of moralizing (e.g., being-available-to = being-helpful-to, of benefit-to). That this would be a mistake to suppose is clear once it is realized that not only lovers and friends, but enemies and antagonists are but different ways of being-available-to. Lying to or deceiving someone, using someone, as also expressing enmity towards someone, are all forms of thou-orientation which in one way or another seek to take advantage of the other, and as such presuppose the vivid presence of the other as thus able to be used, lied to, etc. And this, too, is found in the etymology of "avail": to make use of, to take advantage of, in the sense of to avail oneself of. Presence as availability signifies only that the selves thereby "tuned-in" with one another have established between themselves the kind of complexly reflexive relatedness I stressed earlier. As friends are intimates (but typified nonetheless), so are enemies. Indeed, what follows from the study thus far of vivid presence is that its radical opposite is not at all enmity, but rather (as Kierkegaard also saw) either *apathy*, or what might be called "*hard-heartedness*," i.e., a positive "tuning-out" (not "in") of the other. Apathy towards persons is exactly defined by the *inability* (episodic, momentary, or habituated) of a self to "meet" another self with more than surface presence. Hard-heartedness is similarly a failure to "meet" another, but by positive choice, a being *unwilling* to meet the other. Both of these, like availability, show a number of forms—all the way from a kind of inner exhaustion and lethargy to being uncaring and unwilling to put out the effort; or from various forms of impatience to sadism.

So far as apathy and hard-heartedness are concerned, then, by closing the self off from others, they are forms of conduct which not only impact others but also the self, and, like the case of ignoring the other, can easily eventuate in a crucial curtailment of the sense of self, result even in that loss of self which is manifested in bestiality and barbarianism. And, as Bettelheim noted even as regards young infants, "when the infant is kept from being active in the relation [of nursing] on his own terms ["hard-heartedness"], or when his actions evoke no response ["apathy"], he becomes flooded with impotent rage, a helpless victim of inner tensions" (5, p. 19). Erikson, indeed, terms this experience "the ontogenetic source of the sense of evil, a 'basic mistrust' which combines a sense of mistrustfulness and of untrustworthiness" (22; 5, p. 19).

The catch of such experiences is that, far from destroying availability, they merely make a different use of it: they *are made available* to the self by the other self who practices them. As the modes of apathy and hard-heartedness impact the self who practices them, *so are they thereby made available to the other as modes of conduct by which the self comes, or can come, to see itself defined*. At the core of it is, again, the complex reflexivity: the self/other relation, which is itself a relation wherein each relates at once to the relation and in the relation to itself and to the other similarly self-related self. *To relate myself to my own self in the relation to another who ignores me, or who brutalizes me, is to be enabled to see myself and my relations to other selves in precisely the same ways, hence to enable* (even: to invite, to encourage) *these other selves to relate that way to me, and to still other selves*—and on, in an endless cycle. The only way out of that cycle, it seems, is either, in the case of the still infant self, the withering withdrawal of autism or psychosis, or the development of what is thus empowered in that self; or, in the case of the already emerged self, the various forms of adult sicknesses of the spirit: neurosis, paranoia, schizophrenia, and other forms of self-rupture, self-curtailment, or violence. That, or suicide.

On the other hand, the more such experiences become the prominent ones by which self and other are enabled to apprehend themselves, the less are self and other presenced to one another, and consequently the less can one speak of either self or the other self. If such conducts, then, curtail the vivid presence of selves by their negative thrust, we can seize upon another crucial feature of that presence: the encouraging, enabling, empowering of self to be precisely *its own self* in mutuality with the other self, which is a *potency*. That potency is precisely the opposite of curtailment: namely, *freedom*. As Marcel expressed it very early in his career, to be open to the other's being himself is at once to be enabled to apprehend and to be myself: apprehending the other as freely being able to be is apprehending myself as freely being able to be. "I help him in some way *to be free*, I collaborate in *his* freedom . . . on the other hand, it is qua freedom that he is truly *other* . . . " (*73*, p. 154). Hence in the embrace of the enabling distance, one allows the other the space (reach) and time (span), his own, to be or become in his own way. *"Presence" is thus "co-presence" in such a case.* As Pietro Prini said in his lucid study of Marcel, "I find myself and I 'am' in the other, as the other finds himself and 'is' in me, both of us being the active mediators of our truest personality. *Esse est coesse*" (*92*, pp. 109–10).

For this kind of "fullness" (*77*, p. 49) to emerge, it is not enough that you and I are merely *willing* to understand each other; we must each *be able* to do so, and *be enabling* to one another. But to be enabling to the other perforce requires that I be willing and able *to be taken* as "thou" by him. To be able to give, freely and openly, is one thing; but "giving" has its mutual requirement, being able *to receive* the other's giving—and mutually for the other.

Hence so far as each self allows or enables genuine co-presence to occur as the texture of their vivid presence, this contexture includes as an essential constituent a "testing" of its own kind. Fundamentally, the contexture of co-presence is able at any moment to be betrayed, to be deceived, to be destroyed. Essentially going on in its own time, our co-presence is a kind of bond, a pact, or a promise. Thus our being able and willing (wanting) to live-it-out is precisely a "test" of it. As Ricoeur stressed in his first book, on Marcel and Jaspers, the *time* of this free and freeing co-presence "admits of an essential disgrace, what one could call its disjointedness [*décousu*]: successive *durée* is never apprehended in its totality, but drop by drop" (*96*, pp. 110–11). And, he points out, this lived-time of co-presence invites us to see there less of an error than a temptation and, if I give in to it, a betrayal: but, it is necessary to comprehend that the possibility of either the one or the other is inscribed in our temporal condition as a test. *For, every test is an invitation to betrayal.* (*96*, p. 113)

To enter into co-presence is thus a unique "ordeal" (*épreuve*), having as its "stake" (*enjeu*) precisely that co-presence itself, hence the self and the other self. Seen from either self's perspective, what is at stake is at once the other self and "our" relationship itself; hence *both* the other self and our relationship are essentially able to be betrayed, and in betraying either, the other is also betrayed, as am I myself. Precisely this is the essence of freedom (Marcel). So long as one, as we say, "keeps faith" with the other and "our" relationship, what then becomes opened for us is a new dimension: as Marcel put it, "a new category, the site of which we can only faintly discern," that is "depth" (*76*, I, p. 207).[13]

THE PHENOMENON OF "DEPTH": THE SECRET

The very presence of such complex, reflexive relations in the vivid presence of selves signifies, among other things, a remarkable possibility of reverberation, echoing, resounding, repetition, reiteration, and the like. Still, as has been pointed out, even though not every vivid presence is also a co-presence (intimacy-relation), the vivid presence is rich with such possibles. I think of the reverberations from a single glance, the chills evoked by a simple gesture, the way a single word can echo in the inner spaces of reverie or even in the rush of a crowded street, and so on.

Yet just as it is not the case that vivid presence is always an intimacy or familiarity (co-presence), so would it be improper to assume that co-presence is possible between just any two selves. The experience of the other self as such is always a matter of vivid presence, to be sure; but whether or not this becomes transformed into co-presence (and thus evokes the sense of "depth") is quite another matter—dependent upon the contingencies of circumstance, time, occasion, biographical situation, current interests, habits, etc. Still again, inasmuch as self cannot *in principle* emerge as self except by way of the enabling, *empowering mutuality* with someone—usually, the mother, father, or even siblings—every self has to that extent concretely experienced something at least of vivid co-presence. It may be that this fades, is relatively momentary, that circumstances are such that the emerging self rarely again experiences co-presence, after the essentially necessary initiating, enabling mutuality of emergence. In that case, it may well be that co-presence becomes a kind of nostalgia within the self, haunting echoes of times past and persons gone. Still, even if the now-emerged self does undergo co-presence with another, such relationships do not seem *necessarily* lasting, though they may be that, nor do they seem necessarily possible as regards just any other self. Nor, for that matter, are genuine co-presences possible, it seems, as regards very many other selves. In every case, however, *vivid co-presence is a veritable achievement*, and it is one which, very much like the experiences of "self-disclosure" studied earlier, *deeply marks* the selves co-presenced "with" (*chez*) one another.

Whenever, in Schutz's delightful phrase, we "make music together," we each know—again, deeply and enduringly—that something altogether profound and precious has happened, momentary and episodic though it may be. Artists, performers, athletes, workers, friends, lovers, speakers, know well that distinctive experience when "it's all together." In all the many different sorts of experiences which evoke that wonder *over and at* "our" common endeavor of working together, one thing stands out markedly: the experience of a kind of "depth" and, as we also say, of "warmth." There is here, as it were, a kind of *realization* of what, in vivid presence, is already a kind of promise, is resoundingly potential. The effort to elicit the inner textures of this co-presence, I fully recognize, places me on very much the same sort of difficult terrain I was on in studying self-disclosure. There are good reasons for this felt awkwardness.

Every co-presence with another is not only a kind of *coesse* with the other, but is thereby constituted in respect of, over against, and in a kind of tension to, a "third," an "outside," the "others" who do not share in our co-presence. This phenomenon Marcel calls a "principle of intersubjectivity" (i.e., what I have called "co-presence"): the "secret" (*76*, I, p. 193; *75*, pp. 146, 221). Every co-presence, being the contextural bond of shared reflexivities emphasized already, is established thereby as a positive phenomenon, as unique: it at once "unites" (us) and "excludes" (the "others"). Hence you and I may be close friends, and each of us may have other friends, perhaps some in common; even so, not even "our" common friend can quite experience or be "in" on our unique relationship, our own "secret" bond (nor, if he be a true friend, would he ever try to be "in" on our secret): for "our" bond is what constitutes it as "we." Of course, no co-presence excludes there being other bonds, between you and your friend, me and my other friend, etc. In short, as complex and entangled as are the relations intrinsic to resentment, deception, and the like, we are forced to recognize a quite comparable complexity in the relations of co-presence. Hence it is necessary to speak of *co-presences possible* for any self (and, in general, most of us most of the time do find ourselves with many co-presences with various others).

But, as we all know well, precisely because of the uniqueness of these bonds, I and Thou, *We*, are inwardly co-presenced with one another, hence, as Marcel insists, it is essential to this "secret" that "one does not recognize the right to speak of [it] to the one who has not bodily participated" (*76*, I, p. 197). The attempt to "speak of it," indeed, to "tell" the secret, invariably leaves one "at a loss" for words—for words, too, are contexturally part of the secret, of the sharing, and come to have their own special meanings, special usages, special occasions; as do the gestures, the things spoken about, the myriads of glances, looks, touches, smells, tastes, and attitudes, etc., which constitute our "depth" and "secret."

It seems no exaggeration to say that such experiences seem to elude the effort "to tell"—indeed, even as you and I "speak" to one another, we do not so much "tell" the secret outright as we "tell" it by precisely not "speaking" of it. Our utterances, our speech, are rarely if ever "about" our bond; they rather *exhibit* our bond.

Part of the reason seems to lie in the character of the bond as a disclosure and living-through of *depth*, the "deeps" in which our lives take rise. Though the deeps are distant, they are not alien; as Marcel remarked in an unpublished fragment of his *Metaphysical Journal*,

> an idea is presented as profound for as much as it opens out on [*débouche*] a "beyond" [*au-delà*] which is only glimpsed. . . . The experience of the deep would thus be bound up with the feeling of a promise, the realization of which can only be glimpsed. But what is remarkable here . . . is that this "glimpsed distance" is not experienced as an "elsewhere": it is to the contrary a "completely near"; the distinction . . . between the here and the elsewhere is in this case trascended. This distance is offered us as inward, a domain of which it is necessary to say that it is nostalgically ours—exactly as it is for a man exiled from his home. (*76*, I, p. 208)

This "going-beyond" in spatial terms can be said equally in temporal terms: "the profound idea 'goes far': that means that it announces a road which can only be followed out in time" (*76*, I, p. 209). Like the "here" and the "elsewhere," so "past" and "future"—the "no longer" and the "still to come"—are here transcended: in the embrace of the "profound" one experiences a kind of timelessness, or rather a "time" which is "full of promise," and within which there is the "promise" to keep faith with my co-presenced partner. The time and space of love, of friendship, of caring, is a time and space at once "far" yet "close": the "near" and the "warm" which are yet something which "go beyond" us, are "deeper" than us. It is as though the complex interweavings of our reflexive relatedness to one another and to our very bond itself were now suffused with, transformed into, another dimension: *depth*, the rich reverberations of manifold interreflexive disclosures and promises of the "still to come." Thus do we prize our love, our friendship, "beyond" even ourselves. For thanks to it, as a constitutive moment of co-presence, "I" am fully myself, within the relationship itself wherein "you" are fully yourself.

In different terms, co-presence as the secret disclosure of depth exhibits precisely the complexity of self-relating by which Kierkegaard conceives the self. As self is "that in the relation, that the relation relates itself to its own self," and is empowered as such by its "relating itself in the relation to another self"; so, here, the *reflexive relationship between co-presenced selves is itself a relation that relates itself to its own self*: the "*We*." Whether this "co-selved" relatedness itself also relates itself to another empowering Other—this, I frankly do not know, even though, for reasons beyond mere symmetry, such a suggestion is attractive. I have, in any case, journeyed far enough to make the main point salient: co-presence is itself a reflexive relatedness, experienced as such, and opens up, in "secret," the dimensions of "the profound" wherein I and thou, wherein We, find ourselves radically illumined. This is, as I suggested, a "pact" which is continually "tested" in the course of our "time" and "space" together (precisely as is "self" itself)—hence it is *a free because freeing bond*, open by essence to temptation, betrayal, but also open to our continuing to "make music together" and thereby, in the deepest sense, "grow older together."[14]

SUMMARY: ON WHOLENESS

It should not be forgotten, of course, that though the kinds of experiences differ, the vivid presence with the other is also a reflexive relatedness, experienced as such. It differs from co-presence, as already indicated, mainly by its not being necessarily a relation of intimacy, the bond of "depth" and the "secret." But, as with every relationship of self, it is essentially itself a relationship to which selves relate themselves while in the relation relating themselves to each other and to each self. There is educed here, as elsewhere, a "wholeness," even though it shows differences from other sorts of "wholeness."

It was pointed out earlier how Scheler emphasizes that the perception of our fellow-men is not "first of all" sensory apprehension of their bodies (unless we are conducting a medical exam, for example, and even then that apprehension is grounded on the relation of vivid presence), and "then" (on that basis, by inference or analogy) or "apprehension-*that*" there is a "psyche" attached to that body—"as in my own case." His refutation of this entire way of posing the issue is completely definitive. To deny that style is not, however, to deny that the other person is embodied, nor that I apprehend that body. To the contrary, what (among other matters) I can and do perceptually apprehend is precisely that body; but not that simpliciter. Rather I apprehend the *concretely embodied other self, always within specific contexts of actually "having to do" and reckoning with the other self.*

How this "being-with-others" at all emerges for self—that is one crucial question, which I took up in the previous chapter. What is intrinsically involved in the concrete experiencing of the other self by self—that has been the theme of the present chapter. And, beyond seeing how closely bound are these two issues, what has become clear is that this experiencing of the other self is not only indubitably accomplished (the very emergence of self within the empowering mutuality by the emerged self testifies to this), but can be explicated in respect of its essential moments. These were found to be located in the experience of vivid presence, with its complex spatial, temporal and reflexive characters—which make it possible for there to be the range of "availing" experiences and those of co-presence. The status of these claims, then, is that they are *transcendentally eidetic*: conditions for the very possibility for the embodied presence of selves, in any conceivable "world."

Throughout, moreover, I have maintained that self, as the reflexivity of the complexure of human life (the complex ordering of the contextures of mental life, embodying organism, and environing milieu), is fundamentally *enabled-to-be* by the other self—likewise a "complexured" reflexivity. Hence the "experience of the other," I claimed, has to be understood as a highly complex relationship: namely, a relation between self-and-other-relating embodied reflexivities. Borrowing and extending (and, I have admitted, possibly doing an injustice to) Kierkegaard's terms, what I find exact, if thus extended, is this: the "relationship" which is vivid presence is a relation such that, in the relation the "relation relates itself to its own self." But inasmuch as we have to do, here, with relata that are themselves reflexively self-related to their own relations and in these relations to themselves, the relationship between them is correspondingly complex. *Each self* (for shorthand) *relates itself to the relation-to-the-other, and in that relation to its own self as thus related-to-the-other-self.*

Such locutions, even though I have grown used to them in trying to think clearly about contextures in general, can be translated into simpler ones, *if it is kept rigorously in mind what such terms designate.* Permit several of Laing's superbly drawn and elegant "webs of *maya*":

> They are playing a game. They are playing at not playing a game. If I show them I see they are, I shall break the rules and they will punish me. I must play their game, of not seeing I see the game. (*67*, p. 1)

Here the scenario is familiar enough; little comment is needed. Only this, perhaps: playing at not playing a game, one can suppose they have some cognizance of this (short of absolutely successful double-think); but their awareness is an awareness of not wanting to be aware of their playing at not playing a game. Hence if I tell them (one thinks of Hicky in O'Neill's *The Iceman Cometh*), I break the rules, embarrass them into explicitly admitting both the game and their sham. This is not proper, and would turn them on me. Etc.

Or consider this one:

> There must be something the matter with him
> because he would not be acting as he does
> unless there was
> therefore he is acting as he is
> because there is something the matter with him.

He does not think there is anything the matter with him because
    one of the things that is
    the matter with him
    is that he does not think that there is anything
    the matter with him
therefore
    we have to help him realize that,
    the fact that he does not think there is anything
    the matter with him
    is one of the things that is
    the matter with him (*67*, p. 5)

Again, this is familiar enough: one thinks of the clear double-bind, for instance.

She wants him to want her
He wants her to want him

To get him to want her
    she pretends she wants him

To get her to want him
    he pretends to want her

Jack wants	Jill wants
Jill's want of Jack	Jack's want of Jill
so	so
Jack tells Jill	Jill tells Jack
Jack wants Jill	Jill wants Jack

a perfect contract (*67*, p. 48)

Indeed! And, a nicely spun whirligog, too: in the relation to Jack (Jill), Jill (Jack) relates herself (himself) to Jack (Jill) and in the relation (pretends) to herself (himself) as related (overtly: "wanting") to him (her). But now, finally:

Jack can see he sees
    what he can see Jill can't see
and he can see
    that Jill can't see that she can't see
but he can't see WHY
    Jill can't see that Jill can't see.

Jill
    can see that he does not understand her
and can see that he can't see that he doesn't:
and she can see

> that he can't see that he can't see
> she sees he can't see he doesn't.
> Why does she still feel confused?
> She cannot understand why he can't see that
> she sees that he can't see that he does not understand (*67*, p. 75)[15]

I can see, and I know this clearly, that you have hurt me with your words; I know that I didn't do anything to warrant your hurting me, and it is especially painful that you don't see even that you've hurt me and are wondering why I am so grieved; why can't you see that you've hurt me twice—by doing what you did, and not seeing that you did it to me? Etc.

That is: Jack and Jill are each respectively aware of themselves, aware of the other, aware of their respective relations to the relation between them, and therefore aware of what they take the other to be aware of in the relation between them, "and so forth." But just as such (as Laing calls them) "knots, tangles, fankles, *impasses*, disjunctions, whirligogs, binds" (*67*, "Preface") are possible solely by virtue of the complexly related reflexivities, so, too, are the rhythmed play and interplay of the varieties of friendship, love, helping, and caring—which, for their part, have an equally complex structure—although in an age of suspicion this may be more difficult to appreciate, in view of the tendency to reduce that complexity to one or another form of "fankle."

What at every point we have to reckon with are modulations of vivid presence, which is to say, of "*integral wholes*"—or better, of *contextures*. These contextures, furthermore, are at once embodied and environed, and to use Scheler's terms, "are incorporated into *combinations and structures of quite a different kind*" (*107*, p. 262) by the self, by the other self, by the selves together as a vividly presenced "we." That the selves thus brought to mutual presence may exhibit "disjunctions," "whirligogs" and the like in their respective "combinations" is no more true than that they may also coalesce perfectly in the union of co-presence. What holds as possible for the emergence of self, continues to hold for adult, emerged selves—though with, it seems, greater complexity and enrichment. What music we make together, whether jointly or disjointly, harmonied or in discord, will vary, but always "we grow older together" and the tapestry of our lives both reveals and tells the textures of that incredible fabric.

Afterword

WHEN it is realized that human life is ineluctably bound to specific historical and social circumstances, and this fact is, as Dilthey put it, "followed to its last consequences," we are squarely confronted with a central impasse. On the one hand is the relativity of every kind of human apprehension and the recognition that every phenomenon, precisely by being within its own historical and social setting, is thereby finite. On the other hand, there is "both the demand of thought and the striving of philosophy for universal knowledge" (Dilthey). There results an apparently inescapable "anarchy of opinions," a veritable bedlam of views contending for that universality but always vying harshly with one another.

Confronting precisely that situation, Husserl wrote in 1910 that "the spiritual need of our time has, in fact, become unbearable. . . . [I]t is the most radical vital need that afflicts us, a need that leaves no point of our lives untouched" (*50*, p. 140). Indeed, practically every thinker of our times has found it necessary to work from within that very context, to confront what have come to be called the "crises" of our times in science, ethics, religion, and human life itself (cf., e.g., *86*; *106*).

Realizing that this "anarchy of opinions" poses its own kind of significant issues, I nevertheless sought to detect what this impasse brings into question, what is thereby posed to us as essentially problematic. Dilthey, Ortega, Husserl, and others see this as the *phenomenon of life*, but few thinkers have pursued this with as much historical care and insight as has Hans Jonas. I thus found it both natural and appropriate to follow his critical journey through the currents of thought in modern times. The result of this inquiry is to have shown that it is not just "life," but specifically *human* life which has become deeply enigmatic in our times. Max Scheler, too, saw this, and toward the end of his life wrote that never before in human history has man become so problematic *to himself* as in our times:

> If we ask an educated person in the Western world what he means by the word "man," three irreconcilable ways of thinking are apt to come into conflict in his mind. The first

is the Jewish-Christian tradition of Adam and Eve, including creation, paradise and fall. The second is the Greek tradition in which, for the first time, man's self-consciousness raised him to a unique place on the grounds that he is endowed with "reason." . . . The third idea is that of modern science and genetic psychology, which also has a tradition of its own. According to this view, man is a very recent product of evolution on our planet, a creature distinguished from its antecedents in the animal world only by the degree of complexity of energies and capacities already present on the subhuman level. These three ideas are not compatible with each other. Thus . . . we do not have a unified idea of man. (*106*, pp. 5–6)

If I read the winds of our times fairly, the very ideas to which we have long grown accustomed as presumable vehicles for understanding ourselves and our world—such as "object," "subject," "absolute," "relative," "empirical," "a priori," but also "sanity," "madness," "normal," "abnormal," etc.—have seriously cracked, split, and are no longer readily efficacious. Indeed, Scheler was probably too sparing to mention but three great ideas of man: if one thinks of the tenets of Marxism, the greater variety of notions within Christianity and Eastern religions, or those of Freud (the "humiliations" to self-love), it seems we do indeed confront the anarchy Dilthey feared. Yeats' vision of fifty years ago ("The Second Coming") is remarkable:

> Things fall apart; the centre cannot hold;
> Mere anarchy is loosed upon the world,
> The blood-dimmed tide is loosed, and everywhere
> The ceremony of innocence is drowned.
> The best lack all conviction, while the worst
> Are full of passionate intensity.

As Ortega remarked trenchantly, speaking of that passionate intensity, "the demagogues, impresarios of *alteración* . . . harass men so that they shall not reflect. . . . And by all these means they succeed in throwing men into a passion, in putting them, between ardors and terrors, *beside*, that is, *outside of, themselves*" (*86*, p. 33).

To pose the question of human life, however, leads to a number of questions, at the center of which is that concerning the human *living body*. While Jonas, too, sees this, I found that his response involved both a methodological confusion bearing directly on the issues, and a curious failure to press the inquiry into the living body, guided by the "evidences in our own case." But it is imperative at all times to keep rigorously to the demands of the problematic, to determine just what is the intrinsic sense and experience of the living body: *the embodying organism*. Careful study of that, it was quickly clear, continually urged other questions: of self, consciousness, the complex experience of the other self. But at this stage of the study, it was evident that the embodying organism itself had not yet been adequately understood: it is a "whole" composed of "parts" and "members." Thus the fundamental question had first to be resolved, for, it also became clear, even those concerning self, consciousness, and the other self could not be accounted for without deeper study of the "whole/part" relation.

Posing that question, especially in the effort to make final sense of embodiment, led directly to the phenomenon of context, margin, and, most importantly, *contexture*, as delineated by Gurwitsch in his seminally important theory of the "field of consciousness." It became necessary, however, to deepen and criticize his analysis considerably, and crucial to test it in the case of the embodying organism. I maintained that the latter is also a contextural phenomenon, of its own kind, and went on to try to show that consciousness itself, the temporal stream of mental life, is also a contexture of its own kind. The study of these two contextures, together with Gurwitsch's careful analysis of the perceptual milieu as a contexture, made it clear that *self* is the principal feature of this *complexure*—namely, *reflexivity*. The then necessary turn to the other self, as a constitutive moment in the emergence of self, and as contexturally bound to the self in their mutual experience of one another, finally, showed the central place of vivid presence and co-presence.

I fully recognize that much has not been done here. A full constitutive, genetic explication was only partially indicated; the regions of sociality beyond vivid presence were not even hinted at, even though it might well be that the present study is a kind of prolegomenon to a theory of sociality; and, finally, I did not lay out clearly just what *method* was used, nor its "logos"—i.e., my *methodology*. If, as I maintained, hermeneutics, or at least Ricoeur's version of it, cannot be regarded as the fundamental philosophical discipline, then what is?

Because the latter cluster of issues must be appreciated as fundamental and as inseparable in any case from "content" and "results," I clearly owe some further remarks on methodology. But, as I have already dwelled on this extensively in other places (see *123*; *124*; *125*; *129*; and *132*), I shall here keep these concluding remarks quite brief, and focus on what the present study has done by way of advancing this issue.

Three things, then, on my "way" of proceeding here. First, I take it that the method of free-phantasy variation (*124*; *125*) is far and away the most significant and important phenomenological method, the most powerful and most fruitful. Compared with it, all talk about the so-called "epochē" and "reduction" is decidedly secondary. Second, I made abundant use of the results and observations of a number of clinical and empirical scientists (see *123*; *126*), noting, in my critical consideration of Schutz's reflections on Scheler, that this is to be philosophically understood as *eidetic ideation* and not as empirical generalization. The fundamental rationale for this, and for free-phantasy methodology more generally, I suggest implicitly throughout, is to be found in the "nature" of human embodied life itself, *reflexivity* and *possibilizing* being the relevant features here.

Third, I made use of a number of clinical cases whose nature is that they reveal a prominent *absence* of the phenomenon in question (brain-injured patients, autistic children). These three points, but especially the last, strike to the core of my method. And, as noted in dealing with Ricoeur's hermeneutics, the method of free-phantasy variation (both uses of empirical cases, it should be noted, are instances of the method), even though barely touched upon in the literature, is of foundational significance for philosophy, and the entire range of empirical sciences.

As I indicated, the present study makes an advance in methodology, beyond anything currently in the literature, and beyond my own previous work on the problem. That advance, or variation in method, might be called the *method of prominence by absence*, and deserves a few words.

The basic key of free-phantasy variation generally is that one explicitly endeavors to consider a range of *actual and especially possible affairs as examples* of some kind or sort. But with the present issue, the range of examples (which could have been merely possible ones) is of a *different order* from the more usual sort of examples. Looking carefully at a variety of cases of brain-injured patients, a critical "ability" *was made prominent* (clinically, but also philosophically) *by its very absence* (or impairment and relative absence): what I came to analyze as "possibilizing." Similarly, a brief survey of autistic children made it *prominent* that little if any of the complex of experiences inherent to emerging as self, being with others, etc., was present, but was precisely *absent*. How is this striking prominence by absence to be accounted for?

Two steps should help here. (1) Gerhard Bosch makes a telling comment while considering the usual medical ways of theorizing. Pointing out how Kanner, Asperger, and others "reduce the phenomenon of autistic existence to symptoms within the framework of a scientific-biological pathology," and then proceed to look "behind" these "symptoms" for "functional disturbances" clustered into a "syndrome," Bosch then emphasizes,

> but it has to be recognized that if we approach the problem in this way we cannot see the character of autism as a specific modification of human existence. In a clinical description guided by such a syndrome the observations will be grouped around the fundamental disturbances as more or less direct derivatives of them. The necessary isolation of the individual symptoms from each other and the reduction of the patient under observation to a complex of symptoms is supplemented by an intuitive empirical description of the patient's behavior. This description, however accurate it may be, *is not made use of as a source of evidence* for a theoretical consideration of autism. . . . On the one side [in Asperger's case] there is the characterological conception of the totally autistic nature with its resulting restricted contact with the surrounding world, and on the other side there is a very rich description, intuitively

guided, of typical autistic behavior and experience to which, however, the author [Asperger] does not return in his consideration of the character of autistic existence. (*7*, p. 50; *my emphasis*)

Nevertheless, it is precisely because of these rich clinical descriptions that we are able vividly to "see" these patients, not only recollect similar cases, but even recognize conducts in ourselves and others which are "like" autism, and can even construct *possible* conducts and cases.

Without identifying it as such, perhaps without even recognizing it, what Bosch in fact is pointing to is nothing but the *functioning of the free-variational method* of a certain kind and level. The "clinical descriptions" make something invariant stand out. But reviewing these cases also makes it apparent that these children manifest a *critical absence*. That is, confronting the range of (actual and possible) conducts *confronts one with oneself* (the clinical observer with himself), precisely by means of the failure of one's efforts to "meet" the child, to enter a relation of vivid presence, much less co-presence. On the other hand, by forcing the observer to confront himself, *he or she is forced to a recognition—however faint or episodic—of that failed vivid presence* and its central significance. Thus the variety of responses by family, medical or non-medical observers—of facing an "abyss," a "glass wall," etc.—can be seen as *modes of self and other recognition*, evoking an awareness of self in respect of its crucially constitutive moment: the other self.

(2) A second step can thus be taken. If we ask, as we must, how that series of recognitions, that forcefulness of failed encounter—or, more generally, the meeting with significant otherness and difference—is possible, it is necessary, I believe, to call attention to what has been at the focus all along in this study: the phenomenon of contexture. In particular, it is necessary to pay careful attention to one of its fundamental features: "*good continuation.*" Although Gurwitsch does not give it much attention (*31*, pp. 150–53), it seems to me to have great importance here.

Gurwitsch points out that "parts capable of fitting into the system [i.e., an incomplete contexture] as already delineated are necessitated. . . . The incompleteness of the system appears in that these parts are experienced as in need of support and supplementation along the lines of, and in accordance with, their functional significance" (*31*, p. 151). For any contexture which is incomplete or impaired, the *present parts demand, require and tend toward completion by means of parts which "fit" the lines of continuation* (completion) *already established*. Correlatively, to the extent that the incompleteness is as yet relatively ill-defined, and hence the lines of continuation relatively open, the parts which can come to function "appropriately" are much more numerous, precisely because of the relative openness of lines of completion; the more defined is the incompleteness, the fewer the parts which can "fit." Hence "the condition imposed upon continuation is fittingness of that which is to follow with that which has been presented thus far" (*31*, p. 153).

It is clear that this principle marks out the "sorts" of constituents which, by conforming to the prevailing functional significance, are able to "fit in." In this sense, *the prevailing but incomplete contexture inherently establishes a functionally significant resemblance or similarity: only those constituents* ("parts", "examples") *which are able to take on the relevant functional significance already established are "fit" for inclusion.* Thus a certain melody, as yet not completed, *itself* sets out lines of completion, into which, say, the noises of popcorn being munched do not "fit"—even though they are auditory phenomena, these noises do not exhibit the relevant functional significance, cannot maintain the contextural balance of intrinsic referencings along with other "parts," hence effectively inhibit, interfere with, or even (possibly) destroy the integrity of the melodic contexture (i.e., make it such that the melody can't be heard: "I can't tell what's being played!").

In the same way, what Bosch calls the "rich, intuitively guided, clinical descriptions" are precisely what *cannot* be ignored in trying to understand (hence, treat) autistic children, as well as those suffering from other afflictions. These descriptions set out, make salient, or *establish* a contexture, hence set out relevant lines of completion—i.e., "resemblances." It is therefore no surprise whatever that, as Bosch points out, such descriptions can so readily call to mind other cases, remind us of past cases, make us think even of vaguely similar cases, etc. *What is at work is the law of good continuation.*

But by the same "logic" (*logos of experience*), *as positive resemblances are set out and lines of completion established, so does the contexture "rule out" any and all "parts" which fail to "fit"*—i.e., fail to reveal the functionally significant character of the contexture. As the melody "rules in," so does it "rule out." And, as in certain circumstances what is contexturally "ruled out" can intrude itself annoyingly—precisely by being "unfitting"—so in other cases. An *enclave* or *absence* which is functionally significant is thereby "present" and "prominent" through its "absence." Thus if a crucial passage in a symphony is left out, or if the chords are "wrong" (e.g., out of tune), this (like every disturbance to contextural balance) *makes itself vitally felt and known.* Here, too, the law of good continuation is at work: *precisely what is "called for" announces itself by its very failure to appear, or to appear in the right way*—i.e., with the appropriate, already established functional significance. It is no surprise either, then, that the "failed meeting" in the case of autism makes itself vitally known and patent: *the contexture itself shows forth its enclave, and thereby calls attention to its very incompleteness or impairment.* Hence "similarity" or "resemblance" *is an inherent feature of the contexture itself* (a demand of its "good continuation"). *The only condition, therefore, which effectively vitiates this fundamental sense of similarity (good continuation) is the absence of a contexture: were experience not already autochthonously organized, however minimally, it would be eidetically impossible for "order" to arise, hence knowledge. The transcendental condition for the possibility of knowledge and experience thus turns out to be the autochthonous organization of experience according to the principle of "field": context, contexture, margin.* Given such organization—and, in particular, the extension and deepening of our understanding of it as suggested in this study—then the critical problem is resolved. *The "principle of good continuation" turns out to be, both in positive and negative ways, the fundamental epistemological and methodological one—* given that it issues from the "field" theory of organization.

Finally, then, when Husserl wrote of that crucial "coincidence in conflict" concerning free-phantasy variation, it is necessary to recognize again the presence here of contextural laws: principally, of closure and good continuation. What is "sufficient" to warrant an eidetic claim is exactly the same phenomenon of "fittingness" and "good continuation." *A range of "examples" is sufficient to warrant judgments to the very extent that there are lines of continuation set out, thus defining in advance the relevant or functionally significant ("resembling") further examples—"significant" just inasmuch as they, too, exhibit the "invariant," i.e., the relevant functional significance, and thus serve to "continue" the contexture in a "good" manner.*

The consequence of these considerations is also clear. The method of free-phantasy variation is itself the "way," the method, for detecting and grasping contextures. Out of the *context* or *field* of actual and possible examples ("parts") there emerges a *contexture* ("whole"): the invariant, the common, the *eidos. In brief: what are called "essences" turn out to be contextures appearing (reflectively) from a wider context, a field. The "essence" of whatever it may be is thus a "whole": that is, a system (significance) which is the totality of the functional significances (intrinsic references) exhibited by each of the actual and possible constituents ("examples").* In simpler terms, the essence of, say, human life, is a *significance*, i.e., a meaning whose "content" is precisely the "invariantly common" system of functionally significant constituents—human beings (actual and possible) (*123*).

In these terms, clearly, not only is "eidetic" philosophy of necessity closely bound to "empirical" disciplines and sciences, not only are the latter bound to the former, but the variety of epistemic claims made by both show a remarkable commonality: both are *specifically* contextural (have their "place" within their own respective contexts), and *generically* contextural (have their "place" with respect to one another). Not only is it useful and helpful for philosophy to call on empirical inquiries, and vice versa, *it could not be otherwise.* The only way (method) for eidetic affairs to be grasped is by way of their exemplifications; and the only way empirical (de facto) affairs acquire their sense and direction is by reference to what is exemplified by the instances studied therein. Of course, just as there were important differences found as regards the different sorts of contextures (embodying organism, mental life, milieu), so will there be important differences found with this form of contexture (i.e., "the *eidos*"). Nevertheless, the delineation of the fundamental features of contextures— intrinsic references, functional significance, good continuation, etc.—makes it quite plain that the study of "what is essential to" whatever it may be is a contextural study. Similarly, the theory of "method"—i.e., methodology— turns out as well to follow the lines of contextural organization. In a word, what I have suggested here is that *free-phantasy variation, fully understood, is intrinsically bound to and arises from the phenomenon of contexture.*

Husserl's insight into the necessity to "fertilize our phantasies," ignored though it has been, *turns out to have been of the utmost importance (46, p. 132). The "possibilizing" which is fundamental to the presence of self, as to the vivid presence and co-presence with others, turns out to be the fundamental "method" for understanding life itself. Life makes itself known and knowable by life; the methods for disclosing human life are found in the tapestry of human life itself.*

Thus, finally, forced to confront the impasse signaled by Dilthey, we have found that the *only possible response* to it is to recognize that *the impasse is itself a disclosure of human life,* not something somehow alien but deeply familiar. The fundamental problematic of modern times—life, human life— alone holds the crucial clues to its being met and surmounted, and the integrity of life reclaimed.

Bibliography

1. James Agee, *A Death In The Family*, a novel (New York: Avon Book Division, The Hearst Corporation, 1957).
2. Suzanne Bachelard, *A Study of Husserl's Formal and Transcendental Logic*, tr. L. E. Embree (Evanston: Northwestern University Press, 1968).
3. Peter L. Berger, *The Noise of Solemn Assemblies* (Garden City, N.Y.: Doubleday and Co., 1961).
4. Henri Bergson, *Matière et mémoire* (Paris: Presses Universitaires de France, 54th éd., 1953).
5. Bruno Bettelheim, *The Empty Fortress: Infantile Autism and the Birth of the Self* (New York: The Free Press, 1967).
6. Ludwig Binswanger, "The Case of Ellen West," in Rollo May et al., eds., *Existence: A New Dimension in Psychiatry and Psychology* (New York: Basic Books, Inc., 1958), pp. 237–364.
7. Gerhard Bosch, *Infantile Autism. A Clinical and Phenomenological-Anthropological Investigation Taking Language as the Guide*, tr. D. and I. Jordan, fwd. Bruno Bettelheim (Berlin/New York: Springer-Verlag, 1970).
8. Ray Bradbury, *Dandelion Wine*, a novel (New York: Bantam Books, 1957).
9. Franz Brentano, *Psychologie vom empirischen Standpunkt*, Bd. I, hrsg. u. einl. O. Kraus (Hamburg: Felix Meiner, 1955; from the 1874 ed.).
10. F. J. J. Buytendijk, *Attitude et mouvements. Étude fonctionnelle du mouvement humain* (Paris: Desclée de Brouwer, 1957).
11. Dorion Cairns, "An Approach to Husserlian Phenomenology," in F. Kersten and R. Zaner, eds., *Phenomenology: Continuation and Criticism. Essays in Memory of Dorion Cairns*, Phaenomenologica 50 (The Hague: Martinus Nijhoff, 1973), pp. 223–38.
12. ———, *Conversations With Husserl and Fink*, ed. The Husserl Archives, intro. R. M. Zaner, Phaenomenologica 66 (The Hague: Martinus Nijhoff, 1976).
13. ———, "Perceiving, Remembering, Image-Awareness, Feigning-Awareness," in F. Kersten and R. Zaner, eds., *Phenomenology: Continuation and Criticism. Essays in Memory of Dorion Cairns*, Phaenomenologica 50 (The Hague: Martinus Nijhoff, 1973), pp. 251–62.
14. J. Preston Cole, *The Problematic Self in Kierkegaard and Freud* (New Haven: Yale University Press, 1971).
15. René Descartes, *The Philosophical Works of Descartes*, 2 vols., tr. E. S. Haldane and G. R. T. Ross (New York: Dover Pub., Inc., 1955).

16. William Dilthey, *Gesammelte Schriften*, 17 Bds. (Stuttgart: B. G. Teubner; Göttingen: Vandenhoeck and Ruprecht, 1914–1974), Band V: *Die geistige Welt*; Band VII: *Der Aufbau der geschichtlichen Welt in den Geisteswissenschaften*. ["Ideas Concerning a Descriptive and Analytic Psychology (1894)", translated by R. M. Zaner, and "The Understanding of Other Persons and Their Expressions of Life", translated by K. L. Heiges (respectively from Volumes V and VII of Dilthey's *Gesammelte Schriften*), have been recently published, with an Introduction by R. A. Makkreel, under the title, *Descriptive Psychology and Historical Understanding* (The Hague: Martinus Nijhoff, 1977).]

17. Leon Eisenberg and Leo Kanner, "Childhood Schizophrenia: Symposium 1955," *American Journal of Orthopsychiatry*, 26 (1956), pp. 556–66.

18. _____. "Early Infantile Autism, 1943–1955," *American Journal of Orthopsychiatry*, 25 (1956), pp. 3–14.

19. T. S. Eliot, "Burnt Norton," in *Four Quartets* (New York: Harcourt, Brace and World, Inc., 1943).

20. H. Tristram Engelhardt, Jr., "Bioethics and the Process of Embodiment," *Perspectives in Biology and Medicine*, Vol. 18, No. 4 (Summer, 1975), pp. 486–500.

21. _____, *Mind-Body: A Categorical Relation* (The Hague: Martinus Nijhoff, 1973).

22. Eric Erikson, *Identity and the Life Cycle* (New York: International Universities Press, 1959).

23. Eugen Fink, "Operative Begriffe in Husserls Phänomenologie," *Zeitschrift für philosophischê Forschung*, 9 (1957), pp. 321–37.

24. Sigmund Freud, *On Creativity and the Unconscious*, sel., intro. and annot. B. Nelson (New York: Harper Torchbooks, Harper and Row, Pubs., 1958).

25. John F. Fulton, ed., *Howell's Textbook of Physiology* (Philadelphia: Saunders, 15th ed., 1946).

26. William Golding, *The Spire*, a novel (New York: Pocket Books, Inc., 1966).

27. Kurt Goldstein, *Aftereffects of Brain Injuries in War* (New York: Grune and Stratton, 1942).

28. _____, *Language and Language Disturbances* (New York: Grune and Stratton, 1948).

29. Richard A. Griffith, "Anthropodology: Man A-Foot," in S. F. Spicker, ed., *The Philosophy of the Body* (Chicago: Quadrangle Books, 1970), pp. 273–92.

30. Aron Gurwitsch, "An Apparent Paradox in Leibnizianism," *Social Research*, Vol. 33, No. 1 (Spring, 1966), pp. 47–64.

31. _____, *The Field of Consciousness* (Pittsburgh: Duquesne University Press, 1964).

32. _____, *Studies in Phenomenology and Psychology* (Evanston: Northwestern University Press, 1966).

33. William Heberden, *Commentary on the History and Cure of Diseases* (Boston: Wells and Lilly, 1818).

34. Martin Heidegger, *Being and Time*, tr. J. Macquarrie and E. Robinson (New York: Harper and Row, Pubs., 1962).

35. André Hellegers, "The Beginnings of Personhood: Medical Considerations," *The Perkins School of Theology Journal*, Vol. 27, No. 1 (Fall, 1973), pp. 11–15.

36. John Nicholas Hines, "Person and Word," *International Philosophical Quarterly*, Vol. XIV, No. 3 (September, 1974), pp. 329–41.

37. William E. Hocking, "Marcel and the Ground Issues of Metaphysics," *Philosophy and Phenomenological Research*, Vol. XIV, No. 4 (June, 1954), pp. 439–69.

38. William Horosz, *The Crisis of Responsibility. Man as the Source of Accountability* (Norman, Okla.: The University of Oklahoma Press, 1975).

39. Richard Hughes, *A High Wind in Jamaica*, a novel (New York: Modern Library, Random House, 1929).

40. Edmund Husserl, *Analysen zur passiven Synthesis (1918/1926)*, hrsg. M. Fleischer, Husserliana Bd. XI (The Hague: Martinus Nijhoff, 1966).

41. _____, *Cartesian Meditations*, tr. D. Cairns (The Hague: Martinus Nijhoff, 1960).

42. _____, *The Crisis of European Sciences and Transcendental Phenomenology*, tr. and intro. D. Carr (Evanston: Northwestern University Press, 1970).

43. _____, *Erste Philosophie (1923/24)*, Zweiter Teil, hrsg. R. Boehm, Husserliana Bd. VIII (The Hague: Martinus Nijhoff, 1959).

44. _____, *Experience and Judgment*, rev. and ed. L. Landgrebe, tr. J. S. Churchill and K. Ameriks (Evanston: Northwestern University Press, 1973).

45. _____, *Formal and Transcendental Logic*, tr. D. Cairns (The Hague: Martinus Nijhoff, 1969).

46. _____, *Ideen zu einer reinen Phänomenologie und phänomenologischen Philosophie*, Erstes Buch, hrsg. W. Biemel, Husserliana Bd. III (The Hague: Martinus Nijhoff, 1950).

47. _____, *Ideen zu einer reinen Phänomenologie und phänomenologischen Philosophie*, Zweites Buch, hrsg. M. Biemel, Husserliana Bd. IV (The Hague: Martinus Nijhoff, 1952).

48. _____, *Lectures on Internal Time Consciousness*, ed. M. Heidegger, tr. J. S. Churchill (Bloomington: Indiana University Press, 1964).

49. _____, *Logical Investigations*, 2 vols., tr. J. N. Findlay (New York: The Humanities Press, 1970; from the 2nd rev. ed., 1913).

50. _____, "Philosophy as Rigorous Science," in E. Husserl, *Phenomenology and the Crisis of Philosophy*, tr., notes, and intro. Q. Lauer (New York: Harper Torchbooks, Harper and Row, Pubs., 1965), pp. 71–147.

51. Aldous Huxley, *The Doors of Perception* (New York: Harper and Bros., Pubs., 1954).

52. William James, *The Principles of Psychology*, 2 vols. (New York: Henry Holt and Company, 1890).

53. Hans Jonas, *The Gnostic Religion: The Message of the Alien God and the Beginnings of Christianity* (Boston: Beacon Press, 1958; 2nd enlarged ed., 1963).

54. _____, "On the Power or Impotence of Subjectivity," in H. T. Engelhardt, Jr. and S. F. Spicker, eds., *Philosophical Dimensions of the Neuro-Medical Sciences* (Dordrecht/Boston: D. Reidel Pub. Co., 1976), pp. 143–61.

55. _____, *The Phenomenon of Life: Toward a Philosophical Biology* (New York: Delta Books, Dell Pub. Co., 1966).

56. _____, *Philosophical Essays: From Ancient Creed to Technological Man* (Englewood Cliffs, N.J.: Prentice-Hall, Inc., 1974).

57. Leo Kanner, "Autistic Disturbances of Affective Contact," *Nervous Child*, Vol. 2 (1942), pp. 217–50.

58. _____, "Early Infantile Autism," *Journal of Pediatrics*, 25 (1944), pp. 211–17.

59. _____, "To What Extent is Early Infantile Autism Determined by Constitutional Inadequacies?" in *Genetics and the Inheritance of Integrated Neurological and Psychiatric Patterns, Proceedings of the Association for Research in Nervous and Mental Disease*, Vol. XXXIII (Baltimore: The Williams and Wilkins Co., 1954), pp. 378–85.

60. Leon Kass, "Regarding the End of Medicine and the Pursuit of Health," *The Public Interest*, No. 40 (Summer, 1975), pp. 11–42.

61. Søren Kierkegaard, *Fear and Trembling* and *The Sickness Unto Death*, tr., notes, and intro. W. Lowrie (Princeton: Princeton University Press, 1954).

62. _____, *The Concept of Dread*, tr., notes, and intro. W. Lowrie (Princeton: Princeton University Press, 1944, 1957).

63. Kurt Koffka, *The Growth of Mind*, tr. R. M. Ogden (London: Kegan Paul, 1924).

64. H. Kohut, "Introspection, Empathy and Psychoanalysis," *Journal of the American Psychoanalytic Association*, Vol. 7 (1959), pp. 459–87.

65. Alexandre Koyré, *From the Closed World to the Infinite Universe* (New York: Harper Torchbooks, Harper and Row, Pubs., 1958).

66. Donald B. Kuspit, "Fiction and Phenomenology," *Philosophy and Phenomenological Research*, Vol. XXIX, No. 1 (September, 1968), pp. 16–33.

67. R. D. Laing, *Knots* (New York: Pantheon Books, 1970).

68. _____, *Self and Others* (New York: Pantheon Books, 1969).

69. Alan Leveton, "Time, Death and the Ego-Chill," *Journal of Existentialism*, Vol. VI, No. 21 (1965), pp. 69–80.

70. David Michael Levin, "Induction and Husserl's Theory of Eidetic Variation," *Philosophy and Phenomenological Research*, Vol. XXIX, No. 1 (September, 1968), pp. 1–15.

71. John Macmurray, *The Self as Agent*, The Gifford Lectures (New York: Harper and Bros., Pubs., 1957).

72. Rudolph Makkreel, *Wilhelm Dilthey: Philosopher of the Human Studies* (Princeton. Princeton University Press, 1975).

73. Gabriel Marcel, *Être et avoir* (Paris: F. Aubier, Éditions Montaigne, 1935). [Eng. tr.: *Being and Having: An Existentialist Diary*, tr. K. Farrer (New York: Harper Torchbooks, Harper and Row, Pubs., 1956.]

74. _____, *Homo Viator*, tr. Emma Craufurd (Chicago: Henry Regnery Co., 1951).

75. _____, *Metaphysical Journal*, tr. B. Wall (Chicago: Henry Regnery Co., 1952).

76. _____, *Le Mystère, de l'être*, 2 tomes (Paris: Aubier, Éditions Montaigne, 1951). (This is the French version Marcel prepared from his Gifford Lectures of 1949–50; there are a number of important differences in the texts, enough to warrant referring to the French, written and published a bit later than the English version.)

77. _____, *Position et approches concrète du mystère ontologique*, intro. M. de Corte (Paris: J. Vrin, 1949).

78. Julián Marías, *Reason and Life: The Introduction to Philosophy*, tr. K. S. Reid and E. Sarmiento (New Haven: Yale University Press, 1956).

79. Maurice Merleau-Ponty, *Phénoménologie de la perception* (Paris: Gallimard, 1945). [Eng. tr.: *Phenomenology of Perception*, tr. C. Smith (New York: The

Humanities Press, 1962).] (I have cited the English version due to its availability, even though I feel that parts of the translation are open to serious criticism.)

80. V. C. Morris, *Existentialism in Education* (New York: Harper and Row, Pubs., 1966).

81. ———, *Philosophy and the American School* (Boston: Houghton-Mifflin, 1961).

82. Clark E. Moustakas, ed., *Existential Child Therapy* (New York: Basic Books, 1966).

83. Maurice Natanson, *The Journeying Self: A Study in Philosophy and Social Role* (Menlo Park, CA/London: Addison-Wesley Pub. Co., 1970).

84. John O'Neill, *Sociology as a Skin-Trade. Essays Toward a Reflexive Sociology* (New York: Harper Torchbooks, Harper and Row, Pubs., 1972).

85. José Ortega y Gasset, *Concord and Liberty*, tr. Helene Weyl (New York: W. W. Norton and Co., Inc., 1946).

86. ———, *Man and People*, tr. W. R. Trask (New York: W. W. Norton and Co., Inc., 1957).

87. Blaise Pascal, *Pensées*, tr. W. F. Trotter (New York: Modern Library, Random House, 1941).

88. Wilder Penfield, *The Mystery of Mind*, with discussions by W. Feindel, C. Handel, C. Symonds (Princeton: Princeton University Press, 1975).

89. Jean Piaget, *The Origins of Intelligence in Children*, tr. M. Cook (New York: International Universities Press, 1952).

90. Herbert Plügge, "Man and his Body," tr. E. Eng, in S. F. Spicker, ed., *The Philosophy of the Body* (Chicago: Quadrangle Books, 1970), pp. 293–311. [From Herbert Plügge, *Der Mensch und sein Leib* (Tübingen: Max Niemeyer Verlag, 1967), pp. 34–42, 57–68.]

91. Adolf Portmann, "Biology and the Phenomenon of the Spiritual," in Joseph Campbell, ed., *Spirit and Nature: Papers from the Eranos Yearbooks*, Vol. I, Bollingen Series XXX (Princeton: Princeton University Press, 1954), pp. 342–70.

92. Pietro Prini, *Gabriel Marcel et la méthodologie de l'invérifiable*, lettre-préface de Gabriel Marcel (Paris: Desclée de Brouwer, 1953).

93. Paul Ramsey, "The Indignity of 'Death with Dignity,' " *The Hastings Center Studies*, Vol. 2, No. 2 (May, 1974), pp. 47–62.

94. Paul Ricoeur, *Freedom and Nature: The Voluntary and the Involuntary*, tr. and intro. E. Kohák (Evanston: Northwestern University Press, 1966).

95. ———, *Freud and Philosophy. An Essay on Interpretation*, tr. D. Savage (New Haven: Yale University Press, 1970).

96. ———, *Gabriel Marcel et Karl Jaspers: Philosophie du mystère et philosophie du paradoxe* (Paris: Éditions du Temps Présent, 1947).

97. ———, "Phenomenology and Hermeneutics," *Nous*, 9 (1975), pp. 85–102.

98. ———, *The Symbolism of Evil*, tr. E. Buchanan (Boston: Beacon Press, 1969).

99. Rainer Marie Rilke, *Letters to a Young Poet*, tr. M. D. Herder Norton (New York: W. W. Norton and Co., Inc., rev. ed., 1954)

100. Robert Russell, *To Catch An Angel*, an autobiography (New York: Popular Library, 1963).

101. Gilbert Ryle, *The Concept of Mind* (New York: Barnes and Noble, 1949).

102. Giorgio de Santillana, *The Crime of Galileo* (Chicago: The University of Chicago Press, 1955).

103. Jean-Paul Sartre, *Being and Nothingness. An Essay on Phenomenological Ontology*, tr. H. Barnes (New York: Philosophical Library, 1956).

104. _____, *The Transcendence of the Ego*, tr. F. Williams and R. Kirkpatrick (New York: The Noonday Press, 1957).

105. Max Scheler, *Formalism in Ethics and Non-Formal Ethics of Value*, tr. M. S. Frings and R. L. Funk (Evanston: Northwestern University Press, 1973).

106. _____, *Man's Place in Nature*, tr. and intro. H. Meyerhoff (Boston: Beacon Press, 1961).

107. _____, *The Nature of Sympathy*, tr. P. Heath, intro W. Stark (New Haven: Yale University Press, 1954).

108. _____, *Selected Philosophical Essays*, tr. and intro. D. R. Lachterman (Evanston: Northwestern University Press, 1973).

109. Alfred Schutz, *Collected Papers*, 3 vols. Vol. I: *The Problem of Social Reality*, ed. and intro M. Natanson, Phaenomenologica 11; Vol. II: *Studies in Social Theory*, ed. and intro. A. Brodersen, Phaenomenologica 15; Vol. III: *Studies in Phenomenological Philosophy*, ed. I. Schutz, intro. A. Gurwitsch, Phaenomenologica 22 (The Hague: Martinus Nijhoff, I: 2nd ed., 1967; II: 1964; III: 1970).

110. _____, *Reflections on the Problem of Relevance*, ed., annot., and intro. R. M. Zaner (New Haven: Yale University Press, 1970).

111. _____, and Thomas Luckmann, *The Structures of the Life-World*, tr. R. M. Zaner and H. T. Engelhardt, Jr. (Evanston: Northwestern University Press, 1973).

112. J. P. Scott and J. L. Fuller, *Genetics and the Social Behavior of the Dog* (Chicago: University of Chicago Press, 1965).

113. Roger Shinn, "Personal Decisions and Social Roles in a Pluralistic Society," *The Perkins School of Theology Journal*, Vol. 27, No. 1 (Fall, 1973), pp. 58–63.

114. Herbert Spiegelberg, "On the 'I-Am-Me' Experience in Childhood and Adolescence," *Review of Existential Psychology and Psychiatry*, Vol. V (1964), pp. 3–21.

115. Erwin W. Straus, "Aesthesiology and Hallucinations," in Rollo May et al., eds., *Existence: A New Dimension in Psychiatry and Psychology* (New York: Basic Books, Inc., 1958), pp. 139–69.

116. _____, "Born to See, Bound to Behold," in S. F. Spicker, ed., *The Philosophy of the Body* (Chicago: Quadrangle Books, 1970), pp. 334–61.

117. _____, *Phenomenological Psychology. Selected Papers*, tr. in part E. Eng (New York: Basic Books, Inc., 1966).

118. Carl Stumpf, *Über den psychologischen Ursprung der Raumvorstellung* (Leipzig, 1873).

119. J. H. Van Den Berg, "The Human Body and the Significance of Human Movement," *Philosophy and Phenomenological Research*, Vol. XIII, No. 2 (December, 1952), pp. 159–83.

120. Alphonse de Waehlens, *Une philosophie de l'ambigüité* (Louvain: Pub. Universitaires de Louvain, 1951).

121. Richard M. Zaner, "The Alternating Reed: Embodiment as Problematic Unity," in J. Y. Fenton, ed., *Theology and the Body* (Philadelphia: The Westminster Press, 1974), pp. 53–71.

122. _____, "Context and Reflexivity: The Genealogy of Self," in H. T. Engelhardt, Jr. and S. F. Spicker, eds., *Evaluation and Explanation in the Biomedical Sciences* (Dordrecht/Boston: D. Reidel Pub. Co., 1975), pp. 153–74.

123. _____, "*Eidos* and Science," in Joseph Bien, ed., *Phenomenology and the Social Sciences: A. Dialogue* (The Hague: Martinus Nijhoff, 1978), pp. 1–19.

124. _____, "Examples and Possibles: A Criticism of Husserl's Method of Free-Phantasy Variation," *Research in Phenomenology*, III (1973), pp. 29–43.

125. _____, "The Art of Free-Phantasy in Rigorous Phenomenological Science," in F. Kersten and R. Zaner, eds., *Phenomenology: Continuation and Criticism. Essays in Memory of Dorion Cairns*, Phaenomenologica 50 (The Hague: Martinus Nijhoff, 1973), pp. 192–219.

126. _____, "The *Logos* of *Psyche*: Phenomenological Variations on a Theme," to be published along with other papers given in a symposium, "Philosophy and Psychology" at the 100th Anniversary meeting of The American Psychology Association, New York City, September 5, 1978.

127. _____, *The Problem of Embodiment. Some Contributions to a Phenomenology of the Body*, Phaenomenologica 17 (The Hague: Martinus Nijhoff, 1964).

128. _____, "The Radical Reality of the Human Body," *Humanitas*, Vol. II, No. 1 (1966), pp. 73–87.

129. _____, "Reflections on Evidence and Criticism in the Theory of Consciousness," in L. E. Embree, ed., *Life-World and Consciousness. Essays for Aron Gurwitsch* (Evanston: Northwestern University Press, 1972), pp. 209–30.

130. _____, "Theory of Intersubjectivity: Alfred Schutz," *Social Research*, Vol. 28, No. 1 (Spring, 1961), pp. 71–93.

131. _____, "The Unanchored Leaf: Humanities and the Discipline of Care," *Texas Reports on Biology and Medicine*, Vol. 32, No. 1 (Spring, 1974), pp. 1–18.

132. _____, *The Way of Phenomenology. Criticism as a Philosophical Discipline* (New York: Pegasus Press, Bobbs-Merrill Pub. Co., Inc., 1970).

Notes

TO INTRODUCTION TO PART I.

1. This essay, (see *16, V*, pp. 139–240), which I have translated, and "Das Verstehen anderer Personen und ihrer Lebensausserung," from Bd. VII, tr. Kenneth Heiges, have been published with an Introduction by Rudolph Makkreel, under the title *Descriptive Psychology and Historical Understanding* (The Hague: Martinus Nijhoff, 1977).

TO CHAPTER 1

1. This was the basic point of his lecture, "On the Theory of Responsibility," presented on December 2, 1975, to the Seminar on Bioethics, conducted by Professor Frederick Carney and myself at Southern Methodist University. Personal conversations revealed that his main project is to develop a general ethical theory, based on the new foundations of a conception of responsibility. (Jonas has since completed this study: *Das Prinzip Verantwortung* Frankfurt/ Boston: Suhrkamp Verlag, 1979.)

2. As Jonas emphasizes, "since the point of departure in either case is partial with respect to integral reality, they severally embody the internal contradiction of a partial monism"—i.e., the failure to reduce mind to matter or matter to mind (*55*, p. 17).

3. "Was": that passage is from Jonas' opening lecture course on "The Problem of Life in the Theory of Being," delivered at Hebrew University in Jerusalem, in 1946 (see *55*, p. 156, n. 3).

4. This, it should be noted, is precisely the point, and almost the formulation, made by Gabriel Marcel in the 1920's and 1930's (see *75*, pp. 17–18, 125, 245, et passim). Others of Marcel's works, of course, deepen the theme of the "body-qua-mine" quite substantially. See below, Chapters 2 and 3 for further references to his and others' works on this.

5. As will be seen when I consider Paul Ricoeur's theory of self, precisely this "effort" is fundamental to the "self." See below, Chapter 6.

6. "Only living things have needs and act on needs. Need is based both on the necessity for the continuous self-renewal of the organism by the metabolic process, and on the organism's elemental urge thus precariously to continue itself. This basic self-concern of all life . . . manifests itself on the level of animality as appetite, fear, and all the rest of the emotions (*55*, p. 126).

7. Although neither Husserl nor Merleau-Ponty are mentioned by Jonas, here or elsewhere so far as I know, there is a notable parallel. (See *44*, pp. 72–86, 381–89, and *79*, p. 363, where the "*Urpräsenz*" and "*Entgegenwärtigung*" of human life is laid out, based on Husserl.)

8. It will be necessary to return to these important themes later. See below, Chapters 3, 8, and Afterword.

9. Apparently this "Note" was written a good deal after the original essay; no mention of this is given, nor is there any dating of the Appendices to the various essays.

10. Still another striking parallel is found here, namely, with the fascinating work of the biologist Adolf Portmann (see *91*, especially pp. 344–57).

11. It is surprising that there is hardly a word on his methodology, and almost nothing on reflection; this, as will be seen later, is on the contrary a central requirement for any philosophical theory, Jonas' as well. See below, Chapter 6 and Afterword.

12. As Aron Gurwitsch expressed the point, "every philosophical system is subject to the obligation of accounting for its own possibility. . . . Less radically expressed, there must be no incompatibility between the doctrinal content of a philosophical theory, that which is maintained and asserted in it, on the one hand, and, on the other, the mere fact of the formulation of the theory in question" (*30*, p. 47).

13. See below, Chapters 4 and 5, where the relevant issues and references are given.

TO CHAPTER 2

1. See below, Chapter 6.

2. Cf. Horosz (*38*) for an intriguing argument against "totalisms" as such. I find myself, even while having some problems with his work, far closer to this than to any "totalism."

3. See *The Problem of Embodiment (127)* for the main references to Marcel, Sartre, Merleau-Ponty, and Husserl. But see also Max Scheler (*105*, especially pp. 404–24); Erwin Straus (*115*; *116*; *117*); Paul Ricoeur (*94*, especially pp. 199–337); and H. Tristram Engelhardt, Jr. (*21*).

4. As will be seen in the next chapter, the biology developed by Adolf Portmann, Kurt Goldstein, Erwin Straus, and others, differs radically from that presupposed by Hellegers.

5. As Hellegers insists, "Science can not establish any truths except those which it predefines. It cannot give *meaning* to events; it can only define them and, within the limits of methodology, predict them. As scientists we are the supreme 'bookies' of this world" (*35*, p. 13). I note without comment that this "predictivist" stance is not unproblematic; and that the difference (if any) between "giving meaning" to, and "defining" events, is rather elusive. One must wonder how to handle the "predefinition" which science supposedly gives as opposed to the "definition" it also supposedly gives to all events, without, however, somehow, giving them "meaning."

6. The operative terms "when" and "begins," for instance, could well be of central ethical significance. If, as Hellegers says (*35*, p. 12), one cannot talk about "irreversibly individual human life" until after implantation, even though "new human life quite clearly begins at fertilization," and one argues for the presence of a "soul" when that irreversible point is reached, then these medically determinable

"facts" are eminently relevant for the ethical decision about abortion. And this is merely one instance.

7. This, as will be seen shortly, has deep historical roots specifically with Descartes' dualism.

8. "It is a being because it is there," says Hellegers (*35*, p. 14), in an apparently naive realism, one which is, however, a clearly theoretically naive realism, and not at all what is within commonsense life itself.

9. On the analogy of Dilthey's charge to the explanatory psychology of his day: having little to say about psychic life (*Seelenleben*), he pointed out that such a psychology was in truth a science (*logos*) without a soul (*psyche*)—that being the last phenomenon that psychology, so-called, was interested in studying (see *16*, V, pp. 139–240).

10. Or, one could say as readily, the wholeness of the live body is not the wholeness of a cadaver.

11. As he points out, "disease" is *not* the opposite of "health," but is rather expressive of, and sensible only with, a different model of human life, body, and medicine— presumably, a model which is to be regarded as unacceptable.

12. It should be noted, however, that Kass still flirts with the contrary model of the body when he uses "state" language—i.e., language expressive, not of *activity* or process (*dynamis*), but of *passivity* (*stasis*): "state of being active" is a case in point.

13. This, as already mentioned, is by no means novel. Decades ago, Bergson, Scheler, Marcel, Husserl all insisted on the point; and as we shall see in the next chapter, so did the biologist Portmann, the neurologist/psychiatrist Straus, and the physician/philosopher Goldstein.

14. Why only "two"? Surely an action, if susceptible of "more than one" description, may well be describable in *many* ways: think only of Aristotle's "many ways" in which Being is said; or think of "raising the arm with the fist closed" and, depending on the context, how variously it may be described: a test for a medical examination, a political gesture, an erotic gesture, a symbol of social solidarity, a cheer at an athletic contest, and still other ways.

15. As I suggested in *The Way of Phenomenology* (*132*, pp. 133, 215, n. 15), "consciousings" may be preferable, to avoid prejudging any issues.

16. Jonas (*55*, pp. 28–30) seems to me to court disaster even while he perceptively discerns the crucial point. Taking this "muteness" as itself the problem, he seeks to account for how perception yields "decausalized contents," but no traces of its own causal genesis. In the course of this, he points out that causality is not a "datum" but an "actum"—stemming from propriobodily effort, force, hence causality is "only experienced from within when exerted or suffered" (p. 31). But this collapses two very different matters: "causality" as an *experience* of bodily effort, and "causality" as the *genesis* of perception. He holds that it is suppressed in the latter, and generated in the former—but forgets, it seems, that such bodily efforting is no less a matter of sensory experience than cool vision! If so, then "causality" *is* *perceived* (as he says, in fact—without, however, calling it "perception"); it is indeed experienced bodily (and thus as a mode of encounter), and the problem then is what could possibly legitimate Jonas' very problem! Or else the problem is whether there really is a problem of the "absence there [in perception] and not its presence among our ideas being the puzzling fact" (p. 33). The puzzling thing is this

implicit *double* causality, and the oddity of not recognizing bodily efforting as not only "experience" but as truly perceptual (involving both the sensorium and the motorium).

17. Cf. Husserl (*47*, p. 144): "in every experience of spatial, corporeal objects, the animate organism, as the perceptual organ [*Wahrnehmungsorgan*] of the experiencing subject, is co-perceived '*along with* it' . . . " (see also pp. 151–52).

18. See Alfred Schutz's excellent discussion of Goldstein's work on language disturbances (*109*, I, pp. 260–86).

19. Cf. Husserl (*47*, pp. 56, 128;, *41*, p. 97). See also Dorion Cairns (*12*, pp. 4–7, 12, 18–19, 64, 95–96) for fascinating discussions of these kinaesthesias—a topic which centrally occupied Husserl's efforts throughout the 1920's and early 1930's.

20. See *127*, pp. 129–97, for an exposition; and pp. 198–238 for critical remarks. Although I would modify some of the latter today, I still think they are basically correct. As will be seen later, however, critically rejecting one of Gurwitsch's theses about the "insularity" of consciousness, I have come to appreciate more what Merleau-Ponty seemed to have been driving at. Both, however, would have to be submitted to searching criticisms on the issue; I take up Gurwitsch later on.

TO CHAPTER 3

1. A model case in point might be in the medical situation where, for example, I experience a physician's probing and touching of my body, testing its physiologic and neurologic functions. Having my chest examined, I am cognizant of being taken as a body-object, thus apprehend myself as apprehended by him biologically—and thus in a way "realize" my own being-as-biological.

2. Or, it might be suggested, to the extent one seems literally to "be other than oneself," as it were, we might well have to do with markedly pathological conduct: e.g., the patient Alice reported by Alan Leveton, (*69*, pp. 69–80), or some of Binswanger's classic cases (e.g., *6*, pp. 237–364).

3. Goldstein, in his studies of brain-injured patients, stressed precisely this, noting, for example, that the patient suffering visual agnosia was able to read by means of minute eye and head movements. Not every patient with visual agnosia can be expected to do this, he points out; hence the necessity for clinical treatment being handled with extraordinary care and sensitivity to the context of each patient's life, even patients revealing apparently "the same" pathology.

4. This feature of concrete bodily life is a good case in point of what has been called the "necessary contingency" of human existence by thinkers from Pascal and Kierkegaard to Sartre and Merleau-Ponty.

5. As Buytendijk emphasizes, "it is especially important to realize that man is in this world with his body and that the body itself is a situation. . . ." And, he continues, the body discloses itself as meaningful in its attitudes, gestures, and actions, all of which are inseparably connected to and made possible by the biological structures of the body. Studying these, one can come to an understanding of the distinctively "feminine" and "masculine" *Unwelten* (see *10*, pp. 200 and 204–08). The point I must stress here, though, is the profound sense of irrevocableness which is made present by that "biological structure" of the body: not only does it "make possible," it also, and just as decisively, *makes impossible*—even where one can readily admit the prospects for biological modification.

6. This is related directly to what Husserl calls "the logos of the aesthetic world" (from the Greek, *aisthesis*, pertaining to sensory, corporeal life) (see *45*, p. 292). And see above, Chapter 2, where this primordial source of causality was pointed out.

7. More than anything else in an otherwise very troublesome conception of "'1' ambigüité," it seems to me, Merleau-Ponty's point has a profound place precisely here: every awareness necessarily includes this conditioning component as not itself capable *at the same time* of being focalized (see *79, passim*). The only exception to this, it may be, is reflexive awareness of mental processes, although this is by no means clear or obvious on the face of it. (See *127*, pp. 107–16, 199–204 [for the question of reflection], and pp. 152–80, 208–24 [on "ambiguity"].)

8. It seems appropriate to mention here that although I have adopted quite similar modes of expression, even the same at times, I only recently came on Plügge's marvelously insightful work. As mentioned earlier, it was through my reading of Freud—who was addressing himself to quite different issues—that it struck me how well such expressions captured the profound sense of the full phenomena of embodiment (see *128*).

9. "Ambiguity" is also found used in much the same sense, says Plügge, in Pascal: the *Grandeur* and the *Misère* of man, are understood not as two alternatives, two sides of man, but as *one*: *Grandeur* is at the same time *Misère*. So, too, I would add, did Pascal express the mind and body (see *87*, pp. 27–28).

10. The position I took on this earlier (*127*, pp. 218–24) is not as generous as that taken by Plügge here. Still, even though I continue to have serious reservations about whether Merleau-Ponty's work really warrants his interpretation, I am inclined to see Plügge's view as quite fruitful. It would nevertheless entail, I think, some critical modifications in Merleau-Ponty's analysis to secure that interpretation and clearly differentiate "ambiguity" from Merleau-Ponty's equivalently used terms, "generality" and "typicality."

11. Herbert Spiegelberg, in correspondence with Hughes, confirmed that the passage was autobiographical (see *114*, pp. 3–21).

12. This experience, I will later emphasize, is critical for the understanding of "self." See below, Part II, Chapter 7. An interesting variant on Russell's case was reported by Kurt Goldstein (*27*, p. 180). A patient at first totally blind remained relatively calm and unperturbed about his blindness so long as it was total; on recovering partial eyesight, however, he became extremely upset, had difficulty orienting himself, and for the first time spoke of something not being right about his eyes. Depression would hit him: "What's to become of me if I can't see?" he would say!

13. This is Jean Piaget's usage (see *89*, especially Ch. 1).

14. "Their bodies are expanded between mouth and anus as between an entrance and an exit, a beginning and an ending" (*117*, p. 162).

15. Straus shows (*117*, pp. 138–41, 159–61) that the anatomical and physiological structures of the human body are naturally oriented to the upright posture: " . . . there is no doubt that the shape and function of the human body are determined in almost every detail by, and for, the upright posture. The skeleton of the foot; the structure of the ankle, knee, and hip; the curvature of the vertebral column; the proportions of the limbs—all serve the same purpose" (p. 138). Even the structure and shape of shoulder, arm, hand, and head reveal this same purpose (pp. 149–59, 161–64).

16. Portmann continues: "It might further be mentioned that the lumbar cleft in the

spinal column typical of man is already present at the end of the second fetal month—and that this is the earliest distinguishing feature of the human spinal column . . . " (*91*, p. 357).

17. As Straus exphasizes with wonderful clarity: "Because upright posture is the leitmotiv in the formation of the human organism, an individual who has lost or is deprived of the capacity to get up and keep himself upright depends, for his survival, completely on the aid of others. Without this help, he is doomed to die" (*117*, p. 139). This leitmotiv is thus that of medicine as well—indeed, of all of the "caring" professions. It is precisely here, along with the intrinsic integrity of the human embodying organism, that one finds the basis of ethical and value concerns.

18. It is interesting to imagine freely several kinds of variations on this. (1) As Straus suggests, we can note the intrinsic awkwardness, but also the distinctive way in which things, others, and ground appear when we "get down on all fours." (2) Equally revealing is the fascination we experience when we see a simian "standing up and facing us"; although we "know" that such an act is not native to the animal, this quasi-upright posture seems uncannily "human(oid)" and becomes a source of wonder, just as the belly-crawl of the snake fills us with other feelings.

19. Straus points out, too, how the formation of the face (nose, eyes, ears, jaw, and the subtle differences between the musculature of the animal jaw and the human mouth) is a prerequisite not only for language, but also for the perception of noises as sounds, and the expression of the rich variety of wishings, willings, feelings, etc., by subtle mimic and phonetic muscles (*117*, pp. 162–63).

20. Precisely here is revealed the core of what Goldstein calls the figure-ground relation.

21. Portmann mentions that parallel to the "development of the frontal pole runs a development of the anal pole"—so much so, that the scrotum can become one of the ornamental forms having great "representational value" (*91*, p. 353). As Straus points out, and as his former co-worker, Richard M. Griffith, indicates in delightful detail, with the achieving of upright posture, a significant transformation takes place: the "bottom," "end," or "tail" is no longer—despite our common language—the buttocks, but the feet. See Griffith's marvelously insightful essay, "Anthropodology: Man A-Foot" (*29*, pp. 273–92).

22. See, for example, the very next sentence after he ostensibly restricts the usages (*91*, p. 352; see also pp. 358, 368, and 370).

TO CHAPTER 4

1. Gurwitsch takes up the heart of Husserl's theory, especially the conception of "moments of unity" or "figural moments" (*figurales Momente*), and I shall consider Husserl's conception at that point.

2. See Gurwitsch's subtle discussion of Piaget (*31*, especially pp. 36–56), where he shows that Piaget's work not only does not require any sense-data theory, but is irrevocably damaged at its root if such a theory is retained. Only by excising that notion, through a phenomenological reinterpretation of Piaget and the phenomena he is concerned with, can one rescue his otherwise brilliant and substantially correct insights.

3. Cf. Husserl (*49*, II, pp. 474–75, 478–81). Even though he does seem to endorse Stumpf (pp. 440–42, 451–52) and explicitly admits that his notion of *Einheitsmomente* is the same as von Ehrenfels' "form-qualities" and Meinong's "founded contents" (*49*, p. 442), it could be argued that Husserl's own analyses sometime seem in conflict with those notions, and far closer to Gurwitsch's notion of "Gestalt-contexture" (*49*, pp. 444, 446–47, 448–49, 453). However that may be, as I mention in the text, Husserl's writings after *Ideen*, I (*46*) seem clearly to diverge from that closer direction of the *Investigations*.

4. See, besides the relevant passages of *Ideen*, I (*46*) cited by Gurwitsch (*32*, pp. 175–286), Husserl's *Nachlass*, especially that published under the title *Analysen zur passiven Synthesen* (*40*).

5. "Indeed, all that Husserl and Stumpf say about the way in which content-parts [i.e., nonself-sufficient parts] are given together applies to the constituents of a Gestalt as to their existence with, and within, one another" (*32*, p. 260).

6. Findlay renders Husserl's sentence differently, thus altering its sense. Husserl's words are: "In *diesem* Sinne sind alle Inhalte unabtrennbar." Findlay translates: "In *this* sense no contents are isolable . . . " (cf. *49*, p. 443; Husserl's original, *Log. Unter.*, V. 2, II, p. 235).

7. Translation slightly revised.

8. Translation here is by Fred Kersten, as it appears in Gurwitsch's essay, "Phenomenology of Thematics . . . " (*32*, p. 260), and is preferable to Findlay's.

9. *31*, p. 4; on p. 344, Gurwitsch is much clearer, distinguishing between "*marginal acts*" and "*marginal data*," where the latter is the "*domain of irrelevancy*."

10. Cf. Husserl (*46*, p. 62).

11. Indeed, Gurwitsch seems to regard the "ground-phenomenon" as "somehow more primitive than, and prior to," the figure-ground structure of perception.

12. From Wertheimer, "Untersuchungen zur Lehre von der Gestalt," II, *Psychologische Forschung*, Vol. IV, 1923. It might be noted that even the first two factors have this significance—although their sense cannot be restricted to their spatial meanings. Thus "proximity" might be understood as a *tendency to convergence*, viz., to *concur* in respect of functional significance; "equality" as a *tendency to be similar*, or *to be assimilable to*, the prevailing functional significances of constituents at hand.

13. As I have tried to show elsewhere, there is a prominent *epistemic* status to incompleteness/completion inherent to science, which defines the sense of "level of inquiry" (see *123*; *126*).

14. As will be seen later, herein lies a fundamental, rarely formalized, methodology which will prove central to phenomenological explicative tasks, and in particular free-phantasy variation. See Afterword.

15. It should be noted here not only that much of what Merleau-Ponty says about perception and Gestalt-psychology had already been discussed by Gurwitsch earlier (on his own, though quite in conformity with Husserl, even where he diverges), but also that Merleau-Ponty takes over these results with only a bare mention of Gurwitsch. (See *79*, p. 47, where Gurwitsch's critical interpretation of Köhler's rejection of the constancy-hypothesis as an incipient phenomenological reduction is mentioned.)

16. I should note, too, that this position was endorsed by me earlier, in criticism of Merleau-Ponty (*127*, pp. 205–08). As will be seen, I did not fully appreciate the problems with this at that time.

17. Gurwitsch takes this phrase directly from Husserl, as he notes (see *46*, p. 93; also, sec. 53).

18. See also his "Phenomenological and the Psychological Approach to Consciousness" (*32*, pp. 89–106).

19. Husserl's words are: " . . . Bewusstsein, in 'Reinheit' betrachtet, (hat) als ein *für sich geschlossener Seinszusammenhang* zu gelten . . . als ein Zusammenhang *absoluten Seins*, in den nichts hineindringen, und aus dem nichts entschlüpfen kann . . . " (see *46*, p. 117).

TO CHAPTER 5

1. As Goldstein pointed out, too, there can be functional modifications in undamaged substrata of the nervous system as an indirect result of the destruction of other substrata—and retained performances will be modified as a result. There are thus *functional units* performing in tandem (cf. *27*, pp. 81–83).

2. Cf. Edmund Husserl (*41*, pp. 72–81) for the technical senses of "static" and "genetic" phenomenological constitution.

3. It clearly makes a difference whether we are talking of a phase which falls, for example, in the middle of a sentence (the "rest" of the sentence's saying being rather well delineated), of a phase which is a hearing of Beethoven's symphony (one note "leans" clearly into those "still to come"), or of a phase falling within a rather more uncertain experience (e.g., what will be experienced just around the bend of a highway being traveled for the first time). Even so, however, protended phases and their intentional objects are generally well-delineated, thanks to the way "the past casts its shadow over the future," in Husserl's well-known phase; i.e., we tend to give *weight* to what has already been experienced.

4. See above, pp. 82–86.

5. Although, it should be noted, there are reasons for doubting whether Gurwitsch's understanding of the margin can be wholly correct: surely, as suggested already, not everything marginal is purely contingent or without internal ordering, even though it presently does not appertain to (is not relevant to) the theme/ field now at hand. This is especially true, as I suggest later, of bodily awareness.

6. Although it is surely true that Husserl would himself *insist* that this point is correct, many of his formulations and analyses leave out the *Leibkörper*. Beyond that, it would be interesting to determine whether Gurwitsch's tendency to regard the body as strictly marginal (or, at least, his ambivalence toward the body) derives from this ellipsis in formulating intentionality.

7. This is Gurwitsch's example, the one which immediately precedes the quotation given above (cf. *31*, pp. 416–18). It is doubtful that Gurwitsch would disagree with the point being made here; still, the claim in question was made by him, hence needs to be criticized.

8. Just for this reason, it might be mentioned, Husserl was long worried about the precise status of the "kinaesthetic" processes which are so closely bound to "willing" and "striving." Though at one point he was inclined to take them as

purely psychical, he was later obligated to take them as bodily (cf. *12*, pp. 4–7, 12, 18–19, 95–96, et passim).

TO CHAPTER 6

1. Cf. also *98*, p. 351: to understand symbols, one must live "in the *aura* of the meaning he is inquiring after."
2. For Ricoeur, it is *only* by directly engaging the philosophical issues within the embrace of the diverse and the contingent that philosophy properly fulfills its nature and task as *concrete*. Anyone who would try to escape his own concrete situatedness "would seek nothing, not being motivated by concern about any question" (*98*, p. 24).
3. As will be pointed out later, though Ricoeur does not here mention it, this traditional logic, as also current logical calculus, themselves stand in need of the same transcendental grounding—as Husserl has shown (*45*, especially Part II).
4. Taken seriously, as will be seen, this will present serious difficulties for the understanding of the status of Ricoeur's own claims: if they are hermeneutical, then they are *essentially* revocable, but more, *must* be in "conflict" with other interpretations, with no apparent way of deciding among them. The question is: must this hold *throughout*, especially for his claim about "desire"? Can there be "conflict" about this? That would seem countersensical; but if there can be *no* conflict on such claims as this, then something fundamental must be changed in the conception of the relations between hermeneutics and transcendental grounding.
5. Ricoeur's aim is to show, by confronting Hegel and Freud, that Freud's "archaism" already has Hegel's "teleology" within it implicitly, and vice versa. They are "dialectical others" (see *95*, Book III, Chs. 3 and 4).
6. This is the *opacity* of symbols, the reason they cannot be placed "objectively" before one, but can only be "lived in" (cf. *98*, p. 15).
7. As has been shown already, the sense of "belonging-to-a-totality," although not analyzed by Ricoeur, is clearly a fundamental problem in his work, especially for a hermeneutics pretending to be "architectonic."
8. I shall return to this later.
9. As I shall suggest later, this entire issue is barbed with great difficulties—indeed, it collapses critically different levels of analysis. "How can a philosophy of reflection nourish itself at the symbolic source and become hermeneutic?" (*95*, p. 41). This is a question whose very possibility of being asked requires that another level of philosophical inquiry is being presupposed. The question, thus, is not itself hermeneutical.
10. Cited by Ricoeur (*95*, pp. 377–78, 421).
11. For Ricoeur, this signifies the same "dispossession." He does not seem to appreciate, though, that this "possibility of deception" is itself quite *evident*, adequately and apodictically!
12. The so-called "antiphenomenology" here seems to me dubious, as I will suggest later. (See, however, *95*, pp. 117–22, 424–25, 428, and 443.)
13. This is "the most fundamental hypothesis of psychoanalysis, the one that qualifies it as *psycho*analysis" (*95*, p. 137).
14. This means in psychoanalysis: "what takes precedence in the order of distortion or

disguise," *not* what is "primordial" in transcendental terms: ground or justification (*95*, p. 154).

15. That is, "the unsurpassable character of desire" (*95*, p. 445).

16. As psychoanalysis has its focal task, theoretically understood, in the "archeology of the subject," it lies at the center of such sciences.

17. This is so, not only because of the advent of Marx, Nietzsche, and Freud—the great "unmaskers"—but also because of the problematic of symbols and myths, speech and language.

18. Indeed, the passages where Husserl is compared to Freud, in the end, are not *systematically* important; they serve mainly to help clarify Freud (*95*, pp. 375–418).

19. Obviously, I am hardly concerned to fault Ricoeur for failing to be Husserlian. Since Husserl has in fact figured prominently in Ricoeur's career, and even in this book in a way, it is important to assess the matter.

20. Nowhere else is the "antiphenomenology" so characterized. It is rather asserted either by itself, qualified by "totally" (*95*, p. 119), called an "inverted phenomenology" (*95*, p. 443), or a "pseudo" or "quasi" phenomenology (*95*, pp. 133–34).

21. See above, footnote 14: the sense of primary, as noted by Ricoeur, too, is radically different for psychoanalysis and for transcendental philosophy.

22. In this, there is a perfect parallel between the study of Freud and Husserl's inquiry into "science" as an "acceptance-phenomenon" (*41*, I). As Husserl found, for example, "evidence," "judgment," "grounding," etc., essential to the phenomenon of science, Ricoeur finds psychoanalysis unintelligible except as a discourse on the subject. It is surprising that Ricoeur never seems to appreciate such parallels as this.

23. Presumably by way of reflection-as-assimilation, i.e., as a participation *in* the matters themselves reflected-on. I later criticize this.

24. And thus, too, for the *theorist*—especially the one who is on the alert for the philosophical significance of clinical phenomena.

25. Clearly, on this score it seems necessary to depart from Husserl's claim that the doxic founds the non-doxic. Here Ricoeur seems on the right track. It is not, however, that one must take the reverse of Husserl (as Ricoeur seems to suggest); rather, at their roots the doxic and the non-doxic are indistinguishably bound up in the single, "powerful" urge-to-be hinted at by Ricoeur in his usage of "effort-to-be." Only subsequent experience, to be traced out phenomenologically, brings about the slow distinguishing and differentiating of these modalities.

26. Precisely what Merleau-Ponty had analyzed as the "*Urpräsenz*" definitive of human being: that the presence-to-self is also a "*dé-présentation*" and "*me jette hors de moi*" (*79*, p. 363 [Eng. ed.]; cf. Fr. ed., p. 417).

27. This was confirmed by Ricoeur personally, during a conversation we had about this chapter. I should add that the chapter was written before I had studied this article.

28. Cf. above, Chapter 4.

TO CHAPTER 7

1. The work of J. H. Fabre is in particular fascinating, Portmann notes, for this study. It is worth mentioning, too, that although Jonas nowhere cites Portmann, his

usage of "inwardness" in connection with metabolism and higher-level organic processes is strikingly like Portmann's (cf. *55*, pp. 75–98). Portmann mentions as well that what he calls "appetence"—seizing upon the link between appetite and appeasement of hunger—"leads to the phenomena of freedom" (*91*, p. 349). And, Jonas, too, in his brief study of moving and feeling, points out the place of appetite (*55*, pp. 101, 103–05) and, as already mentioned earlier, freedom (*55*, pp. 83–86, 99, 106–07).

2. Cf. above, pp. 146–47.

3. I am deeply cognizant of what he says, at the end of *Fear and Trembling*, of "poor Heraclitus": "Heraclitus the obscure, who deposited his thoughts in his writings and his writings in the Temple of Diana . . . said, 'One cannot pass twice through the same stream.' Heraclitus the obscure had a disciple who did not stop with that, he went further and added, 'One cannot do it even once.' Poor Heraclitus, to have such a disciple! By this amendment the thesis of Heraclitus was so improved that it became an Eleatic thesis which denies movement, and yet that disciple desired only to be a disciple of Heraclitus . . . and to go further . . . " (*61*, p. 132). I shall have further occasion to "go further" than Kierkegaard, or better perhaps, to go in a different direction—my only saving grace being that I in no way claim to be Kierkegaard's disciple, but only an admirer. Which might have pleased him.

4. The issue of the other person, which will profoundly flesh out the whole sense of situated reflexivity, will be taken up later. I will join Ricoeur's point, i.e., that "self" is a "desire for other desires," a seeking to be acknowledged and affirmed, but will take this in very different direction. See above, Chapter 6.

5. Cf. Gabriel Marcel's lovely essay, "The Ego and It's Relation to Others" (*74*, pp. 13–28).

6. See also his *Philosophy and the American School* (*81*) and Clark E. Moustakas (ed.), *Existential Child Therapy* (82). I am indebted to Professor Spiegelberg for these and other references.

7. Berger's study, concerned with the middle-class "religious establishment" in American culture, shows with equal eloquence the real depth and complexity of what I have called a barrier to the articulation (not to say even the admission) of experiences of self-awakening. There are many built-in techniques gearing against just such "ecstatic" experiences, which find their way into most facets of our culture, even, as he notes, into psychotherapy and guidance norms: "Our psychologists tell us that the mentally healthy individual is one who is capable of coping with reality. What they commonly overlook is that reality itself is socially constituted," and constituted precisely around such techniques of concealment (*3*, p. 92; see also p. 10).

8. See above, Chapter 6.

9. Spiegelberg (*114*) has collected some additional examples and has kindly furnished me with these and others, as I have shared mine with him.

10. A personal report given to Prof. Spiegelberg by a person who happened to see a copy of his article lying on his desk—the sight of which immediately reawakened the memory.

11. In her *Recherche d'une éternité*; Spiegelberg points out that Maria Le Hardouin confirmed the autobiographical basis of the episode, in a letter in response to his inquiry.

12. Chapter II (Little, 1959).

13. Personal communication, given out with other materials in a session on the "I-am-me" experience during his 3rd Workshop in Phenomenology, Washington University, June, 1967.

14. Just as Ricoeur has also stressed; see above, Chapter 6.

15. Some persons, e.g., C. L., report that they can, once the experience has happened and with practiced concentration, bring on other experiences of the same. Even so, the moment of self-encounter with oneself is, not only the first time, but even subsequently, sudden and astonishing; whether deliberately brought about (which is quite rare, so far as I know) or not, it has the sense of being a decisive happening, and the self which "happens" has the sense of being unasked-for, not chosen but precisely disclosed.

16. Which is just the sense of the experience had by Emily, the young girl in Richard Hughes' novel, *A High Wind in Jamaica* (*39*) when she becomes surprised, during an "I-am-me" experience, *over* finding how readily her legs obey her, and *at* her not having realized this surprising thing before.

17. Precisely the character of the experiential disclosure of one's own embodiment, as was already shown (above, Chapter 3). Given the "nature" of the complexure of life, the contextures of "mind" and "own-body," this fact is no surprise, but expressive exactly of the *situatedness* of reflexivity!

18. As in the "I-am-me" experiences recorded by Spiegelberg.

19. C. L. reports how starkly a window-hook stood out, appearing as a "uniquely transformed" part of her milieu; Maria Le Hardouin speaks of odors and beams of sunlight standing out and becoming almost bodily; other experiences are similarly contextural.

20. C. L. reports that certain of her experiences made her feel as if she were "spinning in a void" and were "terrifying" to her. Tom, in Bradbury's novel, is aghast at the collapse of all firm supports. Duke feels "so scared it running out you ears."

21. Used with the permission of the Estate of Paul Tillich, Robert C. Kimball, Executor. Tillich gave this poem to Spielgelberg over the telephone, promptly, in response to the latter's inquiry about the "I-am-me" experience. It was written when he was about sixteen and still a student at the Gymnasium. A very rough translation might be: "If I am I, / who tells me that I am? / Who tells me what I am, / what I should become? / What is this Becoming, / what the sense of living? / What is Being / and taking leave of earth? / O abyss without Ground, / obscurest depths of madness? / Ah, that I had never viewed Thee / and , childlike, might rest!"

22. Recall, here, Straus' comments about this phenomenon and the "upright posture." (see above, Chapter 3).

23. See above, Chapter 6.

24. Groundlessness is not synonymous with pointlessness or meaninglessness; in the experience of self-awakening, what is disclosed is radical openness in the sense of the setting or "place" wherein "grounds" *are able* to occur.

TO CHAPTER 8

1. This little study of "The Sigh" is one of the most provocative and profound on the phenomenon of "expression." Too, it is, unhappily, one of the least known studies of this critical phenomenon.

2. There are several important connections which need to be mentioned here, even though I can do so only briefly (since their elaboration would require a more extensive treatment than is here possible). On the one hand, it seems clear that there is an intrinsic relationship between "effort" and "possibilizing," as the title of this chapter suggests. As is especially evident in clinical descriptions of seriously ill patients (mentioned in the text, from Plügge), this relationship is such that as the horizon of "possibles" and "possibilizing" decreases (for whatever reason), so does the phenomenon of efforting undergo clear modification. "Efforting" wanes, indeed, precisely in correlation with the circumscribing of the range of "possibles" ("alternatives") available to the patient. Either that, or efforting by the patient becomes unusually, even exaggeratedly focused: on lifting one's arm, turning one's head, pronouncing of words, walking, and the like. Thus it seems to be the case that as possibilizing becomes circumscribed, and the range of available possibles likewise circumscribed, efforting tends to slacken, it ebbs, and this becomes evidenced by the sorts of phenomena Plügge notes: the diminishing of observed "liveliness," the increase of a sense of "burdensomeness" and "onerousness" of the live body, the pallor of the skin, and the like. Conversely, then, the attempt to "heal" or at least to "help" a patient seems rather strictly correlated with the degree to which the patient is able to possibilize: thus, given available techniques, regimens, and procedures for treatment, the prime focus of helping and caring must be on enhancing the available possibles for the patient. Or, the greater the range of the latter, the more likely is it that a patient is enabled to effort in ways which enhance the chances of recovery.

A second point must also be made about possibilizing. It seems clear that my ways of explicating the presence of "problems" in the text conform quite well with what Gurwitsch has analyzed as "reorganization" of experience. The phase of actual achievement of a perceptually segregated unity must not only be accounted for on its own terms (*31*, pp. 34–35), but indeed such apprehension presupposes that the field of experience is already autochthonously organized. More than that, the actual occurrence of that achievement "must be accounted for in terms of reorganization and reconstruction" (*31*, p. 101). If what is "problematic" (unsettling, disturbing, etc.) is to be understood, as I suggest, as a breakdown in the prevailing contextual references—making "lines of good continuation" themselves also problematic, of course—then it seems evident that the reestablishment of contextural balance ("solving the problem," in simplest terms), or the problem of reorganization, is to be understood as a function of *possibilizing*. Reorganization is itself an achievement reached by the *effort* to detect or otherwise establish new or different functional significances among prevailing constituents (or different ones, as the case may be)—and this is clearly a matter of possibilizing or "thinking for the possibly otherwise." The texture of reorganization, as what accounts for the phase of actual achievement, is possibilizing; hence possibilizing accounts for reorganization.

TO CHAPTER 9

1. The idea appears in many of his works—even early ones. Perhaps the central text, though, is *Du Refus à l'invocation* (Paris: Gallimard, 1940). This is translated as *Creative Fidelity*, by Robert Rosthal (New York: Noonday Press, 1964). However,

the translation is unacceptable in many ways, especially in one major way: *disponibilité* is rendered as "disposability," which (even though there is one connotation which captures part of Marcel's meaning: "being at the disposal of") utterly defaces Marcel's idea: "to be able to dispose," the usual meaning—one could hardly find a more accurate way of expressing the *exact contrary* of his central notion.

2. Aside from Bosch's remarkable monograph, there has been to my knowledge only one other effort to understand autism philosophically: John N. Hines (*36*, pp. 329–41), whose fine essay focuses mainly on the "person" as "awording," i.e., Hines sees the primacy of the "lingual milieu" (p. 341) with respect to the foundations for a theory of society and for a theory of "person." He does not, however, attempt to elicit, as I have, the phenomenon of "self" as reflexivity, nor therefore the "relation" between selves as "meeting" (mutuality)—which fails in the case of autism. Still, Hines' essay is a very worthwhile effort, and not at all inconsistent with my reading of autism, nor that of Bosch or Bettelheim.

   There are, as will be seen, a number of intriguing points raised by Bettelheim (*5*, especially Part I), among others his usage of "mutuality," which is close to mine. One needs to reckon with his psychoanalytic approach; interestingly, however, little detectable use is made of that approach in his fascinating discussion of the "birth of self"—and, in fact, I find here many significant themes suggested for the theory of self as emerging along with and among other selves. I return to this later.

3. Bosch, who proceeds by way of a "phenomenological-anthropological" approach, using language as a clue and guide, argues that a multiplicity of theoretical approaches is necessary. He is nevertheless anxious to criticize the commonly received view of science simply presupposed by Kanner and most others (though not Bettelheim)—on the basis, interestingly, of Husserl's *Ideen*, II (*47*). I cannot, of course, enter into any of these disputes here, though it is clear that there are serious methodological and epistemological issues it were wise for philosophers to consider most carefully.

4. That is, a person who would "lie in a corner all the time with eyes closed and ears blocked" (*7*, p. 49). In fact, one of the factors constituting the shock of one's encounter with such a child is just that there are degrees of autistic conduct, hence degrees of commonness with the rest of us.

5. Bettelheim notes the frail girl who completely failed to react to the normally unbearable pain of a ruptured appendix, and who later had to be held by two adults when an injection was necessary (*5*, pp. 59–61; cf. also *7*, Ch. VI).

6. Or, as I should want to insist, if it is ever even to *emerge*!

7. I here recall Marcel's wonderfully exact point: as self, I "produce myself" before the Other, "emphasize" myself; or, *je suis manifeste*!

8. Or, as again Marcel could have said, of mere "mirroring"—thus not "testing" self but rather manipulating self and other, as the *poseur* does.

9. Laing's penetration here is evident: ranging from complementarity, confirmation/disconfirmation, collusion, double-binds and untenable positions, attribution and injunctions, elusion, and still others. His initial schematizing of these (*68*, Appendix, pp. 154–60) is most suggestive, especially in relation to my delineation of the complexities of contextural relations. This schematism was later given more detail in his marvelously sensitive work, *Knots* (*67*).

10. Precisely because of this an intuitionistic philosophy proves to be untenable—a point which Ricoeur has also made. Gurwitsch's field-theory of consciousness shows *why*, however, by showing that the fundamental prerequisite for intuitionism—the thesis that experience can be made to appear stripped, cleansed of all the products of intellectualization, and thus be grasped in its pristine purity—is strictly untenable, since it requires that organization be ephemeral, superimposed on experience, hence removable—which he shows to be totally wrong (cf. *31*, e.g., pp. 29–30, 104).

11. As Scheler showed. See also Schutz's important article on Scheler (*109*), I, pp. 150–79).

12. One need think only of his *Reflections on the Problem of Relevance* (*110*), where Schutz initiates his reflections with his own concrete situation at his desk in Estes Park, Colorado; of the dog, Rover, used in many places; etc.

13. I have begun this analysis, one to which surprisingly little attention has been given despite its evident importance (see *125*, pp. 192–219; *124*, pp. 29–43).

14. I myself am convinced that Schutz is quite wrong about the problems and possibilities of transcendental phenomenology, but believe that Husserl's Fifth Meditation is also wrong in crucial ways, though for different reasons than Schutz adduces. This is not the place for this quarrel, however.

TO CHAPTER 10

1. Self, in Maurice Natanson's term, is a "journeying"—a term which evokes Marcel's *être-en-route* and *être-en-marche* (see *83*; and cf. *74*).

2. K. Koffka notes that "friendliness" and "unfriendliness" are more primitive experiences than, e.g., seeing a blue spot.

3. Other instances come easily to mind: teaching someone to dance, cutting someone's hair, teaching a sport, making a photo for advertising, etc.

4. His other great insight is this: that our perception of other persons is always a perception of "patterns of wholeness." This relates to the second fundamental issue delineated above: the experience of others, which will be taken up in the next chapter. One thing, though: as Scheler must be criticized for his view of the "self in a general sense," etc., so it is necessary to note that there is no *theory* of "wholeness" here.

5. Precisely here is the place of the great myths of battle, of trial, of journey, forging the enrichments of self and others.

6. One should think here of Piaget's observations, especially of the fact that nothing of the patterning by assimilation and accommodation, hence internal organization, could possibly occur without that alertness, effort, and initiating possibilizing activity (cf. *89*, especially chs. 1 and 2).

7. A clear instance of what was earlier emphasized as critical: namely, the phenomenon of upset, of disturbance, and the significance this has for the "self."

TO CHAPTER 11

1. Cf. J. Preston Cole (*14*). Cole's study, in many ways really important in its confrontation of two masters of deception and irony, Freud and Kierkegaard,

nevertheless has almost nothing to say about intersubjectivity. Regarding Kierkegaard, this may be understandable, although that issue is surely no mere "by the way" for the integrity of the conception of self. Regarding Freud, though, it is surprising, inasmuch as psychoanalysis, being profoundly clinical and therapeutic, as well as theoretical, most assuredly does invoke a prominent conception of intersubjectivity: the "work" of the dream-work, of therapy itself, as Ricoeur suggests.

2. Cf., for example, Alfred Schutz, "The Dimensions of the Social World" (*109*, II, pp. 10-27), "Common-Sense and Scientific Interpretation of Human Action" (*109*, I, pp. 10-27), "Scheler's Theory of Intersubjectivity . . . " (*109*, I, pp. 172–79), and "Symbol, Reality and Society" (*109*, I, pp. 312–29); and also *The Structures of the Life-World* (*111*, Chs. 2B and 4).

3. Nor am I concerned with a systematic assessment of Schutz's claim to be giving only a "mundane" analysis; nor, therefore, his criticism of Husserl's "transcendental" analysis. These, important as they surely are, belong to another study.

4. Schutz points out, whenever he introduces the terms, that Cooley, who coined the term (*Social Organization* [New York, 1909], Chs. 3-5), simply identified "face-to-face" with "intimacy."

5. It is noteworthy how little Schutz's basic conception changed from 1932 until his death in 1959. Cf. *Der sinnhafte Aufbau der sozialen Welt* (Vienna: Springer-Verlag, 1932; 2nd unalt. ed., 1960), Sec. IV [Eng. tr. by George Walsh and Frederick Lehnert, *The Phenomenology of the Social World* (Evanston: Northwestern University Press, 1967). This translation is, however, quite unacceptable, as even a cursory comparison with the original quickly shows: inconsistent translations, incomprehensibly reversed, and even omitted, sentences and paragraphs, and even, strangely, paraphrases instead of translations of some passages, etc.]

6. From "The Dimensions of the Social World" (*109*, II, pp. 10-27). This is a

translation by Thomas Luckmann of Sec. IV of *Der sinnhafte Aufbau der sozialen Welt*, op. cit., and is much preferable to the Walsh/Lehnert version.

7. Though Schutz never specifically says so, this clearly indicates two further zones within life-worldly experience: one of the *non*-restorable reach (what can no longer be brought back), and one of *non*-attainability (what is "impossible" to attain, either de facto or in principle).

8. As Schutz says, too, this zone has much flexibility: thanks to technology (aircraft, telephones, telegraph, radio, television, etc.), this zone can be vastly extended.

9. Only Bergson, as Schutz notes, has really looked into this crucial phenomenon. See his *Creative Evolution*, tr. Arthur Mitchell (New York: Modern Library, 1944), pp. 12–13.

10. In classes and seminars he gave, between 1957 and 1959, at the Graduate Faculty, The New School for Social Research.

11. I am here far closer to Scheler, of course, than to Schutz (cf. *107*, pp. 248–59).

12. The recent etymology of "avail" is: from the Middle English "availen," it derives directly from the Old French "*a + valoir*," *to be worth*; hence "to be available" is "to be of worth to," "to be able to be at the disposal of" (*disponsible*, in Marcel's French), "to be efficacious for," "to be of sufficient strength to benefit," etc.

13. As there are variations between the French and the English of these Gifford Lectures, I quote only from the French, which is more adequate and prepared more carefully by Marcel. The English version appeared before the French, having been prepared directly from his actual lectures.

14. While Schutz consistently refrains from conceiving the "tuning-in" relationship as "intimacy," his concrete analyses, e.g., of making music together, seem clearly to take him in the direction I've indicated with my notion of co-presence—thus still allowing, as seems necessary, the distinction Schutz rightly makes.

15. As I noted earlier, in his *Self and Others* (*68*, Appendix) Laing lays out a wonderful formalization of these complexities—enough "p's" and "q's" to capture the heart of the most austere formalist.

Index